BETA DELTA *of* ALPHA CHI SIGMA

A History

Rebis from *Theoria Philosophiae Hermeticae* (1617) by Heinrich Nollius

KEITH A. SCHUETTE
Beta Delta '74

Beta Delta of Alpha Chi Sigma: A History
Copyrighted © 2022 Keith Schuette
By Keith Schuette
Edited by: Dennis Uhlig
ISBN 9781645384489

Beta Delta of Alpha Chi Sigma: A History. Copyright © 2022 by Keith A. Schuette. All rights reserved. Printed in the United States of America. No part of this book may be used or reproduced in any manner whatsoever without written permission, except in the case of brief quotations embodied in critical articles and reviews.

For information, please contact:

Ten16 Press
www.ten16press.com
Waukesha, WI

Dedicated to
All the Beta Delta Brothers, Past, Present and Future

And to
My wife, Linda, who encouraged me "…to go and write."

CONTENTS

Introduction..1

Beginnings...5

The 1940s..65

The 1950s..133

The 1960s..187

The 1970s..235

The 1980s and 1990s..303

The 2000s..339

Conclusion-Aureum Opus..387

Appendices..393

Notes...419

Acknowledgements...481

About the Author..483

INTRODUCTION

For the vessel is a living and corporeal spirit...

—*Paracelsus, The Coelum Philosophorum*

There is a saying that goes "You can choose your friends but not your family." Whoever came up with this epigram was obviously not an alchemist. An alchemist would not be bound by fixed notions, but would seek innovative means to achieve gold. Though there is some truth in this statement in regard to each of us being born into a particular family—a birth in which no personal choice is involved—the statement is still misleading. It does not give us the operational definitions of "family" and "friends." It assumes, especially for "family," an operational definition which renders the term immutable, fixed. But observation often proves that such thinking is inadequate. The careful alchemist knows that what presents itself as fixed may, in fact, not be so; there may exist other processes by which new bonds may be forged. Thus, the theory, the operational definitions, or both, may change.

It occurs that friends and family may both be chosen. Another entity—

a fraternity—abets this dual option. In a fraternity, friendship and family are correlated in a kind of double bond. The creation of this double connection, however, requires an individual's conscious choice. The option may be offered, but acceptance lies in the heart and mind of the recipient.

Once assumed, however, this link—like the alchemical gold—cannot be dissolved. Even though this bond may get stretched over distance and years, it does not break. Like space-time which continually expands, yet keeps the heavenly bodies in steady alignment, the fraternal bond holds the members together. No matter the separation—in time or distance—there exists a common unifying ground, a freely chosen history and promise.

There are several kinds of fraternities—honorary, social, professional. Each offers its own brand of social connectedness. The honorary fraternity provides, perhaps, the least cohesive tie between its members. The social fraternity may offer a familial/social bond but the members may have a variety of different interests. The professional fraternity, however, bolsters both the familial and the social bonds and adds a common interest to the equation, which potentially binds the members even more tightly together.

The Beta Delta Chapter of Alpha Chi Sigma at Missouri S&T has had its bonds put to the test. Memories have receded. Contacts have been lost. Members have drifted apart—perhaps even to the point where some may not "feel" a part of the fraternity any longer. But just as in other families, no matter how separated we may perceive ourselves to be from other members, there is still a transcendent quality of history and relationship that binds us. Our bonds cannot be dissolved. They are like the alchemical gold. But gold can be buried, and forgetting our history can obscure the fraternal bonds which we labored to form.

This recounting of the Beta Delta Chapter of the Alpha Chi Sigma Fraternity is a humble effort to keep before us the gold we so forged and chose.

A Word About Sources and Records

The greatest obstacle in writing this history—which spans nine decades—was a lack of source material. Nevertheless, despite disappointments, my research also yielded unexpected surprises. Going into the project, I believed that many of the early records from the 1930s into the 1950s would probably be missing since—when I pledged in 1974—members were told that much documentation had been lost in a fire. But when Nicole Moon and Kari Knobbe dug through the files, they found, stuck in the back of a bottom file drawer, binders filled with records from those very years. This was one of the pleasant surprises.

However, there were serious disappointments as well. Records covering several periods could not be located at all: the early 1950s, a few years in the mid-1960s, and several years in the 1970s, for example. The greatest difficulty was the paucity of chapter records for the significant swath of time from the mid-1980s through 2015. Of course, there were other sources such as the archives of the Missouri Miner, the Missouri S&T Alumni Magazine and the Rollamo Yearbooks which shed some light on what Beta Delta was up to during those years. I also relied heavily on interviews and conversations with members to flesh out the later years.

Because of the lack of records from 1980 to 2015, I organized the last two chapters differently than the preceding chapters. I combined the 1980s and 1990s in Chapter 6, summarizing the events that characterized those two decades and tabulating the initiates in an excursus. I dealt with the years 2000 through 2021 in similar fashion in Chapter 7, providing a summary of events from 2000 to 2015. Since more detailed records were recovered—during the writing process—for the more recent years (2015 to 2021), I used a more chronological approach in a separate section of that chapter. In the final chapter, I followed the schema of Chapter 6, tabulating the initiates for the years 2000 through 2021, and the officers for the years 2006 to 2014 in an excursus. The only record of officers available for that time period came from the National Office of Alpha Chi Sigma.

In addition, the Membership Register of Beta Delta and the membership records of the National Office of Alpha Chi Sigma were available, which supplied the names of the initiates. I gave the Beta Delta Membership registry precedence over the National Office records, since the chapter registry included the signatures of the initiates. I also noted the discrepancies between Beta Delta's and the National Office's records in the text. For the years from 2006 to 2015, the names of the officers were obtained from the membership records of the National Office, which did list officers prior to 2006. I took two approaches in regard to such lists of initiates and officers: in the first five chapters the nature and extent of the records and the short summaries of material allowed a narrative which could easily incorporate such lists of names. But the dearth of records and the summaries of material that were available for the final years did not readily lend to the inclusion of lists in the text. Thus, in those chapters I included the lists of initiates and, in the case of the officers for the period from 2006 to 2015, in tabular form in the excursus for each chapter.

Finally, I accessed the issues of The Missouri Miner, the MSM Alumnus, and the Rollamo yearbooks through Missouri S&T's Scholars' Mine Special Collections found at https://scholarsmine.mst.edu/library_spec-coll/. Theses and dissertations were accessed through Missouri S&T's Scholars' Mine Student Theses and Dissertations (http://scholarsmine.mst.edu/student-tds).

Keith Schuette
January 5, 2022

BEGINNINGS

...the fixation of spirits, which are flying...

—*George Ripley, The Sixth Gate*

First Contact—Houston Taylor

Every beginning has a beginning. The origins and birth of nations, founders, heroes, and just-plain-old individuals all have a prehistory, a context, from which their birth arose. The Beta Delta Chapter of the Alpha Chi Sigma fraternity is no exception. Beta Delta emerged from circumstances involving the Missouri School of Mines and Metallurgy, the national Alpha Chi Sigma fraternity, chemistry clubs and societies around the country, and the mind of one, energetic chemical engineering student. These elements worked their own alchemy to yield a "Great Work"[1]—the Beta Delta chapter of the Alpha Chi Sigma (AXΣ) fraternity. This Great Work, however, did not simply arise from the mixture of a college, a national fraternity and a student's dream, like some magical entity conjured up by occult phrases spoken over a stew of animal and plant organs. The formation and establishment of Beta Delta came about only after great labor.

In 1920 the Missouri School of Mines and Metallurgy (MSM) was looking forward to the celebration of its 50th anniversary the following year. From its beginning class of 13 students meeting in a building purchased in 1871, intended for the Rolla public schools, MSM had grown to 393 students (for the 1919-1920 school year) and 6 buildings: the Rolla Building built in 1871, the Chemistry laboratory added in 1885 and expanded in 1902, Norwood Hall—known as "the Main Building"—opened in 1903; the Metallurgy Building completed in 1911, Parker Hall opened in 1912, and the Jackling Gymnasium opened in 1915.[2]

Expansion meant more than just an increase in facilities. Significant to MSM and Beta Delta's story, in particular, was the Buford Act of 1915, which established chemical engineering as a degree program. Jonas Viles, an early historian of the University of Missouri, explained at that time, "…the basic difficulty…[for the MSM campus was]…that a mere school of mines, a specialized branch of engineering…could have no reasonable hope…for any very considerable enrollment…."[3] Soon after the Act was passed into law, MSM announced the requirements for electrical, mechanical and chemical engineering, and its intention to offer degrees in those disciplines. The introduction of the chemical engineering discipline expanded the fertile ground in which a fraternity dedicated to the chemical sciences could flourish. Without this expansion the young chemical engineering student who had the vision of a chemistry fraternity on the MSM campus would have had his hopes frustrated. Yet, and perhaps unbeknown to Houston Taylor, the arrival of Director Charles Fulton portended developments beneficial to campus organizations.

The eve of the 50th anniversary ushered in Charles Herman Fulton's directorship (1920-1937). Fulton had a significant influence on the school's development—even beyond his tenure. He came to MSM from Case Applied Science in Cleveland, OH, where he was a professor of Metallurgy. He contributed to the expansion of the curriculum and departments of Economics, Ceramic Engineering and Petroleum Engineering.[4] As impressive as the school's growth was, under the leadership of Fulton it was poised for even greater expansion in curriculum, departments, degrees offered and research.

Beginnings

Similar to these developments at the Missouri School of Mines and Metallurgy, Alpha Chi Sigma, a national professional fraternity of the chemical sciences, was also on a significant growth trajectory despite the upheaval of WWI. After the war, several of the chapters struggled to regain what they had lost during that time. Some had to start with a membership of only a few, others had lost house leases, and still others had lost their records.[5] By 1920, however, Alpha Chi Sigma had grown across the country from the singular Alpha chapter founded in 1902 at the University of Wisconsin to 31 chapters—running through the entire Greek alphabet and into a second set, i.e., Alpha through Alpha Eta.[6]

Within this milieu, a Chemical Engineering student, Houston Taylor, conceived the idea of having a chapter of Alpha Chi Sigma at MSM.

Houston Taylor—Rollamo 1921

The impetus for his vision is unknown. Perhaps he had contact with Alpha Chi Sigma brothers from Delta (Univ. of Missouri-Columbia) or Alpha Epsilon (Washington University-St. Louis) chapters. And if he had the idea, it is also reasonable to assume he shared it with others. In any event, he planted the seed of establishing a chapter of the fraternity at MSM in 1920.

Nicknamed "Porky,"[7] Taylor was a member of Kappa Sigma,[8] a social fraternity; Satyr, a sophomore honorary organization;[9] the Diphenyl Dozen; the Metallurgy and Chemistry Society; the Miner Board (1917-1919); and St. Pat's Board (1918). Taylor served as President of the Metallurgy and Chemistry Society, and he was also Student Assistant in Chemistry in charge of the Analytical Laboratory his senior year—1921.[10]

Taylor's membership in the Diphenyl Dozen was significant for Beta Delta. The Diphenyl Dozen held the same purpose as Alpha Chi Sigma—to support chemists and promote chemistry. Established in 1914, the organization was composed of faculty and assistants of the Chemistry Department, and was the precursor to the Ira Remsen Society—the local chemistry club. In 1923 the Diphenyl Dozen decided to change its name to the Ira Remsen Society. However, this change was subject to the approval of Ira Remsen[11] himself, the chemist who, along

with Constantin Fahlberg, discovered the artificial sweetener saccharin. Remsen was also the second president of John Hopkins University.[12] Remsen granted the use of his name, and in 1923 the Diphenyl Dozen officially became known as the Ira Remsen Society.

Ira Remsen–National Academy of Science [13]

According to the petition submitted to Alpha Chi Sigma, Taylor consulted with the Grand Officers of Alpha Chi Sigma concerning the advisability of forming a petitioning group on the MSM campus,[14] but evidently the pursuit of a chapter did not go beyond this initial consultation. No records have been recovered suggesting otherwise. But the idea of a fraternal order dedicated to the chemical sciences had its first admixture in the retort of the local chemistry club.

Second Contact—Schrenk and Kuechler

Not until 1925 did the notion of establishing an Alpha Chi Sigma chapter arise again. In that year Dr. Walter T. Schrenk, a member of Alpha Chi Sigma (Alpha chapter), who at the time, was an Assistant Professor in Chemistry, and Adolph H. Kuechler, a senior ('25), who was an ac-

tive alumnus through the 1970s, approached the Grand Master Alchemist, Robert M. Burns (Eta chapter),[15] with the question of forming a petitioning group. No definite action was taken until five years later when, in 1930, the local chemical society (Ira Remsen Society) was investigated as a possible petitioning group. The Alpha Chi Sigma officers deemed the Ira Remsen Society un-

Walter Schrenk—1925

suitable, however, and recommended that a separate fraternity be formed, one modeled more closely after Alpha Chi Sigma.[16]

Alpha Chi Sigma was still growing nationwide in the years from 1925 to 1930. In 1925 Alpha Xi was installed as the 38th collegiate chapter in Salt Lake City and in 1930 Alpha Psi was installed as the 47th chapter at the Illinois Institute of Technology in Chicago. In the fall of 1927 a new publication (christened "Chrome and Blue") was established and two new songs were added to the Alpha Chi Sigma songbook: "Alpha Chi Sigma Sweetheart" and "Hexagon Girl."[17] But for a local organization at MSM to join this expanding devotion to chemistry—including laudatory musical odes to the science—much work was needed. With the Ira Remsen Society unsuitable to the task, an entirely new organization needed to be formed, and, compounding the situation, Kuechler was rapidly approaching graduation.

Adolph Kuechler

Kuechler[18] earned a Master's degree with his thesis on "The properties of the fire clays used for the manufacture of zinc retorts."[19] Upon graduation he entered industry. His career included such positions as a construction engineer with Robertson and Company, Int.—a firm of designing and construction engineers headquartered in Cleveland--and with United Gas Co. in Philadelphia, in 1928.[20] With Kuechler leaving the school, Dr. Schrenk became the prime mover to establish an Alpha Chi Sigma Chapter on the MSM campus. Perhaps this was destiny since Schrenk was already a member of Alpha Chi Sigma, having been initiated by Alpha—the founding chapter of the fraternity.

Epsilon Pi Omicron

In pursuit of a proper Alpha Chi Sigma-recognized petitioning group, members of the Ira Remsen Society, in 1932, petitioned the Senior Council of MSM for recognition as an organization by the Missouri School of Mines and Metallurgy. On the approval of the Senior Council, Epsilon Pi Omicron was officially established, and became the "prima materia" for the work leading to Beta Delta. The ostensible intent of the group was to bring chemists closer together "…to promote a feeling of good fellowship among them, to stimulate interest in research in chemistry…[and]…to bring the men in the industry in closer contact with the student chemists."[21] The nascent organization recognized the importance of those in industry being materially involved in the students' learning of the latest methods used in the industry. The chosen name, Epsilon Pi Omicron, then, reflected the intent of the founding members. The Greek letters Ε, Π, Ο stood for the Greek words ἐπιτηδεύμα (epitedeuma, research), προβασς (probasis, advancement) and ὁμιλια (homilia, fellowship).[22] The need for a professional chemical fraternity was also evident in comparison to other departments on the campus which had already established their own professional fraternities while the Chemistry Department lacked such an organization.

The actual purpose of the newly formed Epsilon Pi Omicron was four-fold: 1) to strive for the advancement of chemistry, both as a science and as a profession; 2) to foster a spirit of good fellowship among the students of chemistry; 3) to instill the spirit of research; and 4) to petition the national Alpha Chi Sigma fraternity for a chapter at the Missouri School of Mines and Metallurgy. The similarities to the stated purposes of Alpha Chi Sigma indicated that Epsilon Pi Omicron had patterned itself according to the recommendations of the Grand Officers.

Along with the declared purpose, the fraternity developed an initiation ritual—to be conducted semi-annually—based on the purposes of the fraternity. The charter members who constituted Epsilon Pi Omicron included: Thomas G. Day, Pres.; George Hale, Vice-Pres.; Milton L. Herzog, Secretary; Philip C. McDonald, Treas.; Thomas Donahue, Historian; John S. Sabine, C. S. Abshier, L. Merchie, H. E. Boyd, R. L. Cunningham, Mason Larwood, Clemens R. Maise, James H. Tobin, Arthur H. Walther, T. Burnham, Richard A. Parker, W. A. Westerfeld, and G. S. Richardson. Other members, including Dr. Schrenk, Dr. Howard L. Dunlap, Dr. Clarence J. Monroe, and Prof. Karl K. Kershner, were also elected into the fraternity. At the time of its formation, Epsilon Pi Omicron also pledged the following: T. J. Stewart, H. A. Brisch, W. B. Danforth, W. A. Howe, H. F. Lange, J. I. McCaskill, B. A. Menke, N. R. Pulley and J. Smith.[23]

Members were selected on the basis of the following qualifications: 1) the candidate must have an acceptable general personality and general adaptability; 2) the candidate must have signified some branch of chemistry as his/her life's work; 3) the candidate must have an average substantially above an "M"[24] which is the scholastic average of the entire student body; 4) the candidate must have completed at least three semesters of college work; and 5) the candidate must be only non-Semitic members of the Caucasian race.[25] This last requirement would become a major point of contention in the late 40s and early 50s, leading to a significant controversy within the fraternity and a subsequent change in its Constitution.

Obligations to the college did not end with the requirements of the Senior Council of MSM. On May 17, 1933, H. H. Armsby, Registrar and Student Advisor, informed T. G. Day, President, Epsilon Pi Omicron, that the organization, along with others, was to present its constitution and by-laws to the faculty in September. In addition, the presentation was to include reasons why the organization should be permitted to continue at MSM and proof that continuance of Epsilon Pi Omicron would be in the best interest of the school.[26] Those reasons justifying Epsilon Pi Omicron's continuance were laid out in newly elected President George Hale's reply:

To the Missouri School of Mines and Metallurgy Faculty:

We, the members of Epsilon Pi Omicron, respectfully submit herewith what we believe to be justifiable reasons for our existence on the MSM campus.

<u>First,</u> we feel that Epsilon Pi Omicron fills a definite need. Twenty percent of the students on this campus are registered as chemists and chemical engineers. There is no other organization which is devoted entirely to chemists, and which is qualified to accomplish our purposes which are, namely:

- *To bring together the students of chemistry as chemists and to establish a professional feeling.*

> • To establish professional contacts between our members and our graduates who are active in the industry, and
> • Through seeking membership in Alpha Chi Sigma, to further and strengthen these contacts.
>
> Secondly, Epsilon Pi Omicron is a scholastic organization.
> • We insist upon scholastic ability as a criterion of membership.
> • We stimulate interest in current chemical literature through discussions which form a part of our regular meetings.
> • Individual members respond enthusiastically to requests for papers and talks on chemical subjects.
> • We point with pride to the fact that last semester Epsilon Pi Omicron ranked scholastically above all other organizations with the exception of Phi Kappa Phi and Tau Beta Pi. This ranking did include the grades of our graduate student members.
>
> We refer you to the letters of recommendation from all of the members of the Chemistry faculty who have seen fit to lend their support as members of Epsilon Pi Omicron.[27]

A significant hurdle the precursor to Beta Delta had to work through was the matter of members also belonging to competing fraternities. Dr. Schrenk pursued this matter early in the life of Epsilon Pi Omicron. He was concerned about dual membership of Epsilon Pi Omicron members, later to become Alpha Chi Sigma members, in other engineering fraternities. The outcome of this issue was significant for the future when the members would become Alpha Chi Sigma brothers. According to a letter dated February 23, 1933, from E. J. Schrader, Grand Scribe, Theta Tau[28]—a professional engineering fraternity founded at the University of Minnesota in 1904—to Mr. Alex Gow, Theta Tau Chapter at MSM, Dr. Schrenk had discussions with a Prof. Vawter who reported the discussion to Schrader. Vawter reported that Schrenk had stated that Alpha Chi Sigma did not consider Theta Tau as a competitor, which was information obtained from someone at Alpha chapter. In response Schrader shared the rules of the Professional Interfraternity Conference, of which both fraternities were members, which stated that fraternities were not permitted to take members of other fraternities in the same or overlapping disciplines or categories. Schrader reviewed Theta Tau's decision, reached at their 1921 Convention, to initiate chemical engineers. Schrader pointed out in a letter to Alpha Chi Sigma Grand Master Alchemist, Stroud Jordan (Rho) dated March 11, 1922, that since Theta Tau had placed chemical engineers on its eligibility list, this made Theta Tau a competitive chemical engineering fraternity as far as Alpha Chi Sigma was concerned, and, as such, Alpha Chi Sigma's membership would not be permitted to join Theta Tau.[29]

In 1933 Dr. Schrenk again raised this pertinent question of dual membership with the Supreme Council (SC) of Alpha Chi Sigma. The issue, once again, involved the mutual ban on cross membership between Theta Tau and Alpha Chi Sigma. When he formed the local chemistry fraternity, Schrenk questioned whether or not the ChEs who were Theta Tau members could also be members of Alpha Chi Sigma. The question was considered in SC Proposition 654 on Aug. 5, 1933—"Shall inter-election with Theta Tau be permitted?" The motion to permit failed in a vote of 4 to 1, with only GMA Marion E. Dice voting yes. The Supreme Council presented documentation on the reasoning to reject the motion in a letter from Grand Professional Alchemist H.E. Wiedemann to Dice:

> *See my letter to E. Dice of May 6, 1933: Mr. Marion E. Dice, 3119 E. Grand Ave., Huntington Park, Calif.; Dear Marion: Dr. W. T. Schrenk (Alpha) recently wrote about the present status of the local chemical fraternity which was organized with the express purpose of petitioning Alpha Chi Sigma at some future date for a charter. Theta Tau has a chapter at Rolla and it admits chemical engineers as well as other engineers and the Grand Scribe of Theta Tau writes Schrenk that his fraternity considers Alpha Chi Sigma a strictly competitive fraternity. He, E. J. Schrader - Grand Scribe, (Reno, Nev.) quotes Jordan under date of March 11, 1922 as follows: "If Theta Tau places chemical*

engineers on her eligibility list, this makes her a competitive chemical engineering fraternity as far as Alpha Chi Sigma is concerned, and as such she becomes a competitor of Alpha Chi Sigma and our membership will not be permitted to join her ranks." Schrader further states that in one instance, at Columbia, a man was initiated into Theta Tau who was already an Alpha Chi Sigma. As soon as this was found out the Theta Tau initiation was declared null and void and the man was released from all obligations. Under these circumstances it seems to me that we should consider Theta Tau competitive and not permit inter-election. Several years ago, I told Schrenk that as far as I knew there was no conflict between the two organizations but later developments indicate to me that there is. In order to get an expression of opinion I will ask John to circulate a proposition to the council. I am not trying to rush anything at Rolla School of Mines but if the boys want a local built along lines acceptable to Alpha Chi Sigma we should clarify the situation in respect to Theta Tau. Best Wishes. Yours in the Double Bond, Wiedemann.[30]

This resolution of Proposition 654, prohibiting cross election between Theta Tau and Epsilon Pi Omicron, provided clarity in the pledging and initiation process for the fledgling fraternity, and eliminated a potential barrier to the future petition to join Alpha Chi Sigma.

The matter of dual membership was pursued, as well, with the social fraternity Triangle in the fall of 1934 and spring of 1935 since several members of Epsilon Pi Omicron were also members of Triangle. Though no documentation has been preserved, it is reasonable to assume Dr. Schrenk was either in correspondence or conversation with the President of the MSM Chapter of Triangle, Mr. James P. Sloss, for a letter was written to Mr. Sloss on December 15, 1934, in response to a question that was proposed to him, presumably by Dr. Schrenk. Sloss passed the question along to one of the national officers of Triangle. The Grand Scribe, L. S. Gaston of Triangle, replied that the committee which was assigned to settle questions of dual membership presented both a majority and minority report. The majority favored dual membership while the minority did not. It was ruled by the council of Triangle that dual membership with Epsilon Pi Omicron would be permitted as long as it maintained a strictly professional character. If, at any time, Epsilon Pi Omicron would operate a house in competition with other groups on campus, the permission would be withdrawn.[31]

In a letter dated December 22 to Dr. Schrenk from H. E. Wiedemann, Grand Master Alchemist, Alpha Chi Sigma, Wiedemann interpreted the decision of the Triangle National Council, and clarified that the ruling would carry over when Epsilon Pi Omicron affiliated with Alpha Chi Sigma. Wiedemann added that Mr. Gaston intimated that if a chapter of Alpha Chi Sigma maintained a house, inter-election would not be authorized. This placed Alpha Chi Sigma in an awkward position. If Alpha Chi Sigma chapters did not have houses, then Triangle members would be permitted to join, and if chapters had houses, this permission would be canceled.[32] In further correspondence from Wiedemann, dated January 4, 1935, he provided background on Triangle. In 1935 Triangle comprised only 12 chapters, of which only six had houses. Further, Triangle was organized as a college fraternity limited to engineering students, and duplication of membership with other fraternities that maintained houses was not permitted with either general or engineering organizations. Wiedemann clarified that since Triangle was a purely social fraternity, Alpha Chi Sigma's constitution allowed Triangle members to become Alpha Chi Sigma members. However, if an Alpha Chi Sigma chapter maintained a house, then its members would not be eligible for membership in Triangle. Consequently, if Alpha Chi Sigma members affiliated with Triangle at a college where Alpha Chi Sigma had no house but then later established one, an anomalous condition would occur. The Alpha Chi Sigma members who had joined Triangle before the house was established could be affiliated with Triangle. However, those who came into Alpha Chi Sigma after the house was established could not join Triangle. Wiedemann then summarized that the members of Epsilon Pi Omicron could belong to both organizations until a chapter of Alpha Chi Sigma at Rolla would establish a chapter house.[33]

Writing a purpose statement, obtaining organizational approval, and clarifying membership questions, alone, however, was not enough to get the new organization established. Members would eventually graduate and move on. A steady flow of new members and an established procedure were needed if the organization was to become viable. Over the next few years the fraternity grew very slowly, initiating only four men in 1933. The following year, on April 24, 1934, the fraternity grew by an additional 8 members, having initiated: Frank Zvanut, Lester Poese, Harold Haffner, Herbert Mortland, W. Neel, Oscar Fager, Edward Fiss and Ralph Striker. After the initiation and banquet, the group retired to the Chemistry Building, where Dr. Schrenk gave a talk on Alpha Chi Sigma.[34] This was the beginning of a long tradition of holding banquets to honor the newly initiated after the initiation ceremony. In 1935 six new members were initiated, in 1936, five (see Appendix A—Epsilon Pi Omicron Members, Initiates and Officers).[35]

Other elements required for the vitality of an organization are traditions and customs. Of course, once Epsilon Pi Omicron affiliated with Alpha Chi Sigma, the new chapter would plug into the established traditions of the fraternity. But for a local chapter to work out its particular identity, it also needed to have its own peculiar customs and traditions. Once Epsilon Pi Omicron was formed, semi-monthly meetings were held at which current problems of interest to chemists were discussed in addition to the usual business topics faced by the fraternity. Epsilon Pi Omicron's activities were well-known on the campus, and were often reported in the Missouri Miner—the campus newspaper. These activities often included demonstrations of "...a chemical nature" in Rolla and the surrounding towns.[36] One of these took place on November 21, 1934, when the fraternity held a special banquet to honor Dr. Wiedemann, by this time, a consulting chemist from St. Louis, who spoke on "Sulphur: Its Production and Uses."[37] The talk was accompanied by a motion picture provided by the US Bureau of Mines, which was filmed at the sulphur fields of Texas and Louisiana, and explained the extraction of sulphur using the Frasch process.[38] It is assumed this talk went well, since there are no reports that it "stunk." At another lecture, in April, 1936, Epsilon Pi Omicron members listened to Dr. Strathmore Ridley Barnott Cooke explain how the 92nd element, Uranium, was discovered to be present not only on earth but also beyond the earth in other regions of the universe.[39] Though the Supreme Council had ruled there could be no cross membership between Theta Tau and Alpha Chi Sigma, this did not stop the two organizations from participating in each other's activities. (Dr. Cooke was a member of the campus's Iota chapter of Theta Tau.)

Addresses to the members were not restricted to special guests and persons of note. Members, even pledges, presented talks as well. At a meeting, for example, in 1935, C.R. Maise and H.G. Thompson spoke on "Handy Kinks in the Laboratory" and "Relations of Carbon and Silicon," respectively. Maise's talk consisted of suggestions on how to keep laboratory breakage down and why "…it isn't nice to call the stockroom man bad names when you see your bill at the end of the year." Thompson's presentation compared the properties of Silicon and Carbon compounds. Maise was already a member while Thompson was pledging the fraternity at the time.[40]

Members[41]

Epsilon Pi Omicron 1934

Top Row: H. Lange, G. Hale, P. McDonald, T. Donahue; Bottom Row: A. Walther, B. Menke

Epsilon Pi Omicron 1934[42]

Epsilon Pi Omicron 1935

Top Row: H. Brisch, R. Cardetti, W. Danforth, E. Fiss, O. Fager, H. Haffner, W. Howe; Bottom Row: H. Lange, C. Maise, B. Menke, H. Mortland, W. Neel, J. Sabine, F. Zvanut

Epsilon Pi Omicron 1935[43]

Epsilon Pi Omicron 1936

First Row: J. Sabine, G. Schaumburg, A. Haussmann, C. Maise, E. Fiss.

Second Row: R. Striker, R. Lange, H. Thompson, E. Smith, E. Volz.

Third Row: F. Zvanut, J. Campbell, O. Fager, R. Cardetti, Hill, R. Tittle.

Epsilon Pi Omicron 1936[44]

Missouri School of Mines and Metallurgy 1936

Finally, in 1936, Epsilon Pi Omicron attained its fourth objective. This maturation, however, was the result of contributions by MSM, the Chemistry and Chemical Engineering Departments, and Alpha Chi Sigma—all of which were striving successfully toward their own goals.

By 1936, the campus included 9 buildings: Rolla Building, which housed the Missouri Bureau of Geology and Mines and the Missouri Geological Survey; the Chemistry Building; the Metallurgy Building; Parker Hall, which housed the administrative offices, library and an auditorium; Jackling Gymnasium; the Mine Experiment Station Building (1923), which housed the Mississippi Valley Station of the United States Bureau of Mines and the State Experiment Station as well as the Mining and Ceramic Departments. The school, however, had not only expanded its facilities. Courses leading to degrees offered in 1936 included metal mining engineering, coal mine engineering, mining geology, petroleum engineering, chemical engineering, ceramic engineering, ceramic technology, metallurgy and general science.[45]

The Chemistry and Chemical Engineering faculty had expanded significantly as well since the early days, and, in 1936, it included Schrenk, Ph. D., Professor of Chemistry and Head of the Chemistry Dept.;[46] Howard Leroy Dunlap, PhD, Professor of Chemical Engineering; Clarence John Monroe, PhD, Associate Professor of Physical Chemistry; Karl Kenneth Kershner, MS, Professor of Chemistry; Thomas Gordon Day, PhD, Instructor in Chemistry; John Shaw Sabine, MS, Graduate Assistant in Chemistry; Leroy Augustave Bay, BS, Graduate Assistant in Chemistry; and Vincent Smith, MA, Graduate Assistant in Chemistry.[47]

Though a slump in enrollment occurred after the peak year of 1931 due to the economic depression, enrollment in 1936 was over 400—a 9% increase from the previous year. Nevertheless, the Great Depression continued to adversely affect employment opportunities throughout the early '30s.[48]

Alpha Chi Sigma 1936

Meanwhile, notable events for Alpha Chi Sigma occurred in 1936 as well. One of the most significant events for the collegiate members of Alpha Chi Sigma occurred at the 14th Biennial Conclave which was jointly hosted by the Alpha Delta Chapter at the University of Cincinnati and the Cincinnati Professional Chapter. The Conclave moved to make the trial pledge manual—introduced in the previous Conclave—a permanent part of the pledge program. This established a uniform body of knowledge throughout the collegiate chapters which initiates were expected to know and which would aid the passing on of traditions from one generation of members to the next.

Other events of note that year included the grant to the Cleveland Professional Group to change its status to the Cleveland Professional Chapter and the permission for 61 Alpha Chi Sigma alumni living in Baton Rouge to form a professional chapter. And on September 15, 1936, Alpha Chi Sigma filed for incorporation as a non-profit in the state of Indiana.[49]

The Petition and Installation

In September, 1935, at the first business meeting of the year, the members of Epsilon Pi Omicron made tentative plans to petition Alpha Chi Sigma for affiliation in the early spring.[50] Earlier a series of actions had been taken paving the way for the formal petition. The Supreme Council passed proposition 713 on September 15, 1934, permitting Epsilon Pi Omicron to submit a preliminary petition for affiliation, and then on January 26, 1935, passed proposition 726, which permitted Epsilon Pi Omicron to submit a formal petition for affiliation.[51] All of Epsilon Pi Omicron's plans came to fruition, when, in early 1936, it formally petitioned Alpha Chi Sigma to grant a charter and establish a chapter at the Missouri School of Mines and Metallurgy:

> ### *To the Supreme Council and Chapters of Alpha Chi Sigma*
>
> We, the undersigned active and alumni members of Epsilon Pi Omicron, recognizing the benefits of such affiliation, do hereby petition that Alpha Chi Sigma Fraternity grant this organization a charter and establish a chapter at the Missouri School of Mines and Metallurgy. We pledge ourselves to uphold the standards and ideals of Alpha Chi Sigma and to abide by its rules and by-laws should a charter be granted.
>
> —The Petition—Reprinted

The petitioning group included members of the faculty, actives and alumni. Among the faculty signers were Dr. Schrenk, Dr. Dunlap, Dr. Monroe, and Dr. Day. In support of the petition, Charles H. Fulton, Director of the School of Mines and Metallurgy, University of Missouri, and H. H. Armsby, Registrar and Student Advisor, Missouri School of Mines and Metallurgy, wrote letters of recommendation to the Supreme Council of Alpha Chi Sigma.[52]

The Installation

On Saturday, May 2, 1936, Epsilon Pi Omicron became Beta Delta, the 52nd chapter of Alpha Chi Sigma. The installation was conducted by Grand Master Alchemist (GMA) H. E. Wiedemann (Alpha Epsilon). The installation team consisted of members from Delta Chapter at Missouri-Columbia, Alpha Epsilon chapter at Washington University in St. Louis, and the St. Louis Professional Chapter. The ceremony was presented by the Delta and Alpha Epsilon Chapters with G. F. Breckenridge, Delta; Frank Bruner, Delta; Ross Heinrich, Delta; Joseph Holmes, Delta; Lowell O'Daniel, Delta; Edward Ray, Delta; Alpha Gilliam, Alpha Epsilon; Ralph Sherwin, Alpha Epsilon; and Elmer Wirts, Alpha Epsilon participating.

The 25 charter members—who were listed alphabetically on the charter—were Leroy A. Bay; Harry C. Berger; Herman A. Brisch; Richard Cardetti; Robert L. Cunningham; Thomas G. Day; Thomas S. Donahue; Howard L. Dunlap; Oscar H. Fager; Edward C. Fiss; Arthur P. Hausmann; Milton L. Herzog; Peter A. Jenni; Howard F. Lange; Clemens R. Maise; Erwin C. Meckfessel; Leo H. Merchie; Herbert G. Mortland; John S. Sabine; Walter T. Schrenk; Elmer L. Smith; Ralph H. Striker; Hoyt G. Thompson; Elmer W. Volz; and Frank J. Zvanut.[53]

After the initiation ceremony, the Grand Chapter adjourned, and a meeting of Beta Delta convened to elect and install officers. The following were elected:

> Master Alchemist—Elmer W. Volz
> Vice Master Alchemist—Richard J. Cardetti
> Reporter—Arthur P. Hausmann
> Recorder—Harry C. Berger
> Treasurer—Clemens R. Maise
> Alumni Secretary—Thomas G. Day
> Chapter Advisor—Walter T. Schrenk

Following the election, addresses were given by: Counselor Breckenridge; Counselor Van Dorn; Brother Schrenk, faculty advisor; Brother M.

L. Griffin, secretary, St. Louis Professional Chapter; Brother Decker, president, St. Louis Professional Chapter; and GMA Wiedemann.[54]

An official proclamation declaring the establishment of Beta Delta was given to the chapter and reads as follows:

Acting under the authority of the Grand Chapter and at the direction of the Supreme Council, I hereby proclaim that the Beta Delta Chapter was established under the laws of the Fraternity at the Missouri School of Mines and Metallurgy in Rolla, Missouri, May 2nd, 1936.

Those persons listed in the petitioning group who were regularly initiated on that date are declared to be charter members. They are authorized to elect officers, conduct business, and initiate members under the provisions of the Constitution and By-laws of the Fraternity.

Until such time as the formal charter shall be engrossed and delivered this document constitutes authority for Beta Delta to operate as a chapter of Alpha Chi Sigma.

Signed, H.E. Wiedemann
Grand Master Alchemist

—The Proclamation Declaring the Establishment
of Beta Delta—Reprinted

Beta Delta Installation (November 1936 *Hexagon*, Vol.27 (2), 56.

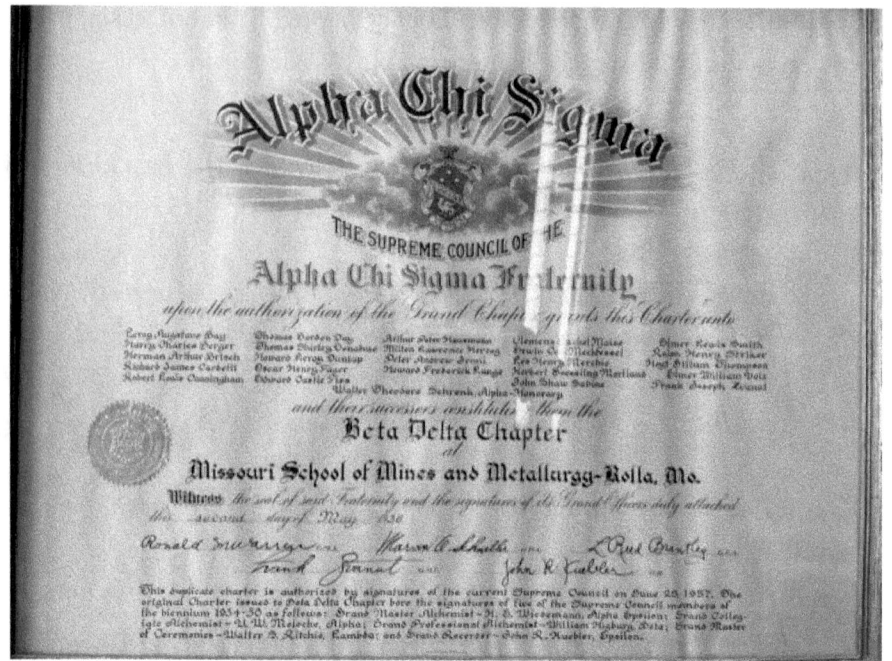

Beta Delta Charter (Duplicate)

The installation ceremony was conducted in time for Beta Delta to be represented at the 14th Biennial Conclave held in Cincinnati, Ohio, that summer. C. R. Maise represented the newest collegiate chapter of the fraternity. Later, in October, the fledgling chapter conducted the first initiation ceremony of its own, welcoming into membership Clarence J. Monroe and Lester Poese.[55] However, Dr. Monroe was prevented from being available in Rolla at the time of initiation due to the illness of his mother. So his initiation was delayed. Also, another special circumstance surrounded Dr. Monroe's initiation. Since Monroe was active throughout the development toward affiliation, the Supreme Council voted to permit him to be considered initiated as of May 2 and be listed as a charter member. However, the chapter decided to initiate him, not as a charter member, but as the first initiate of Beta Delta.[56]

Addressing the issue of Dr. Monroe's initiation, the meeting of May 6 or 8 (The date of the document was not clearly distinguishable) assigned instruction of the candidate to Dr. Schrenk, unless Dr. Dunlop chose to do so, and appointed the participants in the ceremony. In other business, Maise was elected to represent Beta Delta at the 14th Biennial Conclave which was held in Cincinnati, Ohio, the week of June 16-20. Brother Hausmann was chosen to act as an alternate in the event Maise could not attend, and Brother Fager moved that the chapter's funds be placed at Maise's disposal, which motion passed. Also, during this second meeting, it was decided to produce a newsletter, and that the responsibility for its publication would fall to the Alumni Secretary, Thomas Day. Erwin Meckfessel was appointed to assist Day. Keys to files were made available to the Reporter, Arthur Hausmann, and Day. During the discussion of the newsletter, Brother Fager suggested that flowers be sent to Day who was confined to the Rolla hospital at the time. The other members agreed, but the reason for Day's hospitalization was never disclosed. On a final note, Treasurer Maise reported the cost of Installation at $28.83, a quarter of which, $7.50, was spent on cigars.[57]

The last meeting of the spring semester was held on May 20. The primary order of business at this meeting was the initiation which was scheduled for May 22, but the chapter decided to postpone the initiation until the fall (No reason was recorded). Other business entailed the appointment of LeRoy Bay and Elmer Smith to audit the treasurer's books. There was also discussion of the local dues from professional members, but no decision was made. Finally, one last important matter was resolved. The ash trays left over from the Installation would be kept for future use, it was decided. However, there was no mention of left over cigars.

On September 16, the first meeting of the fall semester was held. After the call to order and the roll call, the first item on the agenda was Brother Maise's report on the Conclave. Appointments were then made of the participants in the upcoming initiation. Other business included the decision to have an informal Smoker for all chemists, the assignment of Maise and Sabine to make the necessary arrangements for the Smoker, a decision to move the chapter's files from Dr. Schrenk's office to Dr. Day's, and an agreement to credit all Epsilon Pi Omicron pledge fees toward the Alpha Chi Sigma initiation fee.[58]

At the October 7 meeting, the chapter decided to hold the initiation for Dr. Monroe and for one other candidate, Lester Poese, on October 23. A final list of eligible candidates for the fraternity was presented: 23 Sophomores, 8 Juniors, 2 Seniors, and 4 Graduates (of which Dr. Frank Conrad was one). To be eligible for induction, the chapter decided, those invited needed at least a 1.2 grade point average. (It must be pointed out that the grading scale at the time was different from the one in existence currently. The highest score possible was E, worth 3 points, while M, worth 1 point, was comparable to average.) Mimeographed sheets of eligible names were made available to members for review so a vote could be held at the next meeting. There was discussion of possibly inviting those from other disciplines which were not "pure chemistry or chemical engineering," but no final decision was made.

Since the Ira Remsen Society was still active in 1936, Brother Bay made a motion at the October 7 meeting that Ira Remsen and Alpha Chi Sigma sponsor speakers jointly except those whose talks would not be open to the public or whose expenses were paid by another group. The motion was accepted. Other items presented during that meeting included the reading of letters from Lester Poese and Leo Merchie, who had graduated in the spring, and a letter from the Grand Master Alchemist. (This letter was not included in the minutes and there was no reference to which letter it might have been.) Finally, before adjournment, the following committees were appointed: Pledge and Finance—Maise and Meckfessel; Grades—Cardetti and Sabine; and Speakers—Bay and Cunningham.[59]

At the next meeting on October 21, the chapter determined that the minutes should be more formally recorded and typed. Brother Maise moved that the Recorder purchase a special notebook and rewrite and type the minutes, for the year, to date. The motion carried. In addition, the Pledge Committee reported on three practices by other chapters in regard to pledge fees. These included: a) all fees to be dropped at the end of the year; b) $5.00 dues to be paid per year; and c) the same dues to be paid as actives paid. Sabine moved that plan "b" be adopted at the first of the school year; that motion carried. There was also discussion about the necessary equipment and materials needed for the initiation and about how prospective pledges ought to be approached. A vote on the eligible candidates followed: 29 were invited to pledge. At the end of the meeting, letters from alumni Richardson and Smith were shared by the Alumni Secretary.[60]

In keeping with the earlier decision to honor Dr. Monroe as the first initiate, Beta Delta initiated him on October 23. Lester Poese became Beta Delta's second initiate.

As early as the fall of 1936 certain customs and programs began to coalesce for Beta Delta: pledge requirements, regularly scheduled initiations, and periodic speakers were a few activities taking shape. Having regularly scheduled speakers for Beta Delta began with Mr. Merle L. Griffin of the Shell Petroleum Company, who addressed the chapter on November 18, 1936.

At the November 4 meeting, Hausmann moved that the Initiation ceremony for the full class of inductees would be held on Tuesday evening, November 17. Cardetti seconded the motion and the motion carried. Other business included an announcement of the Rollamo picture-taking and a suggestion that a schedule of the chapter's activities was needed. Brother C. Maise, Dr. T. Day and Dr. Schrenk were appointed as the Calendar committee. Finally, a letter from Frank Zvanut to Dr. Schrenk was read, but the subject matter was not revealed in the minutes.[61]

Whether or not the initiation ceremony of November 17 actually occurred remains a mystery since there was no mention of it in the meeting minutes. Moreover, Beta Delta's records and those of the National Office of Alpha Chi Sigma indicate different dates for those names appearing on the list of prospective pledges from October 7. The National Office recorded January 1, 1937, as the initiation date for Herbert F. Crecelius, Robert P. Cherry, and Dr. Frank H. Conrad. Both Beta Delta and the National Office record February 5, 1937, as the initiation date for Russell L. Yungbluth, William T. Pearl, and William B. Dunlap. (See Beta Delta, 1937, below.)

Another reason for the uncertainty surrounding the November 17 initiation date stems from the meeting minutes of November 23. At that meeting, Brother Bay moved that an initiation be held on December 11. This raises the question: Was the initiation scheduled for November delayed to December 11 for some reason? Unfortunately, chapter records provide no answer. Perhaps there was significance in the final item of business during that meeting: the approval of the purchase of 50 copies of the booklet, "Professional Fraternities."[62]

Discussions on how to formally identify and approach potential pledges began in December, 1936. At the meeting on December 6, pledges were once again discussed. It was decided that lists of all prospective rushees, the names of actual rushers, and accurate dates when persons were asked to pledge be kept. There was also discussion about the fireside meeting to be held on December 16 at Tom Day's house.[63]

According to the minutes of the meeting on December 16, Dr. Conrad and Edward Ballman were pledged at that time, but, again, there is no mention of the initiation that was scheduled for December 11. Also, neither the National Office's or Beta Delta's records indicated an initiation on November 17 or December 16. At that meeting the members were encouraged once again to have their pictures taken for the Rollamo.[64]

Beta Delta 1937 to 1939

1937

During the next few years, Beta Delta continued to work diligently to establish itself as an important member of the MSM community. Much of its effort centered on building the membership numerically and strengthening the group's fellowship activities. During the winter of 1936-1937, the St. Louis Professional Chapter helped Beta Delta become integrated into the national fraternity by including it and fellow collegiate chapter Alpha Epsilon on the invitation list for the St. Louis Professional Chapter winter meeting. This resulted in a total of eighty-five brothers gathering at the Busch brewery for lunch, hearing a presentation on the fermentation process, and, finally, taking a tour of the brewery.[65] Though Beta Delta members had become initially acquainted with members of the St. Louis Professional Chapter and Alpha Epsilon during the installation, this event further cemented a warm relationship and fraternal spirit among these three chapters.

The following spring, the chapter had to focus on the initiation of its first sizable pledge class (9 pledges) and their initiation, and anticipate its first anniversary. At the first celebration of its founding, former Grand Master Alchemist, Wiedemann of Alpha Epsilon, who had presided over Beta Delta's initiation a year earlier, was once again the honored speaker.[66]

Business meetings at the start of Beta Delta's second year reflected the chapter's commitment to grow and flourish. The first meeting of the spring semester on January 6 focused on two matters: creating the pledge quizzes for prospective pledges and electing new officers. Those elected were: Elmer Volz, Master Alchemist; Robert Cunningham, Vice Master Alchemist; Harry Berger, Recorder; Arthur Hausmann, Reporter (appointed); Clemens Maise, Treasurer; Peter Jenni, Master of Ceremonies; and Thomas Day, Alumni Secretary.[67] According to correspondence with the Grand Recorder from the spring of 1937, R. L. Yungbluth either assumed or shared the Reporter duties.[68]

Attracting new members and settling membership questions regarding competing fraternities were not the only membership problems facing Beta Delta. An issue which had been looming throughout the chapter's first year was finally taken up for consideration at the second meeting on January 20: how would the chapter determine the status of the delinquent members of Epsilon Pi Omicron who had become Alpha Chi Sigma members? Sabine moved that the old members of EΠO should not be considered for membership until they paid their dues, at which time they could be considered as new members. That motion was rejected; unfortunately, the minutes do not record if or how the issue was resolved. Perhaps the matter was tabled for a future meeting. New officers were also installed at that time.[69]

Also, at the January 20, 1937, meeting, a letter from Grand Master Alchemist Ritchie was received, but, once again, its contents were not recorded. The initiation was discussed and a practice date was set for January 29. The actual ceremony was scheduled for February 5.

Though no mention of the February 5 initiation was made in the meeting minutes, the chapter and the National Office records both reflect that the event occurred as discussed above. According to the records of the National Office, Russell L. Yungbluth, William T. Pearl, and William B. Dunlap were initiated on February 5. Beta Delta's records, however, also had Robert P. Cherry initiated on that date.

There was another singular membership decision at the time which was not lost on the chapter. Almost two decades had passed since Houston Taylor's first hopes were voiced in 1920, and much had transpired in the life of Epsilon Pi Omicron and Beta Delta since then, but the young chemical engineering student who started it all was not forgotten by the students in the late 1930s who benefitted from his earlier aspirations. In appreciation for his dream of seeing an Alpha Chi Sigma chapter at MSM, the members of Beta Delta decided to invite him to become a member. On February 22, 1937, the chapter requested Dr. Thomas G. Day, Alumni Secretary, to write to Taylor, who was living in Keokuk, Iowa, employed by Taylor's Laboratory—Bacteriological and Chemical, at the time. The letter conveyed the wishes of the membership to sponsor his election should he accept. Sadly, there is no documentation in the chapter's archives to indicate whether Taylor replied or not. There must have been previous correspondence, however, since Taylor had sent a letter to Day, dated December 20, 1936, in which he acknowledged the honor accorded to him by Beta Delta. He pointed out at that time that he would not be able to take advantage of the opportunity but did not want to close the option for membership should he be in a position to accept at a later date. Unfortunately, there was no evidence in Beta Delta's membership list or the national office's records that he elected to join.[70]

During the business meetings at this time, the details for inviting potential pledges, conducting initiations, building fellowship, promoting the chemical sciences, and governing the chapter were refined. At the next meeting on record on March 4, after the formalities of the call to order and the roll call, a letter from Grand Recorder Kuebler to the treasurer was shared. Evidently, there was a committee tasked to develop a letterhead for the chapter, and Cardetti reported on the committee's behalf. It was decided that the coat-of-arms of the fraternity should be included, and Cardetti was requested to obtain a copy of it. (The minutes do not reflect that this request was ever carried out.) The committee dealing with the freshman Smoker reported that it would be held on April 1, that it would consist of games, cards and refreshments, and that prizes would be awarded to the winners. Also, Cunningham of the Scholarship committee presented a list of freshman chemistry students as prospective pledges. Maise moved that only those having a grade-point average of 1.5 or better be accepted for pledging. The motion was accepted. One particular student, Schaumberg, was also accepted as a pledge candidate and was to be invited. Further business centered around the issue of the chapter's by-laws. Maise's proposal that a committee be appointed to write new by-laws was adopted, and a by-laws committee, consisting of Pearl, Thompson and Sabine, was appointed. In addition, an Auditing committee of Volz and Sabine was also established.[71]

In these formative years, the young chapter was not left to fend for itself. Chapters from the surrounding area warmly welcomed the fledgling organization. One such instance was an invitation from Delta chapter in Columbia. In a letter sent to Brother Yungbluth to share with the members of Beta Delta, Herb Volkening, Master Alchemist of Delta Chapter, invited Beta Delta to a dinner-dance held on Wednesday evening, April 21. The occasion was the celebration of Delta's 30th anniversary in Alpha Chi Sigma.[72] No record exists indicating whether or not Beta Delta responded, but very likely at least several members would have attended the event. The chapter was also guided through the mechanics of Alpha Chi Sigma's reporting and documentation procedures by the Grand Recorder, John R. Kuebler and his secretary, Winifred Koon. Significant correspondence was shared between the Office of the Grand Recorder and the chapter during the spring of 1937 concerning the reporting of initiates, the chapters' financial obligations to the "Hexagon" for those transferring to professional membership, and those initiation cases involving special circumstances of particular pledges.[73]

Also, the Grand Recorder offered sage advice on maintaining the viability of the chapter in a letter dated April 24, 1937, sent to R. L. Yungbluth but addressed to the chapter as a whole. The Grand Recorder cautioned the young chapter on two matters. The pertinent sections read as follows:

> First: pledging of men should take place in such a manner that the collegiate active membership maintains a good reserve of juniors and late sophomores. If not, when spring comes around, 'there ain't no chapter'—or the membership is so reduced that the chapter must be built up again.

> Second: I want to warn the chapter about the post-installation slump. Very frequently, we find, after those whose enthusiasm and energy brought the chapter into being are gone, there is a slide to mediocrity, loss of campus prestige, and a general weak pulse. There can be no let down from year to year, or resting on the oars. For a chapter to maintain excellence it must continually keep the grease off its vest, its hair parted, and lodestone out of its pants. When a local affiliates with Alpha Chi Sigma and assumes the national name, it does not acquire a magic possession which will maintain its operation. Local reputation depends upon local effort.[74]

(This advice was not only sound when it was offered, but continued to prove pertinent throughout Beta Delta's history. As will be seen later in these pages, a time would come when the chapter forgot this advice and suffered greatly for the forgetting.)

Edward A. Ballman was initiated on April 30, and on May 19, according to the National Office records, Jack W. Moore and Leo M. O'Hara were initiated. The chapter also recorded two additional inductees on April 30: Herbert F. Crecelius (National records indicate January 1) and Walter E. Duncan. Beta Delta records also show that Frank H. Conrad was initiated on May 19, though the National records had an initiation date of January 1.

The last meeting of the spring semester, held on May 20, tackled two important items of business. The first was a proposal by Maise that the chapter, at the year's graduation exercises, extend an award to the student, in either Chemical Engineering or Chemistry, with the highest grade point average for four years. The award would consist of a junior membership for one year in the American Chemical Society and a one-year subscription to the Journal of Industrial and Engineering Chemistry. The other line of business was the installation of officers for the fall semester: C. R. Maise, Master Alchemist; E. Ballman, Vice-Master Alchemist; H. F. Crecelius, Recorder; W. T. Pearl, Treasurer; and W. Dunlap, Master of Ceremonies.[75]

Fall semester activities got started at the September 15 meeting in which the Communications committee shared a letter from H. H. Armsby, Registrar of the Missouri School of Mines and Metallurgy, acknowledging the graduation award. Armsby's letter read in part, "May I offer my congratulations to Alpha Chi Sigma for their action in establishing the Alpha Chi Sigma award. This is a very much worthwhile activity for your fraternity and I shall be very glad indeed to include a notice of it in the Commencement Program."[76] A letter from the American Chemical Society acknowledging receipt of the payment and application for junior membership was shared as well. The brothers then decided to give a Smoker on September 29 for the upper-classmen taking chemistry, and an initiation for three eligible candidates on October 8 was also planned. In addition, the following committees were appointed: Advisory—C. R. Maise, W. T. Pearl, W. T. Schrenk, and Dr. Breckenridge; Auditing—E. Ballman, J. W. Moore, and W. E. Duncan; Membership—E. Ballman, L. M. O'Hara, and H. F. Crecelius; and Scholarship—C. R. Maise, W. B. Dunlap, and J. S. Sabine. The Scholarship committee was delegated to make the arrangements for the Smoker.[77]

After the Smoker, a follow-up meeting was held on October 6. To determine qualified candidates, E. Ballman moved that those having a grade point average of 1.00 or above be considered for pledging. He also provided a list of qualified candidates. These included three seniors, 16 juniors, five sophomores, and four graduate students. A Pledge Program committee, consisting of Dunlap and Ballman, was appointed and a Calendar committee of "Doc" Day and J. S. Sabine was also established. Finally, plans were made for a shared speaker with the Ira Remsen Society. Ballman's motion carried, provided both parties agreed to share the speaker and the speaker retained the option to address only Alpha Chi Sigma.[78]

Evidently, the initiation planned for October 8 was not held. There is no record of the event, and neither the Beta Delta Membership records nor the National Office records list anyone being initiated on that date. Presumably the three pledges referenced in the September 15 meeting were Merritt M. Francis, Robert Alfred Carter, and Jack Ralph Glatthaar, who were initiated on December 3, according to the Beta Delta Membership list. The National Office records are in agreement, except for Carter who was initiated on January 1, 1938, according to those records.

On November 3, Dr. Malcolm Dole gave a talk entitled "Isotopes of Oxygen and Hydrogen in Nature" before the members of Beta Delta and the Ira Remsen Society. Apparently both organizations and the speaker agreed upon a shared event.[79]

At the next meeting on November 10, a vote was taken to determine which of the prospective candidates should be invited to pledge. Two seniors, six juniors, four sophomores, and three graduate students were asked to join the chapter. The Program committee also recommended that four pledge meetings be held from the time of the formal pledging to the initiation to acquaint the pledges with the history, customs, and other pertinent knowledge about Alpha Chi Sigma. Pledge quiz dates of November 17, 18, and 19 were set in preparation for the December initiation. Finally, a letter from the Grand Collegiate Alchemist regarding the standing of the fraternity, and an announcement of the scholarship award to be given at Conclave, were shared.[80]

A week later, on November 16, the formal pledging ceremony was held for six of the prospective candidates invited to the previous Smoker. Those who decided to pledge included: William H. Webb, Merritt M. Francis, Robert A. Carter, Hill, Lee Roy Johnson, and Jack R. Glatthaar. (It is unclear who Hill was. No first name was given. A Eugene Hill was initiated in 1939, but given the time discrepancy, Its unlikely that this would have been the same person.)[81]

Alpha Chi Sigma and the Ira Remsen Society met in another joint session on November 17. This time members heard Hugh Berry of the Shell Petroleum Corporation speak about "Various Problems Encountered by the Chemical Engineer."[82]

As mentioned earlier, Francis, Carter and Glatthaar were initiated on December 3, while Webb and Johnson were not initiated until February 11, according to the Beta Delta membership records. The National Office records, however, listed Webb's initiation on January 1, 1938, and only Johnson's on February 11.

The last meeting of the semester occurred on December 15. This was a short meeting at which members discussed the progress made on the ash trays which were being made by the pledges (Apparently, the ash trays left over from the installation of the chapter in 1936 were lost, broken, overused from rubbing out cigars, or just no longer aesthetically appealing.) The members were also reminded to have their pictures taken for the Rollamo, and Christmas cards received by the chapter were passed around. After the meeting was adjourned, a social gathering was held to decorate the Christmas tree in the chapter room. Holiday refreshments were served.[83]

Left to Right: Top Row: H. Berger, E. Ballman, R. Cunningham, R. Cardetti, E. Volz.

Second Row: R. Cherry, F. Conrad, H. Crecelius, T. Day, A. Hausmann.

Third Row: P. Jenni, C. Maise, W. Schrenk, J. Sabine, H. Thompson

Beta Delta Chapter 1937[84]

1938

The first official business of 1938 was conducted at a very short meeting—lasting only 10 minutes—on January 5. The purpose, ostensibly, was to review the status of the pledges' ash tray and plaque projects. (Calling a special meeting to ascertain the status of ash tray designs seemed to indicate two important factors in the life of the chapter: the initiative of each of the pledges and—perhaps more crucially—the importance of smoking.) Those pledges who were finished with their projects were: Runyan, Glatthaar, Francis and Carter. The others still working on theirs at the time were: Elliott, Hill, Webb, Cowan, and Volz (Herbert). At the end of this mini-meeting, it was also announced that elections would be held at the next meeting.[85]

During the January 19 meeting, the initiation to receive Lee Roy Johnson and William H. Webb (Later to become one of the chapter's most active advisors) into membership was planned for the following month. Afterwards, the following officers were elected: C. R. "Doc" Maise, Master Alchemist; J. R. Glatthaar, Vice-Master Alchemist; J. W. Moore, Reporter; Carter, Recorder; W. T. Pearl, Treasure; and M. M. Francis, Master of Ceremonies. (Somewhere along the line, Brother Maise picked up the same appellation applied to professors. Presumably, this came about because of his status as a graduate student and laboratory assistant.)[86]

At the meeting preceding the initiation ceremony, on February 2, the officers elected for the spring semester were installed. Vice-Master Alchemist, Glatthaar, then presented a list of potential pledges from the Chemical Engineering department. Brother Ballman moved that only persons having a grade point average greater than 1.00 be considered for eligibility. This stipulation still resulted in 19 prospective pledges. Following the presentation of the prospective pledges, Brother Crecelius proposed that a banquet be held for the pledges Webb and Johnson at 6:00pm, February 11, at the Houston Hotel in Newburg.[87]

Within a week of the initiation, another business meeting was called on February 16. The first order of business, of course, was the ashtray issue. VMA Glatthaar announced that the cast for ash trays and for a series of plaques had been completed. Pledge issues were a second order of business: a by-Law establishing the amount of the fees was proposed by the By-Laws committee and presented by Dr. Day. From those prospective pledges listed at the February 2 meeting, 10 were invited to pledge. Brother Pearl was then elected as Beta Delta's Conclave delegate; Brothers Glatthaar and Crecelius were elected as the first and second alternates, respectively.[88]

About this time, a letter dated February 24, 1938, addressed to all Counselors, Master Alchemists and Masters of Ceremonies, arrived in the chapter's mailbox. Grand Master of Ceremonies (GMC), Harold P. Gaw had several concerns in regard to the pledge examination. First, he reiterated the requirement that the examination was to be given to all candidates prior to initiation. He wrote that he had not received examination papers for all those initiated, which caused him to question whether the examinations were being properly administered. He pointed out the importance of the examination in offering new members a better insight into the origin, scope and functions of Alpha Chi Sigma. His letter also admonished the chapter to use the official list of questions which was given in the Pledge Manual and the Ritual. Gaw acknowledged the official list was less than perfect but requested that it be used until improvements could be made. He also pointed out that Edict #7 on page 31 of the Constitution specified that the examination papers were to be forwarded to the GMC. Evidently, some of the chapters were sending papers to the Grand Recorder's office, instead.[89]

The next business meeting on March 2 reviewed the status of organizational and social activities necessary to the life of the chapter and its relation to the larger campus life. A letter was received from the Grand Recorder concerning the Conclave delegates, and ensuring a proper flow of information between the Grand Chapter and Beta Delta. Within Beta Delta the status of activities and duties of the pledges were discussed in anticipation of the initiation. And in regard to the larger campus community, the chapter planned a dinner dance for a time later in the semester with Brothers Ballman and Sabine assigned to determine an estimate of the cost. In addition, Brothers Johnson and Pearl were appointed to confer with Dr. Mann, Professor of Engineering Drawing and Descriptive Geometry, and Dr. Dodd, Professor of Ceramic Engineering, in preparation for the upcoming Engineers' Day. The event, which scientists, engineers, teachers, and students attended to view and participate in exhibits presented by various companies and departments at the school was scheduled for April 21-23.[90]

A few days later, on March 7, a formal pledge ceremony was held in which brothers Parker, Magill, and Stewart were pledged. As was the custom, coffee and doughnuts were served afterwards. The next day, March 8, Beta Delta, in keeping with its commitment to jointly sponsor speakers, invited, along with the Ira Remsen Society, Dr. Ellis I. Fullner, Professor of Biophysical Chemistry at Iowa State College. Dr. Fullner's address was entitled "Industrial Adaptations of Fermentation."[91]

On March 17, Brother Yungbluth received a special request from Paul Bender of Chi chapter at Yale to visit Beta Delta. The visit, however, was not just a social call. Brother Bender also requested that a meeting with Professor Graine be arranged for April 4. His purpose was to solicit suggestions from Dr. Graine regarding which localities would offer the greatest possibilities for securing as many different mineral specimens as possible.[92]

Apparently, the day-to-day life of the chapter would not be complete without an occasional update on the status of the ashtrays. At the business meeting on March 30, right after the roll call, reading of the previous meeting's minutes and the Treasurer's report, the first order of business was the report on the ashtray project. Brother Glatthaar reported that pledges Rhea and Stewart had been working with Dr. Herold, PhD, Ceramics Instructor,[93] to prepare the mud for the ashtrays. Other business which followed the discussion of the repository of cigars and cigarettes included: a letter from the Grand Recorder which invited all members to attend Conclave (though the chapter could only afford to send one) and the appointment of Brother Ballman to survey members and pledges on their willingness to pay $3.00 for a dinner dance.[94]

April 13 marked a major milestone in the ashtray saga. The first ashtrays were removed from the cast, and arrangements were made with the pledges to provide the finishing work. The only other item discussed was the humble dinner dance which was planned for some time in May. Of course the usual coffee and rolls were served after the meeting.[95]

Two weeks later, after the climatic successful cast removal, the ashtray project's importance waned. The major topic of the April 20 meeting was Beta Delta's founding. Brother Moore motioned that the chapter hold its anniversary banquet at the Edwin Long Hotel at 6:30pm on May 2. Brother Pearl then followed with a motion to hold the initiation ceremony on Friday, May 6. Both motions passed. Brothers Moore, Pearl, and Crecelius were assigned to get out a newsletter announcing both events.[96]

Early in the history of the chapter, talks and discussions were often held on the subject of alchemy—its persons, history, and concepts. These were conducted, not just by active members, but by pledges as well. For instance, in early April, at a pledge meeting, C. L. Cowan, and H. A. Volz, who were pledging at the time, gave such talks.[97] Documented evidence of a meeting in May also reports a presentation from E. R. Elliott on "Paracelsus," an alchemist of the early 16th century and the appointed physician of the city of Basel. Much has been said of Paracelsus, but of particular note was his emphasis on direct observation.[98] He had learned of mining and metallurgy practices and related occupational diseases first hand. From this experience, he developed his techniques for gaining knowledge primarily through personal observation and, to a lesser extent, through academic studies.[99]

The second Beta Delta Anniversary Banquet, held on May 2, 1938, at the Edwin Long Hotel in Rolla, established the celebration as an annual event. St. Louis chapter members were present for the festivities.[100]

Finally, on May 4, officers were elected in preparation for the fall semester, establishing the election of officers for each semester as a precedent-setting practice. The newly elected officers were: W. T. Pearl, MA; J. R. Glatthaar, VMA; H. F. Crecelius, Master of Ceremonies; M. M. Francis, Treasurer; and R. A. Carter, Recorder. W. T. Pearl was selected as the delegate to the Conclave in New Orleans. The chapter also decided to purchase a pennant for Brother Pearl to take to Conclave.[101]

During this meeting, the Alpha Chi Sigma Award offered by Beta Delta was made permanent. Brother W. E. Duncan made the motion to secure this award for future members. The chapter was also honored to have Section Counselor Breckenridge from Columbia in attendance at this meeting.[102]

On May 6, according to the Beta Delta membership records, H. A. Volz, John C. Magill, Clyde L. Cowan, and Robert M. Stewart were initiated. Dr. Gerald Breckenridge, along with two members of Delta chapter attended the ceremony.[103]

By the end of the 1938 spring semester, the swirl of elements in the retort started to clarify. The procedures and patterns of activities were coalescing: elections and initiations were occurring on a schedule, ensuring the continuing life of the chapter; formal recognitions such as the Alpha Chi Sigma Award and regular talks on the chemical sciences became established, promoting the chemical sciences; and social events with other chapters were held, building the bonds of friendship. Over time these activities would further coalesce and precipitate into long-standing traditions and customs.

During the summer, the members of Beta Delta were saddened to learn of the death of one of the charter members, Peter A. Jenni, a native of Crystal City, MO. Jenni died of pneumonia on June 29. Born on May

17, 1915, he graduated in 1937 with a BS in Chemical Engineering, and he was working as a research chemist for Portland Cement Co. at the time of his death.[104]

Returning in the early fall of 1938, first on Beta Delta's agenda was a meeting, September 21, to organize a Smoker from which prospective new members could be selected. Brother Glatthaar presented a list of students, with their grade point averages, from the chemical engineering department who were eligible for membership. Brother Maise moved that only those with a grade point average of 1.00 or greater, as previously required, be considered. A vote was taken, and out of the list of sophomores, juniors and seniors, 23 were approved. Beyond this business item, Master Alchemist Pearl made the following appointments: Smoker Entertainment committee—T. Stewart, C. Maise, C. Cowan, and W. Pearl; Membership committee—J. Glatthaar, E. Volz, and T. Stewart; Auditing committee—J. Glatthaar, W. Webb, and C. Cowan; Scholarship Committee—W. Pearl, J. Magill, and L. Johnson; and Advisory committee—W. Pearl, M. Francis, Dr. Schrenk, and C. Maise. In addition, Cowan was appointed editor of the newsletter.[105]

The Smoker for potential pledges was held on September 28 at the Edwin Long Hotel. The gathering topped all previous attendance records: 50 people. The event was deemed by the brothers to be a great success. The attendees "…smoked, sang, and played their troubles away…. Fun and general nonsense… were the order of the day." Shortly after the Smoker, a second meeting was held to select those who would be asked to pledge. During the meeting, W. T. Pearl reported on the 15th Biennial Conclave in New Orleans, and Dr. Schrenk told of plans for a joint meeting and initiation with chapters from the University of Missouri and Washington University in St. Louis.[106]

The pledge class, gathered from the Smoker invitees, was the first class to be instructed using a formal pledge manual. The first edition of The Pledge Manual of Alpha Chi Sigma Fraternity had become available. That fall, Walter Schrenk was appointed the Midwestern District Counselor on June 25, 1938, per Supreme Council proposition 885, filling the post vacated by the resignation of Gerald Breckenridge.[107]

On October 30, Beta Delta hosted its first Midwest District Jamboree at the Edwin Long Hotel. A committee of Beta Delta brothers served to greet and welcome the visitors. At 12:30 a turkey dinner was served in the College Inn at the hotel, after which the women guests were escorted on a tour of the campus and the members convened their meeting. The formal program began with the pledging of Mr. Anastasoff of Alpha Epsilon chapter. Brother Wiedemann, chair of the program committee, called on Brother Harry Curtis (Eta), Dean of Missouri University Engineering School, to speak. Curtis gave an account of what Alpha Chi Sigma had meant to him. Next, the Master Alchemists from Delta, Kappa and Alpha Epsilon shared the activities of their chapters over the past year. Brothers Huff and Schneller from the St. Louis Professional Chapter followed with an account of their activities as well. Also, Chapter Advisors Breckenridge (Alpha Epsilon) and Gardner (Delta chapter) spoke on the problems of their particular chapter and their endeavors to promote a more active membership. The final speaker was Dr. Schrenk who read several letters expressing approval and encouragement for this type of gathering. A high light of the event was a trip to Merrimac Springs.[108]

At the November 16 meeting, Master Alchemist Pearl read a letter from the Grand Recorder, which announced that the fraternity was putting together pictures of the chemistry buildings of the colleges at which Alpha Chi Sigma had chapters. These pictures were to be published in the "Hexagon." Brother Duncan consented to take several pictures of MSM's chemistry building. It was also determined that the initiation ceremony would be held on December 10. For the ceremony, Brother Pearl assigned brothers Moore, Carter, Crecelius, Volz, Cowan, Johnson, Francis, Duncan, Magill, and Stewart as the participants. Brothers Cowan and Webb were assigned to assist Brother Glatthaar in the set-up, while Brother Francis was asked to make the arrangements for the banquet to be held in honor of the new members.[109]

Before the holidays, on December 10, the ranks of Beta Delta were increased by the induction of seven new initiates: Robert K. Carpenter, Joseph M. Coon, Thomas L. Harsell, C. Rampacek, John James Parker, William R. Rhea, and James R. Runyan.[110]

Beginnings 43

E. Ballman   C. Maise   W. Pearl

J. Moore   H. Crecelius   Hill

J. Sabine   W. Schrenk   T. Day

H. Thompson   J. Glatthaar   W. Duncan

L. O'Hara   J. Runyan   M. Francis

Beta Delta Chapter 1938—Rollamo 1938

1939

New Year's Eve may have marked the end of one year and the beginning of another, but the business of Beta Delta progressed seamlessly. The move from the initiation activities at the end of the fall semester transitioned smoothly into the election of officers and another initiation in February.[111] By this time the customs of having talks or presentations at meetings, and banquets honoring new initiates had become the norm.

The elections for the spring semester were held on either January 18 or 25. Those elected included: W. T. Pearl, Master Alchemist; Jack Glatthaar, Vice-Master Alchemist; Marvin Coon, Reporter; Lee Roy Johnson, Recorder; M. M. Francis, Treasurer; R. M. Stewart, Master of Ceremonies; and Dr. T. G. Day, Alumni Secretary. The honored guest at the election meeting was A. Schueller of G. S. Robins Chemical Company who spoke on the value of Alpha Chi Sigma to the graduate engineer.

It was not all business at the start of the year, however. On January 24, Beta Delta was invited to a dinner and dance on February 4, a Saturday, in St. Louis. The affair was arranged by the District Area Committee for the fraternity.[112]

The initiation ceremony was planned at the next meeting on February 1. Two new men were pledged to the chapter: Bill Enderson and David Boltz. The members set the date of the initiation as February 25, and the following were assigned as the participants: Carpenter, Rampacek, Coon, Parker, Cowan, Rea, Francis, Magill, Runyan and Stewart. Also, a new committee—a Master of Ceremonies committee which consisted of Brothers Stewart, Crecelius, Cowan and Carpenter—was appointed. Another assignment was given to Brother Harsell to put together a list of eligible candidates for membership. There was also a discussion of whether a petitioning organization at Clemson College of North Carolina should be admitted to the Alpha Chi Sigma fraternity. The members voted in favor of admitting the new chapter. There is mention for the first time in these minutes of a Mass meeting. And a film and discussion were also suggested. Nothing else was recorded about the nature of this meeting. (Were these cryptic references the antecedents to the future practice of Mass Meetings and/or Mass Transfer?)[113]

At the February 15 meeting, the initiation plans were finalized. Beyond that there was discussion of the need for a more active social life for the chapter. In that vein Brother Pearl suggested that Beta Delta join with Tau Beta Pi in sponsoring a dance in the early spring. Another social function, the mass meeting, which was initially raised at the previous meeting, was further discussed. The idea of a film was dropped in favor of inviting a speaker. If a speaker was not available, a film on petroleum might still be shown. Other items on the agenda were the status of the newsletter and methods to increase attendance.[114]

The initiation ceremony came off as planned. Four new Alpha Chi Sigma brothers—Edward E. Elliott, Hubert Allen Hayden, Donald George Crecelius, and John Vincent Cramer—joined the fraternity.[115] Afterwards, a banquet was held to honor the initiates at the Houston House in Newburg. Games of pinochle and bridge were enjoyed later in the evening. Apparently, students who had been indoctrinated in the ways of rowdy St. Pat's festivities were still able to enjoy a relatively tame evening.

On the Wednesday following the initiation ceremony, March 1, the regular business meeting was held. The members decided that the dance, previously discussed, should be held on April 15. The arrangements were assigned to Brothers Maise and Elliott. In regard to the mass meeting, Mr. Kingsley, a patent attorney, was consulted for the occasion. Further, the chapter reached a consensus that a social event ought to be held once a month. After discussion of possible social events, the meeting turned to the more mundane concerns for ensuring the function of the fraternity. Two new committees were appointed. The By-Laws committee consisted of brothers Carter (chair), Coon, and Cramer, and the committee to examine the problem of delinquent dues included brothers Pearl, Francis and Maise. In addition, dues owed by pledges were reviewed, and a list of prospective pledges was provided for a vote. All those on the list had met the grade point requirement and therefore were eligible for pledging.[116]

Talks and lectures at this time were not restricted to meetings and banquets. Dr. Schrenk was still very energetically giving his talks outside of the classroom. In March he gave several lengthy lectures and demonstrations on the peculiarities and properties of liquid air. These lectures began with a discussion of the physical and chemical properties of liquid air, and then he demonstrated how intense cold affected other substances. He boiled liquid air on carbon dioxide ice. He made a hammer of frozen mercury. He even made a spring out of lead by freezing it.[117]

On March 28, Tuesday evening, Beta Delta members drove to Columbia for a short business meeting with Delta chapter. Plans were made for a Jamboree on May 7 preceded by a dance on May 6. The Beta Delta members were promised dates with the women from Stevens College, a private women's college in Columbia, MO. Also on March 28, Brother T. G. Day hosted a dinner for the Beta Delta members at his home. Some of the brothers who attended the dinner had hoped to find out what questions might be asked on the organic chemistry quiz Dr. Day was giving the following morning.[118]

A lull in activities occurred in April, but May more than made up for the inactivity. About a dozen Beta Delta members spent the weekend of May 6 and 7 as guests of the Columbia Chapter which had also invited the Kansas University and Washington University chapters and the Professional groups from Kansas City and St. Louis. Fourteen were initiated into the fraternity including three from Beta Delta—William Enderson, David F. Boltz, and E. Clark Romine—and eleven others from the visiting chapters.[119] That Saturday evening the visitors were honored with a banquet and dance. Only two Beta Delta members required dates; all they had to do was provide their respective heights, and the arrangements were made.[120] Whether they enjoyed the evening, however, was a question that was not answered in the minutes. Among the speakers at the banquet were Dean Curtis, head of the College of Engineering at Missouri University in Columbia, MO, and Dr. Schrenk, who was still head of the Chemical Engineering Department at MSM. The next day, Sunday, a District meeting was held during a picnic. The meeting was followed by a baseball game between the professional members and the collegiate members played during a continual downpour.[121]

A week later, Beta Delta members held a combination picnic-meeting, on May 16, in honor of the departing seniors. Delta Chapter was invited as well, but no one was able to attend. Dr. and Mrs. Schrenk served as hosts.[122] Croquet and cards were played, followed by a business meeting to install new officers—Hubert Hayden,[123] MA; Robert K. Carpenter, VMA; Merritt Francis, Treasurer; Donald Crecelius, Recorder; T.G. Day, Alumni Secretary; Clyde Cowan, MC; and Joseph Coon, Reporter. Hosting outings became a regular practice for the Schrenks. That summer, their annual lawn party for Beta Delta Chapter members was another social success story.[124]

Occasionally, throughout the chapter's history, an officer may not have been able to complete his or her term in office. In October, in a special election, Clark Romine was elected to replace M. Francis as Treasurer when Francis failed to return to school.[125] Romine was elected by acclamation at the October 5 meeting. Other items covered at this meeting included: an invitation from the chapter at Lawrence Kansas inviting Beta Delta to join in an initiation ceremony; an invitation from the St. Louis Professional chapter for a picnic, which the brothers decided to hold at Rolla; and a request from Theta Tau to join them in sponsoring a dance held on November 11.[126]

Shortly after the special election, three Chemical Engineering students were initiated into Alpha Chi Sigma along with six pledges from Kappa Chapter, Kansas University, in a joint initiation ceremony held on October 14 at Lawrence, Kansas. Those initiated into Beta Delta were Carl Cotterill, Caesar Leslie, and Andy Cochran.[127] Two actives, D. G. Crecelius and L. E. Henson, and Dr. Schrenk, District Counselor, journeyed to Lawrence, Kansas to take part in the initiation which was held in the chemistry building. The initiation lasted until midnight and was followed by a "midnight lunch and bull session." The Beta Delta entourage left early Sunday morning and enjoyed a tour of the Lake of the Ozarks before returning to Rolla.[128]

Pledging was not over for the semester, however. On October 26, a Smoker was held in which the entertainment consisted of a series of tests. One of the contests, conducted by Prof. Day, involved boiling water, which was similar to pinning the tail on the donkey. Apparently, everyone got stuck before the water was even warm. "Doc" Maise presided over another contest of identifying lab apparatus by touch. Those observing the participants concluded that they had "…developed their sense of touch by feeling other things beside lab apparatus."[129]

At a business meeting a few days later on November 1, Brother Enderson inquired about the ash tray project. Evidently, interest had not completely died, but members were not much interested in reviving the idea. Instead, a new pledge project was proposed: making silvered retorts. In addition, a preliminary vote was taken on prospective pledges who had attended the Smoker.[130]

Shortly after the Smoker, Beta Delta hosted a Jamboree on November 4. The Kappa (Kansas), Alpha Epsilon (St. Louis), and Delta (Columbia) chapters as well as the St. Louis and Kansas City Professional chapters were invited. The first feature of the day was a visit to the blast furnaces and springs at Meramac, a new experience for many of those attending. (The furnaces were used during the Civil War for the production of cannon and cannon balls. They did not go out of use until richer ore fields were found in Michigan.) Brothers Bill Enderson and William Webb then took charge of registration. A noon luncheon was held at the Edwin Long Hotel followed by a business meeting. During this meeting, Mrs. Schrenk escorted the women on a tour of the MSM campus and buildings. This was followed in the afternoon by a gathering at the Schrenks' home where the customary softball game was played between the collegiates and the professionals. The professionals came out on the long end of the 29 to 13 score. The score, however, did not tell the whole story. To mollify the Professionals over their previous defeat the Collegiates gave them a lead (The size of the lead was not recorded). But the Collegiates had not considered the quality of the bats they were playing with. Though the bats were supplied by the Athletics Department, they could not stand up to the ferocious hitting. By the sixth inning, all the bats were shattered, and the Collegiates could not come back from the huge, self-inflicted deficit. Afterward, everyone proceeded to the College Inn where the chapters held a joint business meeting. Mr. and Mrs. Merle L. Griffin (Alpha Epsilon) were also present at the Jamboree and enjoyed the festivities.[131]

At the November 15 meeting, Brother Henson reported that the dance jointly sponsored with Theta Tau on November 11 was a success. It was also decided that the prospective pledges would be voted on in groups of five, and that formal pledging would be held on November 28 for those who accepted the invitation.[132]

An interesting invitation was passed along to the Beta Delta brothers from the Grand Recorder. In a letter dated December 1, 1939, John R. Kuebler announced that Henry Harrison, a poetry publisher out of New

York was seeking submissions for a planned publication, *The Greek Letter*, an anthology of poems by members of fraternities and sororities, edited by Helen Bryant. There was no record that any Beta Delta brothers submitted any poems.[133]

Once formal pledging was completed, the chapter quickly established tasks for the pledges. At the December 6 meeting, the active members agreed that those initiated before January would present "scientific" reports at the banquet on the night of initiation. Also, the sophomore pledges would work on product boards for the halls. A final project for the pledges was to fix the lock on the file cabinets. In preparation for the upcoming initiation, a mock initiation was conducted, twenty copies of the pledge manual were purchased, and—believe it or not—the ashtray project was resuscitated when Dr. Schrenk made a passing remark that "something should be done about the ashtrays." (Evidently, whatever the issue was, it was a perplexing one for the chapter.)[134]

The Smoker and the pledging efforts resulted in four new initiates into the fraternity on December 16: Eugene Hill (His initiation date is shown as January 1, 1940, in the National Office's records), Carl Zvanut, Sebastian L. Hertling, and Harold Nicholas. The actives who participated in the ceremony included Brothers Carpenter, Crecelius, Coon, Enderson, Henson, Boltz, Cowan, Cochran, and Leslie. The honorary banquet was once again held in Newburg. The new members read the "scientific" papers they had prepared for the evening. The initiates' topics included: "Entropy Strainers" by Brother Hill; "Specific and Selective Seductive Capacity" by Brother Hertling; "Production of Butter from Butter of Antimony" by Brother C. Zvanut; and "Production of Ethyl Urinate" by Brother Nicholas. The banquet ended with card playing which lasted until after midnight. The fate of the ashtrays remained unresolved.[135]

During these years before the country entered WWII, the chemical sciences and the fraternity were not the only focus of members' lives. Some excelled in unrelated avocations, which has held true throughout the chapter's history. One such brother was C. R. 'Doc' Maise, who loved being involved in theatrical activities. In January of 1939 his crew produced the play, "It's the Climate"—a three-act comedy about Hollywood—which was part of the General Lecture Program, a series of various lectures, concerts, and performances presented throughout the school year. Plays were a common feature of the Lecture Program. Other examples included "Tea for Three" and "Mistress of the Inn" from 1930.[136]

The great expenditure of commitment and effort that led to the establishment of Beta Delta—and cemented its identity—had extended over two decades from the kernel of an idea to the enactment of regular practices and customs. The fruits of such an endeavor, however, would quickly be put to the test. The war years of WWII would place a significant strain on the young organization.

C. Cowan   H. Crecelius   J. Glatthaar   T. Harsell

L. Johnson   C. Maise   J. Moore   W. Pearl

W. Rhea   R. Stewart

Beta Delta Chapter 1939—Rollamo 1939

Excursus: Founders/Signers of the Petition

Faculty

Dr. W.T. Schrenk

Walter T. Schrenk—Rollamo 1936

Walter T. Schrenk came to MSM in 1923. He was born 24 May, 1891, at Golconda, IL, and he received his elementary education there. He then attended Monmouth College, Monmouth, IL, earning a BS degree in 1915, and after graduation he spent two years teaching chemistry and physics at Genesco, IL. In 1917, Dr. Schrenk resigned as principal of the high school at Galena, IL, in order to accept an instructorship and engage in graduate work in the Chemistry department at the University of Wisconsin, which led to his Master's and Doctor's degrees in 1919 and 1922, respectively. He wrote his doctoral thesis on "The Action of Selenium Oxychloride on the Different Coals."[137]

When the government established a chemical warfare service plant at Edgewood, Maryland, in April, 1918, Schrenk was one of the scientists sent to organize the plant and laboratory and get operations started. While there, Schrenk conducted research and did control work on chloropicrin, phosgene and mustard gas. In 1923, he resigned his position at the University of Wisconsin and accepted the position of assistant professor of chemistry at the Missouri School of Mines and Metallurgy where he taught Analytical and Inorganic Chemistry. A year later he was promoted to Associate Professor. His next promotion came in 1929 when he became a full Professor of Chemical Engineering. He would go on to serve as Chair of the Chemistry and Chemical Engineering Departments from 1928 to 1956, as a consultant with the Missouri Mining Experiment Station from 1929 to 1961, and as a consultant with the Mississippi Valley Research Station from 1929 to 1946. Both consulting positions were in conjunction with the US Bureau of Mines.[138]

From early on in his career, Schrenk was known for his entertaining talks regarding issues in chemistry. In 1923 he gave an in-depth lecture on Selenium Oxychloride for the Ira Remsen Society. The emphasis was on the compound's unique properties—its power to dissolve coal and rubber and its action as an "anti" knock compound for gasoline engines.[139]

Schrenk's talks did not only pertain to industrial chemistry. His lectures also addressed the societal implications of industrial processes. A talk given to the Ira Remsen Society in 1927 entitled "Pollution of Certain Missouri Streams" discussed the relation Chemical Engineers might have with polluted waters and demonstrated how the Chemical Engineer might be confronted by pollution problems. He also specifically pointed out the common substances causing pollution: waste products from canneries, sawdust which killed fish by clogging their gills, oil and gas by-products, dyes, mine washings and different types of sewage. In 1927 he spoke to the Public Health Association in Jefferson City on "The Iodine Content of the Municipal Water Supply in Missouri." He was considered an authority on the subject because of his considerable research in the area.

His lectures, however, were not restricted to academics and the technical disciplines. He also participated in the Popular Lectures series at MSM which was open to the general public. In 1925, for instance, he gave a well-attended talk on "The Chemistry of Every-Day Life," which, according to the Miner newspaper, was of great interest to the audience.[140]

Schrenk was more than a respected professor. He was popular socially as well. In March, 1925, he received a particularly coveted honor: knighthood bestowed by St. Patrick, who made his appearance (through a chosen representative), during the St. Patrick's festivals in Rolla.[141]

As part of his teaching duties, Schrenk participated in the Summer Sessions which the Missouri School of Mines and Metallurgy conducted as a service to the people of the state. The Summer Session program was established to prepare students and teachers for future courses. In pursuit of that objective the faculty, the facilities, and all the equipment of the School of Mines were made available. For those who participated in the summer program, the State Department of Education granted full credit toward the various courses for which the students and teachers prepared.[142]

In addition to his faculty duties, Schrenk was also active in many organizations. He was a member of Sigma Xi, a scientific research honor society; Phi Kappa Phi, an honor society; Gamma Alpha, a graduate scientific society; Alpha Chi Sigma (initiated Alpha 1917); Acacia, a social fraternity; the American Chemical Society; the Missouri Academy of Science; Square and Compass, a Masonic fraternity; and the Ira Remsen Society.[143]

Throughout his distinguished career, Dr. Schrenk contributed numerous articles on analytical and inorganic chemistry to the Journal of the American Chemical Society, the Journal of Industrial and Engineering Chemistry's analytical edition, Water Works Engineering, and the US Bureau of Mines Information Circular. He also contributed heavily to the technical series of bulletins of the Missouri School of Mines and Metallurgy.[144]

Howard Leroy Dunlap

Howard Leroy Dunlap-Rollamo 1936

Howard Leroy Dunlap, PhD, Professor of Chemical Engineering, joined the faculty of MSM in 1917 as an Assistant Professor, a position he held until 1919, when he became an Associate Professor in 1919. In 1930 he earned a Professorship of Chemical Engineering and served in that capacity until the fall of 1936, whereupon he resigned to accept a position at Ohio University in Athens, OH.[145] Prior to that he had earned a BS degree from Ohio University in 1912, an MA degree from Ohio State in 1914, and a PhD degree from Ohio State in 1925. He was a member of Phi Kappa Tau—a social fraternity; Sigma Xi; Phi Kappa Phi; the American Chemical Society; the Missouri Academy of Science; the Ira Remsen Society (originally the Diphenyl Dozen); Epsilon Pi Omicron; and Masonic organizations such as the Trowel Club and Square & Compass. He was also a member of the Metallurgical and Chemical Society in which he often presented addresses such as the one he gave in 1920—"The Recovery of Sulfur from Hydrogen Sulfide."[146]

During the summers, Dr. Dunlap held positions in experimental work at a number of well-known corporations including: Goodyear Tire and Rubber Co. (1919 and 1920); White Star Refinery, Wood River, Il (1921 and 1924); Phillips Petroleum Co., Bartlesville, OK (1926, 1927, 1928, 1930 and 1933); and the State Experiment Station, Missouri (1918).

Prof. Dunlap also contributed articles on organic chemistry and petroleum technology to numerous publications: Chemical and Metallurgical Engineering, the Journal of Industrial and Engineering Chemistry, the Journal of the American Chemical Society, the Oil and Gas Journal, and the Bulletin of the Missouri State Experiment Station.[147]

Besides his academic credentials, Prof. Dunlap was much appreciated by his students. One evening he invited his students to his home to honor an associate. After the evening, his students described the event as "... one of the most delightful and enjoyable evenings they ever spent in Rolla."[148]

As good as his credentials were, a particular class session revealed Prof. Dunlap's chemical knowledge was keener in some respects than others. He had trouble, for example, trying to explain to a freshman class the cause of the foam on soda water and beer. He admitted he did not know much about soda water as he had never worked in a soda fountain. The question remains to this day: Had he ever worked in a brewery?[149]

Professor Dunlap was born on 22 Jan., 1885, in Flushing, Belmont County, Ohio, to Joseph Calvin Dunlap 1858-1938, and Clara Pleasant (Clements) Dunlap (1862-1928). He preceded his wife, Kathryn Roeser Dunlap (1889-1969), in death on 9 Jan., 1964, at the age of 78 in Athens, Athens County, Ohio.[150]

Clarence John Monroe

Clarence John Monroe, PhD, Associate Professor of Physical Chemistry in 1936, earned a BS degree from Chicago University in 1917 and a Fellowship, PhD, from the University of Chicago in 1921. He joined the faculty of MSM in 1921 taking the position of Assistant Professor, which he held until 1927, at which point, he was given the title Associate Professor. He was in charge of Physical Chemistry since starting with MSM.[151]

Clarence John Monroe—The Rollamo 1936

Dr. Monroe was a member of the American Association for the Advancement of Science, the American Chemical Society, the Missouri Academy of Science, Sigma Xi, and Epsilon Pi Omicron. He contributed various articles on different phases of physical chemistry to the Journal of the American Chemical Society, the Journal of Chemical Education, and the Missouri Geological Survey Reports.[152] In addition to his contribution to the chemical literature, Dr. Monroe gave presentations to various organizations around the country. One of these, delivered at the meeting of the St. Louis section of the American Chemical Society in 1932, explored the precipitation of large crystals and oolites of the insoluble carbonates of calcium, manganese, cadmium, and other elements in silica gel.[153]

In 1948, Monroe transferred from MSM to the Chemistry Department at the University in Columbia as an Associate Professor.[154]

Karl Kenneth Kershner

Karl Kershner, Professor of Chemistry, earned his MS degree from MSM in 1920, and joined the faculty that same year as a Professor of Chemistry. He wrote his master's thesis on "The preparation and physical properties of benzene--and toluene—sulphonamides."[155] He was a member of the American Chemical Society, Tau Beta Pi, Phi Kappa Phi and Epsilon Pi Omicron. Prof. Kershner developed his own laboratory manual which was used in both general chemistry and qualitative analysis classes. Many of his articles on qualitative aluminum tests appeared in the Journal of Chemical Education.[156]

Karl Kenneth Kershner—Rollamo 1936

In 1948 Kershner transferred from MSM to the Department of Agricultural Chemistry of the College of Agriculture at the University of Missouri in Columbia where his title was Assistant Professor.[157]

Thomas Gordon Day

Dr. Thomas Gordon Day, PhD, Instructor in Chemistry, came to MSM in 1930 as a graduate assistant in chemistry. He earned a BA degree from Carroll College in 1930, an MS degree from the Missouri School of Mines and Metallurgy in 1932, and his PhD from the University of Missouri in 1935. Day wrote his Master's Thesis on "Factors affecting the electrolytic deposition of small amounts of lead as lead dioxide and the composition of the deposit" under the guidance of his advisor, Dr. Schrenk.[158]

Upon completion of his graduate work, he became an Instructor in Chemistry in 1935 at MSM. He was a member of the American Chemical Society, Sigma Xi, Phi Kappa Phi, and Epsilon Pi Omicron.

Thomas Gordon Day—Rollamo 1936

Actives

The actives of the petitioning group included: Leroy Augustave Bay, Herman Arthur Brisch, Clemens Raebel Maise, John Shaw Sabine, Frank Joseph Zvanut, Oscar Henry Fager, Edward Castle Fiss, Elmer Lewis Smith, Ralph Henry Striker, Hoyt Gillum Thompson, Harry Charles Berger, Richard James Cardetti, Arthur Peter Hausmann, Peter Andrew Jenni, Robert Cauthorn Lange, Grant Walter Schaumburg, and Elmer William Volz.

Frank Joseph Zvanut

Frank J. Zvanut 1932—Rollamo 1932

Of all the charter members, besides Dr. Schrenk, the most significant perhaps was Frank J. Zvanut. At the time of the formation of Beta Delta, Brother Zvanut was not only a member of Epsilon Pi Omicron and a signer of the Petition, but he was also a member of the Orton Society (Ceramic Engineering organization), Tau Beta Pi (Engineering Honor Society), Sigma Xi (Scientific Research Honor Society), Alpha Psi Omega (National Theater Honor Society), Ira Remsen, Phi Kappa Tau (Social fraternity), and Phi Kappa Phi (Honor Society).[159]

Zvanut was an Assistant in the Ceramic Department at the time of the Petition. He was awarded his BS in Ceramic Engineering in 1932 from the Missouri School of Mines and Metallurgy and his MS in Ceramic Engineering in 1933 from the University of Washington, Seattle. When the Petition was submitted, he was a candidate for the PhD in Ceramic Engineering, which he finally earned in 1937.[160] He wrote his bachelor thesis on "The effect of different rates of ram movement on the transmission of pressure in dry pressed bodies." His doctoral thesis explored the "Pyrochemical changes in Missouri halloysite."[161]

Zvanut became instrumental in the life of Alpha Chi Sigma. He was appointed the East Central District Counselor in 1941.[162] He went on to join the Supreme Council in 1954 and served as Grand Master of Ceremonies from 1954 through 1957, Grand Master Alchemist from 1960 to 1962, and, subsequently, as a member of the Order of Altotus. In 1957 he had the honor of signing the replacement Charter for Beta Delta. The original was lost in a fire in the Chemistry Building.

Throughout the remainder of his life, Zvanut was an active MSM alumnus. He was a member of the Ark-La-Tex Section of MSM-UMR Alumni Association and served as President of the Section from 1982-1987.[163] He and his wife, Kathryn, were regular attendees of the annual Homecoming event and members of the Century Club—donors who made gifts of $100 or more to either the MSM-UMR Alumni Association or to UMR.[164] His later career involved working as a research and manufacturing sales representative in Mexico for Ferro Corp. and Cabot Corp.

Zvanut was an avid tennis player and later in life, on his birthdays, he would play the same number of games as his age.[165] For example, on his 73rd and 77th birthdays he played 73 and 77 games of tennis, respectively. Born in St. Louis on 30 Aug., 1911, to Frank Joseph Zvanut and Margaret Petrovich, he married Kathryn Haymes (1914-2001). He passed away on 2 May, 2004, in Tyler, Texas.[166]

Frank J. Zvanut 1982[167]

John Shaw Sabine

A graduate assistant in Chemistry from 1931 to 1935, Sabine was a candidate for PhD, at the time of the petitioning. He had previously earned a BS degree from Mississippi State in 1931 and an MS degree from the

Missouri School of Mines and Metallurgy in 1933, his thesis was "A study of methods for separating the elements that interfere in the electrolytic deposition of lead as lead oxide."[168] His advisor was Dr. Schrenk. He was a member of Beta Kappa, Scabbard and Blade, and Epsilon Pi Omicron.[169]

Leroy Augustave Bay

Bay was a graduate assistant in 1935. Having earned his BS degree at MSM, he became a candidate for his Masters in 1935. Under the supervision of Dr. Schrenk, Bay wrote his Master's thesis on "A study of methods for the recovery of silver, bromine, iodine, and sodium thiosulfate from used photographic fixing baths."[170] He was a member of Epsilon Pi Omicron.

Herman Arthur Brisch

Brisch, an assistant in the Chemistry Department, received his BS in Chemical Engineering in 1935 and was a candidate for an MS degree in Petroleum Engineering in 1936. He was a member of Epsilon Pi Omicron and the Ira Remsen Society.

Clemens Raebel Maise

"Doc" Maise, a Laboratory Assistant, earned a BS degree in Chemistry in 1934 and was a candidate for an MS in Chemistry in 1936. Maise wrote his master's thesis on "The catalytic vapor phase hydrolysis of benzene and toluene."[171] His advisor was Dr. Thomas Day. He was also a member of Epsilon Pi Omicron and the Ira Remsen Society.

Maise 1934—Rollamo 1934

Oscar Henry Fager

Fager was a candidate for BS in Chemical Engineering in 1936. He was a member of Epsilon Pi Omicron, Ira Remsen, Blue Key, Interfraternity Council, and Triangle.

Edward Castle Fiss

Fiss was also a candidate for BS in Chemical Engineering in 1936. He was a member of Epsilon Pi Omicron, Ira Remsen, Phi Kappa Phi, Tau Beta Pi, Lambda Chi Alpha, Rifle Club and the Officers Club.

Elmer Lewis Smith

A candidate for BS in Chemical Engineering in 1936, Smith was a member of Epsilon Pi Omicron, Ira Remsen, Phi Kappa Phi, and Tau Beta Pi.

Ralph Henry Striker

Striker, an Assistant in Chemistry, was working on his BS in Chemical Engineering at the time of the petition. He was a member of Epsilon Pi Omicron, Ira Remsen, Phi Kappa Phi, Tau Beta Pi, Blue Key, and the Officers Club.

Hoyt Gillum Thompson, Harry Charles Berger, Richard James Cardetti, Arthur Peter Hausmann, Peter Andrew Jenni, Robert Cauthorn Lange, Grant Walter Schaumburg, and Elmer William Volz were all candidates for BS in Chemical Engineering in 1936. They were also members of Epsilon Pi Omicron, and—except for Hausmann, Lange, and Schaumburg—were members of Ira Remsen. In regard to membership in other organizations, this group demonstrated a variety of interests: Thompson was a member of Triangle; Cardetti and Hausmann were members of Mercier; Lange was a member of Blue Key and Pi Kappa Alpha; and Schaumburg was a member of Kappa Sigma.[172]

Alumni

A number of alumni also signed the petition. These included: Harold Edgar Boyd, Robert Louis Cunningham, Warren Bowditch Danforth, Thomas Shirley Donahue, Harold Joseph Haffner, George Augustus Hale, Milton Lawrence Herzog, Howard Frederick Lange, Mason Burt Larwood, Philip Coleman McDonald, Erwin Carl Meckfessel, Bert Allen Menke, Leo Henry Merchie, Herbert Geesling Mortland, Lester Ernest Peeze, George Shackelford Richardson, James Hugh Tobin, and Arthur Harris Walther.[173]

THE 1940s

Fixation is right disposing a Volatile or Fugitive thing to abide and endure in the fire...

—Geber, Summa Perfectionis

The Times

In 1931 Japan invaded Manchuria. In 1935 Italy invaded Ethiopia (Abyssinia). In 1937 Japan attacked China again. From 1936 to 1939, Spain was devastated by civil war. Germany invaded Poland in 1939. By 1940 the seams of the world were being torn apart, and when all the dust settled at the end in 1945, no country on Earth was left unscathed. Everyone lost: loved ones would not return home or would come home with grave physical and/or psychological injury; some had no homes to which they could return; cities had been reduced to rubble; populations had been devastated; economies had collapsed; humans had inflicted unimaginable atrocities and horror on each other. Fortunately, much of the western hemisphere was not in the eye of this raging storm. Yes, there were lives lost—and not to diminish that unbearable sorrow—but the Americas were spared the devastation the rest of the world experienced. Other than the rationing of goods and materials or the constant worry of whether loved ones fighting in the European or Pacific theaters were still alive, life in the United States functioned in relative peace.

During this time, the Missouri School of Mines and Metallurgy saw many of its young men leave for war. Some returned; others did not. Following the attack on Pearl Harbor on Dec. 7, 1941, the tendency among students was to rush to enlist. But Dean Curtis Laws Wilson encouraged students to remain in school and complete their education. He did not discourage the patriotic enthusiasm of the students, but he effectively pointed out that in this war, technology was a critical element, and there would be great demand for engineers and scientists both during the war and when it was over. The school was primarily called upon not so much for brawn, Wilson explained, but for brain power to contribute to the war effort. MSM was encouraged to redouble its efforts to turn out engineers and scientists who could support the production of materiel and the development of technology needed to fight this world-encompassing conflict.

As in the case of the First World War, MSM was dedicated to the nation's winning the war. An Engineering Defense Program was established as early as February, 1941. Its purpose was to provide technically skilled personnel for the military and defense industries. In the summer of '42, the program became known as the Engineering, Science and Management War Training Program, and it was conducted in cooperation with the Department of Education. From June, 1942, through the summer of 1943, 830 students completed the program. Because of the need for expediency in meeting the demands of the war, graduation requirements were reduced from 150 credit hours to 144 and the additional military and special lectures required the acceleration of the availability of technically proficient personnel.[1]

Before the United States entered the war, expansion of MSM facilities was underway as evidenced by the construction of the new Chemistry Building. By the end of the fall semester of 1940, the north half of the new building, which would house the Chemistry and Chemical Engineering Departments, was already nearing completion. The building was turned over to the School of Mines in February of 1941, and the department of Chemical Engineering and the Organic Processing department moved in immediately. Construction of the southern half would not start until 1949 when funds were made available.[2]

While the tragic struggle ensued on the world stage, the vision of a greater School of Mines and Metallurgy and the further expansion efforts had to be put on hold. The demands of the war after 1941 did not allow funding and materials for such endeavors. Not until the end of the war in the summer of 1945 did funds and materials become readily available again for expansion. The late forties saw a return to the growth envisioned by Dean Wilson when the state legislature approved additional funding in July 1946, for the badly needed new power plant, along with a dormitory, and signaled the resumption of the expansion plans.[3]

When the war ended in 1945 the nation celebrated, and MSM made plans for its 75th anniversary celebration the following year. The honor of heading the committee responsible for this milestone event was bestowed on none other than Beta Delta's Walter Schrenk.

Alpha Chi Sigma

In the summer of 1940, while blood was being shed in Europe and Asia, a model initiation[4] of Linus C. Pauling (Sigma-Berkeley) was conducted at the 16th Conclave, June 21-25, held in Berkeley, CA. When Beta Delta received a letter from Sigma chapter in Berkeley recommending Professor Pauling for membership in Alpha Chi Sigma, the chapter unanimously approved the recommendation.

The year before America's entry into the war (1941), Alpha Chi Sigma established the Grand Chapter Safety Program to encourage the promotion of safe laboratory practices by the collegiate chapters at their respective schools.[5] As part of that program, Alpha Chi Sigma became an Associate Member of the National Safety Council.[6] The NSC was, and remains, a 501(c)(3) nonprofit, public service organization promoting health and safety in the United States. Headquartered in Itasca, IL, NSC is a member organization, founded in 1913, and granted a congressional charter in 1953. It emerged from the 1912 Cooperative Safety Congress held in Milwaukee, WI. At the second congress in 1913, the National Council on Industrial Safety was organized, which in 1914 changed its name to the National Safety Council. The goal of the organization was to promote the safety of human life in industries in the United States. The Supreme Council voted that year to purchase a copy of the National Safety Council's book, "Student and Employee Safety in Colleges and Universities," for each collegiate chapter, District Counselor, and Supreme Council member. Later, in 1943, the Office of Civilian Defense in Washington, D.C., sent a letter of commendation to Alpha Chi Sigma for its outstanding safety program. The fraternity had developed a strong safety program to ensure safe laboratory practices at each of its chapters.[7]

As in much of the rest of the world, the war years brought a pause to Alpha Chi Sigma's activities. Beyond the establishment of the chapter safety programs no significant events occurred until after the war's end. In 1946, signs that the war was over and life was returning to normal for Alpha Chi Sigma included the creation of the Detroit Professional chapter and the return to active status of Beta Epsilon (Clemson), which had been one of the "war inactive" chapters.[8]

Beta Delta

1940

While the world sank into chaos, Beta Delta carried on with its own sort of order on the MSM campus. Pledgings, initiations, elections, and fellowship activities continued to take place, ensuring the continuance of the chapter. But the war, which was looming over the horizon for the United States in 1940, would present a serious challenge for Beta Delta. Young men leaving college to join the ranks of the armed forces, coupled with graduating seniors, would reduce the ranks of the chapter, threatening its existence and undoing the "Great Work" begun in the 1930s.

Though a storm was brewing in Europe, the dark clouds had not yet reached America's horizon in 1940, and Beta Delta's story was allowed to unfold in a sequence of intertwining and integrated activities. The chapter continued to focus on growing its membership and on more mundane matters, which were crucial to its life and fellowship. Continuing the work begun in the late 1930s, membership growth, fellowship and promotion of the chemical discipline dominated the chapter's efforts in the early years of the decade. Smokers, Jamborees, Founders' Day Celebrations, technical addresses and talks, initiations, and social events that had become customary in the 1930s continued throughout the 1940s and became established traditions. Each practice, however, was unique and stamped with the conditions and circumstances of the time.

The year began with a review of the ashtray project, of course. At the meeting of January 11, Dr. Schrenk announced that a report on the ashtrays would be given soon. (By this point the ashtrays had become a default pledge project; each pledge class was now required to make them.) Otherwise, business conducted during that meeting included: the pledging of Professor Yates, the fixing of the lock on the file cabinet, and the purchasing of a gift for Mrs. Day for her help in the preparations for the last initiation ceremony. In addition, officers were elected for the spring semester: William Enderson, Master Alchemist; Dave Boltz, Vice-Master Alchemist; Harold Nicholas, Reporter; Julius C. Leslie, Recorder; E. Clark Romine, Treasurer; Andy Cochran, Assistant Treasurer; Don G. Crecelius, Master of Ceremonies; and Clemens R. Maise, Alumni Secretary. The officers were to be installed at the next meeting on January 24.[9]

Beta Delta was confronted not only with its own particular membership questions. It also faced membership issues brought up by the national fraternity. At the meeting on February 7, MA Enderson read a letter from the national chapter concerning three constitutional amendments and read the actual proposed amendments as well. The chapter voted to approve amendments no. 23 and no. 24. Amendment 23 involved a revision to Article 8, paragraph 9 of the Articles of Organization to change the requirement that there be one district counselor for every five chapters and allow the Supreme Council to determine the number of district counselors and the number of chapters in each district. Amendment 24 involved Article 8, paragraphs 3 and 4 of the Articles of Organization changing the rules about collegiate chapters initiating professional members. The amendment proposed the change that any professional member could be initiated at any collegiate chapter. Amendment 25, which involved a revision to Article 8, paragraph 11(a) simplifying the process of expelling a professional member, was voted down by the chapter.

During that same meeting assignments were made for the upcoming initiation and committees. Also, Brother Henson gave a report on the newsletter and asked for suggestions in regard to content and a possible name. D. Boltz announced that Oliver Smith, Edmund Butch and Robert Pohl desired to be initiated on February 24. The last item on the agenda was the preliminary vote on pledges for the semester.[10]

Spring 1940 Committees and Assignments

Advisory	Pled	Schol	Social	Initiation Assign- ments	Initiation Assign- ments
W. Enderson	S. Hertling	W. Enderson	C. Maise	R. Carpenter	W. Enderson
E. Romine	W. Webb	J. Leslie		H. Crecelius	C. Cowan
Dr. Schrenk	D. Boltz			W. Dean	E. Hill
W. Dean				S. Hertling	J. Leslie
				C. Zvanut	

Except possibly for the ashtray pledge project, the actual pledging and initiations had not settled into a steady rhythm as yet. But gradually the logical order of events began to fall into place. The first initiation ceremony of the year was held on February 24, and a week later, a formal pledging ceremony was held for those voted on at the end of February. According to the National Office records, four new initiates were received into the fraternity on January 1: Edmund R. Butch, Eugene F. Hill, Oliver V. Smith, and Charles A. Schaeffer. Beta Delta records, however, indicated that Butch, Smith and Robert A. Pohl were initiated on February 24.[11]

During the meeting on March 4, in a short pledging ceremony, Virgil Johnson, Jennings Lambeth, James Mack and James Nevin were pledged. The custom of formal pledging was becoming the routine business of the chapter. Following the formal pledging, a vote was taken on the potential candidates to represent Beta Delta at Conclave. Those eligible were W. Dean, H. Nicholas, C. Zvanut, A. Cochran, O. Smith and R. Pohl. Brother Nicholas was elected to be the delegate with Brother Dean as the first alternate and Brother Cochran as the second. Amazingly, the ashtray project was relegated to third on the agenda. Dr. Day read a letter from Frank

Zvanut concerning the pledge work on the ashtrays, which was followed by a technical discussion about their manufacture. Before proceeding further, inquiries would have to be made about where a metal die might be produced, so an end to the saga was still not in sight. The next order of business was the preparation for Founders' Day, to be held on May 4, which had taken a backseat to the ashtrays on the agenda. Master Alchemist Enderson announced that Past Grand Master Alchemist Weidemann consented to be the principal speaker at the event.[12]

On March 20, at the regular business meeting, it was revealed that the Cleveland Professional chapter was ahead of the curve in the production of ashtrays. Dr. Schrenk read a letter from Brother Frank Zvanut, which reported that the Cleveland Professionals were already manufacturing and selling ashtrays for $0.50 each, $5.00 a dozen or $33.00 a hundred. In fairness to Beta Delta, the professional members were already working in industry so they had the edge on the students.[13] This on-going—rather minor pledging project—had become emblematic of the chapter's objectives. The project strengthened the bonds of friendship among pledges, actives and professionals; it provided at least a modicum of learning for the members in their ambitions as chemists, through the technical discussions and execution of the manufacturing processes involved; and—though Beta Delta did not have to re-invent the proverbial wheel this time—it advanced chemistry as a science by encouraging future chemists and chemical engineers to hone their knowledge and skills. So, even seemingly small actions by the chapter served to facilitate a closer affiliation of future scientists and engineers.

The spring semester pledge roll was increased by one, when Lawrence R. Hinken was formally pledged at the business meeting on April 3. Also on the agenda: Brother Maise gave a report on the preparations for Founders' Day and the associated banquet and announced that pledges could attend. Then VMA Boltz reported that the pledges had issued a challenge to the actives for a baseball game and that the actives had enthusiastically picked up the gauntlet. In further business, MA Enderson explained that Saturday, May 4, was set for the initiation. Of course, the meeting could not come to an official end without another mention of ashtrays. Brother

Butch read a letter from his father regarding some "historic ashtray," and announced that a sample would be sent.[14]

As pledging continued, mundane business matters and event preparations continued on pace. On April 17, Brother Henson and Brother Zvanut gave reports on the progress of the newsletter and the scholarship report, respectively. MA Enderson announced that he would plan a meeting of the Advisory committee to review the by-laws. He also shared news on the preparations for Founders' Day and the banquet to be held at the Houston House in Newburg. The St. Louis Professional chapter would attend and would stay through Sunday, May 5, to participate in the softball game. Then the ashtrays were brought up again. MA Enderson appointed Brother Leslie to survey the actives and pledges to determine if they would purchase ashtrays at $0.20 each. In addition, Brothers Hertling and Maise discussed the proposed "Handbook Award" which would be presented at the beginning of the following year. The award, an Alpha Chi Sigma honor, would consist of a chemical handbook to be given on the second Friday in February at the Mass meeting. It would be given to a sophomore, enrolled in Chemical Engineering or Chemistry, with the highest scholastic average. All the recipient's credits would have to be earned at MSM, and, in case of ties, duplicate awards could be given. At the end of the meeting, Brother Henson volunteered to captain the actives' softball team against the pledges on Sunday afternoon, April 28.[15]

Just prior to the Founders' Day and the initiation events, another meeting was held on May 1. At the outset it was announced that the pledges squeaked by the actives in the ballgame, winning 12 to 11. (Dear Reader: Take a stab at the next agenda item!) Brother Carpenter moved that Beta Delta purchase 100 ashtrays. The members then elected officers for the fall. Those elected included: William K. Dean, Master Alchemist; Carl M. Zvanut, Vice-Master Alchemist; Robert Pohl, Recorder; Ed Butch, Treasurer; and Don G. Crecelius, Master of Ceremonies. The newly elected officers would be installed at the next meeting on, Thursday, May 9.[16]

The Founders' Day celebrations opened with an initiation on Saturday afternoon, May 4. In addition to initiating its own pledges—James Mack, Charles Schafer and Jennings Lambeth—Beta Delta also initiated four

Kappa (Kansas) pledges and two Delta (Missouri-Columbia) pledges. The Beta Delta members who participated in the initiation ceremony included Brothers Cochran, Crecelius, Dean, Maise, Butch, Zvanut, Cowan, Henson, and Hertling. Several members of the St. Louis Professional Chapter were on hand to help out with the ceremony, and the initiation banquet was held that same evening at the Houston House in nearby Newburg. After dinner, Brother Wiedemann, Past Grand Master Alchemist, gave a short talk, which was followed by remarks from Brothers Huff, Swanger, Schneller and Kopfstein from the St. Louis Professional Chapter. In addition, Brother Miller from Delta chapter and Brother Olmstead from Kappa chapter spoke. All together 47 members of Alpha Chi Sigma—actives, pledges, and professionals—were present at the banquet. Members from Alpha Epsilon chapter, who had been invited, were unable to attend.[17] The next day was spent at Dr. Schrenk's home playing softball, roasting hot dogs and enjoying the remainder of a beautiful spring afternoon. Once again, the actives left the field with their tail between their legs, losing to the pledges and professionals 7 to 6 in the softball game.[18]

In Europe, meanwhile, more dark clouds were gathering as the Allies evacuated the ports of Norway, and Germany planned its imminent invasion of Belgium, France, the Netherlands, and Luxembourg, for May 10, 1940.

Just days after the initiation, a separate pledging ceremony was conducted for Ashton P. Renwick at the business meeting on May 9. Since the Conclave in Berkeley was approaching, this meeting also gave members an opportunity to express their opinions on the topics that would come before the delegates. Installation of officers for the fall semester followed; because Brother Pohl was absent, he would be installed at the first meeting after the summer.[19]

The fall semester of 1940 was a very active time for Beta Delta. It included a Rush Party, a Jamboree, a trip to Delta Chapter and the initiation of new pledges. Before all of these, however, the members were enlightened by an interesting talk on September 25. Jack Pearl, Class of '39, an Inspecting Engineer for the United States Rubber Company, addressed the chapter on synthetic rubber and its uses.[20]

The Rush Party (Smoker) was held at the Edwin Long Hotel in Rolla on the evening of October 9. During the dinner, Brother Dean and Dr. Schrenk extolled the aims and advantages of belonging to Alpha Chi Sigma, and Dr. Thomas Day and Brother Maise added their input. After dinner, the group played various games—including a Smell Test, an Apparatus Test, a Qualitative Test, a Boiling Water Test, an Ad Test, a Shooting Test, and Bingo—until the store of prizes was exhausted. A card game followed, during which, a rousing songfest exalting the engineering feats of old St. Patrick broke out. The preliminary vote on the prospective pledges was taken on October 23; twenty-one of the candidates passed.[21]

The Jamboree, the second annual such event, was held on October 27 and attended by 53 members from Delta Chapter, the St. Louis Professional Chapter, Kappa Chapter and Alpha Epsilon Chapter.[22] Three MSM alumni were among the St. Louis Professional contingent—L. E. Henson, S. L. Hertling, and Jack Gatthaar. The most outstanding attendee, however, was Dean Harry A. Curtis, PhD, ChE, of the University of Missouri's College of Engineering. Dean Curtis had been an Alpha Chi Sigma brother for 28 years by 1940 and had held almost every national office. He was instrumental in the formation of the professional branch of the fraternity, and, as of the fall of 1940, a member of the committee for the National Defense Program (see the Excursus at the end of the chapter).

Upon completion of registration at the Edwin Long Hotel, a banquet was held at the College Inn. After dinner, Dr. Schrenk showed movies of the sixteenth Biennial Conclave held at Berkeley, California. Short talks were also given by Dr. T. Day, and Harold Nicholas, both of Beta Delta Chapter. W. K. Dean, Master Alchemist, Beta Delta, conducted the meeting. After the dinner and meeting, a softball game was played between the professionals and the collegiate members; the professionals won by a score of 18 to 5. Given Dr. Schrenk's history as an avid baseball player and excellent pitcher, it's likely the game was his suggestion.[23] Throughout the weekend, many of the attendees expressed a desire to see Meramec Springs on the Meramec River near St. James, MO. A local Beta Delta member, Jim Mack from Kansas City, MO, (a 1941 grad) obliged to serve as guide and conducted a tour of what is considered one of the most beautiful spots in Missouri.[24]

Once the Jamboree was over, the final vote on the candidates for pledging was held on October 28. Several additional candidates who could not attend the Rush party were added to the list, so a total of 28 were invited to pledge. During this meeting, the chapter also decided that Beta Delta would join in the sponsorship of the Tri-Tech Dance. The following were appointed to serve on the Tri-Tech Dance Committee: C. Schaeffer, Chair; J. Mack; H. Crecelius; and W. Dean.[25]

On November 13, the following pledges were invited to join the chapter: Kulifay, Johnson, Berndt, Couch, Christiansen, Carmack, Flood, Conary, Krummel, Gobush, and Johnson. The initiation was set for November 30 with the following active members participating in the ceremony: Cochran, Crecelius, Mack, Pohl, C. Schaeffer, Zvanut, Smith, Nicholas, Lambeth, and Francis. A practice initiation was held on November 29, the Friday night before the big event. A final vote was taken on additional new pledges that night as well. (Apparently, in the drive to increase membership numbers, pledge classes were beginning to overlap.) The new pledges were: Pietz, Stehlau, Roszkowski, Wyman, and McLean.[26]

At a meeting on November 27, the pledges to be initiated on November 30 were assigned topics to report on at the banquet after the initiation. These assignments included: Oscar M. Muskopf—Vitamin K9P; Roy H. Carmack—Ethyl Lactate; George R. Couch—Specific and Selective Seductive Capacity; Frank E. Johnson—Ethyl Urinate; Robert C. Wright—Entropy Strainer; Ashton Renwick—How to Make Rose Water; and Melvin C. Flint—Production of Butter from Butter of Antimony.[27]

Those initiated that fall (November 30) were: Renwick, Wright, Flint, Johnson, and Muskopf. Beta Delta records also included: Couch and Carmack (The National Office recorded an initiation date of January 1, 1941, for Couch and Carmack). The initiation ceremony was held in the Chemistry Building and was followed by a banquet at the Houston House in Newburg. Dr. Doisey, Prof. of Biochemistry and Dr. Laird, Prof. of Physical Chemistry, both of St. Louis University, were guests of Dr. Schrenk at the banquet.[28]

At the last meeting of the semester, MA Dean appointed the following committees: Auditing committee—J. Mack, R. Carmack, and C. Zvanut;

Membership committee—C. Zvanut, M. Flint, and A. Cochran; Scholarship committee—W. Dean, O. Muskopf, and J. Lambeth; Budget committee—E. Butch, W. Dean, Dr. Day, and J. Mack; and Beta Delta Data Committee—H. Nicholas, O. Muskopf, M. Flint and R. Wright. The minutes of this meeting mentioned the name of the chapter's newsletter, the Beta Delta Data, for the first time.[29]

The semester ended with a visit of Beta Delta brothers to the Delta Chapter in Columbia where Dr. Schrenk once again showed his movies of the Jamboree.[30]

Top Row: R. Carpenter, A. Cochran, C. Cotterill, C. Cowan, D. Crecelius.
Bottom Row: W. Enderson, H. Hayden, J. Leslie, C. Maise, E. Romine, R. Wright.
Beta Delta Chapter 1940— Rollamo 1940

1941

The beginning of the second semester of the '40-'41 school year saw the campus in the midst of a serious influenza epidemic which threatened to shut down the school. In January, 75 students were infected and the Health Director, Dr. E. E. Feind, reported the school hospital was filled. Any increase in the number of sick students, he warned, could shut the school down. The Rolla public schools remained open, but they were also in the same precarious situation as the college. Originating in California, the influenza epidemic had rapidly spread across the nation; its extent was second only to the great epidemic of 1918.[31] Fortunately, symptoms were not severe; they consisted of listlessness, fever, headache, and general bodily aches. Though new cases were still being reported at the start of the semester, by mid-January the rate had declined significantly.[32]

Membership concerns remained at the fore at the beginning of 1941. The first meeting of the semester, January 8, covered two proposed by-laws and the election of officers for the spring. The first by-law proposal, which the members voted to adopt, dealt with pledges who failed to return their pledge pins upon initiation; it stipulated that those failing to return their pins would be assessed the cost of the pin. The second by-law proposed that actives who had unexcused absences from meetings be fined $0.10 for each unexcused absence. This proposal was defeated. During this meeting, the chapter also elected officers for the semester; they included: Carl Zvanut, Master Alchemist; Robert Pohl, Vice-Master Alchemist; Edward Butch, Treasurer; Charles Schaeffer, Recorder; Jim Mack, Master of Ceremonies; Oscar Muskopf, Reporter; and William Webb, Alumni Secretary. These officers were installed on January 22.[33]

Another effort at the start of the decade to facilitate membership and fellowship was the move to hold more joint initiations with other chapters in the district. Two such ceremonies occurred in 1941—one with Kappa Chapter in January and another with Alpha Epsilon in December. In spite of the epidemic, Beta Delta initiated four members—James Cornelius Johnson, Michael Gobush, Stanley M. Kulifay, and Clyde H. Krummel—at a joint meeting on Saturday, January 11, in Lawrence, KS, with Kappa Chapter, which initiated six new members. The event was also attended by representatives of Delta (Missouri-Columbia), Nu (Penn State), Alpha Phi (Tennessee), Kansas City Professional and St. Louis Professional chapters. The following Sunday afternoon a dinner was held in honor of the initiates with Dr. Schrenk, District Counselor, presenting a talk on the progress of Alpha Chi Sigma in the district. Dr. Day, Ed Butch, Carl Zvanut, Les Olmstead, and Walter Dean accompanied the initiates to Lawrence.[34] Later, on February 15, six additional pledges were initiated: Herbert P. Brueschke, Elmond L. Claridge, Joseph P. Berndt, Hugh Haines, Don R. Strehlau, and W. E. Yates. With another pledge class duly initiated, a new pledge class needed attention. At the next business meeting, on January 22, it was decided that the next pledge project would be to grow a large crystal to be exhibited either on Engineer's Day or at the dedication of the new Chemistry building.[35]

Also in January, it was announced that C. R. 'Doc' Maise was leaving the Chemistry department staff after six and a half years to accept a position with the Titanium Pigment Division of the National Lead Company. (The company, known today as NL Industries, is a lead smelter located in Houston.) In 1907 the National Lead Company entered the consumer market for titanium paints, creating the product line known as "Dutch Boy." The Dutch Boy brand was sold to Sherwin-Williams in 1980.[36] Maise, who had received both his Bachelor's and Master's degrees at MSM, was replaced on the Chemistry department staff by Dave Boltz, who also received his Master's at MSM (His thesis, "The volumetric determination of alumina in clays and related minerals," was advised by Dr. Schrenk).[37]

Though most of the committees were appointed at the last meeting of 1940, several new committees were formed on February 5. The Auditing committee consisted of R. Pohl, J. Mack and J. Lambeth. R. Pohl, M. Flint and R. Carmack comprised the Entertainment committee, and R. Pohl, R. Wright and F. E. Johnson made up the Membership committee. The new Scholarship committee included R. Pohl, O. V. Smith and M. Flint. During this meeting, it was also announced that the following pledges would be initiated: Bruesche, Yates, Berndt, Claridge, Harness, and Strehlau.[38]

Prospective pledges eligible for the next pledge class were selected at the following meeting on February 26. Of those invited to pledge ten had accepted and were formally pledged on March 11. They included: Kurusz, Kisslinger, Harris, Schilling, Beach, Kadera, Perkin, Schmitz, Classen, and Vaughn. After the formal pledging, during the business meeting, Dr. Day informed the chapter that the Time Magazine quizzes had been ordered. These would be used to compete for the book award. Also the Scholarship committee was tasked with reviewing the scholastic averages of the sophomores enrolled in the Chemistry department to determine who should receive the annual handbook award.[39]

The fidelity of Beta Delta extended not only to Alpha Chi Sigma's objectives, but was maintained for one of Epsilon Pi Omicron's objectives as well—to have students informed of the latest methods used in industry. On March

26, Mr. E. C. Hunze, a graduate of MSM, Class of '26, now with the Aluminum Ore Company of America in E. St. Louis, spoke before the members of Beta Delta on "Cryolite, the New Insecticide." He was prominent in the Insecticide Division of the Aluminum Ore Company and his talk was based on research into the use of aluminum compounds as insecticides. He was accompanied by J. R. Fox, Jr., Secretary of the St. Louis Section of the American Institute of Chemical Engineers. A dinner followed the presentation. Another instance of fulfilling this objective occurred on April 23. Paul Krueger of Mallinkrodt Chemical Works in St. Louis addressed the Beta Delta Chapter. The topic of his address was "Chemistry in Modern Illumination." Krueger was a member of the Alpha Chi Sigma St. Louis Professional Chapter and a President of the St. Louis Section of the American Chemical Society.[40]

The following month on April 11, at 5 in the afternoon, the new Chemical Engineering and Chemistry Building was dedicated. Gov. Donnell of Missouri was present with Dr. William R. Chedsey, Director of MSM, who presided over the ceremonies. Dr. Harry A. Curtis (Alpha Chi Sigma member—Eta), Dean of the School of Engineering at the University of Missouri, gave an address, "Chemical Engineering Today and Yesterday." Other notables in attendance included: Senator F. McDavid, president of the board of Curators, Univ. of Missouri; Dr. Frank Whitmore (Alpha Chi Sigma member—Omicron), Dean of the School of Chemistry and Physics of Pennsylvania State College and past president of the American Chemical Society, who gave an address, "The Accelerating Advance of Chemistry"; H. E. Wiedemann, consulting chemist of St. Louis and past Grand Master Alchemist, Alpha Chi Sigma; Dr. Walter T. Schrenk, Alpha Chi Sigma member (Alpha) and counselor of the Midwest District of Alpha Chi Sigma; and W. L. Rathman of the architectural firm Klipstein and Rathman which designed the building. Rathman presented the keys to the building to President Middlebush of the University of Missouri. The Dedication of the new building was part of the closing program of the American Chemical Society national meeting, which was held in St. Louis. The visitors were guided through a tour of the laboratories by the student members of the AIChE and the Beta Delta Chapter of Alpha Chi Sigma. A banquet was held to end the ceremonies with H. E. Wiedemann as toastmaster.[41]

Chemical Engineering and Chemistry Building, April 1941

The initiation ceremony, held May 3, received 14 new members (see the table Spring 1941 Initiates below) from the pledge class formed on March 11. Afterwards, a banquet was held that evening at the Edwin Long Hotel with speeches given by the new initiates and the professionals attending. The next day a picnic was hosted by Dr. Schrenk at his home. Of course, a baseball game was played between the professional and collegiate members. This time the collegiate members trounced the professionals, avenging their poor showing in the Jamboree game the previous fall.[42]

At the meeting of May 7, Brother Pohl proposed a special initiation for a single pledge before the end of the semester if it were not possible to have the pledge initiated by another chapter. The proposal was accepted. Once again, accommodations were made to ensure the growth of the chapter. The person in question was Charles Koch, who in a final vote was found to be eligible.[43] Koch was initiated on May 23.

Spring 1941 Initiates

January 11	May 3	May 23
James Cornelius Johnson	Harold Flood	Charles O. Koch
Michael Gobush	Warren Kadera	
Stanley M. Kulifay	Ira Perkins	
Clyde H. Krummel	Arthur Rose	
	James Nevin	
	Kenneth Schowalter	
February 15	John S. Harris	
Elmond L. Claridge	Frank O. Suessdorf	
Don R. Strehlau	Gilbert R. Shockley	
Joseph P. Berndt	King D. Beach	
William E. Yates	Joseph Schmitz	
Hugh Haines	Edwin J. Claassen	
Herbert P. Brueschke	Henry Kurusz	

On May 14, Robert Pohl was elected as Master Alchemist for the fall semester. Ray Carmack, VMA; Mike Gobush, Recorder; James C. Johnson, Treasurer; and Don Strehlau, MC, were also elected. Carl Zvanut was awarded membership into the American Chemical Society for being the highest ranking senior chemical engineer. And, also in May, Oscar Muskopf, who was initiated in 1940, was elected Vice-President of the Student Council.[44]

As spring rolled into summer, Beta Delta Chapter hosted a dedication of their new Chemistry Building. Later, at the home of District Counselor Dr. Schrenk, Beta Delta chapter defeated the St. Louis Professional Chapter in a friendly game of baseball by the score of 29 to 5, underscoring the point that the collegiate members ruled the diamond.[45]

Though Beta Delta may have enjoyed a leisurely summer relieved of the burden of classes and entertained by baseball games, the members were cognizant of the somber atmosphere hanging over them in the world. In a letter dated August 26, 1941, Grand Collegiate Alchemist, Harold P. Gaw, reminded the chapter of Motion No. 39 which was passed at the 16th Biennial Conclave and gave the Supreme Council instructions to take any necessary action it deemed necessary to safeguard the fraternity during any national crisis. Though the letter did not direct the chapter to take any specific actions, it did lay out the general responsibilities agreed upon by the chapters when they voted to pass Motion No. 39. These responsibilities, as laid out in the letter included:

1. To lend your moral support to the chapter to continue to function if an emergency decimates the active membership.

2. To take charge of all property, if necessary, such as rituals, regalia, records and files, books, and any other similar possessions the chapter might have. See that these are safely stored and where one or more of you will have access to them when necessary.

3. Designate one of your group, if necessary, to be responsible for all chap-

ter correspondence with the national organization.

4. In the event the chapter holds property, make arrangements for continuing to operate the house, or, if necessary, to dispose of it to the best advantage. In case the chapter has a House Corporation, work with their Board of Directors in disposing of the property if necessary. In this connection it would not be a bad idea to lay some plans now in order to be somewhat prepared in the event of an emergency.

5. To conduct any of the regular chapter functions which the group may consider advisable or possible.[46]

Amidst these dire concerns, Beta Delta planned, in the opening meetings of the fall semester, the events and activities that would facilitate the chapter's fellowship and ensure its continuance through troubled waters. On September 17, planning for the Smoker to be held on October 8 was assigned to a committee of Brothers R. Carmack (chair), A. Rose, C. Schaeffer, and H. Brueschke, who would also put together a list of those eligible to pledge. Planning for the Jamboree, held on October 19, was assigned to D. Boltz. Exhibits for Parent's Day, on November 1, became the responsibility of W. Webb, D. Boltz, S. Kulifay, H. Flood, J. Nevin, D. Strehlau, and F. E. Johnson. In addition, based on a letter from the Grand Chapter regarding the Safety Program for all the chapters, Beta Delta's own safety program was launched. Recognizing the importance of communications and publicity, Ed Johnson was appointed as the Miner Reporter and Elwood Conary as Chapter Recorder. Finally, committees were appointed to handle the details of these activities.[47]

Fall 1941 Committees

Auditing	Membership	Scholarship	Budget
D. Strehlau	R. Carmack	M. Flint	J. Johnson
J. Schmitz	S. Kulifay	Harness	Dr. T. Day
J. Harris	H. Kurusz	I. Perkins	E. Classen
			H. Flood

Beta Delta Data	Safety	Chemistry Exhibits	Dance	Bulletin Board
R. Carmack	J. Harris	K. Schowalter	E. Johnson	H. Kurusz
J. Johnson	K. Schowalter	D. Boltz	H. Flood	
K. Schowalter		Kulifay	D. Strehlau	
Shockley				

On October 8, the scheduled Smoker for members and prospective pledges was held in the basement lecture room of the new Chemical Engineering building. The program consisted of a number of "chemical quizzes" requiring smell-o-metric analysis. Unfortunately, no details of the snifter exercise were given in the record. Perhaps it was an experience better left forgotten since immediately following the olfactory test, refreshments were provided by Mrs. T. G. Day—presumably to erase the after-effects of the ordeal. After refreshments, talks on the purpose of Alpha Chi Sigma were delivered by Dr. T. G. Day, Chapter Advisor; Dr. Schrenk, District Counselor; and Robert Pohl, Master Alchemist of the Beta Delta Chapter. The evening ended with card games in the chemical engineering laboratory.[48]

The Fifth Annual Midwest District Jamboree of Alpha Chi Sigma was held in Rolla on Oct. 19, a Sunday. The days' activities opened with registration at the new Chemical Engineering Building followed by a trip to Fort Leonard Wood. At noon, a banquet and business meeting were held at the Pierce-Pennant Tavern in Rolla. In the afternoon, the annual softball game between the collegiate and professional members took place on the upper athletic field. This time the collegiate members "trimmed" the professionals, according to the Miner writer. Speakers at the banquet included Beta Delta's Dr. Schrenk and H. E. Wiedemann of the St. Louis Professional Chapter.[49]

The Smoker, on October 8, yielded ten new pledges from the prospective attendees: J. Brodhacker, H. Scott, W. Hubbard, Marvin D. Livingood, J. Miller, J. Mueller, Robert M. Dunham, C. Wahlbring, L. Grass, and D. Wicker.[50] After the formal pledge ceremony on November 11, Beta Delta held a joint meeting with Sigma Xi at 8 pm in Parker Hall. Dr. Henry E. Bent, Dean of the Graduate School of the University of Missouri, addressed the group on "The Use of Absorption Spectra in Studying Certain Chemical Problems." In his address Dr. Bent described the use of the spectrometer to determine the structure responsible for the color developed by iron and the thiocyanate ions. He also illustrated the use of color developed by organic free radicals by following the course of these substances' reactions in solutions. The presentation was an outline of Dr. Bent's own research.[51]

If it was thought that Epsilon Pi Omicron had become a cipher in an historical ledger by this time, that conclusion was wrong. A series of correspondences, starting with a letter dated October 4, 1941, from George Richardson to Thomas Day through letters between Day and Grand Recorder John Kuebler, reignited an issue involving Beta Delta's predecessor. George Richardson, who was one of the signers of Epsilon Pi Omicron's original petition, expressed interest in becoming a member of Alpha Chi Sigma. At the time of his request, Richardson was a Flight Surgeon with the Air Corps Advanced Flying School at Midland, TX. He had graduated from MSM and the School of Aviation Medicine before his assignment. Day passed on Richardson's request, detailing the circumstances, to Kuebler in a letter dated November 17, 1941. In his response on November 19, Kuebler indicated that membership would be inadvisable at that point. In spite of the circumstances, Kuebler felt Richardson was too closely associated with the medical profession, and he stated that the fraternity required a member to be following chemistry as a profession. Richardson's interest in pursuing a career related to chemistry was not enough. But Kuebler did indicate that according to Alpha Chi Sigma's constitution, legally, Richardson might be eligible, and he left the matter to the discretion of the chapter.

Day conveyed Kuebler's response, along with other obligations, to Richardson in a letter dated November 26. Unfortunately, there was no record of any further correspondence regarding the final outcome of this matter.[52]

Of the pledges recruited at the Smoker, Marvin Livingood and Robert Dunham were initiated along with John Schilling at the joint ceremony at Alpha Epsilon on December 13. The chapter decided that the senior members of the pledge class would be initiated in St. Louis, while the others would not be initiated until January, 1942.[53]

Top Row: E. Butch, D. Crecelius, M. Flint, J. Lambeth; Middle Row: H. Nicholas, R. Pohl, A. Rose, C. Schaeffer; Bottom Row: C. Smith, R. Wright

Beta Delta Chapter 1941—Rollamo 1941

1942

The spring semester of 1942 opened on a positive note at the January 6 business meeting. A letter had been received from the Grand Recorder, John Kuebler, congratulating Beta Delta on the Christmas issue of the Beta Delta Data. After the accolades, the participants for the upcoming initiation were announced; most of the members—Schowalter, Dunham, Shockley, J. Johnson, Rose, Kulifay, Perkins, Renwick, Flood, Muskopf, Claasen, Suesdorf, Schmitz, Nevin, Carmack, Wilson, and Conary—would take part in the ceremony. The election of officers followed: Ray Carmack, Master Alchemist; Oscar Muskopf, Vice-Master Alchemist; Harold Flood, Reporter; Warren Kadera, Recorder; James Johnson, Treasurer; Arthur Rose, Master of Ceremonies; and William Webb, Alumni Secretary.[54]

Beta Delta began the year with a surge of new initiates: Charles H. Sparks, Paul F. Steinhoff, and T. J. Roemer on January 1 (according to the National Office records); and David A. Wicker, John W. Brodhacker, William A. Hubbard, Joseph B. Schmitt, Edward P. Schneider, Bailey W. Hagar, John D. Mueller, Harry S. Scott, and Louis W. Grass on January 10. The Beta Delta Membership records, however, indicated that Sparks and Steinhoff were also initiated on January 10, while Roemer was not initiated until April 11.

But the year began sadly for Dr. Schrenk. On January 22, his wife (Alberta, b. 27 July 1897)[55] died at St. Mary's Hospital after suffering from ovarian cancer. Funeral services were held at the Presbyterian Church in Rolla with the Rev. Frank L. Rearick officiating. Mrs. Schrenk, Dean of Women Students, was for many years an active sponsor of women students at MSM and instrumental in the founding of the coed organization and the Pi Delta Chi sorority. She was also active in the Order of the Eastern Star. Mrs. Schrenk acted as hostess many times at picnics and parties at her home for the sorority, and she co-hosted numerous events with her husband for Beta Delta.[56]

Alberta Schrenk—back row center—Rollamo 1939

On January 27, the following officers were installed at the new Chemistry Building: Ray Carmack, MA; Oscar Muskopf, VMA; Warren Kadera, Recorder; Harold Flood, Reporter; James Johnson, Treasurer; Art Rose, MC; and William Webb, Alumni Secretary. In addition, Brother Harris was appointed as assistant to VMA Muskopf and Brother Scott was appointed Publicity chair. The committees below were appointed to ensure the efficient execution of the work of the fraternity. During this meeting the chapter established new guidelines for a safety program designed to be implemented in all the chemical laboratories, and a series of safety posters and cartoons were displayed throughout the chemistry building. In addition safety talks were presented by seniors to the lower classes.[57] There was no mention that ashtrays posed any safety concerns.

Spring 1942 Committees

Advisory	Auditing	Membership	Scholarship
Dr. Schrenk	O. Muskopf	O. Muskopf	R. Carmack
Dr. Day	J. Berndt	J. Harris	G. Shockley
R. Carmack	H. Kurusz	E. Schneider	A. Renwick
J. Johnson		I. Perkins	

Spring 1942 Committees Cont.

Budget	Beta Delta Data	History	Safety
Dr. Schrenk	H. Flood	W. Kadera	R. Pohl
R. Carmack	E. Claassen	E. Conary	H. Kurusz
J. Johnson	J. Schilling	B. Hagar	W. Hubbard
R. Dunham	I. Perkins	J. Brodhacker	J. Brodhacker
	K. Schowalter	L. Wilson	L. Wilson

During the meeting on March 5, Oscar Muskopf, the Beta Delta Reporter, was recognized by the editors of the Hexagon, the fraternity journal, as the Best Alpha Chi Sigma Reporter. The decision was based on the quality of the material which he submitted to the journal. In recognition of his work, Dr. Schrenk presented him with a professional charm, given each year by the editors of "Polymorphisms" (a column in the Hexagon) to the outstanding Hexagon Reporter. Muskopf also read a letter from the Alpha Iota chapter inviting Beta Delta to submit a design for a fraternity flag. No restrictions were placed on the preliminary design other than the colors had to be the fraternity colors. No size was stipulated except the flag was to be comparable to other fraternity flags (i.e. approximately four to five feet long).[58] A committee—consisting of B. Hagar, J. Nevin and W. Kadera—was appointed to design the banner.

During this meeting, a communication from the Grand Recorder requesting Beta Delta's opinion on the upcoming Conclave scheduled for June 19-23, in Chicago, was read. The chapter, consequently, voted Jim Johnson as its representative to the Conclave. Ira Perkins and Harold Flood were chosen as first and second alternates, respectively. In addition, a committee—C. Schaeffer, D. Wicker, and J. Schmitz—was appointed to compile the chapter by-laws. Before the meeting concluded, Dr. Day, who was the winner of the "Time" current events contest held at a previous meeting, chose a book entitled "Catalysis" as his prize. He announced that the book would be placed in the chapter's clubroom to be available to all the members. A final vote regarding potential pledges for the semester resulted in 16 prospects passing. And the members then heard a report of a trip Dr. Schrenk, Harold Flood, Ed Johnson, Oscar Muskopf, and Ray

Carmack made to Delta Chapter at the University of Missouri where they attended a banquet held at the Tiger Hotel. (The chapter's records do not indicate when this trip took place.)[59]

A week later, on March 17, a formal pledging ceremony was held for Paul F. Shatto, Robert W. Roos, Patrick D. Quinn, Clifton Seymour, Charles H. Sparks, and James H. Bottom. The initiation date was set for Saturday, April 11; all the chapters in the district would be invited. The meeting was then adjourned in time to listen to H. E. Wiedemann's address. Weidemann, who served as past Grand Master Alchemist, and as Missouri State Chemist from 1912 to 1933, spoke on the subject of "The Manufacture and Properties of Chemical Lime."[60]

A month later, on April 11, the following men were initiated: James H. Bottom, Jacob D. Jenkins, James R. Miller, Patrick D. Quinn, Robert W. Roos, and Douglas N. Christensen. Beta Delta's Membership records had also listed Jack Roemer and Charles Sparks among the initiates. Paul Shatto, who had pledged, was not initiated, for some reason. The active members who participated in the initiation rite included: Livingood, Schmitt, Kulifay, Hagar, Schowalter, Steinhoff, Berndt, Harness, Kurusz, Claassen, Nevin, J. C. Johnson, Shockley, Brodhacker, Grass, Scott, Wicker, Hubbard, and Schilling.[61]

Three days later, on April 14, the election of officers for the fall semester was held. The new leaders for the fall included: J. C. Johnson, Master Alchemist; Ira Perkins, Vice-Master Alchemist; Warren Kadera, Recorder; Harold Flood, Reporter; William Hubbard, Treasurer; Henry Kurusz, Master of Ceremonies; and William Webb, Alumni Secretary. Before adjourning, the chapter voted to send a greeting to Art Rose who was in the hospital (No reason for his stay was given).[62]

During April, Beta Delta continued to work on its design for the Alpha Chi Sigma flag—with the hope of winning the nationwide contest. At the meeting on April 27, the design was finalized and preparations were made for its submission. (Ultimately, the Conclave Ritual committee reviewed all the chapters' submissions and selected the design by John Baer of the Alpha Iota chapter). At the same meeting, James Bottom was elected chapter Historian, and James Johnson was selected to represent Beta Delta along with Dr. Schrenk at the 17th Biennial Conclave, to be held in Chicago, June 19-22.[63]

Other business included a decision that Beta Delta hold its own dance on the Saturday night before the Jamboree instead of participating in the Tri-Tech Dance and a vote to send flowers to Art Rose who was still in the hospital. The following committees were also appointed: Advisory—Dr. Schrenk, J. Johnson, and W. Hubbard; Auditing—I. Perkins, J. Jenkins, and J. Berndt; Budget—Dr. Day, Dr. Schrenk, J. Johnson, and W. Hubbard; Membership—I. Perkins, D. Christensen, and R. Roos; Scholarship—M. Livingood, J. Johnson, J. Schilling; and Flag—H. Kurusz, J. Bottom, and P. Quinn.[64]

During the last meeting of the semester, on May 12, the new by-laws were read with the intent to vote on them at the next meeting. The dance date was set for September 19, and Dr. Schrenk showed "moving pictures" of the chapter's activities.[65] Then Reporter Flood read letters from Brothers Carmack and F. Zvanut, and one from Art Rose's mother, dated May 6, 1942:

> *Dear Boys, Your kind thoughtful attention meant so much to all of us at such a critical time and we all want to express our thanks and appreciation along with Art's. We felt a little encouraged when the Doctor dismissed one of the three nurses to day but Son has long way to go for a complete recovery.*

Unfortunately, Art's condition did not improve but declined over the summer, and he passed away on September 9.[66]

In keeping with the chapter's emphasis on safety, Seb Hertling, a Beta Delta alumnus who initiated on December 16, 1939, returned to Rolla on June 25 to give a talk on safety engineering. In 1942, Hertling was the chief safety Engineer at one of the munition factories in St. Louis. He discussed how safety was becoming more and more important in the industry and emphasized that it was a field in which chemical engineers should be interested. Beginning pay for a safety engineer, he reported, was $250 per month—a sizeable starting salary for the time. Though he could not go into great detail because of wartime regulations, Hertling was able to demonstrate just how unbreakable a pair of safety glasses, developed by the American Optical Company, was by bouncing them off a table, onto a wall, and off the floor. The glasses were inexpensive, he explained, but because companies were buying them for their employees, they were difficult to purchase on the open market.[67]

Two committees were appointed at the September 9 meeting to ensure the details were addressed for the dance and Jamboree that were initially planned in the spring. The dance committee consisted of I. Perkins, J. Berndt, D. Wicker and R. Roos, and the Jamboree Food committee members were H. Kurusz, J. Bottom and J. Miller who were also appointed to make the arrangements for the softball field and equipment for the Jamboree ball game. At this meeting it was also announced that Brother Hubbard would receive the Alpha Chi Sigma award for having the highest scholastic average.[68]

The annual Jamboree—determined in advance to be the last such event until the war ended—was held on the weekend of September 20. It began with registration on Saturday morning, climaxed with a dance that evening, and ended with a strong finish on the following day in a game of bat meets leather. After the registration, a tour of the campus was conducted with guides provided by Beta Delta chapter members. Chapters from the University of Missouri, Washington University, and the University of Kansas attended. An alumnus from Tennessee, Gil Shockley, was also in attendance. (Gil had won second prize--$50—for his solution to the problem proposed in the national student design contest sponsored by the AIChE for college seniors in chemical engineering courses. The problem proposed for the 1942 contest entailed designing a plant for the production of aniline from nitrobenzene at the rate of 5 tons per day, seven days per week, using the iron-muriatic acid reduction process.)[69] The Jamboree closed on Sunday at the Schrenk residence with an appetizing lunch. Afterwards, the men and the women split up, each going their separate ways for separate discussions. The men were entertained with anecdotes from the professional members. "Weedy" Wiedemann—known as the ringleader of jokesters—treated the group to some fine humor. (The records do not reveal how the women were entertained.) The evening was capped off with the Varsity orchestra providing swing music for the dance.[70]

On October 13, the traditional Smoker, to which prospective pledges were invited, took place. The invitees were given a series of various chemical tests, which consisted, principally, of the identification of substances used throughout the chemical profession. After the tests, Dr. Schrenk addressed the members and prospective pledges on the function of the fraternity in the professional world. The following evening the chapter met to iron out the problems in the safety program implemented in the school laboratories which had been developed the previous year.[71]

The efforts of Beta Delta members were recognized not only by the chapter or by the larger fraternity. In the October 24 issue of the Missouri Miner, Jim Johnson was honored as the student "In the Campus Spotlight." Johnson, originally from Licking, MO, graduated from Rolla High School, entered MSM in 1939, and earned his BS degree in 1942. He was a member not only of Alpha Chi Sigma, which he served as Master Alchemist and as Treasurer, but was also a member of AIChE, Independents, and the Engineers Club. He served as treasurer for the Independents and was on the Engineers Club Board of Controllers during his sophomore and junior years. He was also active in intramural sports, including football and baseball. In recognition of his scholastic record, he received the Phi Kappa Phi Bookplate award, the Blue Key award, and the Alpha Chi Sigma award for being the highest ranking third semester student in Chemical Engineering.[72]

Formal pledging of those selected on November 4, was conducted on November 18. Following the ceremony the active participants in the upcoming initiation were named. These included: Roos, Wicker, Sparks, Mueller, Schmitz, Brodhacker, Scott, Hubbard, Miller, Kurusz, Flood, Grass, Bottom, and Livingood.[73]

At the meeting on December 2, the date of the initiation was set for either Friday, December 18, or Saturday, December 19, depending on the actual start of the Christmas holiday. And the officers were elected for the spring semester: Dave Wicker, Master Alchemist; Harry Scott, Vice-Master Alchemist; Robert Roos, Reporter; James Miller, Recorder; John Brodhacker, Treasurer; Charles Sparks, Master of Ceremonies; Dave Boltz, Alumni Secretary; and John Mueller, Historian.[74]

Then, on December 18, the last initiates of the year—William F. Walker, Mailand Strunk, who would become chair of the Chemical Engineering department, Paul B. Rothband, Hartley M. Bosworth, Donald O. Reinert, Theodore Dziemianowicz, and Edwin W. Blase—were inducted into the fraternity. The Beta Delta Membership records, however, also listed: Robert L. Ehrlich, Robert L. Heineck, Joseph D. Sheppard, William F. Halsee, Dr. Philip H. Delano, and Clifton J. Seymour. The National Office's records listed these initiates and Henry Rust as January 1, 1943, inductees; it had no record of William Halsee.

For Dr. Schrenk, 1942 ended happier than it had begun. He was remarried on Dec. 30 to Irene Seele Heimberger of Rolla (see the Excursus at the end of the chapter), who was a teacher in the Rolla elementary schools for 12 years. The ceremony, performed by Rev. Rearick of the Presbyterian Church, at the bride's home, was a private affair. In attendance were the bride's brother, Harry Heimberger, his wife, and their daughter, Susan, who acted as bridesmaid. Also present were Dr. and Mrs. E. A. Doisy and their son Dicky. Dr. Doisy, the best man, was Professor of Biochemistry at St. Louis University.[75]

J. Berndt, H. Brueschke, R. Carmack

E. Claassen, M. Flint, H. Flood

J. Harris, H. Harness, F. Johnson

J. Johnson, W. Kadera, C. Krummel

S. Kulifay, H. Kurusz, O. Muskopf

J. Nevin, I. Perkins, R. Pohl

A. Renwick, A. Rose, A. Schaeffer

J. Schilling, F. Schmitz, G. Shockley

K. Schowalter, R. Striker, F. Suessdorf

Beta Delta Chapter 1942—Rollamo 1942

1943

The war continued to disrupt everyone's life, and campus life was no exception. In February the St. Pat's festivities for the coming spring were canceled, but the St. Pat's Board made it clear that the cancellation did not mean the end to the St. Pat's tradition.[76] The ongoing business meetings, the Smokers for prospective pledges, and the biennial initiations provided at least a semblance of normality for the Beta Delta chapter. The first meeting of the spring semester, on January 5, saw the installation of officers and set the banquet for the last initiation on January 10 at the Pennant Tavern. The banquet after the previous initiation was postponed since the ceremony was held on the evening before the Christmas holidays.[77] The following committee assignments were not made until the February 2 meeting:[78]

Spring 1943 Committees

Advisory	Auditing	Membership	Scholarship	Safety
Dr. Schrenk	H. Scott	H. Scott	D. Wicker	C. Sparks
Prof. P. Delano	D. Boltz	C. Sparks	Prof. M. Livingood	P. Rothband
D. Wicker	J. Jenkins	J. R. Miller	E. Blase	J. Sheppard
J. Brodhacker				

On March 2, right after the Smoker, the next group of potential candidates for pledging was selected. At the meeting on March 30, the dates were set for the formal pledging ceremony and the initiation, April 13 and May 1, respectively. The following members were chosen to participate in the initiation rite: Roos, Rothband, Mueller, Blase, Brodhacker, Bottom, Bosworth, Erhlich, Scott, Hubbard, Walker, Miller, Heinech, Sparks, Jenkins, Reinert, Sheppard, and Dziemanowicz. A preliminary vote was then taken on the status of R. Denison who had been overlooked in the previous election. The final vote for Denison's inclusion was passed at the business meeting on April 6, and, ultimately, fourteen young men were invited to pledge.[79]

During this time, efforts continued to strengthen the objectives of the safety program. On March 30, the safety committee reported that the first aid kits in the various chemical stock rooms had been replenished and that new safety charts were being hung at prominent places in the laboratories.[80]

On April 12, a formal pledging ceremony was held for those chosen at the Smoker. The new pledges included William H. Dragoset, Frank Schofro, Earl M. Shank and the following transfer students: Robert A. Denison from the University of Arkansas, Ken E. Rudert from Southeast Missouri State Teachers' College; Alfred W. Thiele, from Southeast Missouri State Teachers' College, and John W. Sjoberg from Southeast Missouri State Teachers' College.[81]

During this time, Beta Delta focused not only on its own fellowship and well-being, but it was always cognizant of the needs of the campus community as well. In April, several Japanese students had lost their belongings when a fire broke out on April 3 at the Tech Club where they were living. In response, the members of Beta Delta decided, at the business meeting on April 27, to contribute to a fund established by the Blue Key Fraternity to offer assistance.[82]

Wayne H. Hoereth, Fred W. Schmitz, Robert R. Denison, John W. Sjoberg, Ivan P. Kinder, Kenneth E. Rudert, Earl M. Shank, William H. Dragoset, Alfred W. Thiele, Henry R. Rust, and Frank O. Schofro were initiated into membership on May 1 and were honored with a banquet after the ceremony. However, the date recorded in Beta Delta's membership records for the initiation was June 1, 1943, and the same records indicated that Henry Kurusz was initiated on May 3. The principal speaker that evening was Grand Collegiate Alchemist L. W. Van Doren of the National Supreme Council. Similar to Dean Wilson's advice for MSM students, Van Doren advised all students in technical schools such as MSM to remain civilians and do the job for which they were being trained. In that way, he explained, they would contribute much more to the war effort than if they were actually in the armed forces. He stressed the point that the war was a technical conflict and that so much depended on technically trained people to win it. Van Doren also spoke of the growth of Alpha Chi Sigma, reporting that the year had seen the fastest increase in membership in the fraternity's history.[83]

At the last meeting of the spring semester on May 11, all the officers were re-elected by acclamation with the exception of the Chapter Historian. Jack Mueller, former Chapter Historian, left school with the reservists at the end of the semester. Fred Schmitz was elected to replace Mueller. The other officers re-elected were: Dave Wicker, MA; Harry Scott, VMA; Bob Roos, Reporter; Jim Miller, Recorder; John Brodhacker, Treasurer; and Charles Sparks, MC.[84]

Usually, meetings were not held over the summer. But 1943 was an exception; business meetings were held in June and July. At the June 22 meeting, a committee, comprised of C. Sparks, J. Brodhacker, and R. Heineck, was formed to plan future meetings and consider whether a Smoker should be held in the fall. Fred Schmitz was installed as Chapter Historian; all the other officers had retained their positions.[85]

At the first meeting of the fall on September 21, the chapter decided to go ahead with a Smoker and appointed the following committee to organize it: D. Boltz, F. Schmitz, C. Sparks and J. Brodhacker. The following week an informal meeting on September 27 was called to announce those prospects eligible for pledging and to set Monday, October 4, as the date of the Smoker. Two additional committees were appointed: Refreshment—J. Brodhacker; and Program—J. Miller (Chair), A. Thiele, I. Kinder, H. Rust, F. Schofro, and F. Schmitz.[86]

During these early years of the war, most MSM students remained on campus and continued their preparations for the technical careers they were pursuing. But, like millions of people all over the country, they did their best to demonstrate their patriotism and often contributed to the war effort. At the October 6 meeting, for example, the chapter decided to purchase a $100 War Bond–not an insignificant contribution for college students at the time.[87]

In October, the Miner reported the dance schedule for the final months of 1943. It had become customary around this time for the various campus organizations, particularly the fraternities, to sponsor dances and arrange for the venue and the band. Beta Delta signed up for the November 27th slot.[88]

On November 3, the following officers were elected for the spring semester: Fred Schmitz, Master Alchemist; I.P. Kinder, Vice Master Alchemist; John Sjoberg, Reporter; Wayne Hoerth, Recorder; Earl Shank, Treasurer; John Mueller, Master of Ceremonies; Robert Heineck, Historian; and David Boltz, Alumni Secretary. At the same meeting, the chapter invited ten new prospects to pledge: Carl B. Yoder, Glennon M. Jost, Donald H. Hessling, Robert L. Banks, James M. McKelvey, John V. Glaves, Paul R. Kasten, William H. Magill, Richard L. Schmitz, and George W. Walpert.[89]

The newly-elected officers were installed on November 17. Plans were made that evening to hold the initiation on December 4, and at another meeting on December 1, the location of the ceremony was determined—the new Chemical Engineering building. The chapter also decided to hold a dance on January 14, if the event could be arranged.[90] In addition, the members were reminded to attend the lecture by Dr. Edward Doisy, a biochemist from St. Louis University on Friday, December 10. Doisy won the Nobel Prize in Physiology or Medicine in 1943 for his work with Vitamin K. He succeeded in producing two variants of the vitamin in pure form, determining its structure and producing it by artificial means. His work was especially important for the treatment of bleeding in small children. Doisy was initiated into Alpha Chi Sigma by Alpha Epsilon at St. Louis University. He was born on 13 November, 1893, and died on 23 October, 1986. (His son, Richard, was initiated by Beta Delta in 1944.)[91]

Edward Doisy-Nobel Foundation Archive

On December 4, all those who pledged in November—except for John Glaves--were initiated. Glaves was initiated later in the spring of 1944, but the reason for his postponement could not be determined. A few days later, on December 8, according to what by now was becoming an expected tradition, a banquet, in honor of the initiates was held at the Pennant Tavern. Following the banquet the new members were asked to share their impressions of the ceremony—a custom started the previous spring. District Counselor Dr. Schrenk reviewed the history of Alpha Chi Sigma, spoke of the future of the organization, and welcomed the initiates into the fraternity. The evening ended with jokes contributed by everyone in "…a friendly atmosphere of fragrant cigar smoke."[92]

Fall 1943 Initiates

George W. Walpert	James M. McKelvey	Robert L. Banks
William H. Magill	Richard L. Schmitz	Don H. Hessling
Glennon M. Jost	Paul R. Kasten	Carl B. Yoder

Top Row: J. Berndt, D. Christensen, W. Hubbard, W. Kadera, I. Perkins, R. Roos, H. Scott; Middle Row: J. Bottom, H. Flood, J. Jenkins, H. Kurusz, P. Quinn, J. Schilling, C. Sparks; Bottom Row: J. Brodhacker, L. Grass, J. Johnson, J. Mueller, T. Roemer, J. Schmitz, D. Wicker

Beta Delta Chapter 1943—Rollamo 1943

1944

The first order of business at the first meeting of the new year, on January 5, was the dance that had not come off as expected the previous semester. Now the members decided that—because Tau Beta Pi and Theta Tau were no longer interested in helping—the event should be dropped. Earl Shank moved that, in place of the dance, some other event should be held to give the graduating seniors an appropriate farewell, but no final action was taken at the time. At the end of the meeting, Sjoberg made a motion, which passed, that the senior with the highest scholastic ranking be awarded a membership in the American Chemical Society.[93]

On January 28, chapter advisor Dr. Thomas Day left MSM for a temporary assignment on the research staff at Columbia University. Though he planned to return after the war, Beta Delta recognized his service to the chapter anyway by presenting him an alumni charm engraved with "To T. G. Day from Beta Delta." The members then chose Dr. Schrenk to replace him as Chapter Advisor.[94]

At the meeting on February 2, the chair of Beta Delta's Safety committee reported that the chapter had joined the National Safety Council (NSC) and was planning to take full advantage of the training programs and safety-related resources available under the Grand Chapter's membership.[95]

Enlistments in the armed forces continued throughout 1944, and members leaving the campus to serve in the war effort led to some depletion in Beta Delta membership numbers. The meeting on February 16, for example, was the last one attended by Brothers Jack Mueller and Wayne Hoereth, Master of Ceremonies and Recorder, respectively, who had been assigned to Officer's Candidate School at Fort Belvoir, Virginia. Both made short remarks to the chapter expressing the pleasure they had experienced as Alpha Chi Sigma members. Their departure left two important offices vacant, however, and necessitated an immediate election. Bill Magill became the new Master of Ceremonies; Bart Yoder, the new Recorder.[96]

After Magill and Yoder were installed as the first order of business at the March 2 meeting, the chapter took up the major item on the agenda–the first ballot on prospective members. Twelve possible prospects were selected. After the election, Hessling proposed that members prepare papers on phases of a chemical engineering student's progress through the course of study, stressing those points that would not ordinarily be covered in the curriculum. Though the reasons for raising this topic were not reported specifically, presumably the school administration was seeking input into the quality of various departments' curricula.[97]

At the next meeting, on March 16, ten prospective pledges passed the final vote. The members then set the calendar for upcoming events: Pledging Ceremony, March 30; Assignments for the initiation, April 6; Beer-Bust on April 15; Chili Supper at Dr. Schrenk's, April 20; and Initiation, April 22.[98] Notable on the calendar was the absence of a Smoker, which was the obvious result of a smaller pool of students during the war from which to select prospective new members. The urgency to maintain an effective membership level became a major concern for the chapter; only three of the prospective pledges—Daniel Thurston Blount, M. L. Custis, Robert E. Murray, and Nils K. Nelson—were formally pledged on April 6. On April 22 Blount, Nelson, Murray, and John V. Glaves were initiated. The reason why Custis was not initiated was not determined.[99]

Low pledge numbers, however, did not keep the chapter from meeting its obligations to fellowship and scholarship. On April 20, Dr. Schrenk hosted a bountiful chili supper after which everyone joined in an evening of card playing. A week later on April 27, the chapter was treated to a talk by Lester E. Olmstead (Kappa Chapter) of the technical staff of the research division of Western Cartridge Company. Brother Olmstead was a graduate of the University of Kansas. His lecture, entitled, "Old Man Corrosion," dealt with nonferrous metals. Before Olmstead arrived at the podium, John R. Kuebler felt the need to give the chapter a "heads-up." He told the members to "keep an eye on" Olmstead. "He's the St. Louis Professional Chapter's treasurer," Kuebler joked. "When he walks through a gathering of fraternity members… dollar bills and chicken feed fly right out of the brothers' pants."[100]

Beta Delta finished the semester on a high note. Collectively, the members achieved a coveted recognition: They attained an average grade point of 1.463, a close second to the average of 1.657 achieved by first place Theta Tau.[101]

The chapter's very last item of business in the spring of 1944 was the election of officers for the fall on May 18. Fred Schmitz was re-elected Master Alchemist by acclamation. The other officers included: William Magill, Vice-Master Alchemist; Carl Yoder, Reporter; James McKelvey, Recorder; Richard Schmitz, Master of Ceremonies; Nils Nelson, Historian; and Marvin Livingood, Alumni Secretary. After the meeting was adjourned, the members watched the movie, "Underwriters Laboratories," produced by the National Safety Council.[102]

In the fall of 1944, General and Chemical Engineering were among the most popular courses at MSM. Of 185 students (88 Freshman, 28 Sophomores, 37 Juniors, 31 Seniors, and 1 graduate student), 35 were registered for General Engineering, and 32 for Chemical Engineering. These numbers should have provided a sizable pool for potential Beta Delta members, but, unfortunately, they did not translate into a large pledge class.

The chapter organized for the coming semester at a meeting held in the chapter's club room in the Chemical Engineering building on September 21. The schedule, this time, included a Smoker for pledges on October 5. An expanded safety program and renovations to the club room were also planned.[103] Other dates were set as well: October 12, regular meeting; October 26, final vote on pledges; November 6, pledging ceremony; and November 22, regular business meeting. The initiation would be held sometime between November 22 and December 13. Eleven students were deemed eligible for pledging. N. Nelson was appointed as master of ceremonies for the Smoker and C. Yoder was assigned—with assistance from all the members—to clean up the club room. The group also decided to hang more safety posters in the freshman lab.[104]

At the October 12 meeting, the date for initiation was set for December 2. Then, for some reason, the election of officers–which had taken place in spring–was completely re-done. This time, Carl Yoder was elected Master Alchemist; Earl Shank, Vice-Master Alchemist and Master of Ceremonies; Robert Murray, Treasurer; Nils Nelson, Reporter; and James McKelvey, Recorder and Historian. The specific reason for this repeat election was not recorded, but, presumably, F. Schmitz, R. Schmitz, J. McKelvey, and M. Livingood either enlisted or were drafted. The motions to combine the VMA and MC positions and the Recorder and Historian positions passed easily, probably because of the reduced number of members, a problem that would be mitigated, it was hoped, by the new pledge class. Eleven potential pledges passed the first ballot after the Smoker. Still, when the new officers took over, Beta Delta had only six active members—the officers and one other. The remainder had graduated previously in May.[105]

Only four initiates were brought into the fraternity on December 2. These included: William Break, a transfer student from Southeast Missouri Teachers' College; Emil Lawrence Bahn, a transfer student from Cape Girardeau; Richard J. Doisy; and Forest O. Sisk.[106] The record from the National Office of Alpha Chi Sigma indicated that only William Break was initiated on December 2, while Bahn, W.P. Eyberg, and Doisy were initiated on January 1, 1945. Only the six actives–and three faculty members–were available to conduct this initiation. Nevertheless, after the ceremony, a banquet was held in honor of the initiates. The new members entertained the small gathering with their life histories and their impressions of the initiation rite. The chapter was honored to have three prominent guests–H. E. Wiedemann, R. R. Cornwall, and J. H. Gardner from St. Louis–in attendance. Wiedemann entertained the attendees with a talk on the history of the fraternity; Gardner and Cornwall spoke about the activities of Alpha Epsilon. Other stories–better left untold–provided a "most enjoyable time."[107]

Top Row: R. Banks, J. Brodhacker, R. Denison, W. Dragoset, L. Grass, R. Heineck, W. Hoereth, W. Hubbard, J. Jenkins, Middle Row: P. Kasten, I. Kinder, W. Magill, J. Miller, J. Mueller, R. Roos, K. Rudert, H. Rust, J. Schmitz, J. Bottom Row: F. Schofro, H. Scott, E. Shank, J. Sheppard, J. Sjoberg, C. Sparks, A. Thiele, D. Wicker, C. Yoder

Beta Delta Chapter 1944—Rollamo 1944

1945

In February, with the end of the war in sight, petitions to restore the St. Pat's festivities circulated around the MSM campus. Students wanted to get back to some sense of normality, and what better way to do that than with a rousing week of Irish celebration? Canceled since the fall of 1942, when the St. Pat's Board was disbanded, the popular event was rescheduled by the Student Council, for the week of March 17th. The decision had positive results; campus life brightened. So, too, did Beta Delta's academic achievement and social life. An outstanding accomplishment was the chapter's winning the highest scholastic distinction for campus organizations: first place in the semester's academic standing with a cumulative grade point average of 1.718. Sigma Pi ranked second with a 1.689 average, followed by Theta Tau at 1.625. (MSM grade points at this time were based on a three point system first developed in 1922. Using the existing grade designations of E, S, M, I and F, points per credit-hour were assigned as follows: 3 for E, 2 for S, 1 for M, 0 for I and -1 for F. The words for which the letters stood can be surmised but were never mentioned in the records. This grading system remained in effect until the 1957-58 school year when it was changed to a 4-point system.)[108]

On March 8, a Thursday evening, Beta Delta held its spring Smoker in the Chemical Engineering Lab. Active and prospective members played various games such as the qualitative tests, "Hit the Pot," and "Pin the Electron in the Atom Orbits" (while blindfolded). Since cigarettes were still in short supply, a contest to see who could roll the best cigarette followed. The winner was not recorded, but the prizes were a box of stationary for the best RYO (Roll Your Own) and for the worst–a sucker. Afterward, hot dogs, doughnuts, and soda were enjoyed by all.[109]

On May 5, six pledges were initiated: Thomas Dean Daniels, William L. Griffith, Oscar M. Olsen, Walbridge P. Eyberg (National Office records indicated he was initiated on January 1), William Kelmer, and Charles W. Wehking. Following the ceremony, a banquet was held in the initiates' honor at the Houston House in Newburg.[110] Two days later, on May 7, 1945, Germany surrendered to the allies, bringing the European Theater of the war to an end.

In the summer of 1945 the Board of Curators at the University of Missouri, upon the recommendation of the Dean, Curtis L. Wilson, appointed a committee of ten faculty members to prepare a program for MSM's 75th anniversary. The committee, chaired by Dr. Schrenk, was in charge of planning and supervising the programs, ceremonies, and other events to be held in the fall of 1946. In anticipation of the war in the Pacific ending soon, large numbers of alumni advocated for an extensive homecoming celebration which could be observed in conjunction with the 75th anniversary event of the school.[111]

In the summer, good news spread across the nation. On August 15, the Japanese surrendered to the Allies, and the war finally came to an end. Beta Delta members, like the rest of the country, got back to business in earnest. The fall semester began with a renewed optimism. At the first meeting, on September 21, most of the officers, who held their positions in the spring, were reinstated by acclamation: Nils Nelsen, Master Alchemist; Dick Doisy, Vice-Master Alchemist; Bill Kehner, Treasurer; Dean Daniels, Reporter; and Larry Bahn, Master of Ceremonies. The only new officers–Bill Break and Bob Heineck–were elected Recorder and Historian, respectively, by acclamation as well. (No records were found attesting to an election of officers in the summer of 1945.) Also, at the September 21 meeting, the schedule for the fall semester was announced: the Smoker, October 4; the First Election, October 18; the suggested date for the Initiation, December 6. In addition, a program committee–Bahn, Olsen, and Break–was appointed.[112]

At the meeting on October 18, after the officers were re-installed, 13 pledges were announced as eligible for initiation. The chapter invited Alpha Epsilon, by letter, to attend a joint initiation, and the following active members–Kehner, Bahn, Doisy, Break, Livingood, and Olsen–were assigned to participate in the initiation ceremony.[113]

Two brief meetings were held before the initiation. At the first, on November 1, the chapter decided to have Brother Heineck approach the administration to determine if MSM would be willing to help pay for the periodical, "National Safety News," for 1946. Even with fewer members, the chapter held on to its commitment to the safety program. At the second meeting, on November 15, the members changed the date of the initiation to December 8 and arranged for a banquet to follow at the Houston House in Newburg. In addition, a former student, Virgil Johnson, who had been in the armed forces and returned, was given permission to pledge in 1946.[114]

Grand Recorder John Kuebler was among several brothers who gathered in Rolla to attend the joint initiation of Alpha Epsilon (Washington University, St. Louis) and Beta Delta.[115] The following pledges were initiated on December 8: Wilbur P. Tappmeyer, Albert V. Malone, James J. Casler, Virgil A. Johnson, Donald A. Branson, Alfred T. Marsh, Eric Rolaff, Robert G. Barrick, and Robert E. Johnk.

Beta Delta Chapter 1945—Rollamo 1945

1946

The first meeting of the spring semester, on January 3, began with a welcome from Nils Nelson and Dr. Schrenk to the new membership: Dr. A. T. Marsh, Wilber Tappmeyer, Robert G. Barrick, Bob Johnk, Don Branson, Eric Rolaff, V. A. Malone, Jim Casler, and V. A. Johnson. Prof. William H. Webb, who had just returned from the European Theater, gave an account of his experience since leaving MSM. The chapter then elected officers for the spring semester. These included: Dean Daniels, MA; Wilbur Tappmeyer, Reporter; Bob Johnk, Treasurer; and Eric Rolaff, MC.[116] In addition, a party was planned for later in the month to honor the graduating seniors.

The new officers were installed at the next meeting on January 16, and Brother Rolaff was also appointed to chair the Smoker committee. The date of the Smoker, however, was not set until the following meeting on February 7, and it was announced, at that time, that Beta Delta and AIChE would hold a joint meeting on February 28.[117]

With the war over, and the immediate crisis of low membership levels behind it, Beta Delta turned its attention to more substantial membership issues. At the meeting on March 7, the chapter engaged in a lengthy discussion regarding the problem of the racial barrier inherent in the wording of the membership requirements and decided that this issue should be raised by Beta Delta's delegate at the 18th Biennial Conclave, which was scheduled for June 12-16 at the Coronado Hotel in St. Louis. Virgil Johnson, a junior and a major in the army, who had left the school in 1941 and had just returned for the spring semester, was elected to this important delegate position. His alternates were Kenneth Schowalter and Robert Johnk. The preliminary vote for prospective pledges was also taken at this meeting—19 prospects passed. Two weeks later, on March 21, the final vote took place. Thirteen candidates were invited to pledge. Eleven accepted.[118]

At a joint outing with Theta Tau at Buehler Park, on April 6, Beta Delta announced its new pledges: Roy V. Denton, Marion F. Hawthorne, Ivan Lampe, J. Hartley Locher, Arliss V. Martin, Robert K. Neuman, David P. Petersen, Howard Gene Russell, Herbert B. Sachs, William L. Shivelbine and Charles L. Rakestraw.[119] Later, on April 27 all of these pledges, except for Ivan Lampe, were initiated and honored with a banquet held at the Houston House in Newburg afterward. Two days before the initiation, on April 25, a business meeting was held to elect new officers for the fall semester. The new leaders included: Virgil Johnson, MA; Jim Casler, VMA; Albert Malone, Recorder; Rick Rolaff, MC; Bob Johnk, Treasurer; and Bill Magill, Historian.[120]

The officers elected on April 25 were installed at the May 8 meeting. During this meeting, two letters were read. The first, from Sigma Chapter, indicated that they intended to propose an amendment to the constitution at the Conclave in the summer that would eliminate the bar to membership for those of Semitic descent. The second letter, from Alpha Epsilon thanked Beta Delta for the joint initiation the previous December and invited the chapter to their initiation on May 11.[121]

The semester closed with a small disappointment. Beta Delta's collective grade-point average (1.660) slipped from first place—which it held since the spring semester of 1945—to third place behind first place Theta Tau (1.813) and second place Women Students (1.732).[122]

The consequences of WWII raised new technical issues which would require adjustments in the education of those pursuing the chemical sciences. With the dawning of the age of atomic energy, the use of such an unparalleled energy source became a frequent topic of speeches and debates at the university. On June 18, a roundtable discussion was held on the MSM campus concerning this subject. The principal speakers included Mr. Anderson, head of the Metallurgy Department at the Bureau of Mines at Rolla, Dr. Schrenk, Director of the Chemical Department at MSM, Rev. Ralph Hicks of the Rolla Ministerial Association, Prof. Sam Lloyd of the Economics Department of MSM, and Eddie Sowers, editor of the Rolla Daily News. MSM's Dean Curtis L. Wilson was the final speaker. In his speech, Dr. Schrenk explained the chemistry of atomic energy and focused primarily on the theory of decomposition of radioactive material. (Schrenk had taught—and encouraged—many of the people involved in the "Manhattan Project." His insights and suggestions played a significant role in the development of the atomic bomb.)[123]

Another consequence of the dissipating clouds of war was a return to normalcy. Activities and events which had been suspended returned. At a meeting on October 3, the awarding of a Perry's Chemical Handbook to the Chemical Engineer with the highest grade point in the sophomore class—an honor that was discontinued during the war due to the lack of students and money—was re-inaugurated. During this meeting plans for the annual Jamboree—also suspended previously—got underway. In addition, Dr. Webb was elected to succeed Dr. Schrenk as Chapter Advisor, but Schrenk would continue to hold the position of District Counselor. The final order of business was the matter of securing guides for Engineer's and Parent's Day. Dr. Frank H. Conrad, Associate Professor of Chemical Engineering, announced that Beta Delta would furnish 20 guides for the Chemistry department tours. Presumably there was no problem meeting this goal, since students who volunteered or had parents attending were excused from classes.[124]

On October 13, Beta Delta Chapter (Missouri-Rolla) hosted the Midwest District Conclave and Jamboree held at Buehler's Park in Rolla. The highlight of the Jamboree—after the regular business meeting—was the picnic at the home of District Counselor Schrenk. Alpha Epsilon Chapter (Washington U) and the St. Louis Professional Chapter joined forces and claimed a moral victory when they lost by only eight runs, 10 to 18, to Beta Delta in a raucous baseball game. Life for Beta Delta was truly returning to better days.[125]

Even scholastic averages ticked higher. In the fall, when the academic status of the fraternities was announced, Beta Delta made a comeback. Once again, the chapter came out at the top of the ranking with a grade point average of 1.866.[126]

Getting back to business on October 17—after the big baseball victory—the chapter laid out the schedule for the rest of the semester: November 7, Smoker; November 23, Dance jointly sponsored with Tau Beta Pi and Theta Tau; and January 4, Initiation. A food committee for the Smoker was appointed and a discussion about who to invite ensued. Since the number of students eligible for pledging was rather larger than usual, it was decided to invite only the juniors and seniors, and the sophomores with the highest grade point averages. Drs. Caldwell and Fisher (both Assistant Professors of Chemical Engineering) were also invited. The participants for the initiation ceremony were then assigned.[127]

The Smoker was a success with 14 potential pledges passing the preliminary vote. On November 23, the long-expected Tri-Tec Dance, which had been enjoyed for many years before the war, returned to the campus. Beta Delta, along with local chapters Tau Beta Pi and Theta Tau, hosted the event which proved to be extremely successful. The dance, at the Jackling Gymnasium, marked a significant renewal of social activity on campus—a harbinger of good things to come.[128] Earl Jackson and His Men of Note, a well-known band throughout the East and Midwest at the time, was engaged by the three fraternities to provide the music.[129]

The final vote for pledges was held at the December 5 meeting; twelve candidates were invited to officially join the chapter. The date of the initiation ceremony was finalized for January 5, 1947.[130]

Front Row: W. Tappmeyer, R. Heineck, N. Nelson, W. Kehner, D. Daniels, W. Break, R. Barrick; Back Row: R. Johnk, D. Branson, J. Casler, E. Rolaff, O. Olsen, R. Doisey, L. Bahn, J. Monroe, W. Schrenk, M. Livingood

Beta Delta Chapter 1946—Rollamo 1946

1947

Beta Delta started the new year with a business meeting on Thursday, January 2. There were only two items on the agenda for the meeting: confirming the assignment of initiation participants and electing officers. The officers elected were: Mailand R. Strunk, Master Alchemist; Bob Neuman, Vice-Master Alchemist; John Sjoberg, Reporter; Hawthorne, Recorder; Herb Sachs, Treasurer; Roy Denton, Master of Ceremonies; Bill Break, Historian; and Don Brice, Alumni Secretary. The meeting concluded with the announcement that H. E. Wiedemann would be among the guests attending the banquet.[131]

At the initiation, 16 new members were welcomed into the fraternity (see below), but, for some unreported reason, the banquet which usually followed the initiation ceremony did not take place; it was postponed to some future unspecified date instead.[132]

January 1947 Initiates

Francis O. Roderique	Rayburn A. Wilks	Vincent V. Valleroy	William H. Gammon	Robert J. Armstrong
Harold J. Withrow	Joe Collins	Paul L. Moore	Robert L. White	Samuel E. Martin
Donald G. Lowder	Vincent V. Valleroy	John D. Vaden	Charles N. Hudson	Albert L. Vandenburg
Stanley E. Bye				

The officers elected on January 2 were installed at the meeting on January 16. Then Virgil Johnson reported on the 18th Biennial Conclave which was held in St. Louis (Beta Delta alumni Edward Schneider and Frank Zvanut also attended). Johnson was on the committee appointed to write a resolution to repeal the by-law barring people of Semitic descent from joining the fraternity, but the Grand Chapter did not reach a conclusion on the issue. Other Beta Delta members—Robert Johnk, Walter Dean, Wilbur Tappmeyer and William Break—also attended and had parts in the model initiation (See Note 4) of Francis J. Curtis, Vice-President of Monsanto.[133]

The Smoker, originally scheduled for March 20, was delayed for two weeks until April 3, possibly because of the large number (44) of eligible prospects invited. At the final vote, on April 16, 19 candidates were asked to pledge with formal pledging scheduled for April 22. During that meeting, the initiation was re-scheduled from May 2 to May 4, and participants assigned: Valleroy, Withrow, Tappmeyer, Mueller, Wilks, Bosworth, Casler, Break, Gammon, Locher, Malone, Johnk, Schmitz, Martin, Walpert, Vaden, and Van Amburg.[134]

Improving members' understanding of technical matters in industry was not forgotten amidst the planning and execution of pledging, social events, and usual business matters. Later that spring, on April 17, Beta Delta held a joint meeting with the AIChE in the Old Chemistry Building, Room 103. The speaker for the evening was Mr. G. C. Cunningham, Superintendent of Operations at the Shell Refining Company in Wood River, IL. Cunningham, a graduate of MSM, spoke on "Petroleum Refining" and showed films demonstrating the refining process.[135]

Beta Delta concluded the spring semester with an eventful week in early

May. On May 1, new officers were elected in preparation for the fall. Robert Armstrong, Master Alchemist; Rayburn Wilke, Vice-Master Alchemist; Charles Hudson, Recorder; Samuel Martin, Master of Ceremonies; Fred Rodrique, Historian; and Stanley Bye, Alumni Secretary were the chapter's new leaders. Of the nineteen new members who were initiated on May 4, two of them, Bill Bernard and Ed Busche, were from the Alpha Epsilon chapter at Washington University. Following the initiation, a banquet was held in honor of the new initiates, according to the chapter's custom, at the Edwin Long Hotel in Rolla. After what was reported as a "…delicious dinner," the gathering heard from several members of the professional chapter of St. Louis including Wiedemann, past Grand Master Alchemist of the fraternity. Other guests included faculty members of the Washington University Chemistry Department and members of Alpha Epsilon. In addition to the formal words presented by the professional members, countless humorous incidents were shared—to the delight of the attendees. Mailand Strunk, Master Alchemist of Beta Delta, was toastmaster for the evening.[136]

May 1947 Initiates

Earl E. Hoehn	Don W. Detjen	Schuyler Kingsland	Frederick T. Crossman	Maurice F. Wetzel
William D. Carter	Glenn E. Brand	George E. Purdy	Robert C. Booth	
Joseph F. Miazga	Walter S. Knecht	James F. Walker	Bernard A. LaRose	
Gene A. Tyrer	Hampden O. Banks	Jorge Jackson	Robert Stahl	

Also in May, officers were installed on the 15th, and a Scholarship committee, consisting of S. Bye and S. Kingsland, was appointed to nominate the recipients of the chapter's awards for the senior and sophomore with the highest scholastic average in chemistry or chemical engineering. The senior winner would receive a one-year subscription to the American Chemical Society; the sophomore with the highest average would win the choice of a Perry's, Lange's or Chemical Rubber Handbook. On May 17, Beta Delta concluded the semester with an outing—the location not specified.[137]

Many of the students who suspended their education to serve in the armed forces during the war returned to the campus when the war ended. One such student was A. L. Van Amburg, a Chemical Engineering student, who had served in the Marine Air Corps. After returning, during his junior year, Van Amburg was awarded the A. P. Greene Scholarship in July. The scholarship—worth $300—which recognized the most outstanding junior, was presented by Dr. A. P. Greene, President of the A. P. Greene Firebrick Company, Mexico, MO. Van Amburg was selected by a faculty committee of which Dr. Schrenk was a member. A member of Alpha Chi Sigma and AIChE, Van Amburg was elected president of the local AIChE chapter for the following semester.[138]

On Sunday, July 27, the St. Louis Professional Chapter members, along with their wives or dates, were invited by Beta Delta for an outing and ballgame. Following the established tradition, Dr. and Mrs. Schrenk hosted the outing at their home. The repast included large quantities of baked ham, cheese, baked beans, potato chips, sodas and BEER—quite a combustible fare.

The ball game followed the lunch, of course. This time, the playing field was a cow pasture near the Schrenk's home, a location which required special clean-up for Beta Delta members the previous week. (Chapter members quickly learned that not all cow chips are pleasantly dehydrated.) For the first six innings, the teams were evenly matched, but the students moved out ahead and eventually prevailed, 7 to 4. The wife of Dr. Conrad, Assistant Professor of Chemical Engineering, was not happy with how the game was being called. She expressed her dissatisfaction on several occasions by throwing beer bottles at Doc Schrenk. The game was remembered for the enthusiastic cheering, angry jeering and the bellowing of cows.[139]

Despite the economic hardships immediately following the war, in 1947 Gov. Donnelly approved funding for an addition to the Chemistry Building. At the time, no date was immediately established for the construction of the new addition, but MSM was fortunate to get the governor's backing since many of the schools around the state had seen their funding and budgets slashed.[140]

The fall began officially with the Midwest District Jamboree in Rolla on

October 12. The usual cast of participants—the St. Louis and Kansas City Professional chapters along with collegiate chapters Kappa, Delta, Alpha Epsilon and Beta Delta--attended the event. At the meeting held in conjunction with the Jamboree, the following committees were established:[141]

Fall 1947 Committees

Advisory	Auditing	Membership	Scholarship	Budget	Program
R. Armstrong	R. Wilks	R. Wilks	R. Armstrong	R. Armstrong	J. Collins
H. Sachs	V. Valleroy	J. Vaden	S. Kingsland	H. Sachs	P. Moore
DC Schrenk	A. Malone	G. Brand	J. Jackson	DC Schrenk	
W. Webb				R. Stahl	
				V. Valleroy	

The Smoker was held on October 16 with invitees taking the traditional tests and winning prizes for the highest and lowest scores. Those present ate hot dogs, drank cokes, smoked cigarettes or cigars, and played card games until late into the evening. No one mentioned ashtrays.[142] The evening's activities resulted in 26 potential new members—all of whom formally pledged on December 4. After the formal pledging ceremony, Ed Schneider, along with Les Olmstead, Hank Kurusz and Mack Barlow of the St. Louis Professional chapter spoke at the meeting. Schneider discussed "The Problems and Opportunities Which Confront the New Engineer in Industry." The others also gave brief talks on their respective jobs. Afterward, the chapter joined the guests in a round table discussion of various topics.[143]

The final meeting of the fall, on December 18, saw the formal pledging of three additional students. And Brother Rodrique was named the winner of the Junior Scholarship award for 1946-47. Changes to the requirements for this award, drawn up at a meeting on November 6, included: 1) the award should be presented to the junior in chemistry or chemical engineering with the highest scholastic standing, 2) the winner should be named at the end of each spring semester, 3) to be eligible, the winner must have earned from 110 to 128 credit hours, 4) the candidate must have matriculated at MSM for at least two semesters, 5) the candidate must have completed one year of organic or physical chemistry, and 6) the award should be presented at the most convenient public gathering after the beginning of the fall semester.

During this meeting, it was announced that the initiation of 26 new pledges would be held on January 11, 1948, with the customary banquet to follow at the Houston House in Newburg. It was also decided that the chapter would not send a delegate to the pre-Conclave meeting which was held on December 29-30, 1947. And finally, officers for the spring were elected: Samuel Martin, Master Alchemist; Stanley Bye, Vice-Master Alchemist; William Gammon, Reporter; Robert Stahl, Recorder; Earl Hoehn, Treasurer; Don Detjen, Master of Ceremonies; R. R. Cornwall, Alumni Secretary; and Schuyler Kingsland, Historian.[144]

Occasionally a tribute was paid to all the hard-working chemists on campus—albeit with tongue in cheek. One of these rare accolades appeared in the Miner on September 24, 1947:

Ode to a Chemist
By McCallister

A green little chemist on a green spring day

Mixed some green chemicals in a green way

Now the green little grasses tenderly wave

O'er the green little chemist's green lil grave.[145]

4th Row: W. Break, R. Neuman, S. Bye, E. Rolaff, J. Sjoberg, W. Shivelbine, M. Strunk, S. Martin, R. Johnk, D. Petersen, J. Collins, D. Lowder;

3rd Row: V. Johnson, H. Withrow, G. Walpert, J. Casler, J. Vaden, W. Gammon, A. Van Amburg, H. Sachs, W. Magill, J. Glaves;

2nd Row: J. Schmitz, F. Roderique, K. Rudert, P. Kasten, R. Armstrong, D. Brice, W. Tappmeyer, C. Hudson, A. Martin, R. White;

1st Row: C. Rakestraw, J. Locher, R. Denton, A. Malone, J. Mueller, P. Moore, R. Wilks, M. Hawthorne, V. Valleroy.

Beta Delta Chapter 1947—Rollamo 1947

1948

In 1944, during the worst of the war years, Beta Delta's numbers had fallen to a low of only six active members. Since those dark days, the chapter's numbers had slowly–but steadily–increased. But with the reception of 28 new members on January 11, 1948, the group's membership swelled beyond everyone's expectations. Suddenly, chapter meetings felt crowded and boisterous. (See the table below for a list of all the new members). After the initiation, the chapter quickly installed officers on January 15 and appointed the following committees on February 5: Advisory—S. Martin, E. Hoehn, District Counselor Schrenk and Chapter Advisor Webb; Membership—S. Bye, W. Hellwege, and Griessen; and Scholarship—S. Martin and J. Miazga. The addition of so many new members, it appeared, would make it possible for the chapter to renew its commitments to advancing the chemical sciences, assisting its members in their careers in the field, and encouraging stronger bonds of friendship within the group.[146]

January 1948 Initiates[147]

Edward A. Geiss	Donald F. Carney	John H. Rice	Max L. Kasten	Joseph A. Coffman	Winston C. Moss
Adolph F. Hemme	J F. Middeler	Aurelius K. Allen	Henry P. Schweder	Norman A. Niederstadt	John W. Ehrler
Robert S. Ferry	C. J. Hyslop	Leroy W. Fuller	Carl H. Goller	M. R. Rohr	Emory Fisher
Paul F. Shatto	Fred G. Koenig	William H. Hellwege	William H. Hiatt	Earl W. Loucks	
Michael J. Ditore	Louis E. Frank	Robert A. Isringhaus	Charles L. McGehee	Frank L. Brice	

At the February 5 meeting, letters were read from H. E. Wiedemann, thanking the chapter for the flowers he received from the members on the death of his wife, and from the General Lecture Series announcing the next event on February 17 at Parker Hall. An attendance contest was suggested–with the losing team paying the larger portion of a beer-bust.

The chapter's most significant concern at the start of 1948, however, centered on the fraternity's membership requirements. The issue of racial and ethnic discrimination raised at the March 7 meeting in 1946, was not acted on at that time, but it had not been forgotten either. Now, during the February 18 meeting, a discussion was enjoined regarding the restrictions of the membership clause in the fraternity's by-laws. The issue would be further discussed, it was decided, at the April 1 meeting, when the full membership would be present to better determine if the chapter favored repeal or modification of the by-law in question. The results of that vote would determine the position Beta Delta's delegate—R. Booth—would take at the national Conclave held in Cleveland, OH. The group then selected Brothers Gammon and Hoehn as Booth's first and second alternates, respectively.

Two other matters regarding membership were also raised at the February 18 meeting. The first was a proposal to increase the number of credit hours necessary to qualify for an invitation to the Smoker to 75. The second was the happy report that made the first change imperative; Beta Delta numbers had jumped to 54 collegiate members, 2 professional members, and seven professors. Evidently, most of the group felt that some method was needed to limit the increasing number of students interested in joining the fraternity–a spectacular change of opinion from the membership dearth in 1944.[148]

Beta Delta members struggled with one other membership issue at this time. At the March 4 meeting, a question was raised as to whether a student with a degree in chemistry from another college who was currently studying ceramics would be eligible for membership. The Advisory committee split evenly on this matter. Upon the vote of the entire membership, it was decided that initiations remain restricted to those enrolled in either chemistry or chemical engineering. This question would soon become another significant issue requiring a decision by the Grand Chapter.[149]

During the winter of 1948, television came to Rolla, Missouri. Across the country, television was being touted as one of the advantages of "big-city life," and—though Rolla was hardly a "big city" in 1948 (According to the 1950 census data, the population of Rolla was 9354)—the community was able to enjoy this marvel of modern technology due to the ingenuity of two MSM students—John Stanley and John Warsing. Though they were not Beta Delta members, Stanley and Warsing were able to provide television reception in Rolla which was over 100 miles from the nearest television antenna in St. Louis. And they did it in their spare time! As partners in the Guarantee Radio Co. in Rolla, they understood that television was much like FM radio, which was limited to line-of-sight transmission. Even though Rolla was 500 feet higher in elevation than St. Louis, which favored line-of-sight transmission, successful reception was dependent upon an antenna and receiver system of extremely high sensitivity and selectivity. Warsing and Stanley modified the conventional television receiver to provide much greater selectivity with higher gain and developed a directional antenna with a gain about twice that of the conventional antenna of the same dimensions. Their initial TV installation was on display in the lobby of the Edwin Long Hotel very soon after they invented it. Rolla had arrived.[150]

On April 15, one of the chapter's founders, alumnus Clement "Doc"

Maise, returned to campus to speak at a joint meeting of Beta Delta and the AIChE, which was held in the Old Chemistry building. Maise's talk, "Scientific Aspects of Crime Detection," elaborated on the use of the scientific method in that very specialized field. Maise knew what he was talking about; he had been with the FBI for six years prior to taking a position as Associate Director of the St. Louis Police Laboratories. The spring pledging ceremony was also held on April 15, but it was abbreviated to allow more time for Maise's address.[151]

In preparation for the fall semester, officers were elected on April 29. Those newly-elected included: Robert Booth, Master Alchemist; Carl Goller, Vice-Master Alchemist; John Ehrler, Recorder; Adolph Hemme, Master of Ceremonies; and James Walker, Historian. Their installation was held on May 6.[152]

A crucial piece of business before summer vacation remained, however. R. Booth had to be given his instructions as delegate to the Conclave in Cleveland. At the meeting on May 20, the membership tasked him with bringing up the following points: Beta Delta (1) favored raising the fee for initiated members from $15.00 to $20.00, (2) opposed increasing the collegiate dues, (3) supported reducing the maximum fine for loss of any section of the ritual from $15 to $5, (4) opposed a policy that required someone initiated at one chapter to be voted on before affiliating with another professional or collegiate chapter, (5) opposed the initiation of premedical candidates for Bachelor of Science degrees, (6) supported the repeal of the membership requirement barring persons of Semitic descent, (7) opposed the present system of excluding someone because of one "blackball" for possible personal reasons, (8) opposed redistribution of financial obligations or readjustment of voting powers because the professional branch was larger than the collegiate branch, (9) favored the Grand Chapter's creating a special fund for loans to collegiate chapters for the purpose of starting new chapter houses–provided this would not result in a significant increase in chapter dues, (10) favored requiring that professional delegates pay their own expenses at Conclave, since professional members did not pay into the fund for this purpose, and (11) opposed any limitation on the number of candidates who could be proposed for membership in any one year. Though the chapter spent a good deal of time voting on each of these issues, Brother Booth was not required to follow the group's recommendations. Instead, he was allowed to exercise his discretion.[153]

After the Smoker on March 25, and the subsequent requisite activities,[154] Beta Delta initiated another large group of new members—25 in total--on May 2 (See the table below) and later, in the evening, held a banquet in their honor at the Edwin Long Hotel. Guests attending were H. E. Wiedemann and Marvin Schneller, members of the St. Louis Professional Chapter. During the celebration, Dr. Schrenk was welcomed back after his accident, the nature of which—and the extent of the injury—were not recorded.[155]

May 1948 Initiates[156]

Don H. Telthorst	Vernon A. Chapman	Wilbert E. Bach	Edward A. Koziboski	Raymond Lieb
George W. Jamieson	Charles H. Hoppe	Elmer C. Breidert	Arthur W. Helwig	Robert Ferry
Glenn E. Merritt	Frank W. Bergman	Richard E. Driscoll	Reagan H. Young	Don Carnay
Nick Holloway	James C. Schmitt	Howard M. Casselman	William E. Smith	C. J. Hyslop
Robert T. Knauer	Edgar E. Thielker	Werner C. Born	Lloyd DeHekker	

In the fall, work continued on the south addition to the Chemical Engineering Building. The new construction, which also included an extension to the west of the south end of the building, was expected to be completed in 1949.[157]

Campus life got back into the full swing of things, and Beta Delta, too, ramped up its activities after the summer lull. More than 70 people attended the Smoker on October 21 at which the winners of the senior and junior scholarship awards were announced: M. Rohr and L. Frank, respectively. The Jamboree—now known as the Midwest District Conclave—followed on the heels of the Smoker, on October 24, a Sunday. It included a luncheon, another spirited ball game and a "beer bust." The committee responsible for the event's success consisted of R. Lieb (chair), R. Driscoll, W. Smith and F. Koenig.[158]

Brief meetings were held on December 2 and 16 to close out the semester. On December 2, the participants for the initiation ceremony were assigned, and the Safety committee reported that safety sheets had been circulated to the freshmen and that posters had been put up in the labs. At the December 16 meeting, the initiation date was set for January 9, and the Houston House was chosen for the banquet. Afterward, Kansas Professional member Olmstead spoke to the group on "The Applications of X-Ray Analysis in Industry."[159]

Since the initiation was scheduled for January 9, the names of no new members were recorded at the end of 1948, but the chapter's records indicate that 20 new members were initiated in 1949—four on January 1, the rest on January 9. (See the names of the new initiates in the table at the start of 1949.)

1948 also saw the continuation of the significant controversy for Alpha Chi Sigma which arose, originally, over concerns aired as early as 1946. The resolution of this issue would ultimately force a change to the fraternity's Constitution. On November 18, 1948, Alpha Zeta Chapter (MIT) voluntarily returned its charter to the Grand Chapter in protest over the restrictive membership provisions in the by-laws, which limited membership to non-Semitic Caucasians. There had been efforts, prior to the 1948 Conclave, to remove the restrictive sections, but no official action had been taken. When the proposal came before the Conclave, there was no opposition to the removal of the restriction, but the wording of the new by-law became a matter of debate. The restrictive language barring "Semitic Caucasians" was changed to individuals who were "socially acceptable," and the matter was referred to committee. Brother S. Radke, representing Alpha Zeta, however, did not accept this action, and upon returning to MIT, convinced the Alpha Zeta chapter to withdraw from the fraternity before the Membership Qualifications Committee completed its report.

The Supreme Council reached out to Alpha Zeta to reconsider. The Supreme Council insisted that Alpha Chi Sigma had never discriminated on the basis of religion, and that Alpha Zeta was misinterpreting the meaning of "socially acceptable." The request for reconsideration failed. Consequently, the Supreme Council placed Alpha Zeta on probation (Supreme Council Proposition #1431-2/28/49), and would not revoke the charter.

The Grand Chapter considered expelling all the members involved with the "illegal self-dissolvement," but it did not act upon that consideration. It did, however, reclaim all Grand Chapter Property.

It took another four years to completely eliminate the restrictive clause from the by-laws, but by then MIT was no longer interested in having an Alpha Chi Sigma Chapter, and the Supreme Council no longer had any interest in starting one there.[160]

Fourth Row: S. Kingsland, S. Martin, C. Hudson, W. Hellwege, R. Stahl, J. Ehrler, D. Peterson, H. Schweder, F. Crossman, J. Miazga, R. Booth, D. Detjen, J. Vaden.

Third Row: A. Allen, H. Withrow, D. Lowder, C. Goller, J. Rice, W. Gammon, V. Valleroy, L. Fuller, F. Roderique, J. Collins, E. Hoehn, J. Glaves, W. Knecht, M. Wetzel.

Second Row: F. Koenig, C. Wehking, P. Shatto, J. Coffman, S. Bye, R. Wilks, R. Armstrong, J. Jackson, W. Walker, P. Kasten.

First Row: A. Hemme, D. Brice, Tyrer, E. Geiss, J. Middeler, M. Rohr, W. Carter, C. McGehee

Beta Delta Chapter 1948—Rollamo 1948

1949

After the Christmas holidays, the first order of business was the election of officers on January 6. The new officers were: Carl Goller, Master Alchemist; Adolph Hemme, Vice-Master Alchemist; Arthur Helwig, Reporter; Elmer Breidert, Recorder; Robert Knauer, Treasurer; M. Rohr, Master of Ceremonies; and William Smith, Historian.[161] The new Beta Delta initiates—joining the membership for the first time—were:

January 1949 Initiates[162]

Thurston B. Howard	August J. Vogler	James D. Tschannen	Kurt H. Frank
Loren Lafferty	R. P. Schmitz	Donald J. Dowling	Jack H. Venarde
John T. Hilgenbrink	Franklin W. Wyatt	Alfred T. Klemme	Charles O. Reed
Richard B. Miller	Walter W. Campbell	Walter W. Walker	James E. Wood
Don L. Honerkamp	Donald Peterson	Roland J. Niederstadt	Dale L. Kingsley

The chapter did not pause to rest on its numerical laurels at the start of 1949. The next Smoker was scheduled almost immediately for March 4. Invitations were extended to all eligible sophomores, juniors, and seniors—a whopping total of 99 students in all. Two special guests, Dr. R. A. Cooley, and Dr. E. C. Henley, both Associate Professors of Chemistry, were also invited.

Consistent with its commitments to reach as many students as possible and to increase their technical and industrial knowledge, Beta Delta continued its practice of combining activities with other organizations. On February 11, the chapter joined ranks with AIChE and attended a presentation by Virgil Hullette on Process Development" and watched the movie, "From Test Tube to Tank Car," which demonstrated the steps necessary to convert a laboratory reaction to a successful, full-scale, commercial process.[163] Another such joint venture took place on May 12 when Dr. Odin Knight spoke to the combined group on "The Engineer's Place in a Chemical Plant." Dr. Knight, employed by the Commercial Solvents Corporation in Terra Haute, Indiana, was head of the technical personnel and design departments. His BS, MS, and PhD degrees were all in engineering.[164]

Chapter activities continued at a steady pace through the spring semester. Election of officers for the fall took place at the meeting on April 21; the new officers included: Arthur Helwig, Master Alchemist; Lloyd DeHekker, Vice-Master Alchemist; Walter Campbell, Recorder; Robert Ferry, Reporter; rank. Frank Wyatt, Historian, and Elmer Breidert, Master of Ceremonies. Two weeks later, on May 1, the chapter inducted 25 new members into the fraternity (See the table below). The initiation banquet, honoring the new members, was held at the Edwin Long Hotel. Dr. Schrenk gave his obligatory talk on the history of Alpha Chi Sigma.[165]

May 1949 Initiates

George A. Rees	Arthur R. McDermott	Raymond H. Maag	Paul A. Haas	Warren W. Rutz
Norman A. Vaniman	Ralph E. Coffee	George Dillender	H. C. Iten	Robert L. Lucker
C. W. Keller	Ivan L. Gray	William L. Utnage	Leonard E. Dieckman	Richard B. Miller
Andrew M. Taylor	Robert A. Cooley	E. D. Schrader	Otis R. Ummel	John T. Hilgenbrink
Herman N. Bockstruck	James R. Murrell	John R. Atwell	Stuart S. Brown	Donald Peterson
John F. Hernan				

The final business of the chapter in the spring was the appointment of standing committees; Beta Delta members were intent on ensuring that their large group would be ready to meet its obligations as soon as school started again in the fall. The committees they formed reflected the chapter's hopes that Beta Delta would continue to flourish as the decade drew to a close:

Fall 1949 Committees[166]

Program	Membership	Budget	Attendance
E. Breidert (Chair)	L. DeHekker (Chair)	R. Knauer (Chair)	W. Campbell (Chair)
J. Venarde	J. Tschannen	A. Helwig	G. Jamieson
H. Iten	N. Vaniman	A. Vogler	W. Burch*
A. McDermott	R. Miller	L. DeHekker	J. Maurer*
	W. Bach		
	I. Gray		

Safety	Banquet	Beta Delta Data	Miner Correspondence
A. Klemme (Chair)	W. Campbell (Chair)	F. Wyatt (Chair)	R. Miller
N. Niederstadt	G. Jamieson	R. Ferry (Advisor)	
	W. Utnage		

* Unique in these committees is evidence of the practice that allowed pledges to become committee members.

At its first meeting of the fall semester of 1949, on Thursday, September 15, Beta Delta hosted three guest speakers—H. E. Wiedemann, Ed Schneider and Hank Kurusz. Wiedemann, a Past Grand Master Alchemist, better known as "Chief" to the "chems," gave a short history of Alpha Chi Sigma, which was mainly for the benefit of the new members, initiated the previous spring, and for the fall pledges. Schneider, MSM '43, and Kurusz, MSM '42, were both employed by Monsanto Chemical Company in St. Louis. They conducted a round-table discussion on the topic, "What Industry Expects of the Engineering Graduate," which included a review of the many career fields available to the chemical engineer.[167]

The chapters of Alpha Chi Sigma were not always left to fend for themselves. Periodically they were inspected by a District Counselor who would review the health of the chapter and offer support from the Grand Chapter when needed. On October 6, Beta Delta was inspected by Dr. Chamberlain, District Counselor and a professor of Chemical Engineering at Washington University in St. Louis.[168] The inspection entailed meeting with the officers, examining the financial accounts with the treasurer, reviewing the professional activities of the chapter, and inspecting the initiation regalia. Dr. Chamberlain attended a regular chapter meeting as part of the inspection and afterward gave an informative talk on graduate studies.[169]

On Sunday, October 16, seventy-five brothers from area chapters met in Rolla for the Midwest District Conclave. Delegations from Delta, Alpha Epsilon, and Kappa chapters along with the St. Louis Professional chapter, attended. Beta Delta Chapter played the host. Registration was held at the Chemical Engineering Building, but the assembly quickly moved to the home of GMC Schrenk. As usual, the meeting was not the most significant activity of the day. The event everyone was waiting for was the baseball game in which the collegiate members "…were out to avenge" their defeat the previous year. The collegiates expected to regain possession of the coveted "…handsomely painted baby's potty," also known as the Wiedemann Cup. The collegiates' victory was decisive—a 28 to 13 pounding. Another report had the final score at 28 to 18.[170] Either way the collegiate members ruled the diamond that day. As he was leaving the playing field, one of the professional team members was heard "congratulating" a collegiate player with the passing remark: "I hope you get as much out of the cup as we put into it."[171] Sideline activities during the day included cork-ball,[172] beer drinking, and casual discussions among the attendees. The event ended after a hearty supper repast.

Several days after the Jamboree, Hugh Berry of the Shell Oil Company spoke to the chapter at its October 20 meeting. His presentation, "Crude Oil Evaluation" brought members up to date on the latest trends in the petroleum industry.[173]

On November 6, a Sunday, 13 pledges were initiated into the fraternity. The ceremony was held in the new Chemical Engineering and Chemistry Building under the direction of Elmer Breidert, Master of Ceremonies. The new actives included: Wallace W. Short, John E. Maurer, Walter L. Hampson, William D. Burch, Maurice K. Rausch, Robert E. Dieckgrafe, Harlow M. Keeser, Dale W. Heineck, Hilbert W. Crocker, William E. Rushton, Richard W. Ladd, William B. Vase, and Ross F. Crow.[174]

A week later, on November 15, Beta Delta—hoping to maintain its stunning membership growth—held another Smoker in the Chemistry Building in which "Feel-otative and Smell-otative" quizzes were the order of the day. One doctor of chemistry, who was not specifically identified, mistook acetic acid for hydrochloric acid. And a certain instructor of organic chemistry had a little trouble as well. He left the "Feel-otative Analysis" with a wry grin muttering something about a horse. The take away that evening was that even the "Profs" were fallible. The students who were invited to pledge after the meeting were scheduled for induction on January 8, 1950.[175]

In addition to its regular activities Beta Delta sponsored a number of other notable events during the 1940s. Its annual dance, the "Tri-Tec" with Tau Beta Pi and Theta Tau, became a popular affair each year. Its Chemical Magic Show, performed at Parent's Day, proved to be a hit for several years running. In addition, the chapter maintained the Safety Program throughout the Chemistry Building, published the newsletter—the Beta Delta Data—twice a year, and maintained the Beta Delta Club Room.[176]

Nevertheless, two membership issues that had plagued the fraternity since 1946 still lingered. The discriminatory language in the by-laws remained on the books and would not be properly revised until the 1950s.

The controversy over which academic disciplines qualified for membership in the fraternity would prove even more challenging; it would not be settled until the 1960s.

Fourth Row: H. Bockstruck, W. Smith, W. Knecht, L. Frank, N. Holloway, N. Niederstadt, D. Dowling, D. Peterson, R. Niederstadt, D. Honerkamp, F. Wyatt, C. Goller, R. Driscoll. Third Row: E. Breidert, E. Thielker, T. Howard, J. Schmitt, R. Young, W. Gammon, J. Middeler, J. Miazga, W. Walker, E. Geiss, D. Branson, J. Schmitz, A. Klemme, D. Kingsley, H. Schweder. Second Row: Prof. F. Conrad, W. Griffith, A. Hemme, D. Brice, E. Hoehn, F. Walker, L. DeHekker, A. Vogler, D. Telthorst, R. Knauer, G. Jamieson, W. Campbell, J. Ehrler, K. Frank, G. Tyrer, H. Withrow, C. Reed, R. Booth. First Row: B. Hagar, R. Isringhaus, V. Chapman, C. Hoppe, A. Helwig, J. Venarde, W. Bach, R. Ferry, J. Coffman, W. Carter, E. Koziboski, M. Rohr, J. Wood.

Beta Delta Chapter 1949—Rollamo 1949

Excursus: Notable Persons

Harry A. Curtis

Born in Sedalia, CO, Feb 16, 1884, Dr. Harry A. Curtis received his BS in Chemical Engineering from the University of Colorado in 1908 and his AM degree in 1910. He earned his PhD degree from the University of Wisconsin in 1914. He was recognized with a Doctor of Science degree from both Colorado and Wisconsin universities and an honorary Doctor of Engineering degree from the University of Louisville.

Curtis served on the faculties of the University of Colorado, Northwestern University, and Yale University in addition to the University of Missouri where he was Dean of the College of Engineering. He also served as a chemist with several industrial firms during his career; he was chair of the Division of Chemistry and Chemical Technology of the National Research Council from 1930-31, and he was, at one time, director of research for the Vacuum Oil Company (Currently Mobil Oil Co.). From 1930 to 1938, he served the Tennessee Valley Authority (TVA) as Chief Chemical Engineer, resigning that position when he became dean of the College of Engineering at the University of Missouri in Columbia. He was also a member of the board of directors of the Oak Ridge Institute of Nuclear Studies. Toward the end of his deanship at the University of Missouri in March, 1949, the students in the College of Engineering made him "editor" of the St. Pat's issue of The Missouri Shamrock—the official student publication. Dr. Curtis wrote one of the issues—a 44-page tome titled: "St. Patrick Was an Engineer."[177]

After 11 years as dean, Curtis returned to the TVA. In 1949, he was appointed Director of the Tennessee Valley Authority by President Harry S. Truman—replacing Dr. Harcourt Morgan who had retired from the agency. Curtis remained with the TVA until his retirement in 1957.

Dr. Curtis was initiated into Alpha Chi Sigma at Eta Chapter at the University of Colorado. In addition to his extensive accomplishments, he served as Grand Master Alchemist, Vice-Grand Master Alchemist and Grand Historian for the fraternity. While Grand Historian, he authored an early history of Alpha Chi Sigma, entitled: "History of the Alpha Chi Sigma Fraternity: 1902-1927."

Dr. Curtis passed away on July 1, 1963; the cause of death was abdominal cancer. He was 79 years old.[178]

Irene Heimberger Schrenk[179]

Irene Heimberger was born 2 February, 1902, to Louis and Johanna, Seeley, Heimberger. She was the youngest of three children, having two older brothers—Harry and Carl. Irene's paternal grandparents—Tobias and Elizabeth—were the first generation of Heimbergers to live in Rolla. They were immigrants from Germany who first settled in southern Indiana in the 1850s and then moved to Rolla in 1868.

Irene's father, Louis, the oldest son of Tobias and Elizabeth, followed in his father's footsteps working as a plasterer. Louis also became involved in local politics; he ran for Constable on the Democratic ticket in 1890 and subsequently won that position. Two years later, he was nominated as the Democratic candidate for alderman of the second ward of Rolla. As alderman, he served on the Public Health and Fire Department committees. When his financial situation made it possible in 1891, Louis and his younger brother Andrew purchased blocks 16 and 17 in Rolla, each containing eight lots. In 1893 Louis bought out his brother and constructed the home Irene grew up in.

After she graduated from high school, Irene trained to be a teacher and began teaching at East Elementary School in Rolla. When Louis died in 1931—and Johanna in 1939—Irene inherited the family home.

Walter Schrenk and his first wife, Alberta, moved to Rolla in 1923 when Dr. Schrenk accepted a position on the faculty at MSM. In January of 1942, Alberta died of ovarian cancer. In December that same year, Schrenk married Irene and moved into her home.[180]

Irene became active in university life. She sponsored the University Dames[181] and hosted various outings, luncheons, and dinners for students and university guests at the Schrenk's home. Together, Irene and Walter founded the Order of the Golden Shillelagh (OGS) in 1977. The OGS was conceived as a vehicle to promote the college after it was renamed the University of Missouri at Rolla in 1964.

Walter and Irene lived in their home until their deaths—Walter in 1979 and Irene, on 25 June, 1983.

THE 1950s

Augmentation it is of the Elixer indeede,
In goodnes and quantitie both for white and red
Multiplication is therefore as they doe write,
That thing that doth augment medicines in each degree,
In colour, in odour, in vertue and also in quantitee.

-George Ripley

The Times

Removing the rubble and rebuilding, along with the emergence of a new form of warfare—the Cold War with the Soviet Union—marked the focus of the world after WWII. But MSM did not experience the need to rebuild; instead, it enjoyed the opportunity to build anew during the decade. Major expansions were made. The Chemical Engineering Building was completed during the summer of 1953. The lecture room, the Physical-Chemistry laboratories, the freshman chemistry laboratories, and the instrumental laboratories were the final steps of the project, and they were ready for the fall semester that year.[1]

In addition to the Chemical Engineering building, the school also constructed a new Student Union, a new Electrical Engineering building, and a new Civil Engineering building. Moreover, the construction of a nuclear reactor was initiated at the end of the decade.[2]

Chemical Engineering Building 1951[3]

Organic Labs circa 1950—Rollamo 1950

More than new facilities were established, however. In 1959, MSM offered the new degree of Doctor of Philosophy in Chemical Engineering, and the school was listed in the American Chemical Society Directory of Graduate Research for the first time. Two decades later, in 1980, Judith Flebbe— a member of Beta Delta—would be the first woman to be awarded the Doctor of Philosophy in Chemical Engineering from the yet-to-be-renamed University of Missouri-Rolla.

As countries recovered from the war, the sciences lost one of the world's greatest minds. Albert Einstein passed away in 1955 at his home in Princeton, NJ. He was 76.[4] As Einstein's generation was fading, a new generation was stepping up to meet the modern demands for technical personnel. The Missouri School of Mines and Metallurgy and the professional fraternities, including Alpha Chi Sigma, were on the forefront, providing the means and the support for aspiring scientists and engineers.

Alpha Chi Sigma 1950s

In 1952, after 13 years in which no new Alpha Chi Sigma chapters were installed, the Supreme Council accepted petitions from four organizations in various parts of the country: Beta's Colony at the University of Akron, Nu Tau local chemistry fraternity at North Texas State College, Alpha Chi Chemistry Club at the University of Delaware, and Sigma Chi Alpha local chemistry club at the University of Texas.[5]

That same year the fraternity celebrated its 50th anniversary at the 21st Biennial Conclave in Madison, Wisconsin. The event was especially meaningful since the last three living founders were the special guests: Joseph H. Mathews, Harold E. Eggers and Frank J. Petura.[6]

A significant event for Alpha Chi Sigma during the 1950s was the revision of the fraternity's by-laws to eliminate the restrictive membership clause. The 22nd Biennial Conclave, June 21-25, 1954, hosted by Alpha Upsilon chapter and held at the Kellogg Center of Michigan State College in East Lansing, acted to remove all racial and ethnic restrictions on membership. The delegates felt the qualifications for membership should be determined only by one's proficiency in chemistry and a genuine desire to pursue a career in that field.

Another significant development in the life of the fraternity was the revival of "The Chrome and Blue," a newsletter published for the collegiate chapter officers and District Counselors. At the direction of the Supreme Council in 1957, the Grand Recorder reinstituted the publication, which had ceased in 1946 due to resource constraints brought on by the war (The newsletter was first published in 1927).[7]

The last year of the decade, Alpha Chi Sigma established the Alpha Chi Sigma Educational Foundation for the purpose of recognizing the outstanding senior chemistry student. During its first year the Foundation trustees planned to approach AIChE to offer an award to compliment the Pure Chemistry Award which Alpha Chi Sigma sponsored through the American Chemical Society.[8]

Beta Delta

1950

The 1950s were important years for Beta Delta. Because of its steady reception of new members and the achievements and recognitions of many of these young men, the fraternity earned a positive, forward-looking reputation on the MSM campus. As a chapter within Alpha Chi Sigma, its participatory contribution to overcoming discrimination in the membership qualifications added to its prominence as a competent, professional, and beneficent organization. But, of course, the major focus of the chapter was maintaining the customs and traditions which were established during the 1940s.

(It should be noted that the records for the period from 1951 through 1956 were very limited, and the minutes of the chapter's meetings, in particular, could not be found. This was due, most likely, to the practice, started in the 1970s, to dispose of records more than five years old. Anecdotes also attest to some records being lost in a fire.)

The decade got off to a good start. On January 8, 27 new members were initiated and honored with the traditional banquet held the following

Sunday at the College Inn of the Edwin Long Hotel. Chicken and jokes were the fare and, surprisingly, according to the campus newspaper, the Miner, even the jokes were good. During the meeting the latest issue of the Beta Delta Data was distributed.[9]

January 1950 Initiates[10]

Richard F. Justus	Robert L. Land	Willian M. Boushka	Donald D. Norwood	William B. Heisler	George T. Palmer	Leonard LaPatina
Joseph P. Fris	Charles A. Rice	Edward J. Zeitz	Eugene F. Winter	Robert Olson)Doc Olson)	William B. Vose	Hal G. Lankford
Richard L. Rowton	Eugene F. Sanders	Robert H. Schwaig	Dewey E. Kibler	Theodore H. Gosen	Wayne E. Kottwitz	Richard C. Phelps
George C. Young	Frank Guzzy	Donald O. Schafer	George E. Commerford	Arlen Glen Sliger	Paul Manocchio	

The first week of January also witnessed the election of new officers. These included: W. W. "Red" Campbell, MA; Bob Ferry, VMA; Bill Burch, Reporter; Norm Vaniman, Recorder; Dick Miller, Treasurer; Art McDermott, MC; Jack Venarde, Historian; and Dr. W. E. Clark, Alumni Secretary.[11] They were installed at the next meeting on January 17.[12]

Spring 1950 Committees

Membership	Program	Scholarship	Budget	Safety	Banquet	Outing
R. Ferry	A. McDermott	W. Campbell	W. Campbell	W. Campbell	J. Maurer	G. Dillender
G. Jamieson	E. Koziboski	J. Maurer	R. Miller	W. Kottwitz	W. Heisler	E. Zeitz
E. Sanders	P. Manocchio	D. Honerkamp	J. Venarde	E. Zeitz	W. Keller	D. Schafer
Weiss	D. Norwood			R. Dieckgrafe		J. Hilgenbrink
R. Crow	G. Dillender					
E. Schrader	J. Hilgenbrink					
	D. Kibler					

Committees for the spring were appointed on February 2. The following members—J. Venarde, W. Bach, D. Heineck, A. Vogler, A. Taylor, H. Keeser, W. Vose, R. Ladd, A. Sliger, F. Guzzy, and R. Young—were named to the Beta Delta Data staff. In addition, a committee was formed to investigate possible requirements for future membership. Instead of being appointed, its members were all volunteers: J. Rice, A. Klemme, W. Burch, R. Ladd, R. Schmitz, and J. Maurer. Delegates and alternates for the upcoming Conclave were also elected. J. Venarde was chosen as the delegate with Tachmann and Burch as the first and second alternates, respectively. In regard to Conclave, the chapter decided that the following issues should be brought before the Grand Chapter: 1) Duplicate questions on candidate records, and 2) The requirement that a member be cleared by a collegiate chapter before joining a professional chapter.

Membership issues dealt with more than restrictive entry qualifications or increasing the numbers, however. Occasionally questions arose in regard to removing members. During the March 2 meeting such a case involving the membership of Leonard LaPatina came up. A letter from Brothers A. Helwig and E. Koziboski charging that LaPatina was initiated into Alpha Chi Sigma while on probation was submitted to the chapter. In response LaPatina submitted a letter explaining that he had unknowingly entered incorrect information on the application. However, he admitted his mistake and resigned from Alpha Chi Sigma. But his letter did not settle the matter. At the business meeting on March 2 the chapter received a letter from Grand Recorder, Kuebler, who explained that LaPatina's resignation could not be accepted; the standard expulsion process would have to be exercised. Based on this position, Brother Koziboski moved that LaPatina be expelled because of the mistake on the pledge record, but with a stipulation. Should LaPatina ever meet the scholastic requirements, he could be re-installed into the fraternity through the proper authority of the Grand Recorder.[13]

Beyond the expulsion of LaPatina, the meeting of March 2 focused on responding to questions sent out by the Grand Chapter. The fraternity had been deliberating on the issue of membership standards since the requirement barring persons of Semitic descent from membership was first raised in 1946. The survey of questions submitted to the chapters was part of that larger conversation. The questions were:

> 1. Are you completely satisfied with the provisions and requirements of the present Membership Standards Resolution, Grand Chapter Proposal No. 26, as approved last year?
>
> 2. (According to the minutes, since the chapter's answer to question No. 1 was "Yes," question No. 2 did not have to be answered. Consequently, the minutes did not state what the question was.)
>
> 3. Do you favor removal of all restrictions, expressed or implied, including social acceptability as expressed in the Membership Standards Resolution and in By-Law, article 1, section 2, on membership as pertains to racial groups so as to open membership to all such groups?
>
> 4. Do you favor removal of By-Law, article 1, section 2?
>
> 5. Do you favor the change in the required vote on changes in membership standards from ¾ to a straight majority of the members?

The chapter voted "Yes" to questions 1 and 3, and "No" to questions 4 and 5.

As winter gave way to spring, the students set their sights on the St. Pat's festivities. When the ball was held in March, students were treated to Lawrence Welk and his Orchestra (Welk's musical variety show would become one of the most popular television programs from 1951 to 1982.)

Over the course of the meetings of March 30 and April 6, 16 candidates were approved for pledging. There was no mention of a Smoker in the minutes, so it's unclear how the candidates were approached or how they became acquainted with the members. Nevertheless, Formal Pledging was held on April 30.[14]

On May 4, Jack Maurer was elected Master Alchemist along with Bill Boushka, VMA; Andy Taylor, MC (not of Mayberry), Warren Keller, Recorder; and Richard Phelps, Historian for the fall semester. Dick Miller was the present Treasurer since he was elected for two semesters. Installation was held on May 10. Once again, membership requirements were the major topic of discussion. One particular requirement that was brought up repeatedly and was often subject to differing opinions was the minimum grade point average. At this meeting it was decided to set the minimum grade point average at 1.3 in the prospective candidate's chemistry or chemical engineering courses. A committee of J. Maurer, W. Boushka, J. Venarde, J. Rice and R. Phelps was appointed to investigate the most appropriate method for nomination of pledges. Finally, the chapter gave J. Venarde permission to vote as he saw fit at Conclave.[15]

On May 7, 14 new members were initiated under the leadership of Art McDermott, Master of Ceremonies. Several dignitaries, including Merle Griffin, Grand Professional Alchemist; J. C. Schwarz, Central Professional Counselor; D. F. Chamberlain, Midwest District Counselor; and Beta Delta's own Dr. Schrenk, Grand Master of Ceremonies (1948-1950), attended the banquet at the Edwin Long Hotel (Schrenk would continue to serve as Grand Collegiate Alchemist through 1954).[16]

May 1950 Initiates[17]

Warren V. DeMiller	Peter J. Lucido	Wilson H. Rushford	Robert L. Snell	Dave F. Van Fossen
Donald L. Duncan	Donald C. McCormack	Richard G. Soehlke	Richard Bauer	George P.
Paul L. Hausmann	Edgar Oliphant	Mario R. Trieste	Richard M. Bosse	

The first meeting of the fall, on September 21, tied up loose ends from the summer and made preliminary preparations for the fall semester. Dr. Webb, after auditing the books, reported that several members had graduated over the summer still owing the chapter dues. Because of this delinquency, the chapter's finances were in the red. The chapter decided to contact those who had graduated and were still in Rolla to determine if they wished to remain active. If not, the chapter would report them as inactive and not be liable for their national dues. Dick Miller had graduated over the summer, leaving the treasurer's position open. Joe Fris was elected to take his place. Jack Venarde gave a report on Conclave, and Brother Boushka reported on plans for the Jamboree which was scheduled for October 15. Invitations and programs were already in the mail for the St. Louis Professional Chapter and the collegiate chapters of the District—Delta, Alpha Epsilon, and Kappa.[18]

New committees for the fall were appointed on October 5:[19]

Fall 1950 Committees

Program	Membership	Budget	Safety	Beta Delta Data
W. Boushka (chair)	E. Zeitz (chair)	J. Fris	D. Norwood (chair)	R. Phelps (chair)
R. Bosse	R. Ladd	E. Oliphant	D. Duncan	J. Venarde
R. Land	J. Rice	G. Commerford		
D. Kibler	R. Crow			
	E. Sanders			
	D. Van Fossen			

On October 19, the chapter reviewed and updated its pledging activities. The suggested membership program stipulated that:

> 1. The selection of those eligible would be done in the same manner as it had previously been practiced, and the Smoker be held as usual.
>
> 2. The first vote would be held immediately after the Smoker.
>
> 3. The plaques would be given out immediately after the vote.
>
> 4. The prospective members would be given one month to obtain all the names on the plaque.

5. The pledges must obtain the signatures of the members at their places of residence and not at the school.

6. The pledges must distribute some tokens, such as cigars or candy, to the actives who sign their plaques.

7. During this period, the chapter should sponsor several joint activities for both the prospective members and the actives.

8. Prospective pledges would be expected to give some type of entertainment program for the actives.

These suggestions were discussed at some length. Dr. Schrenk pointed out that the pledges could not be given plaques until they had been formally pledged. This meant that all voting had to be completed before the plaque-signing process could begin.[20]

The members, along with their invited guests, other members of AIChE and the prospective pledges, watched two movies, "Aluminum" and "Magnesium," before the business meeting on November 16. During the meeting, it was decided to invite Dr. Matthews to speak on December 6. All the prospective pledges passed the final vote, and formal pledging was set for Tuesday, November 30. The initiation date for new members was set for January 7, 1951.[21]

The 1950s 143

Fifth Row: W. Hampson, J. Maurer, M. Rausch, D. Carney, D. Kingsley, W. Utnage, J. Hernan, R. Phelps, W. Burch, R. Miller, R. Dieckgrafe, G. Young, G. Commerford, T. Gosen, J. Hilgenbrink, Barker. Fourth Row: S. Brown, C. Ummel, A. Klemme, D. Norwood, H. Crocker, W. Heisler, C. Keller, J. Atwell, E. Zeitz, G. Dillender, W. Walker, E. Thielker, F. Guzzy, D. Kibler, R. Maag, MacDonald, E. Schrader. Third Row: A. Taylor, E. Winter, G. Jamieson, R. Schmitz, J. Coffman, R. Ferry, R. Niederstadt, A. McDermott, E. Koziboski, J. Venarde, J. Fris, W. Campbell, N. Vaniman, R. Ladd, C. Reed, W. Short. Second Row: R. Crow, I. Gray, R. Coffee, C. Hoppe, P. Haas, A. Sliger, E. Sanders, R. Schwaig, R. Rowton, F. Wyatt, D. Honerkamp, E. Breidert. First Row: D. Peterson, R. Olson, H. Lankford, W. Bach, A. Helwig, H. Iten, C. Rice, G. Rees, R. Lucker.

Beta Delta Chapter 1950—Rollamo 1950[22]

1951

On January 7, 15 new initiates were welcomed into Beta Delta. The National Office reported that only 14 were initiated on that date, but according to the January 12, 1951, issue of the Miner, a graduate student, Ormond K. Lay, was also initiated. Besides Lay, the other initiates were: Glen E. Benedict, John W. Iselin, Robert O. Wickey, David L. Conklin, John P. Greiten, Howard W. Westerman, John F. McIntyre, Herbert L. Bowkley, George J. Freebersyser, Thomas H. Lentz, Charles E. Steinmetz, Kenneth L. Birk, Milton M. Silver, and Mark F. Winton. The ceremony was presided over by Master of Ceremonies, Andy Taylor and John Maurer, Master Alchemist.[23]

Officers elected for the spring semester were: William Burch, Master Alchemist; Richard Phelps, Vice-Master Alchemist; Richard Soehlke, Reporter; Charles Rice, Recorder; Eugene Sanders, Treasurer; Andrew Taylor, Master of Ceremonies; and Richard Ladd, Historian.[24]

Another initiation was held in the spring. On April 29, eleven new members officially joined the fraternity: Richard W. Arter, Edward L. Creamer, William G. Petty, Juergen J. Bloess, Merville E. Doyle, Philip J. Quatrochi, Melvin E. King, James E. Akers, Charles A. Weeks, and Ralph W. Carl. The Beta Delta membership records also listed Glenn Hook.

In the fall, Beta Delta hosted the annual Alpha Chi Sigma Midwest Jamboree at Dr. Schrenk's home. Attendance for the event totaled 72 and included GPA Merle Griffin from New York. The highlight of the weekend was a football game between the collegiates and professionals. The winners' trophy, known as the Wiedemann Cup, named for the former GMA, went to the collegiates.[25]

The year ended with the initiation of an additional 13 members on December 16: C. R. Custer, George S. Morefield, Jean E. Hacker, Jacob J. Kadnar, James A. Cooley, John P. Friedrich, Richard O. Holland, James A. Bottorff, Charles A. Hewett, Edward L. Roster, Jerry S. Klobe, James E. Walizer, and Elwood L. Knobel.

First Row: D. Kibler, G. Freebersyer, D. Duncan, J. Greiten, A. Taylor, W. Burch, J. Maurer, W. Short, E. Schrader, M. Trieste, R. Phelps, C. Rice. Second Row: H. Westerman, R. Crow, D. Norwood, E. Sanders, G. Dillender, H. Crocker, E. Zeitz, R. Wickey, R. Ladd, R. Dieckgrafe, F. Guzzy, J. Iselin. Third Row: W. Keller, W. Boushka, R. Bauer, D. Schafer, G. Commerford, W. Vose, K. Birk, J. Fris, D. Van Fossen, J. Venarde, R.Soehlke.

Beta Delta Chapter 1951—Rollamo 1951

1952

1952 saw continued progress in the Chemistry and Chemical Engineering departments on the MSM campus, and the success of the Beta Delta chapter was significantly bound to that growth. The two departments were the primary source of new members for Beta Delta, and their classes were instrumental in the education of the chapter's members.

In February of 1952, Dr. Schrenk provided a recap of the current state of the Chemical Engineering Department in an article he wrote for the Missouri Miner:

> *The department has been advised of its accreditation on the basis of an inspection in the fall of 1950. It is now recognized by the American Institute of Chemical Engineers, the American Chemical Society, and the Engineers' Council for Professional Development.*
>
> *Through the efforts of President F. A. Middlebush, Dean Curtis L. Wilson, and the Board of Curators, a bill for an appropriation of $240,000 is now in the hands of the State Legislature for the completion and equipping of the Chemical Engineering building. There is a good probability that the bill will be passed. This will enable the department to complete the expansion program started in 1941. When this is done, the department of Chemical Engineering will be well equipped with respect to building, equipment and staff, and better able to perform its duties of training chemical engineers.*
>
> *The growth of this department during the last ten years has been healthy and above normal. The students graduating in Chemical Engineering during the past several years have been above average in number because of the return of many veterans to school after service in the armed forces. This excess has been absorbed by industry, and the need for trained personnel in chemistry and chemical engineering is an ever expanding one and far greater than the number of graduates. This excessive demand for graduates in chemistry and chemical engineering will continue for many years to come.*

The Missouri School of Mines and Metallurgy has emphasized applied chemistry in all engineering curricula since its founding in 1871. Graduates majoring in this curriculum have made outstanding records in the various fields of industry. The Chemical Engineering curriculum was adopted in 1917 and since that date 593 students have graduated with a BS degree and 63 have received the MS degree.

The large majority of these men hold positions for which they received training at the Missouri School of Mines and Metallurgy. They are to be found in all types of chemical industry in the United States and foreign countries as well as in teaching positions on the faculties of colleges and universities. Graduates are filling positions of responsibility in all fields of chemical engineering and many have achieved eminent success. The Chemical Engineering curriculum closely follows recommendations of the American Institute of Chemical Engineers. It presents a thorough training in mathematics, physics, chemistry and economics as well as the principles of chemical engineering.

The study of the principles of chemical engineering begins in the sophomore year and extends through the senior year. Unit operations, thermodynamics and chemical engineering design are especially emphasized.

Graduate courses are maintained in the principal branches of chemistry and chemical engineering which makes available a large selection of well-rounded courses for the MS degree in Chemical Engineering or chemistry major.

The department is housed in a relatively new building, half of which was completed in 1942. The four story building containing an area of 47,000 sq. ft. was completed as far as funds would permit in 1949. It is a modern fire proof structure of skeleton concrete, buff brick exterior, concrete interior with walls and floors of concrete. It contains offices, class rooms, lecture rooms and laboratories for chemistry and chemical engineering. The section constructed in 1949 has not been fully completed and equipped.

> The chemical engineering laboratory is well equipped to give training in the various unit operations. Special apparatus is available for graduate study in this field.
>
> The department maintains a comprehensive research program. A contract with the Atomic Energy Commission for the determination of the rate of rapid reactions is in progress. In addition to this, each senior member of the staff is performing and directing research projects of graduate students. This research has resulted in the publication of many articles in the current scientific literature.

Dr. Schrenk continues, in this article, to review the Chemistry and Chemical Engineering staff. Besides himself, the faculty member of particular note was Dr. William H. Webb. Dr. Webb, while a student at MSM, was initiated into Alpha Chi Sigma by the Beta Delta Chapter in 1938. Originally Dr. Webb came to MSM with a BS degree (1936) from Mississippi State College and completed the requirements for a MS degree at MSM in 1939. He was a member of the staff from 1939 until his retirement, except for the interval from July, 1942, to January, 1946, when he was in the US Army, and the period from June, 1948, to September, 1949, when he was on a leave of absence for completing the requirements of his PhD degree at the University of Wisconsin (1949). Dr. Webb specialized in inorganic and analytical chemistry and taught undergraduate work in these fields. He also taught graduate course work in instrumental analysis. His published works included an article on germanium.

Dr. Schrenk, Professor and Chairman of the Chemical Engineering department, was on staff continuously at MSM since coming to the institution in September of 1923. He specialized in analytical chemistry, water and fuel technology, and inorganic chemistry. He directed the research work of candidates for the MS degree, and two of his students had secured PhD degrees by 1952.[26]

Unfortunately, the funds to complete the Chemistry and Chemical Engineering building project, anticipated by Dr. Schrenk so hopefully in his February recap, did not come through in March. The State Senate unexpectedly made cuts to the budget and, at least for the immediate future, eliminated any plans the Rolla School might have had for any further expansion of its facilities. It is interesting this cut came at a time when chemists and chemical engineers were being demanded by both industry and government. According to the Miner, even Fortune Magazine documented the great shortage of and demand for engineers.[27]

Beta Delta, true to its objectives, did all it could to carry out its activities, providing support to future chemists and chemical engineers who were so vitally important in the country's post-war economy. In the spring, on May 4, the chapter welcomed nine new members: William E. Blair, James B. Miller, Robert J. Van Duyne, Alfred F. Moeller, Bernard O. Zamudio, Donald E. Puyear, Robert B. Puyear, Robert H. Towell, and Claude W. Ashburn. Beta Delta membership records also included Jerry Lynch. Officers elected for the fall included: Dewey E. Kibler, Master Alchemist; Thomas Lentz, Vice-Master Alchemist; Eugene Sanders, Treasurer; and George Freebersyer, Historian. Dr. Webb was still the chapter's advisor.

The school year came to a close in May, and campus life quieted. The summer promised excitement for Alpha Chi Sigma, however, as it approached a momentous milestone—its 50th anniversary. The event was celebrated at the 21st Biennial Conclave, held the week of June 20, at the University of Wisconsin in Madison. The Conclave also marked a special occasion for Beta Delta. Dr. Schrenk was elected Grand Collegiate Alchemist (GCA). Frank Zvanut and Edward Creamer represented Beta Delta at the event.[28]

In the fall, the annual Midwest District meeting was held at the home of Dr. Schrenk. Members from Delta, Alpha Epsilon, and Beta Delta collegiate chapters along with the professional chapter from St. Louis attended. Guests, in addition to Professor Schrenk, Grand Collegiate Alchemist, included: H. Schwarz, Grand Professional Alchemist, Merle L. Griffin, Grand Master Alchemist, and Dr. Chamberlain, District Counselor. Among the faculty present were Norman Smith, O. K. Lay, F. H. Conrad, W. H. Webb and R. R. Cornwall. When the business was concluded, the annual softball game between the professional and collegiate members was played. The collegiate members, deeply disappointed by their loss to the professionals (who took home the Wiedemann Cup) found solace, however, in beer libations afterward.[29]

And with a stiff upper lip, Beta Delta marched on into the fall semester of 1952. New pledges were selected at a Smoker in September. These included: LeRoy Gockenbach, Joseph Kolasch, Harvey Schulte, James Tietjens of St. Louis, Allan Holiday, of Carthage, IL, Lloyd Mason, of Hannibal, MO, Lawrence Kickham of East St. Louis, IL, and William Hays of Decatur, IL. Of these only Holiday, Kolasch, and Schulte were initiated on December 14. Gockenbach was not initiated until May of 1953. (There is no record of Lloyd Mason being initiated though he is shown in the picture below taken for the Rollamo Yearbook.)[30]

First Row: R. Wickey, D. Duncan, K. Birk, C. Weeks, R. Arter, G. Freebersyer, E. Creamer. Second Row: W. DeMier, G. Hook, J. Kadnar, J. Bloess, R. Rowton, P. Hausmann, J. McIntyre, L. Mason. Third Row: J. Bottorff, J. Hacker, P. Egan, R. Soehlke, H. Westerman, T. Lentz, J. Klobe, R. Custer, Sanders. Fourth Row: C. Hewett, G. Palmer, D. Van Fossen,

Beta Delta Chapter 1952—Rollamo 1952

1953

During the Fourth Annual Honors Convocation held on April 30 in the Parker Hall Auditorium, Robert Custer, Master Alchemist, introduced Jerry Lynch and Robert Puyear and announced that they would be co-recipients of the Alpha Chi Sigma Award. In addition to the high honor, they received a one year membership in the American Chemical Society and a copy of Lange's Handbook of Chemistry, respectively. Both were lauded for their proficiency in their studies, their engineering promise, and their participation in numerous campus activities.[31]

Two weeks later, on May 10, nine new members were initiated: Charles S. Barkley, Harvey L. Lewis, LeRoy G. Gockenbach, Lawrence T. Kickham, Samuel U. Barco, William R. Chastain, Philip P. Corneli, and James W. Stump. According to the Beta Delta membership list, Robert J. Kornfeld was also initiated at the ceremony.

Except for the usual business meetings, the early fall of 1953 appeared to be relatively quiet for Beta Delta. The annual Jamboree and a pledging ceremony rounded out the year for the chapter. The Jamboree was held at the Schrenks' home on Sunday, October 18. Guests included eight members of the Alpha Epsilon Chapter at Washington University, three members of Delta Chapter at Mizzou, 13 members from the St. Louis Professional Chapter, and one member from Kappa Chapter in Lawrence, KS. A conference was held in the morning for the collegiate members (The purpose was not stated). Following a picnic dinner, members of the collegiate chapters defeated the St. Louis Professional members 23-3 in the annual softball contest and regained the Wiedemann trophy.[32]

The semester ended with a pledging ceremony on December 9 for eight pledges: Charles R. Altheide, Richard G. Beecher, J. Max Brawley, Frank B. Damerval, Paul R. Douglas, Larry N. Fussell, Bobby L. Jones, and Kenneth G. Riley. One of the projects required of these pledges would be the completion of the chapter room in the Chemical Engineering Building.[33]

Officers 1953[34]

Office	Spring	Fall
Master Alchemist	Robert C. Custer	James E. Akers
Vice-Master Alchemist	Richard W. Arter	Ralph W. Carl
Reporter	Paul J. Egan	Edward L. Creamer
Recorder	Sam Zamudio	Richard W. Arter
Treasurer	Robert J. Van Duyne	
Master of Ceremonies		Robert Custer
Historian	Donald Puyear	
Alumni Secretary	Dr. G.E. Brandt	
Chapter Advisor	Dr. William Webb	Dr. William Webb

First Row: Custer, Carl, Akers, Creamer. Second Row: Egan, Towell, D. Puyear, Moeller, Schulte. Third Row: R. Arter, R. Holland, A. Holiday, L. Gockenbach, R. Van Duyne, J. Kolasch, B. Zamudio.

Beta Delta Chapter 1953—Rollamo 1953

1954

All of those who pledged the previous December plus one more—Peter Yiannos—were initiated on January 17. Records show an initiation date of Jan 1, 1954, for Frank Damerval and John J. Howard who were not listed as pledges at the December 9 ceremony. The initiation ceremony and the business meeting were conducted under the auspices of the officers for the spring semester—Robert H. Towell, Master Alchemist; Alfred Moeller, Vice-Master Alchemist; Samuel Barco, Reporter; William Chastain, Recorder; and Philip Corneli, Treasurer.[35]

At the Fifth Annual Honors Convocation on April 29, Robert Towell, Master Alchemist, presented the Alpha Chi Sigma Junior Award—a copy of Lange's Handbook of Chemistry—to LeRoy Gockenbach. Then, on behalf of Merck and Company and the Chemistry Department, he awarded copies of the Merck Index to Charles Barkley and Robert Riegel.[36] (The Merck Index is an encyclopedia of chemicals, drugs and biologicals with monographs on specific compounds or groups of related compounds. It was first published in 1889 by the German company Emanuel Merck. Today it is published online by the Royal Society of Chemistry.)[37]

A second initiation ceremony took place on May 9. Six new members were welcomed into the fraternity: Charles J. McCoy, John W. Folk, Everett J. Collier, Dale J. Schillinger, James A. Unnerstall, John J. Howard, and David W. Bunch.

On June 24, GMA Merle Griffin finally put the issue of the restrictive membership clauses, initially raised in the 1940s, to bed. He issued Constitutional Interpretation #47, which stated: "The phrase 'socially acceptable to the Grand Chapter' as used in By-Laws, Article 1, Section 2, is hereby interpreted to be applicable without prejudice to all racial categories of persons." Nevertheless, there was still a concern that Blacks were not granted equal access to facilities at a few of the universities where there were Alpha Chi Sigma chapters.

In the early 50s, the Membership Standards Committee had submitted Grand Chapter Proposal #26, Instructions on Selection and Election of Candidates for Membership. Its Paragraph C still contained restrictions on the admission of Blacks. Motion #15 at the 22nd Biennial Conclave deleted Paragraph C, eliminating all the restrictive clauses. However, still concerned about the possibility of Black brothers transferring to a chapter where university rules still segregated students by race, the committee added Motion 14 (which would go into effect only if Motion 15 passed) which required another declaration to the pledge card that stated, "I understand that when I become a member of Alpha Chi Sigma, the fraternity shall bestow upon me all of its rights and privileges. If these rights and privileges are restricted in any locality due to State, Municipal, or Institutional laws and regulations, or local customs, for any reason or of any nature *beyond the control of the fraternity*, I hereby agree to respect such restrictions and be bound by them". *The purpose of this statement was to ensure that Alpha Chi Sigma chapters complied with the requirements the universities and colleges had for fraternities to be recognized organizations.* Thus, relative to the policies and practices of some of the universities and colleges, and prior to the Civil Rights Act of 1957, Alpha Chi Sigma was in the forefront of eliminating racial and ethnic discrimination.[38]

During the same Conclave, two members of Beta Delta were elected to positions of distinction on the fraternity's Supreme Council. Dr. Schrenk succeeded Griffin, who was working for the Shell Oil Company in New York, as GMA, and Dr. Frank Zvanut was elected Grand Master of Ceremonies (GMC).[39]

The celebratory news surrounding the elections of Schrenk and F. Zvanut in the summer came to an end in the fall. In October Paul Joseph Egan died of leukemia. Egan had been active in Beta Delta as its Reporter in the spring of 1953. He graduated in June of 1954 with a BS in Chemical Engineering and was working for US Steel at the time of his death. Besides his membership in Alpha Chi Sigma, he was a member of the American Institute of Chemical Engineers, Pi Kappa Alpha, and Gamma Delta, the association of Lutheran students.[40]

In December, members of Beta Delta attended the Founders Day celebration in St. Louis. Hosted by the St. Louis Professional chapter, the celebration was held at Belvedere Joe's Restaurant in St. Louis on the evening of December 4. Grand Master Alchemist Schrenk addressed the gathering. At the same meeting, Beta Delta was honored to receive three new initiates—Charles A. Wentz, Maurice LeGrand, and Dale G. Smith—who were privileged to take the final step of the initiation process.[41]

First Row: P. Egan, W. Chastain, S. Barco, R. Towell, P. Corneli, A. Moeller; Second Row: R. Beecher, D. Puyear, R. Puyear, B. Zamudio, A. Holiday, R. Kornfeld; Third Row: L. Gockenbach, K. Riley, J. Stump, M. Brawley, R. Van Duyne, L. Kickham, P. Douglas. Fourth Row: R. Miller, R. Jones, F. Damerval, L. Fussell, H. Schulte, L. Yiannos

Beta Delta Chapter 1954—Rollamo 1954

1955

The second half of the 1950s saw a significant increase in the awards and distinctions bestowed on Beta Delta members. On January 25, 1955, Dr. Schrenk had the opportunity to speak on one of his favorite topics. He addressed the Kansas City Paint, Varnish and Lacquer Association and the Kansas City Production Club at their annual meeting held at the Hotel Phillips in Kansas City. He elaborated on the progress of the Paint Technology Course at MSM, which both organizations supported. After Schrenk's speech, David E. Eichelberger, President of the Kansas City Association, commented on the importance of this project. He explained that since there were so few schools offering such technology, Dr. Schrenk's efforts were of interest to paint manufacturers throughout the Midwest and to suppliers of raw materials used in manufacturing paint. This kind of recognition would become commonplace for Schrenk in the next few years.[42]

But Dr. Schrenk was not the only one making news. In April, an article in the school newspaper, the Miner, cited two Beta Delta brothers for their outstanding contributions to campus life. Dick Douglas, originally from Jefferson City, was the recently elected Editor-in-Chief of the newspaper. He was also a member of Theta Kappa Phi, a social fraternity of Catholic men, and AIChE. In addition, he served as Vice-President of Theta Kappa Phi and was on the Rollamo Board.

The other Beta Delta brother who was recognized in the Miner article for his outstanding participation in campus activities was Jerry McCoy. A high school senior from Sikeston, MO, McCoy, too, was on the Miner staff. He was also an active member of Tau Kappa Epsilon social fraternity, Blue Key, Tau Beta Pi, and the "M" club—an athletic organization comprised of those who lettered in one of the varsity sports.

More distinction for Beta Delta brothers was in the offing. At the Annual Honors Convocation on April 28, 1955, held in the Parker Hall Auditorium, Charles R. Altheide, Vice-Master Alchemist, presented the Alpha Chi Sigma Senior award to J. Warren Stump and the Junior Award to Richard G. Beecher. Altheide also introduced the newest members to the chapter: David W. Bunch, Everett J. Collier, John J. Collier, Maurice LeGrand, Charles J. McCoy, Dale J. Schillinger, Dale G. Smith, James A. Unnerstall, and Charles A. Wentz. Later, on December 15 at the Christmas Convocation, David Bunch was the recipient of the American Institute of Chemical Engineers' Junior Scholarship Award, and Leslie Daniels was also awarded an AIChE scholarship, both presented by Prof. F.H. Conrad, a Beta Delta brother.[43]

1955 saw another significant increase in the chapter's membership. On April 29, fourteen new students were initiated: Paul L. Passley, Clarence J. Vetter, John F. Rasche, Albert G. Sturdevant, Donald C. Knobeloch, Robert L. Wilkins, David E. Troutner, Carl E. Burkhead, John H. Rother, Dale W. Harris, Robert W. Sucher, Jimmy C. Johnson, Jerry D. Vie, and Joseph F. Louvar.[44]

Then, at the end of the following semester, on December 11, 18 additional members were received: Paul W. Leming, Royce M. Scott, Wilbert Falke, Samuel A. Bradford, James E. Fick, William L. Kennedy, John C. Gavan, Clifford J. Rapp, John R. Knapp, Robert M. Smith, Leo N. Yiannos,

Delbert C. Grantham, Panayotis P. Demopoulos, Marshall L. Severson, and Richard W. Niccolls. According to the Beta Delta membership records, Edwin L. Warneck, Leslie C. Daniels, and James F. Struesse were also initiated. According to the National Office records, five new members—Warneck, Jerry J. Carr, Struesse, Leslie Daniels, and Robert F. Bridger—were received on January 1. However, the Beta Delta records indicated that Carr and Bridger were not initiated until May 6, 1956.

Officers 1955[45]

Office	Spring	Fall
Master Alchemist	Roy Chastain	Richard G. Beecher
Vice-Master Alchemist	Lawrence Kickham	Larry N. Fussell
Reporter		Robert L. Jones
Recorder		Charles R. Altheide
Treasurer	Philip Corneli	Kenneth G. Riley
Master of Ceremonies	Harvey Lewis	Frank B. Damerval
Historian		Dale J. Schillinger/Maurice LeGrand
Alumni Secretary		
Chapter Advisor	Dr. William Webb	Dr. William Webb

The 1950s

First Row: J. Stump, L. Kickham, R. Beecher, W. Chastain, H. Lewis, R. Altheide, K. Riley. Second Row: H. Schulte, L. Gockenbach, J. Unnerstall, J. Kolasch, L. Fussell, J. Cooley, M. LeGrand. Third Row: J. Howard, D. Schillinger, R. Jones, C. McCoy, P. Yiannos, D. Bunch, C. Wentz.

P. Corneli; Faculty Advisor, Dr. William Webb

Beta Delta Chapter 1955—Rollamo 1955

1956

1956 ushered in a significant milestone at MSM, a consequence of a development begun at the University of Missouri in 1953. Journalism professor Edward C. Lambert established a full-time commercial TV station to provide first-hand experience for journalism students there. He aired his first successful broadcast on December 21, 1953. The station produced an analog signal on VHF and carried programs from all four major networks, though it was primarily an NBC affiliate.[46]

Early in 1956, the MSM Chemical Engineering Department produced its first TV program for the station. The only evidence of this achievement, however, was an article in the Miner on the same day as the broadcast, March 2, 1956. The program was broadcast in the early evening over station KOMU-TV in Columbia, MO. Three members of the MSM faculty—Dr. Frank Conrad, Dr. Glenn Brand, and Dr. Schrenk—participated in the discussion that was aired that night. The subject of the show was "Chemical Engineering: Behind the Paint Industry." In fact, the actual process of making paint was demonstrated in living black and white.[47]

The year was also noteworthy for Beta Delta because one of its outstanding members achieved the prestigious distinction of winning the Atlas Power Scholarship. The award, according to the May 18 issue of the Miner, was presented to Robert Bridger on the bases of his academic record, his personal references, and his visit and interview at the Atlas Power headquarters in Wilmington, Delaware. The Scholarship carried a stipend of $1000 and covered most of Bridger's expenses for the 1956-57 school year. Bridger, a transfer student from the Junior College in Joplin, MO, where he earned a grade point of 3.0 out of a possible 3.0, won the freshman mathematics award, and served as president of the sophomore class, was one of only 21 students selected from the 112 applicants from across the state to win the award. In addition to the scholarship, Bridger was also afforded the opportunity to gain practical employment experience at one of Atlas' explosives, chemical, or activated carbon plants or at one of its research laboratories.[48]

May, 1956, also saw Beta Delta maintain its very large membership. Fourteen new students—Gerald W. Schaeffer, Arthur D. Kiehne, Dudley Thompson, Joseph R. Aid, Richard L. Bruce, Thomas J. Meyer, James W. Johnson, Ron Jurenka, Carlton C. Summers, Donald R. Parille, Ronald E. Harris, Gerald L. Stevenson, Frank J. Berveiler, and Ronald F. Vetter—were initiated on May 6. The chapter's membership records also included J. James Carr and Robert Bridger, so even with the loss of 14 seniors and 3 graduate students, the chapter still had 46 active members. Toward the end of the spring semester, C. J. Vetter was elected Master Alchemist for the fall, and Jim Fick was chosen, along with Frank Zvanut, to represent Beta Delta at the 23rd Biennial Conclave held at State College, Pennsylvania. Before the semester ended in May (the chapter's records do not give a date), the traditional softball game was played. Despite the umpiring, Beta Delta, with help from Delta Chapter, defeated the St. Louis Professional Chapter and retained the Wiedemann Softball Cup.[49]

Dr. Schrenk's efforts to promote paint technology continued in 1956. In May the Chemical Engineering Department received a new piece of equipment for use in the course on Technology of Protective Coatings. The machine—the Kady Mill—was designed to break up agglomerates of pigment crystals, which attract each other during the production process and form particles that are too large to be properly dispersed. The Kinetic Dispersion Corporation of Buffalo, N.Y., through Mr. C. E. Kew, who was an MSM graduate in Electrical Engineering, had contacted Dr. Schrenk earlier with their intent to donate the equipment to MSM. Mr. Wheeler, who was a Technical Sales representative for the Corporation, presented the "mill" to the department and demonstrated its operation to the Chemical Engineering students.[50]

The beginning of the fall semester saw a significant change in the faculty of the Chemical Engineering department—a change that must have seemed unexpected at the time. Dr. Dudley L. Thompson, formerly with the faculty of Virginia Polytechnic Institute, replaced Dr. Schrenk as chair of the department. The specific reason for Schrenk's stepping down is not mentioned in Beta Delta's records. Perhaps he simply wished to reduce his academic responsibilities, but he retained his teaching and advising obligations until he retired officially in 1961.[51]

In September, the Miner announced that J. Johnson, a chemical engineering major, was named the winner of the 1956-1957 Archer-Daniels-Midland Company scholarship. Johnson, one of 14 recipients selected from 12 colleges and universities, spent September 6-7 as a guest of ADM in Minneapolis, exploring how campus laboratory work applied to industrial research and production. Thomas L. Daniels, president of ADM, one of the world's largest processors of agricultural products and sperm whale oils, explained the purpose of the scholarship to a Miner reporter: "It's typical of what large companies are doing to cope with the serious shortage of scientists and engineers in public service and industry." Johnson, who attended high school in Clayton, OK, graduated in 1947, and received a Bachelor of Science degree in chemistry and mathematics from Southeastern State College, Durant, OK, was a worthy recipient of the scholarship. He was listed in Who's Who in American Universities and Colleges in 1953 and had served two years in the U.S. Army. Initiated into Beta Delta in the fall of 1956, he served as Master Alchemist the following spring.[52]

September, 1956, also marked the occasion of a very large donation to the Chemical Engineering and Metallurgical departments. A grant of $3900 from the Atomic Energy Commission, for the study of the dissolution and corrosion of nuclear metals in acids, was a boon for Professor O. K. Lay of the Chemical Engineering department (and a member of Beta Delta) and A. Nieman, a Metallurgical graduate student, who were conducting research in this field.[53]

Lay and Schrenk—Rollamo 1957

Two other important awards were presented to Beta Delta members in 1956. John C. Gavan, a senior in Chemical Engineering who had been initiated on December 11, 1955, won recognition as the first student in the St. Louis area to be eligible for a college education under the Wars Orphan Education Program. And, on December 12 at the Christmas Convocation, held at the Parker Hall Auditorium, Dr. Frank H. Conrad, representing the American Institute of Chemical Engineers—and a member of Beta Delta himself—presented the Junior Scholarship Award to Leslie Daniels. The award consisted of a certificate, a student membership pin, a one-year student membership in AIChE, and a two-year subscription to Chemical Engineering Progress, a magazine of the American Institute of Chemical Engineers which covered such topics as current and future chemical engineering projects, technical issues in safety, environmental management, the handling of solids and fluids, and other technological information. (Today, the magazine is published digitally).[54]

No students were initiated in the fall (The reason for this could not be determined).

Officers 1956[55]

Office	Spring	Fall
Master Alchemist	Charles Altheide	C. J. Vetter
Vice-Master Alchemist	Kenneth Riley	D. Bunch
Reporter	C. Alvin Wentz	A. Wentz
Recorder	James Unnerstall	P. Leming
Treasurer	Dale Harris	D. Harris
Master of Ceremonies	David Bunch	C. Burkhead
Historian	Albert Sturdevant/ Dr. R. L. Hicks	J. Louvar
Alumni Secretary		
Chapter Advisor	Dr. William Webb	Dr. William H. Webb

Third Row: R. Niccolls, P. Yiannos, R. Wilkins, A. Sturdevant, W. Falke, J. Stuesse, P. Demopoulos, C. McCoy, C. Burkhead, J. Rasche, S. Bradford, J. Vie, M. Brawley. Second Row: M. LeGrand, R. Scott, D. Harris, D. Knobeloch, K. Schultz, J. Rother, D. Schillinger, P. Yiannos, D. Bunch, C. Wentz, J. Louvar, C. Vetter, C. Rapp. First Row: R. Smith, L. Fussell, R. Altheide, K. Riley, J. Fick, R. Beecher, J. Unnerstall, B. Jones, P. Passley, J. Howard, J. Johnson, M. Severson.

Beta Delta Chapter 1956—Rollamo 1956

1957

Before the end of 1956, several students at MSM expressed interest in pursuing work towards a Doctor's degree in Chemical Engineering. By early September, 1956, Dr. Dudley Thompson, Chair of the Chemical Engineering Department, had petitioned the Graduate School at the University of Missouri for permission for his department to grant the degree of Doctor of Philosophy. A committee, consisting of Dr. Henry E. Bent, Dean of the Graduate School; Dr. A. E. Stern, Chair of the Department of Chemistry; and Dr. J. C. Hogan, Chair of the Department of Electrical Engineering—all at the University of Missouri—along with Dr. D. S. Eppelsheimer and Dr. Thompson at MSM, was appointed to consider Thompson's request. After reviewing the facilities and the qualifications of the staff of the Chemical Engineering Department, the Committee granted its approval—and, starting in 1957, students at MSM were offered the opportunity to pursue a doctorate degree in Chemical Engineering.[56]

After no new students were initiated in the fall of 1956, early 1957 witnessed another large expansion in Beta Delta's membership. On January 6 (National Office records indicate January 13), 14 new members were received into the fraternity: Eldon R. Dille, George A. Chappell, D. R. Edwards, Glenn W. Hoffman, Roger L. Guyot, Mack O. Roberts, Neal L. Lawson, Allen D. Pope, Walter D. Tims, Duane M. Larsen, James A. Chittenden, Donald L. Gillenwater, Harry E. Schaedler, and Richard K. Oberlander. Edwards--now an official member—was recognized once again as the recipient of the Sophomore Scholarship Award and presented with a copy of the Chemical Engineer's Handbook by Charles Wentz, president of the student chapter of AIChE.[57]

The schedule for the spring semester was not set until the business meeting of March 20 which was called to order by Master Alchemist J. Johnson. Plans for the April 3 Smoker were finalized and Brothers J. Louvar and R. Oberlander were appointed to arrange the program for the event. MA Johnson announced the tentative schedule leading up to the Initiation: April 3—Smoker; April 4—Final Vote on Pledges; April 10—Members to contact assigned number of pledges; April 10—Formal Pledging (all members and pledges were required to wear suit and tie); and April

28—Initiation to be held in the ChE Building. The minutes of the meeting noted that a prospective pledge, Samuel Colburn, had been overlooked and was to be invited to the Smoker.[58]

In March, Dr. Schrenk was again on the receiving end of several honors, though they were less solemn than other recognitions he had acquired during his long career at MSM. That month the following "spoof" appeared in the Miner:[59]

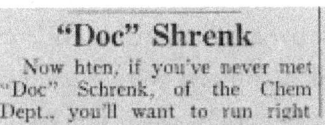

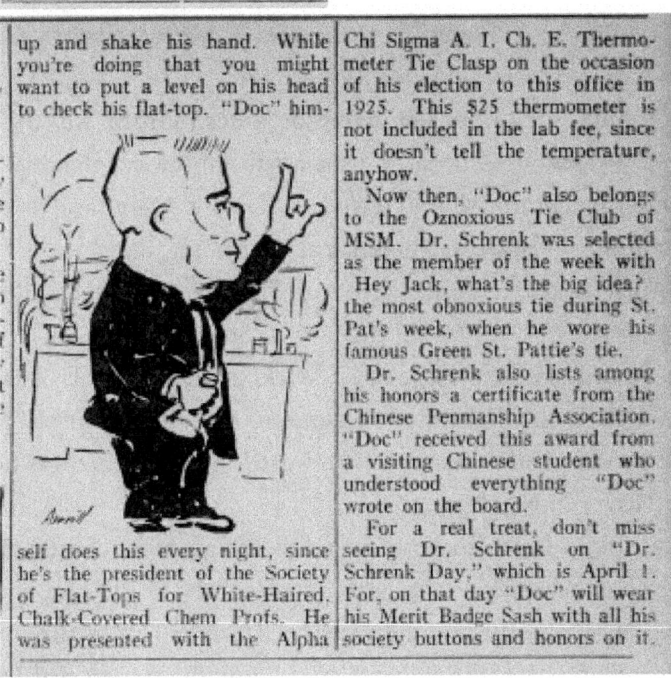

"Doc" Shrenk

Now hten, if you've never met "Doc" Schrenk, of the Chem Dept., you'll want to run right up and shake his hand. While you're doing that you might want to put a level on his head to check his flat-top. "Doc" himself does this every night, since he's the president of the Society of Flat-Tops for White-Haired, Chalk-Covered Chem Profs. He was presented with the Alpha Chi Sigma A. I. Ch. E. Thermometer Tie Clasp on the occasion of his election to this office in 1925. This $25 thermometer is not included in the lab fee, since it doesn't tell the temperature, anyhow.

Now then, "Doc" also belongs to the Oznoxious Tie Club of MSM. Dr. Schrenk was selected as the member of the week with Hey Jack, what's the big idea? the most obnoxious tie during St. Pat's week, when he wore his famous Green St. Pattie's tie.

Dr. Schrenk also lists among his honors a certificate from the Chinese Penmanship Association. "Doc" received this award from a visiting Chinese student who understood everything "Doc" wrote on the board.

For a real treat, don't miss seeing Dr. Schrenk on "Dr. Schrenk Day," which is April 1. For, on that day "Doc" will wear his Merit Badge Sash with all his society buttons and honors on it.

Schrenk obviously had a good sense of humor regarding himself, and students had no trouble playing into that trait.

The Smoker was held as planned on April 3. Dr. Schrenk gave a short talk on the purposes and benefits of membership in Alpha Chi Sigma. This was followed by an advertisement identification contest. Afterwards, refreshments were served and the members and prospective pledges were allowed an informal get-together until 9:30 pm. When the invitees had departed, a meeting of the members was held to cast the first vote to determine who would be invited to pledge.

Following the schedule proposed in March, the second and final vote was held the next day, April 4. And on April 10, the formal pledging ceremony was conducted before the regular business meeting. Those formally pledged included: Hubert Adams, Charles Blake, John Davis, Jesse Dickinson, John Donaldson, Ray Hughs, Clyde King, Patrick Knight, Dale Magre, Gary Patterson, Robert Pfisterer, James Willis, Kenneth Wood, Herman Smith, Richard Spencer, John Taliaferro, Sam Colburn, Ken Howard, and George Staples. A week later, on April 17, officers were elected: D. Harris, Master Alchemist; A. Kiehne, Vice-Master Alchemist; G. Stevenson, Master of Ceremonies; A. Pope, Recorder; and T. Meyer, Historian. Installation of officers was scheduled for May 15.[60]

That month, the Miner reported that James Johnson was the recipient of another award. This time he won a substantial scholarship from the Atomic Energy Commission to pursue a Master's degree and, eventually, a Doctor of Philosophy degree in Nuclear Technology.[61]

On April 28, 15 new members were initiated: Samuel Colburn, Dale M. Magre, John W. Donaldson, Richard K. Spencer, James A. Willis, John P. Davis, George G. Staples, Jesse C. Dickinson, Hubert L. Adams, Herman C. Smith, John D. Taliaferro, Raymond F. Hughes, Gary K. Patterson, Kenneth W. Wood, and Kenneth J. Howard. The banquet was held at the Houston House in Newburg.

In June, Beta Delta finally received its replacement charter. The original document, according to an anecdotal history of the chapter, was lost in a fire along with other important records. A salient feature of the new charter rested in one of the signatories. Among the signers was Frank Zvanut, GMC, who was one of the founders of Beta Delta back in 1936.

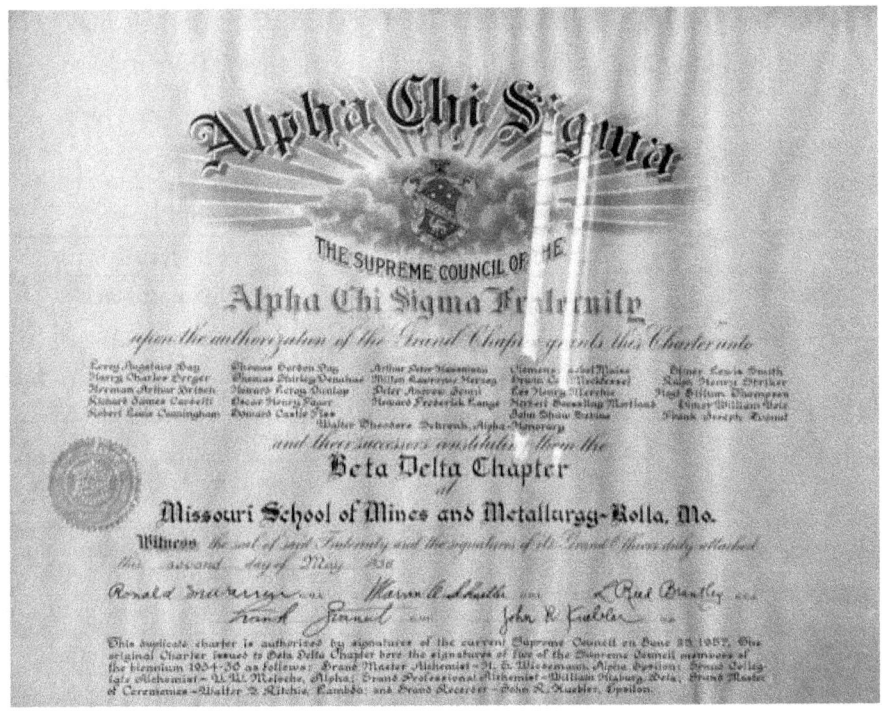

Beta Delta Charter (Duplicate)

The first event of the fall semester was an open house for freshmen and transfer students (and their wives) held on September 18. The scheduled program included a welcome by Dr. Thompson and talks on freshmen chemistry by Dr. Fisher, analytical chemistry by Dr. Webb, physical chemistry by Dr. Sutherlin (or Dr. James), chemical engineering by Dr. Conrad, and protective coatings and water technology by Dr. Schrenk. Tours of the building were also conducted with refreshments served afterward.[62]

If a September meeting was held upon return from the summer break, the minutes were either not taken or they were lost. The first meeting on record was held on October 2; it was called to order by Master Alchemist Harris. He announced that the Alpha Chi Sigma annual conclave of the Central District would be held on Sunday, October 13, at the Airport Park Pavilion in Columbia, MO, and he read a letter from the Kansas State Chapter of AIChE which invited the Beta Delta chapter of Alpha Chi Sigma to attend a get-together on October 25-26. During the meeting, Neal

Lawson and Don Parille announced that they had changed their majors to Metallurgy, but would continue paying national dues. The final order of business was the appointment of committees:[63]

Fall 1957 Committees

Advisory	Program	Auditing	Budget
Dr. Webb (chair)	P. Demopoulos (chair)	A. Kiehne	D. Harris (chair)
D. Harris	L. Yannopulus	J. Willis	J. Rasche
J. Rasche	K. Wood	J. Donaldson	G. Patterson

Safety	Chapter Publications	Scholarship	Memberhsip	Refreshments
G. Hoffman (chair)	T. Meyer (chair)	D. Harris (chair)	A. Kiehne (chair)	R. Vetter (chair)
D. Magre	M. Roberts	N. Lawson	W. Tims	J. Willis
R. Oberlander	R. Overlander	G. Schaeffer	C. Blake	J. Donaldson

Two weeks later, at the business meeting on October 16, it was announced that the fall Smoker would be held on November 6, that pledging would begin on November 20, and that the initiation would be held on December 8. In a final bit of business, Ken Schultz was appointed as an additional member to the Membership committee by MA Harris. After the meeting, William H. Gammon, of the Ashland Oil and Refining Company, presented, "Chemistry as Applied to the Petroleum Industry," which was followed by refreshments in the Unit Ops Lab.[64]

The Smoker was held, as planned, on November 6, with the prospective pledges (12 Seniors, 18 Sophomores, and 22 Juniors) welcomed by VMA Art Kiehne, who also gave a presentation on the Collegiate chapter of Alpha Chi Sigma. He was followed by Dr. Schrenk who spoke about the Professional branch of Alpha Chi Sigma. A chemical equipment identification contest followed—with prizes awarded to the winners. Afterward, the Smoker was recessed for refreshments and an informal get-together. Per custom, the meeting was reconvened after the invitees had left for the first vote on the eligible pledges. Twenty-five of those attending passed the first vote. On the second and final vote, which took place a week later, on November 14, 23 students were officially invited to pledge. The formal pledging occurred on November 21 when 16 of the 23 accepted the invitation.[65]

These sixteen young men were initiated into the fraternity on December 8: Patrick D. Culnan, Ned A. McLeane, Jerry L. Stone, James W. Poarch, Paul E. Minton, James G. Harvey, Ronald C. James, Risdon W. Hankinson, Harold W. Christian, Kenneth W. Shrum, James E. Newton, James L. Hibberd, Richard A. Lawhon, Mohammed R. Arshadi, George H. Graves, and J. G. Hofer. Once again, the initiation banquet in honor of the initiates was held at the Houston House.[66]

The last meeting of the semester was held on December 18 to elect officers for the new year. Those elected were: John Rasche, Master Alchemist; Thomas Meyer, Vice-Master Alchemist; Richard Oberlander, Reporter; John Donaldson, Recorder; John Taliaferro, Treasurer; Panayotis Demopoulos, Master of Ceremonies; Allen Pope, Historian; and Martin, Alumni Secretary (Martin's first name could not be discerned).

In addition to the election of officers, J. Rasche moved that Neal Lawson be placed on an equal status with other members who had changed their majors. The motion carried, and Lawson was allowed to continue paying national dues. A second motion was made—and passed—to have an outing in the spring to revive fraternity spirit. Based on the number of absentees over the past several meetings, it was likely that low meeting attendance led to this action.[67]

During the MSM Annual Christmas Honors Convocation held on December 19, Dale E. Harris, Master Alchemist, introduced the April and December, 1957, Beta Delta initiates—a total of 31 students. The Convocation, which opened with three selections—"A Christmas Story," "Gaudeamus Igitur," and "O Holy Night"—by the 50 member Glee Club, featured the presentation of the AIChE awards to two Beta Delta members. Dr. Conrad presented the AIChE Junior Scholarship Award—which consisted of a certificate, a two-year subscription to Chemical Engineering Progress magazine, a one-year student membership in AIChE and a student membership pin—to Doyle Ray Edwards. Ronald Vetter, president of the student chapter of AIChE and a fellow Beta Delta member, presented the

AIChE Sophomore Scholarship Award and a copy of the Chemical Engineer's Handbook to Gary Kent Patterson.[68]

Officers 1957[69]

Office	Spring	Fall
Master Alchemist	James W. Johnson	Dale Harris
Vice-Master Alchemist	Carl Burkhead	Art Kiehne
Reporter	Leslie C. Daniels	
Recorder	David W. Bunch	Allen Pope
Treasurer	John Rasche	
Master of Ceremonies	Alvin Wentz	G. Severson
Historian	Art Dan Kiehne	Thomas Meyer
Alumni Secretary	Marshall Severson	
Chapter Advisor	Dr. William Webb	Dr. William Webb

First Row: R. Oberlander, D. Parille, P. Leming, D. Bunch, R. Vetter, J. Fick, D. Harris, J. Rasche, L. Daniels, C. Wentz, R. Sucher, R. Bruce. Second Row: T. Meyer, H. Schaedler, E. Dille, M. Roberts, C. Summers, J. Vie, R. Scott, H. Smith, A. Kiehne. Third Row: K. Schultz, R. Edwards, C. Vetter, D. Larsen, N. Lawson, J. Johnson, W. Kennedy, W. Tims, R. Wilkins, J. Howard. Fourth Row: G. Stevenson, G. Schaeffer, D. Grantham, C. Burkhead, A. Pope, F. Berveiler.

Beta Delta Chapter 1957—Rollamo 1957

1958

Not missing a beat after returning to the classroom after the holidays, Beta Delta held its first meeting of the spring semester on January 15. MA Harris opened the meeting by introducing Hugh Smith of the U. S. Bureau of Mines in Bartlesville, OK. Mr. Smith offered a brief overview of the work of the Bureau in Bartlesville and in Rolla. This portion of the meeting was open to the public, and several members of the faculty, a number of students, and several engineers from the Bureau attended.

After the presentation, a closed session was held to conduct business and to install the new officers. MA D. Harris announced that the chapter had received a request for affiliation from Alpha Beta—a new chapter in Houston, TX, which the members voted to approve. This new chapter would become the Beta Omicron chapter of the fraternity. MA Harris also announced that John Rasche was the recipient of the chapter's Senior Award for the year—a one-year membership in the American Chemical Society upon graduation. Harris then installed Rasche as the new Master Alchemist, who, in turn, installed the rest of the officers[70]

During the month of February, the Safety committee, chaired by Glenn Hoffman, distributed safety posters throughout the Chemistry building, and safety booklets were prepared by Beta Delta members. Also, new standing committees were appointed on February 5 with an additional committee of four—D. Gillenwater (chair), K. Schultz, H. Christian, and J. Poarch—appointed to plan an outing sometime in the future.[71]

Spring 1958 Committees

Nominating	Membership	Advisory	Program
G. Stevenson (chair)	T. Meyer (chair)	Dr. Webb (chair)	D. Harris (chair)
R. Hughes	J. Chittenden	J. Taliaferro	J. Newton
G. Staples	G. Patterson	J. Rasche	J. Aid

Spring 1958 Committees Continued

Refreshment	Safety	Chapter Publication	Budget
A. Pope (chair)	G. Hoffman (chair)	A. Kiehne (chair)	R. Edwards (chair)
J. Hibberd	G. Graves	L. Yiannos	J. Taliaferro
J. Davis	R. Lawhon	J. Vie	J. Rasche
G. Hoffman	J. Rasche		
	Dr. Webb		

In the late 1950s, recognition for academic achievement, of course, was not only in the province of institutions of higher learning or industry. High schools all across the country were also rewarding outstanding students with financial assistance to further their pursuit of their educational goals. One such scholarship with special significance for MSM was the Thomas Wallace Kelly Scholarship Fund at Benton High School in Benton, MO. Thomas Kelly graduated from Benton High School in 1936 and enrolled at MSM where he earned a Bachelor of Science degree in Metallurgical Engineering in 1940. While at MSM, he was a member of the Blue Key Honor Society, the Athletic Association Society of American Military Engineers, the Independent Student Organization, and the American Society for Metals.

At the beginning of WWII, Kelly entered military service as a commissioned officer. On July 26, 1944, he was killed in action in France. Having no immediate living relatives, Kelly had arranged for his government insurance to be paid to his former high school to provide scholarships to students desiring to attend MSM. Two Benton High School graduates who benefitted from the Thomas Wallace Kelly Scholarship Fund were Beta Delta members, Maurice LeGrand and Arthur Dan Kiehne. LeGrand enrolled at MSM in September, 1953, and graduated on May 26, 1957, with a Bachelor of Science degree in Chemical Engineering. After graduating, he worked for the Research Division of the Carter Oil Company in Tulsa, OK. Kiehne was a senior in Chemical Engineering at the time these awards were reported by the Miner in 1958.[72]

True to one of its longest standing traditions—established back in the days of its precursor, Epsilon Pi Omicron—Beta Delta held its annual open meeting on February 19. Representatives from the Ohio Oil Company—

Mr. Shirliss, Bob Wilson and Bob Jones—addressed the members and their guests. Their presentation was entitled "Oil Refining and Production." Afterwards, at the closed session, Al Pope was installed as Historian and A. Martin as Alumni Secretary. The remainder of the meeting consisted of committee reports. A few weeks later, on March 5, final plans were made for the upcoming Smoker; nine juniors, seven sophomores, and nineteen freshmen were invited.[73]

In March, 1958, the Beta Delta brothers participated in a major milestone in the social life of MSM—the 50th Anniversary of the St. Pat's festivities. The highlight of the event was the music provided by the great Louis "Satchmo" Armstrong and his All-Star band. At the dance, the "Ambassador of Jazz" played to an overflow crowd of more than 2000 in the Rolla High School auditorium.

Velma Middleton swings "The St. Louis Blues" as Louis Armstrong, Trummy Young and Edmond Hall sound their horns.[74]

The Smoker, held on March 19, opened with introductions and Dr. Schrenk's talk on the history and significant accomplishments of Alpha Chi Sigma over the years. An advertisement game followed by refreshments provided opportunity for existing members to meet the prospective pledges. After the Smoker, a preliminary vote was taken, and 17 prospects were approved. Members also elected Tom Meyer as their delegate to the Conclave which was scheduled for June 23-27. John Donaldson and Harold Christian were selected as first and second alternates, respectively.[75]

The second vote on the pledges was taken at the meeting on April 2; all the candidates from the first vote were unanimously accepted. April 16 was set for formal pledging and May 4 for the initiation date. During the meeting, Glenn Hoffman demonstrated the use of a suction valve for pipettes. Suggestions were also made for additional safety projects, among them one requiring that a record be kept of the cause of all accidents. Before adjournment—which had all the members reciting the objectives of the fraternity—May 2 was set for the spring outing. [76]

While campuswide, students were still reveling in the performance of Louis Armstrong and his band, Beta Delta was planning a significant celebration of its own. On April 19, approximately 200 former students joined by colleagues and friends, paid tribute to Dr. Walter T. Schrenk, the man who made the local chapter of Alpha Chi Sigma possible and who had guided the fraternity from its inception. By 1958, Dr. Schrenk had served MSM continuously for 35 years—26 as head of the Chemical Engineering department. For his dedicated service to the school, the Board of Directors of the Alumni Association voted unanimously to award "Doc" Schrenk with its highest honor for a non-MSM graduate—Honorary Life Membership.[77]

Mrs. Schrenk, Dr. Schrenk, Dr. Conrad, Mrs. Elmer Ellis, Dean Curtis L. Wilson
"Doc" Schrenk Honored as Great Teacher and Leader; at MSM 35 Years
Presented With Collection of More Than 400 Letters

The event was held at the Hotel Edwin Long. Those who could not attend sent over 400 letters of tribute. The highlight of the evening was the address of H. E. Wiedemann, a professor at Washington University in St. Louis, and a life-long friend. Others who paid tribute included: President Elmer Ellis of the University of Missouri; Dean Curtis L. Wilson; Dr. Dudley Thompson, chairman of the Chemical Engineering Department; Dr. C. J. Potter, president of the Rochester Pittsburgh Coal Co., and Dr. Doisey. Dr. Frank H. Conrad, toastmaster at the dinner, presented Schrenk with a bound collection of the letters. The huge volume, covered in rich Morocco leather, was inscribed on the cover with: "35 Years at MSM – Dr. Walter T. Schrenk."[78]

On April 25, an editorial in the Miner heralded the event:

Last week Dr. Walter Schrenk was honored at a banquet held in his honor at the Edwin Long Hotel. We of the Miner staff would like to congratulate him on his 35 years of constant service to the school and the Chemical Engineering Department.

What is more important than his services to the school is the help and guidance that he gave to the many men who have come through his department. This is exemplified by the many fine Chemical Engineers who have graduated. He received many letters from former students, congratulating him and thanking him for the help and assistance which he gave them.[79]

Not long after the celebration of Dr. Schrenk's tenure with MSM, the newly initiated members of Beta Delta were introduced at the Ninth Annual Honors Convocation on May 1 in the Parker Hall Auditorium. Thomas J. Meyer, Vice-Master Alchemist at the time, presented the newest brothers who had been initiated the previous December. However, these members lost their "newbie" status almost immediately. Within a few days of the convocation, another set of initiates would become the chapter's newest members. At this event, John J. Schliermeier announced that Gary K. Patterson (Beta Delta member) was the recipient of the Tau Beta Pi Outstanding Freshman Award. In addition, the American Institute of Chemists,

Chicago Chapter, awards were presented to Beta Delta members, John F. Rasche (outstanding senior in Chemical Engineering or Chemistry) and Gerald Stevenson (outstanding junior).[80]

The spring of 1958 was a very busy time for Beta Delta. In May, a pledge/active outing at Lions Park, marking Alpha Chi Sigma's 22nd year on the MSM campus, was well attended, and it was reported that the event was enjoyable—even though it was difficult to barbecue hamburgers in the rain.

To close the weekend, an initiation ceremony for 13 pledges was conducted on May 4. Louis A. Kuhlmann, Michael S. Herzog, H. N. Grannemann, Gary B. Mason, Allen D. Early, William J. Weber, Hugh W. Haseltine, Allen L. Rouse, Joseph C. Gay, George C. Heilig, James R. Lynn, and Anthony V. Classe became the newest Beta Delta members. According to the records of the National Office, one other member, Kenneth E. Powell, was initiated on January 1. (Beta Delta records showed Powell was initiated on May 4 along with the others.) On the evening following the initiation ceremony, the banquet was held at the Houston House in Newburg. After the banquet, the officers for the fall semester were installed—Allen Pope, MA; Ray Hughes, VMA; and Risdon Hankinson, Recorder. By the spring of 1958, Beta Delta had reached a prominent position on the MSM campus—both in size and influence. According to the May 9 issue of the Miner, the fraternity had become the 4th largest collegiate chapter of Alpha Chi Sigma in the country.[81]

The final meeting of the semester, on May 4, featured four Alpha Chi Sigma brothers from the St. Louis Professional chapter who addressed the local members as a panel. Each represented a different branch of the chemical profession: Mr. Morris—Research and Development; Mr. E. Schneider—Plant Management; Mr. Ross—Private Industry; and Mr. Mann—Sales.[82]

In 1958, another Beta Delta alumnus was recognized for his achievements as a chemical engineer. On May 16, the Miner reported that Robert L. Land, who was initiated in 1951, was awarded a Sloan Fellowship for one year of advanced study at the School of Industrial Management of the Massachusetts Institute of Technology. Land had graduated from MSM in 1951 with a Bachelor of Science degree in Chemical Engineering and was currently the Superintendent of Coke Production in the Coke and Coal Chemical Division of Gary Steel Works in East Gary, Indiana. He was a member of the Blast Furnace and Coke Association, the Hobart Masonic Lodge, and the Gary Junior Chamber of Commerce. According to Professor Howard W. Johnson, director of the Sloan program in 1958, Sloan Fellowship candidates were selected by their companies for having demonstrated executive ability and promise for growth. The fellowship was made possible by grants from the Alfred P. Sloan Foundation, Inc.[83]

The following September saw the beginnings of new facilities on the MSM campus. Work began on the new Student Union Building, and plans for construction of a nuclear reactor were announced. The Atomic Energy Commission would provide the funding for the reactor and related teaching facilities.[84]

At the meeting on October 1, it was announced that the St. Louis Professional chapter would hold their picnic on Sunday, October 12, in St. Louis and that Beta Delta was invited. The primary focus of the business session, however, was on the appointment of committees:[85]

Fall 1958 Committees

Nominating	Membership	Program	Advisory
K. Wood	J. Stevenson	R. Hughes	Dr. Webb
A. Rouse	J. Poach	P. Minton	Dr. Schrenk
R. Edwards	H. Smith	A. Pope	J. Rasche

Safety	Refreshment
R. James	J. Donaldson
G. Staples	R. Lynn
K. Powell	
H. Christian	

1958 was not all about recognitions, scholarships and initiations. Social events—though not always publicized as widely—were held regularly. In fact, the old joke, "I never drink except when I'm with someone or by myself," characterized Beta Delta's philosophy about socializing around campus.

Impromptu events—usually with plenty of beer on hand—were held among the fraternity's own members or in conjunction with another organization. One such joint event—memorable enough to be mentioned in the chapter's minutes—was an outing on October 18 with the student chapter of the American Institute of Chemical Engineers at Lions Club Park.[86]

In October, Leonard E. Henson, a 1940 graduate of MSM in Chemical Engineering, a Beta Delta alumnus, and currently a production superintendent at the Aluminum Company of America (Alcoa) in East St. Louis, returned to MSM to deliver two talks—"Unit Operations in Aluminum Processes" and "What an Engineer and a Company Expect from Each Other"—to the student chapter of AIChE.[87]

At the October 22 meeting, John Donaldson reported on the Conclave held during the summer, which he attended along with Dr. Schrenk. One of the more memorable activities at the event was the initiation of the new Beta Omicron chapter. Other business at the meeting on the 22nd: a decision to hold a joint outing with AIChE on Saturday, October 25, at Lions Park, and a report on the picnic with the St. Louis Professional chapter on October 19 at which Beta Delta won the Wiedemann Cup in the softball game. At the end of the meeting, it was decided that 26 prospective candidates would be invited to the next Smoker.[88]

Also in October, Dean Wilson announced the three winners of the $400 Paint Chemistry Scholarships. One of the recipients, Thomas Meyer, was a Beta Delta member. Meyer, a member of Kappa Alpha social fraternity, the Interfraternity Council, the American Institute of Chemical Engineers, and Alpha Chi Sigma, was currently serving as Beta Delta's Vice-Master Alchemist.[89]

30 active members and rushees attended the Smoker on November 5. As usual, each of the pledges was invited to introduce himself, and Dr. Schrenk gave his customary talk on the meaning of Alpha Chi Sigma. Games were played with notebooks given as prizes. The Smoker resulted in the formal pledging of six pledges on November 19 with Pledge Week following after Thanksgiving.[90]

The initiation ceremony for these pledges took place at 3:00pm on Sunday, December 14, and the banquet was held that evening at the Houston House in Newburg. G. Patterson, J. Stone, R. Lawhon, R. Hankinson, J. Taliaferro, J. Lynn, J. Poarch, G. Heilig, J. Hofer, and G. Chappell were responsible for organizing the initiation program. Several days later, on December 17, the election of officers was held with the following results: Ray Edwards, Master Alchemist; John Donaldson, Vice-Master Alchemist; Kenneth Powell, Recorder; Gary Patterson, Reporter; Ken Wood, Treasurer; Rich Lawhon, Master of Ceremonies; John Hofer, Alumni Secretary; and George Graves, Historian.[91]

By the middle of December, Beta Delta had initiated seven additional members: Robert W. Hill (on November 11, according to the National Office records), Alvin A. Mayer, Ronald G. Whittaker, Dennis B. Redington, Edwin L. Crow, Charles A. Blake, and John F. Mullins. Dr. Frank Conrad, representing the Alpha Chi Sigma fraternity at the 10th Annual Christmas Awards Convocation, introduced these newest members of Beta Delta before the schoolwide gathering. The Convocation was held at Parker Hall on December 18.[92]

Left to Right, First Row: R. Oberlander, W. Tims, A. Pope, L. Daniels, A. Kiehne, D. Harris, J. Stevenson, T. Meyer, J. Rasche, W. Kennedy, H. Smith. Second Row: R. Spencer, J. Donaldson, K. Wood, G. Chappell, J. Chittenden, N. McLeane, G. Hoffman, S. Colburn, J. Knapp, R. Hughes. Third Row: R. Lawhon, R. Edwards, J. Davis, H. Adams, G. Patterson, J. Hibberd, J. Stone, P. Yannopulus, D. Gillenwater, G. Staples. Fourth Row: J. Howard, R. James, D. Magre, H. Smith, M. Arshadi, H. Christian, J. Harvey, R. Vetter, J. Newton, J. Poarch. In Front: J. Willis, P. Culnan, G. Graves, P. Demopoulos, E. Dille.

Beta Delta Chapter 1958—Rollamo 1958

In the midst of all the seriousness and tedious studying at the end of the semester, Beta Delta members could always find a lighter side. One of the jokes circulating at the end of 1958—one that only chemists could love—even made it into the Miner:

> *Prof. Fisher: "What can you tell me about nitrates?"*
> *Chemistry Student: "Well...er...they're a lot cheaper than day rates."*[93]

1959

The first order of business to start off the new semester—and the last year of an extremely successful decade for Beta Delta—was the installation of officers and the appointment of committees on January 7. Officers who were absent were installed at the next meeting on February 4. That meeting also saw the establishment of a committee charged with setting the dates for the chapter's traditional events from Rush Week to the initiation of new Beta Delta members. The dates followed the predictable pattern: March 18—Smoker; April 1—Pledging; April 6-10—Pledge Week; April 19—Initiation and banquet; May 6—election of officers; and May 20—Installation of new officers. The meeting ended with an interesting talk by Dr. James Langston of Hoffman-Taff in Springfield, MO entitled "Problems of the Small Manufacturer in the Pharmaceutical Industry."[94]

Spring 1959 Committees

Nominating	Advisory	Refreshment	Membership
J. Stevenson	Dr. Webb	R. Hughs	R. James
G. Graves	Dr. Schrenk	J. Poarch	C. Blake
A. Early		R. Lynn	H. Grannemann

Program	Audit	Budget	Safety	Publicity
J. Donaldson	G. Heilig	W. Weber	A. Pope	E. Crow
P. Minton	J. Hibberd	J. Taliaferro	G. Staples	J. Mullins
R. Edwards	H. Hasseltine		H. Christian	

In February, 1959, the Miner reported a story that had huge significance on the MSM campus. The school had just been named a recipient of a large grant from the Atomic Energy Commission, the Federal agency created in 1946 to manage the development, use, and control of nuclear energy for military and civilian applications. A substantial amount of the money was designated for the Radiation Lab in the Chemistry department and for other equipment in the Mechanical, Ceramic, Metallurgical and Physics departments. $30,000 of the grant was specifically awarded to the Chemical Engineering department for the development of a prototype required for the production of nuclear fuel by combining uranyl nitrate and nitric acid with tributyl phosphate. The purpose of this project was to prevent accidents by using non-hazardous materials. Those involved in the design or affiliated with the project included: Dr. Dudley Thompson, chair of the Chemical Engineering department and project advisor; Don Puyear (a Beta Delta member) and Medhi Ford, Chemical Engineers who graduated in 1958 and drew up the original design of the prototype; Professor O. K. Lay, Assistant Professor in Chemical Engineering and also a member of Beta Delta; and Bob Shouse, Jerry Hofer (another Beta Delta member) and Jim Hubbard, undergraduates who would be working on specific parts of the prototype.[95]

The skills of Beta Delta members during the 1950s extended far beyond their accomplishments in the classroom or chem labs. Many students demonstrated exceptional athletic ability as well—and not just on the baseball field playing for the Wiedemann Trophy. One student, in particular, represented this facet of the Beta Delta character. On February 12, Joe Gay, a Sophomore Chemical Engineer, who lettered in football for two years, was elected secretary of the Miner's Letterman Club. Besides his athletic exploits, Gay was a member of the Independents, the Tech Club and the Student Council.

At the regular meeting on February 18, a special committee was appointed to design an exhibit for the upcoming Engineer's Day. The group included G. Graves (chair), H. Smith, J. Chittenden, P. Minton, J. Hofer, and R. Hughes. The acquisition of a map showing the locations of former Alpha Chi Sigma graduates for display in the department was discussed.

John Donaldson was assigned the task of finding a suitable map. In addition, a possible future outing was discussed.[96]

A week later, on February 25, George E. Purdy, an alumnus of Beta Delta (initiated in 1947) was the guest speaker at the meeting. Purdy, the Manager of Technical Service and Special Products for the Tretolite Company of St. Louis, which manufactured chemicals for the prevention of corrosion, as well as emulsion-breaking additives, spoke on "Oil and Gas Well Corrosion"—a topic he knew a great deal about.[97]

A total of 45 active members and rushees attended the Smoker on March 18. Drs. Webb and Schrenk gave short talks on Alpha Chi Sigma, and Ken Wood gave an interesting speech on alchemy. A short party game followed (Winners won mechanical pencils.) to acquaint members with prospective pledges. Then, immediately afterward, in a closed session, members discussed and voted on which pledges should be invited to join. All 20 invitees passed the first vote. On Monday, March 23, the 2nd vote was held.[98]

Fifteen of the 20 invitees were formally pledged, and on April 19, all of them—Thomas McCourt, Rich Hallahan, Carl Armstrong, Rich Swanson, Charles Martinek, Ken Snavely, Clifford Larsen, William Koenig, David Bartholic, Ronald Walter, Gary Achenbach, Nich Marvich, Burton Windeknecht, Jerry Janes, and Bennett Atwarter—were inducted into the chapter. At the business meeting which followed, Brother G. Graves reviewed plans for Engineer's Day and requested volunteers to assist him. MC R. Lawhon assigned tasks for those members participating in the upcoming initiation ceremony. And Ray Hughes announced that he would look into the possibility of a joint outing with AIChE.[99]

At the following meeting on April 16, a new nominating committee, composed of Paul Minton (chair), Ed Crow, and Ken Wood, was appointed. Why a new committee was necessary when one had just been appointed at the beginning of the semester was not explained in the minutes. George Graves reported on the Science Fair Day exhibit and explained that AIChE needed help to set up their display and clean the unit operations lab.[100]

The election of officers was held on May 6 with the following results: George Graves, Master Alchemist; Neal Grannemann, Vice-Master Alchemist; Ron James, Recorder; Rich Lawhon, Master of Ceremonies; John Davis, Alumni Secretary; and Allen Early, Historian. After the elections, two brothers from the St. Louis Professional chapter spoke on "Pure Research, Small Business, and Applied Research."[101]

Following the installation of officers at the last meeting of the semester on May 20, Neal Grannemann presented the graduating seniors with pins and a pamphlet to help them get acquainted with the professional chapters available in the area.[102]

Upon returning from the summer hiatus, Beta Delta held its first meeting of the fall semester on September 30. First off, MA Graves announced that immediately following Beta Delta's meeting, the members were invited to the American Chemical Society's meeting in room G-6. Graves also explained that the District Conclave (previously the Jamboree) would be held in Rolla on October 11 and gave the dates for the traditional pledging events for the semester: Smoker—October 21; Pledging—November 4; Pledge Week—November 9-13; and Initiation—November 22. Before the group adjourned to get to the Chemical Society's meeting, standing committees for the fall were appointed.[103]

Fall 1959 Committees

Nominating	Refreshment	Membership	Program
J. Poarch (chair)	K. Snavely (chair)	D. Bartholic (chair)	N. Grannemann (chair)
E. Crow	D. Redington	R. James	H. Adams
R. Hallahan		J. Janes	
D. Bartholic			

Safety	Budget	Audit	Banquet
C. Armstrong (chair)	K. Wood (chair)	K. Wood (chair)	J. Donaldson (chair)
J. Mullins	G. Achenbach	M. Herzog	G. Patterson
	D. Redington	D. Knobeloch	J. Hibberd

The Smoker was held on October 21; 28 members and 10 rushees attended. Each rushee was invited to introduce himself, share his major, and talk about where he was from. Once again, Dr. Webb spoke about the fraternity, and Dr. Schrenk discussed the professional branch. Following these introductory matters, Roy Chastain (MSM 1955) addressed the group on the subject of Labor Relations. Then, as was customary after the rushees had left, another meeting was called for the preliminary vote. All of the prospective pledges were acceptable. (On October 28, nine of them won final approval.) Then, in keeping with the chapter's commitment to safety promotion, the members decided to obtain a film on mouth-to-mouth artificial respiration.[104]

At the November 4 meeting, the pledge project for the current pledge class was the first order of business. The new pledges would once again be expected to prepare a map indicating the home addresses of all Beta Delta alumni. The new pledge class—William Jones, Jerry Finne, Jerry Luecke, John Schwaller, Roger Schild, William Onn, Harvey Dewing, and Gary Vaughn—was then formally introduced. At the end of the meeting, a film about glass and paint production, "Bright New World," was shown.[105]

Two Beta Delta members stood out for their accomplishments in 1959. Robert K. Neuman (initiated in 1946) was named manager of information services in the American Chemical Society's Division of Public, Professional and Member Relations—a prestigious position in which he would be working to coordinate the Society's communications activities. Brother Neuman received his BS degree in Chemical Engineering from the Drexel Institute of Technology in 1943 and his MS degree in Chemical Engineering from MSM in 1947. He was a Chemical Corps lieutenant from 1943 to 1946 and a Captain in the Army Reserves. He was a research engineer for the Koppers Company, Inc. and a production supervisor for Merck & Company, Inc., both in Rahway, NJ, before he joined the staff of the American Chemical Society News Service in 1953. He was also a member of the American Chemical Society, the Chemists' Club of New York, the National Association of Science Writers, and the American Institute of Chemists.[106]

Robert Newman—Missouri Miner 1959

Jerry Stone was the second Beta Delta member who earned high praise for his achievements in 1959. Stone was picked by Blue Key, the national honor society that recognized college students for all-around excellence in scholarship, leadership, and service, for its second Man-of-the-Month. At the time of this recognition, Stone was a senior in chemical engineering and a member of both the American Institute of Chemical Engineers and Alpha Chi Sigma. He was active on the Rollamo Board—as its Business Manager—and on the Student Board of Publications. A member of Blue Key; Alpha Phi Omega, a co-educational service fraternity; and Pi Kappa Alpha, a social fraternity (Historian and Secretary), Stone pledged Alpha Chi Sigma the first semester of his sophomore year and was initiated on December 8, 1957.[107]

Jerry Stone--Rollamo-1959

Beta Delta's meeting on November 18, called to order by Master Alchemist Graves, covered a range of topics. First, Neal Grannemann suggested acquiring a case in which to display the map the pledges had prepared. Apparently, the map showing the present location of Beta Delta alumni was spectacular enough to merit a protective display case. The minutes do not record, however, whether such a case was actually purchased. Then, Treasurer Ken Wood's end-of-the-semester financial report concluded, naturally, with his list of the members who still owed dues. Finally, the important business of selecting the menu for the upcoming Initiation Banquet was debated. Gary Patterson reported that chicken or steak were the options. Unfortunately, once again, the minutes of the meeting were sketchy: there was no mention of how many members "chickened out" or how many "had a beef." After the business was completed, two short films, "The Petrified River" and "Losing to Win," were shown. Between the films, refreshments were served in the Ops Lab.[108]

On November 22, Beta Delta initiated nine new members: William D. Onn, Gerald O. Finne, Gary E. Vaughn, William R. Jones, Roger A. Schild, H. H. Dewing, John J. Schwaller, and Jerome E. Luecke. The customary banquet in honor of the initiated was held at the Houston House in Newburg. According to the Initiation and Banquet summary submitted by Recorder Ronald James, dated November 22, 1959, John Schwaller was the ninth member of the final initiation class of the decade.[109]

Beta Delta earned national distinction, once again, for its steady increase in membership at the end of the 1950s. When the decade ended, Beta Delta ranked third among Alpha Chi Sigma chapters in total number of members—67 brothers. The chapter trailed only Zeta and Beta Nu, who had tied with a membership of 68 each.[110]

First Row, Left to Right: G. Patterson, J. Donaldson, P. Minton, G. Graves, R. Edwards, K. Powell, K. Wood, J. Hofer, H. Christian. Second Row: J. Stevenson, R. Hughs, W. Weber, G. Chappell, N. Grannemann, J. Hibberd, R. Oberlander, G. Hoffman, D. Harris. Third Row: J. Taliaferro, R. Lawhon, R. James, E. Crow, J. Poarch, J. Stone, W. Tims, D. Magre, E. Dille, J. Mullins. Fourth Row: J. Davis, D. Redington, H. Haseltine, A. Rouse, A. Pope, L. Kuhlmann, A. Early, J. Gay, A. Mayer, R. Hankinson.

Beta Delta Chapter 1959—Rollamo 1959

THE 1960s

...therefore... [hear] my Words...search into, and inquire, from them; it is not for the justification of the Work of any Evil Doer, but to give to every good [person] a Reward, that I have Discovered all things which are bid, relating to this Science, and Disclosed and made Plain and Open to you the greatest of Secrets, even the Intellectual Knowledge...

—*Hermes Trismegistus, Tractatus Aureus*

The Times

The 1960s were tumultuous years: the Civil Rights Movement, the Vietnam War, the Hippie/Flower-Power Counter-Culture, the rise of feminism, the Anti-War protests, and the break-up of the Beatles. In spite of the political and social upheaval that marked the decade, perhaps one event united a divided country: the technological feat of Neil Armstrong stepping onto the Moon from the Lunar Landing Module on July 20, 1969.

Eight years earlier, on May 25, 1961, President John F. Kennedy challenged the nation with the goal of landing a human being on the Moon by the end of the decade. This challenge added to the already unprecedented demand across the country for scientists and engineers of all disciplines. Even though MSM/UMR was already positioned to provide technical personnel, the college went a step further and added the aerospace engineering degree option in 1967.

Along with the challenge of reaching for the stars, there was also a significant endeavor to harness the heart of the stars: nuclear energy. MSM had embarked on this journey in the late 50s, and the 60s witnessed major milestones in this effort.

MSM 1960s

The first nuclear reactor in Missouri was nearing completion on the MSM campus in September of 1960 with the expectation it would be open to the public by the spring of 1961. It was built to be used entirely as a teaching facility. As such, it facilitated the study of the properties of metals under bombardment by neutrons and—with this knowledge—was expected to enhance the mechanical and/or electrical properties of metals. The reactor was the swimming pool type—so named since the main reaction took place in a sunken pool. Overseeing the project was the Nuclear Engineering Advisory Committee composed of Dr. Daniel Eppelsheimer, chair (Nuclear Engineering Department); Dr. Aaron Miles; Dr. Harold Fuller; Dr. Ted Planje; and Dr. William Webb (Chemical Engineering Department).[1]

Other developments that affected the university specifically in the 1960s: In 1964, MSM underwent a name change, becoming the University of Missouri at Rolla. Shortly afterwards, the new name was modified further—to the University of Missouri-Rolla (UMR). By 1964, a number of Beta Delta initiates had been appointed to the faculty of MSM: Dr. Dudley Thompson ('56), Dean of Faculty; Mailand Strunk ('42), Chair of the Chemical Engineering Department; and William Webb ('38), Chair of the Chemistry Department.

And in October, 1969, the Old Chemistry Building was extensively damaged by a fire which broke out in a storeroom in the basement. The fire destroyed most of the professors' offices in the building. The Social Sciences Department and the Biochemistry Department sustained very serious damage, and the Chemical Engineering Department also suffered considerable destruction. Two laboratories were completely destroyed.[2]

Alpha Chi Sigma 1960s

In the fall of 1963, Grand Recorder Merle Griffin recommended that a national committee be established to develop a program for collegiate chapters to work with the Boy Scouts. According to the proposal, fraternity members would act as chemistry consultants and help the Scouts earn the chemistry merit badge.[3]

In the summer of 1966, the Supreme Council approved the sponsorship of an award in Chemical Engineering research to be administered by the American Institute of Chemical Engineers (AIChE).[4]

In the same year, GMA Jim Miller issued the landmark Constitutional Interpretation Number 50 which redefined and expanded the fraternity's definition of "chemist." The document settled the debate as to the eligibility of pre-med students, metallurgists and ceramic engineers; from henceforth, all three groups could be accepted into the fraternity.[5]

Toward the end of the decade, two more brothers were honored with Nobel Prizes. Dr. Lars Onsager, Chi (Yale) was recognized with the Nobel Prize in Chemistry for his work on the thermodynamics of irreversible processes, and Dr. Robert W. Holley, Zeta (Illinois), along with two other independent researchers, was awarded the Nobel Prize in Medicine for his investigations into DNA/RNA.[6]

Beta Delta

Many chapter records for the 1960s suffered the same fate as those for the 1950s. Much of the documentation of that period could not be recovered, most likely due to the decision made in 1970 to dispose of records over five years old. Nevertheless, from the Missouri Miner, the Rollamo, the Missouri S&T alumni archives and Beta Delta's membership records it was possible to piece together significant events and accomplishments of the chapter and its members.

Though the recognitions and awards that honored Beta Delta members in the 1950s would continue into the 1960s, the significant increase in the number of Beta Delta members among the faculty would be the chapter's major contribution to the college during the decade. Beta Delta members—Walter Schrenk, Thomas Day, Clarence Monroe, P. G. Herold, Frank Conrad and A. Marsh, to name just a few during the chapter's relatively short history—often took teaching positions after graduating, but during the decade, not only would many additional Beta Delta members join the faculty, but several of them—Dudley Thompson, Wouter Bosch, Mailand Strunk and William Webb—would rise in the ranks and bring national distinction to the chemistry and chemical engineering programs.

1960

The decade began with another collegiate organization wishing to join the Alpha Chi Sigma fold. On March 4 the chapter received a letter from Grand Recorder, Roy Loan, which notified Beta Delta of a petition for affiliation with Alpha Chi Sigma for a collegiate chapter from the Chemistry Club, a local chemical organization at the College of the Pacific in Stockton, California. Beta Delta voted to approve the request, but—for some un-recorded reason—no immediate follow-up occurred.[7]

A few days later, Beta Delta members were treated to an informative presentation by Dr. Charles J. Thelen. Dr. Thelen, an Alpha Chi Sigma member who was working with the US Naval Ordnance Test Station (NOTS), spoke on March 9 at a meeting of the American Institute of Chemical Engineers on campus. In his talk, he described how various compositions for both propellants and explosives were determined. Thelen—who was employed as head of the explosives and pyrotechnics division of the Propulsion Development Department—received his bachelor's and doctor's degrees in chemistry from the University of Iowa. Before NOTS, he was a research associate at the University of California at Los Angeles. He also held memberships in Sigma Xi, Phi Lambda Upsilon honorary chemical society, the American Chemicals Society, and the Research Society of America.[8]

Early in the decade, Walter Schrenk received another significant honor. A letter from J. D. Commerferd, Chair of the Midwest Award, to Dr. Frank Conrad, dated April 1, 1960, acknowledged the nomination of Dr. Schrenk for the 1960 Midwest Award. Faculty members who supported the nomination included: Dr. E. D. Fisher, Prof. of Chemistry; Dr. Wouter Bosch, Prof. of Chemistry; Dr. M. R. Strunk, Assoc. Prof. of Chemical Engineering; Dr. David E. Troutner, Asst. Prof. of Chemistry; Dr. William H. Webb, Prof. of Chemistry; Dr. Dudley Thompson, Chairman & Prof. of Chemical Engineering; Dr. G. K. Lay, Asst. Prof. of Chemical Engineering; and Dr. R. C. Sutherland, Assoc. Prof. of Chemistry.[9]

Sandwiched between the conferral of the Midwest Award on Dr. Schrenk and Beta Delta's upcoming recognition at Conclave, the chapter carried on its business of pledging and initiation. On May 1, eleven new members were initiated: Donald W. Haas, Jerome A. Denzel, Robert A. Steinkamp, Robert L. Gray, Glenn E. Stoner, William A. Scholle, Clinton A. Clark, John S. Bosnak, Duane E. Thurman, Gary D. Fehsenfeld, and James R. Knox.

That summer Gary Achenbach, Edward P. Schneider, and Frank J. Zvanut represented Beta Delta at the 25th Biennial Conclave in West Lafayette, IN. At this conclave, Beta Delta was awarded the top non-house chapter of the fraternity.[10] In July, Beta Delta received the T. Dale Stewart Cup as the outstanding chapter of Alpha Chi Sigma which did not operate a house in the biennium 1958-1960. The selection, made by the District Counselors—sitting as the Efficiency Rating System Committee—recognized Beta Delta's general excellence in chapter operations. The fraternity, according to the committee, had consistently shown a degree of professional interest, a willingness for service, and a competency in the execution of routine duties in an exemplary fashion.[11]

The MSM Chemistry and Chemical Engineering faculty—many of whom were Alpha Chi Sigma members initiated through Beta Delta—continued its service to students on campus, to members of the wider scientific community, and to high school teachers in the first years of the decade. During June and July, 1961, the Department of Chemical Engineering and Chemistry conducted four special paint and polymer short courses: Paint Short Course for Beginners; Coatings Course for Architects, Painting Contractors and Maintenance Engineers; Advanced Paint and Polymer Refresher Seminar; and Paint Short Course for High School Chemistry teachers. Together, the courses had a combined enrollment of over 150 students from 37 different states and four Canadian provinces. Assisting in the courses were 31 guest lecturers. The courses, in their second year in 1961, were held on campus under the direction of Dr. Wouter Bosch, Professor of Paint and Polymer Chemistry at MSM (Bosch would later be initiated by Beta Delta into Alpha Chi Sigma in 1967).[12]

On October 28, the Miner announced that Joseph Gay was named October Man-of-the-Month by the Blue Key organization. The honor was bestowed on an MSM student not only for outstanding participation in extracurricular activities and exemplary scholastic achievement, but also for praiseworthy leadership qualities displayed on campus. Gay, who enrolled in the fall of 1957 in Chemical Engineering and was initiated into Alpha Chi Sigma on May 4, 1958, also served Blue Key as Vice-President, worked as a student assistant in both the Chemical Engineering and Athletic departments, served on Student Council for two years, and held a membership in AIChE.[13]

The end-of-the-year initiation occurred On December 11, when 13 new members were received into the fraternity: Rudolph M. Phillips, Herman R. Miller, Don R. Brown, James H. Stadelman, Alvin N. Hainline, Robert F. Zeitzmann, Wayne E. Blumenberg, Rufus G. Miller, Donald R. Pogue, Daniel R. Middleton, Ronald D. Mitchell, Richard W. Broockmann, and David G. Skamenca. An additional person, W. V. Andoe, had been initiated alone on October 11. A singular initiation such as this would be held only under special circumstances, but the reasons for Andoe's early admittance could not be ascertained.

The 1960 Rollamo reported that K. Snavely, G. Patterson, H. Grannemann, D. Redington, R. James, J. Janes, R. Lawhon and W. Weber served as officers in 1960. Except for Snavely, who served as Reporter (determined by correspondence with the Grand Chapter), the others' positions were not recorded.

The 1960s

In 1960—as it continued to do throughout the decade—Beta Delta conducted bi-weekly meetings featuring guest speakers or professional movies, maintained joint meetings with other collegiate chapters, attended and participated in meetings with the professional branch chapter in St. Louis, gave awards to the highest ranking junior and senior in chemical engineering and chemistry, provided help sessions for freshman chemistry students, and promoted safety in the chemical laboratories.

First Row, Left to Right: R. Lawhon, K. Snavely, R. James, H. Grannemann, D. Redington, G. Patterson, J. Janes, W. Weber, G. Achenbach. Second Row: G. Vaughn, J. Luecke, M. Herzog, C. Armstrong, E. Dille, G. Stone, K. Wood, J. Hibberd, R. Schild. Third Row: R. Hankinson, G. Chappell, J. Jones, J. Mullins, R. Hallahan, C. Larsen, G. Heilig. Fourth Row: R. Walter, B. Windeknecht, H. Adams, D. Magre, D. Bartholic, E. Crow, J. Davis, B. Atwater, J. Harvey, R. Swanson, W. Onn.

1961

On February 8, AIChE presented its Annual Chapter Scholarship Award to AIChE and Beta Delta member, Gary Achenbach, who had been initiated on April 19, 1959. The Award—earned by the student with the highest cumulative grade point average in the Chemical Engineering department during the freshman and sophomore years—was presented by Dr. Frank Conrad, Prof. of Chemical Engineering (initiated by Beta Delta in 1937), who gave Achenbach an AIChE pin and a two year subscription to "Chemical Engineering Progress." Achenbach—who had also won the AIChE freshman award in 1960 for having the highest freshman grade point average in the Chemical Engineering department—had been Vice-Master Alchemist and also represented Beta Delta at the 25th Biennial Conclave in 1960 in West Lafayette, IN. In 1962, Achenbach—like many other altruistic students during the 1960s—suspended his college career to pursue another calling. As a member of the Baptist Student Union, he ventured on a mission to the Philippines during the spring and summer that year.[14]

Gary Achenbach—Rollamo 1962

One of the most notable events at MSM in 1961—and certainly a pinnacle in the life of Beta Delta—was the retirement of Dr. Schrenk. At the 88th Annual Commencement Ceremonies held at Jackling Field on May 28, Schrenk was awarded the title of Professor Emeritus of Chemical Engineering. The Commencement speaker, Francis Cameron, president of the St. Joseph Lead Company in New York, NY, devoted most of his speech to the spectacular achievements and the incomparable service "Doc" Schrenk had demonstrated at MSM during his amazing 38-year career.

Left to Right: Dean Curtis L. Wilson, Dr. Walter Schrenk, and Dr. Elmer Ellis, President of the University of Missouri

Missouri S&T Magazine, June 1961

Of course, these highlights occurred in the midst of the chapter's usual business. In April the following officers were elected for the fall semester: Dennis B. Redington, Master Alchemist; Robert A. Steinkamp, Vice-Master Alchemist; Ronald W. Walter, Treasurer; Jerry Luecke, Recorder; Gary E. Vaughn, Master of Ceremonies; Duane E. Thurman, Reporter; Michael S. Herzog, Alumni Secretary; and Dr. William H. Webb, Faculty Advisor.[15]

On April 30, ten pledges were initiated: Norman T. Miller, Kenneth C. Scott, Michael K. Norman, Jeffrey R. Herbst, Robert V. Rommelman, Bernard J. Moormann, Jo L. Reed, Gerald J. York, David O. Cox, and James R. Frazer.

On October 6, the Miner announced that Beta Delta member Wayne Blumenberg (initiated December 11, 1960) was the recipient of the St. Joseph Lead Company Scholarship plan. The Scholarship provided a $600 stipend per year and could be renewed annually for up to four years, provided the student demonstrated satisfactory work. Blumenberg, who was originally from Farmington, MO, and entered MSM on a Curator's Award, received the Monsanto Chemical Company Scholarship for the spring 1960 semester and the Phi Kappa Phi Book Award for the 1959-60 school year. He was also a member of AIChE and served as a student assistant in the Chemical Engineering department.[16]

Then, on October 11, Beta Delta elected officers for the spring 1962 semester: Bob Steinkamp, Master Alchemist; Rich Hallahan, Vice-Master Alchemist; Roger Schild, Master of Ceremonies; Ron Walters, Treasurer; Dean Culman, Recorder; Duane Thurman, Reporter; and Jerry Luecke, Historian.[17]

On October 21, a Sunday, the Nuclear Training Reactor was dedicated. The ceremony was attended by John M. Dalton, governor of Missouri, Elmer Ellis, president of the University of Missouri, and Dr. Frank Foote, director of the Argonne National Laboratory, who recounted the history of the University of Chicago's first nuclear reactor. The highlight of the dedication was the presentation of a 15-pound block of remi-graphite used in the first reactor in Chicago.[18] Remi-graphite was a synthetic graphite manufactured for use as a moderator or reflector within a nuclear reactor. Graphite was an important material in the construction of both historical and modern nuclear reactors, due to its extreme purity and its capacity to withstand extremely high temperatures.[19]

That same week, the Miner shared the news that John Joseph Schwaller, a Beta Delta member, was the recipient of the J. B. Arthur and Family Scholarship provided by J. B. Arthur, President and founder of the Mexico Refractories Company. The Scholarship, given annually to an outstanding student in Ceramic Engineering, was awarded on the basis of character, engineering promise, scholarship, and leadership. Schwaller, who was initiated into Beta Delta on January 1, 1960, was active in many other campus organizations: Blue Key, the Newman Club, the Rollamo board, the American Institute of Chemical Engineers, Phi Kappa Theta social fraternity, the American Ceramic Society, and Keramos, the professional fraternity for ceramic engineering.[20]

Another Beta Delta brother to receive a scholarship in 1961 was Clifford Keith Larsen (initiated April 19, 1959). He was one of four recipients of the General Motors Scholarship Award, which was given to an incoming freshman and subject to renewal for a four year period. A member of Kappa Alpha, the American Institute of Chemical Engineers; Gamma Delta, the International Association of Lutheran Students; Tau Beta Pi; and the Miner board, Larsen also served as a student assistant in the Chemistry

The 1960s

department. He had previously won the Phi Kappa Phi Bookplate Award and the Gold Key Award.[21] In the summer of 1961, he took part in a Proctor & Gamble training program in which he assisted in the development of a unique business simulation exercise called MATRIX (Management Trial Exercise). The exercise exposed students to the decisions that plant managers are required to make and was conducted in groups of four to twelve. Larsen participated in a group at Proctor & Gamble's St. Louis plant.[22]

The year closed with the initiation of nine new members on December 10: Richard E. Dudley, Tom D. Spence, Ronald K. Riley, Stephen F. Ganz, James A. Baker, Richard A. Ploeger, Kenneth J. Wulfert, Warren R. Needels, and Calvin B. Cobb.[23]

Note: The 1961 Rollamo carried a description of Alpha Chi Sigma but provided no picture of the members, as it had consistently done in previous years.

1962

The faculty of the Chemical Engineering department started expanding the Engineering Biochemistry program in 1961, taking on instruction at the doctoral level for the first time. This effort was continued in early January, 1962, when Dr. Dudley J. Thompson (Beta Delta '56), Chair of the Department of Chemistry and Chemical Engineering, announced, on January 12, that the department had received three additional grants from the National Defense Education Act (NDEA) for studies at the doctoral level in Engineering Biochemistry, bringing the total number of grants to six. At the time, three students (James Click, Thomas Good, and Robert Logan—none of whom were Beta Delta members) were working toward the PhD degree on three NDEA fellowships in the field of Engineering Biochemistry.

In addition to enhancing their academic offerings, the chemistry and chemical engineering professors continued to expand their competencies beyond higher academia into secondary education and industry. On May 18, the Miner reported that a fourth summer session of the Paint Chemistry course would be offered that June and July. Dr. Bosch, Professor of Paint and Polymer Chemistry, would once again be teaching the courses which had achieved national recognition. The 1962 series consisted of the Paint Short Course for Beginners; the Paint Short Course for High School Chemistry Teachers; the Coatings Course for Architects, Painting Contractors and Maintenance Engineers; and two additional offerings—a Polymer Chemistry Conference and an Advanced Paint Refresher Course.[24]

In October, while pledging, Donald Bugg, received a renewal of the St. Louis Section of the MSM Alumni Association Scholarship for the 1962-1963 academic year. Bugg, a member of AIChE and the Independents, also served on the Men's Residence Halls Association (MRHA) Judicial Board.[25]

Two initiations took place during the year. At the one on April 29, Ted A. Baer, F. L. Scott, Paul D. Griffin, William E. Kemp, Edgar L. Moodie, Chester P. Gunn, Daniel Wacker, and James R. Miller became Beta Delta members. The second was held on December 9, at which the following were inducted: William E. McCracken, Thomas A. Hrastich, Donald G. Schnake, Donald A. Bugg, Gene A. Cochran, David F. John, Charles K. Hanna, James A. Schoeffel, Jorge M. Rodriguez, Paul P. DeMay, John L. Cannaday, William I. Winters, Gary L. Kelso, Dale W. Howard, Anthony M. Romano, Dannie R. Clarida, and Warwick W. Doll.

First Row, Left to Right: J. Frazer, D. Skamenca, R. Whittaker, D. Thurman (Vice-Master Alchemist), J. Luecke (Master Alchemist), J. Jones (Recorder), G. York, J. Janes, D. Middleton, R. Steinkamp, R. Rommelman. Second Row: J. Denzel, J. Baker, J. Herbst, M. Norman, R. Schild, G. Finne, H. Swanson, W. Needels, R. Mitchell, J. Mullins. Third Row: R. Walter, C. Cobb, S. Ganz, R. Dudley, K. Wulfert, P. Culnan, H. Miller, R. Miller, D. Haas, C. Larsen.

Beta Delta Chapter 1962—Rollamo 1962

1963

By 1963, interest in the history of chemistry—and in stories of significant figures in the field—appears to have increased on the MSM campus, not only among members of Alpha Chi Sigma and the chemistry community, but to a wider audience as well. An article in the February 15, 1963, issue of the Miner, for example, featuring the influential 18th century French chemist, Antoine Laurent Lavoisier, the "Father of Exact Chemistry," would certainly have been appreciated by more students than just the members of the Beta Delta chapter. Another article, "Louis Pasteur: Father of Research and Processes," appeared in the April 5 issue and would also have appealed to a broad audience. It summarized the life and work of Pasteur, who was renowned in the 19th century for his discoveries of the principles of vaccination and pasteurization. [26]

Between these two stories, the Miner took on an even more ambitious project. In March, it ran a long article summarizing the entire history of the Missouri School of Mines and Metallurgy from 1871 to 1963. [27]

The highlight of the spring semester of 1963, however, was the address, on April 9, by Dr. Wernher von Braun, the world-renowned scientist in the field of space technology. He spoke to a near capacity audience of students in the Rolla High School auditorium about the US Government's plans to send astronauts to the moon. The head of the George C. Marshall Space Center in Huntsville, Alabama, von Braun, incorporating slides throughout his presentation, outlined the various steps necessary in the completion of the Apollo moon-landing project. Born in Wirsitz in Poland, in 1912, von Braun was instrumental in the development of liquid-fueled rockets, including the V-2 used by the Nazis toward the end of WWII. He, along with approximately 100 other German scientists, surrendered to Allied forces in 1945. In America, he was best known for the successful launching of America's first earth satellite, Explorer I. His other accomplishments included the development of the Redstone Intermediate-Range Ballistic Missile and the Jupiter Intercontinental Ballistic Missile. The visit to Rolla was one of only four such trips von Braun made in 1963 for primarily educational purposes. Retiring Dean and Mrs. Curtis L. Wilson were among the special guests at the event. [28]

Werhner von Braun

Two weeks after von Braun's visit, brothers and pledges from Alpha Epsilon made the drive from St. Louis to Rolla to join Beta Delta and its pledges, on April 28, for a joint initiation. Beta Delta's initiates that day were: Kenneth W. West, Jack E. Russell, Timothy C. Judkins, Jay S. Stirrat, Larry A. Michael, James D. Hunter, James M. Lysaght, David S. Shimamoto, and Thomas H. Dunning.[29]

In May, another Beta Delta member joined the esteemed ranks of Fraternity-Man-of-the-Year. On May 10, the Miner announced that the Inter-Fraternity Council had chosen Clinton A. Clark (initiated May 1, 1960) as the Fraternity-Man-of-the-Year for 1962-1963. At the time, Clark was studying metallurgical engineering and had served—or was currently serving—in numerous leadership positions: president of the MSM Student Council, secretary and president of the American Society for Metals, president of Alpha Sigma Mu (the national honorary metallurgical engineering fraternity), vice-president of the Student Union Board, president and vice-president of Blue Key, treasurer of the local chapter of the American Institute of Metallurgical Engineers, and membership officer for the American Foundrymen's Society. He was also a member of Kappa Sigma, Tau Beta Pi, and Phi Kappa Phi.[30]

Just before Thanksgiving on November 24, the following men were received into membership: Jagdish S. Sanghvi, Jerome F. Scego, David P. Alt, Robert T. Montgomery, Frederick B. Rudolph, Marc J. Sims, George M. Breuer, Robert J. Sagan, Charles R. Porterfield, Phillip F. Hodges, and Joseph W. Rizzie.

First Row, Left to Right: D. Middleton, W. McCracken, K. Wulfert (Treasurer), W. Needels (Vice-Master Alchemist), J. Denzel (Master Alchemist), P. DeMay, T. Baer, E. Moodie. Second Row: W. Blumenberg, D. Wacker, R. Zeitzmann, M. Norman, C. Gunn, D. Bugg, J. Baker, C. Hanna, W. Doll, D. Howard. Third Row: B. Moorman, W. Winters, J. Knox, R. Dudley, Miller, D. Thurman, F. Scott, W. Kemp, R. Mitchell, J. Schoeffel.

Beta Delta Chapter 1963-Rollamo 1963

1964

From one semester to the next, Beta Delta members continued to garner all kinds of awards and recognitions. On February 12, Tom Hrastich won the American Institute of Chemical Engineers Junior Scholarship Award at the meeting of the student chapter of AIChE. Hrastich, a member of Alpha Chi Sigma and AIChE, was also active in Tau Beta Pi, Phi Eta Sigma (an honorary fraternity) and Delta Sigma (a social fraternity). In addition, he served as president of the student chapter of AIChE. The Junior Scholarship Award consisted of a certificate issued by AIChE, a two year subscription to "Chemical Engineering Progress," a special membership in AIChE, and either a student pin or lapel button.

At the same meeting, David Shimamoto was honored for earning the highest scholastic average during his freshman year. He, too, received a year's subscription to "Chemical Engineering Progress." Like Hrastich, Shimamoto was a member of Alpha Chi Sigma and AIChE. His other activities included memberships in Engineers Club, Independents, Intra-

Coop Council (treasurer), and Phi Eta Sigma. He also served as treasurer of AIChE and lettered in track.[31]

By 1964, Beta Delta's reputation for fostering outstanding faculty members was spreading far beyond the MSM community. The chapter's alumni were becoming teachers and professors at colleges and universities all over the country. Dr. James M. McKelvey (initiated December 4, 1943) was just one such example. On April 4, Washington University in St. Louis announced that McKelvey would be the new dean of the School of Engineering effective June 30. McKelvey, the chair of the Chemical Engineering Department at the time, received his BS in Chemical Engineering in 1945. During his undergraduate days he was a member of Tau Beta Pi, Blue Key, Pi Kappa Alpha (social fraternity), Interfraternity Council, and the Student Council. He also served as president of the Junior Class and was a student assistant in the Chemical Engineering department. Another example of a Beta Delta member teaching at another college was Neil L. Book who was initiated in 1969. He taught at Tulane University in New Orleans, Louisiana.[32]

On the afternoon of April 10 (The National Office records indicate May 10), Beta Delta initiated 10 new members: Richard C. Porter, Alva H. King, John C. Roeseler, J. D. Bennett, Robert A. Wenom, Gary B. Dreher, Michael D. Moran, Roy Brunson, Onur Engemen, and S. C. Allen.[33] On April 12, the Sunday evening following the initiation ceremony, new and active members enjoyed a banquet at Hull's Colonial Village Hotel and Restaurant in Rolla. Present at the celebration were Dr. Webb, faculty advisor; Edward Schneider, District Counselor; and Bill Morris, former St. Louis professional chapter president, who also counseled the Columbia, MO, and Washington University chapters—Delta and Alpha Epsilon, respectively. During the meeting, Morris commended the Beta Delta chapter for retaining the National Efficiency Trophy throughout the 1960 and 1962 biennial conclaves. The 1964 Conclave would be held in New York City, Morris announced; Paul Griffith and Edward Schneider would be Beta Delta's representatives.

After 93 years, the Missouri School of Mines and Metallurgy finally took on a new name. Acknowledging that MSM's educational enterprise had expanded into a much broader array of engineering and science fields, and recognizing the school's integral place in the University of Missouri schema, University of Missouri President Elmer Ellis announced, on April 14, that the Board of Curators had approved the change in the name; effective July 1, the School of Mines and Metallurgy would become the University of Missouri at Rolla. Under the new affiliation in the University system, the curriculum was restructured into four major divisions, each under its own director. The title of the administrative head at Rolla, Dr. Merle Baker, was changed from Dean to Chancellor of the University of Missouri at Rolla. Under the new format, the School of Engineering was divided into five departments: Chemical, Civil, Electrical, and Mechanical Engineering, and Engineering Graphics. The School of Science now included the departments of Applied Mathematics, Chemistry, Geology and Physics, and the School of Mines and Metallurgy consisted of the departments of Mining, Metallurgical, Ceramic and Geological Engineering.[34]

On May 6, the Beta Delta chapter of Alpha Chi Sigma and the local chapter of the AIChE held a joint meeting at which Mr. George W. McLellan, Coordinator of Technical Information Service for Corning Glass Works, New York, gave a presentation which dealt with new developments in the glass industry.[35]

Once again the Summer Paint Chemistry courses, directed by Dr. Bosch, were offered in June and July. The courses differed somewhat from those offered in the summer of 1963, but covered many of the same topics brought up to date with the latest technological advances; they included: an Introductory Polymer Course; a Conference on the Chemistry and Physics of Polymers; a Coating Course for Architects, Painting Contractors and Maintenance Engineers; a Paint Short Course for Beginners; and an Advanced Paint Refresher Course. The Paint Short Course for High School Chemistry Teachers was not offered.[36]

In 1964 the fraternity was well represented in the administration of the University of Missouri at Rolla. New appointments, announced on September 25, included Beta Delta initiates: Dr. Dudley Thompson ('56) to the Dean of Faculty; Mailand Strunk ('42) to the Chair of the Chemical Engineering Department ; and William Webb ('38) to the Chair of the Chemistry Department. Brother Webb was also District Counselor for the Missouri Valley District.[37]

Department Chairs: Left: Mailand Rainey Strunk. Right: William Hamlet Webb

Rollamo-1965

In September, the Chemical Engineering department added two faculty members: Dr. Harvey H. Grice and Dr. Efton L. Park, Jr., who would later serve as a faculty advisor to Beta Delta. The Chemistry department also took on two newcomers: Dr. Oliver K. Manuel and Dr. Raymond L. Venable, both Assistant Professors.[38]

As Beta Delta alumni gained prominence as faculty members, the recognitions for achievements of its student members continued. On November 6, the Miner reported that Beta Delta member, Charles Kenneth Hanna, was the recipient of the A. P. Green Fire Brick Company Scholarship for the 1964-1965 academic year. The award was made each year to an outstanding senior. Recipients were selected on the basis of character, leadership, and scholastic achievement—all hallmarks of Hanna's career as an undergraduate. He had served as Vice-Master Alchemist for Beta Delta and was also a member of the American Institute of Chemical Engineers, Tech Club, Prospectors Club, and the Independents.[39]

Several weeks later, on November 20, the Miner announced that another Beta Delta brother, Melvin Rueppel, a sophomore, was named recipient of the H. T. Mann Scholarship for the second consecutive year. The scholarship was made available by Besse C. Mann, widow of the late Dr. H.

T. Mann, alumnus and former faculty member at MSM. According to the Miner, Rueppel was a member of Alpha Chi Sigma, which awarded him the Outstanding Freshman Award for 1964. No record was found of his initiation date, however.[40]

On December 5, James Dew was initiated into the fraternity in a separate ceremony (No explanation was given for his early initiation). Then on the next day, the 6th, the following were received into membership: James W. Moore, Lawrence M. Young, Robert W. Whelove, Raymond J. Kruep, Devendra V. Mehta, Craig B. Johler, James J. Beeson, Michael E. Hardy, David E. Wolfersberger, Donald G. Schilling, Constantine Tsimpris, James M. Savage, Terence Towers, Harley D. Hickenbotham, Donald G. Miller, Gary R. Graham, Kent G. Horner, Gary W. Wigginton, Glen L. Mizer, Tom L. McKenzie, and John W. Thurman.[41]

Due to the lack of accurate records, officers for 1964 could not be ascertained with any certitude—except for the offices of Reporter and Treasurer. From their correspondences during the year, it was clear that Thomas Dunning was Reporter for all of 1964, and William E. McCracken was treasurer for at least the spring semester. According to the 1964 Rollamo, C. Hanna was VMA, W. Doll, Recorder, and D. John, MC, but whether these were for the spring or fall semester could not be determined.[42]

First Row, Left to Right: E. Moodie, C. Gunn, R. Sagan, T. Dunning, T. Judkins, W. McCracken (Treasurer), C. Hanna (Vice-Master Alchemist), W. Doll (Recorder), D. John (Master of Ceremonies). Second Row: G. Kelso, D. Alt, C. Cobb, J. Schoeffel, P. DeMay, W. Needels, D. Bugg, T. Hrastich, J. Hunter. Third Row: W. Winters, T. Baer, Miller, G. Breuer, K. Wulfert, G. Cochran, c. Porterfield, J. Russell, D. Clarida.

Beta Delta Chapter 1964—Rollamo 1964

1965

The year began with another award. In February, Dr. Wouter Bosch, professor of chemistry and graduate director at UMR, received the 1964 Service Award from the St. Louis Coating Society. The annual award—inscribed with the citation "For outstanding contributions to the technology and art of protective coating in the specific field of education"—was presented to Bosch at a meeting of the Society in St. Louis. Dr. Bosch was a graduate of the State University of Utrecht in the Netherlands and the University of Minnesota.[43]

A distinction of peculiar interest appears to have had its origins around 1965. The infamous Prof. Snarf Award (see Excursus), though outwardly an insult, was really a "back-handed" compliment often secretly held dear by the recipient—a member of the Chemical Engineering or Chemistry department faculty. The Professor Snarf Award winner—determined by a secret vote of the students—was the "Scrooge" of the instructors, someone "notorious," someone who could handle friendly criticism or take a cynical joke. The Award probably originated prior to 1965, but the earliest documented evidence of its existence appeared in an article in the Miner in April, which cited evidence from correspondence between George Breuer, Reporter, and Merle Griffin, Grand Recorder.[44] The contest to select the recipient was used to raise funds for a worthy project. In 1965, for instance, the proceeds went toward improvements in the safety conditions of the Chemical Engineering building and resupplying laboratory first aid kits.[45]

The new initiates on May 9 were: James J. Schlosser, William J. James, and Jacques L. Zakin. Honored attendees at the banquet, held at the Crystal Room, were Dr. Dudley Thompson, Dean of the Faculty; Dr. Mailand Strunk, Chair of the Department of Chemical Engineering; and Dr. William Webb, Chair of the Department of Chemistry and Midwest Counselor for Alpha Chi Sigma.[46] In addition to the honored initiates, the winners of the Alpha Chi Sigma awards were also recognized: Dennis Krauss, Freshman Award; Gary Graham, Junior Award; and Thomas Dunning and Donald Bugg, co-winners of the Senior Award. During the banquet, Dr. K. G. Mayhan, the current chapter advisor, introduced Dr. Efton Park, who would soon take over that role. Dr. Mayhan was taking a one year leave of absence for postdoctoral work at the Mellon Institute. It was also announced that the money received through the voting for the Prof. Snarf Award—a vote was cast for each donation of a minimum amount, which was not stated in records from that time—would be used in the Alpha Chi Sigma Safety Program.[47]

Life for Beta Delta members, mid-way through the decade, was not just about recognitions and awards, of course. Members attended business meetings each month, maintained their service obligations, and enjoyed frequent social activities. District events—including installations of new chapters and the annual Jamboree—were still very much a part of the chapter's life. On October 19, for example, Grand Master Alchemist Burton Tiffany invited Beta Delta members to attend the installation of Beta Rho's newest inductees on October 30 at Kansas State University in Manhattan, Kansas. Beta Rho, a Kappa Chapter Colony, had only recently been established on March 10, 1964. It is likely that a contingent of Beta Delta brothers made the trip to Manhattan, but their attendance at the installation could not be confirmed.[48]

The annual Jamboree was held on October 24 at the Lions Club Park in Rolla. The events included the traditional picnic and softball game between the St. Louis Professional chapter and the collegiate chapters. The invitation encouraged the professional members to bring a "crying towel" since the collegiate members would be winning the big game. When Alpha Epsilon was not able to attend, however, the collegiate team was clearly at a disadvantage. Unfortunately, the score of the game has not survived and so the outcome remains a mystery. According to a record from 1966, however, Beta Delta was still in possession of the Wiedemann Cup at that time, so apparently the collegiates came away with the victory.[49]

To wrap up the semester an initiation ceremony was held on December 12. Fourteen new members—Lawrence J. Mikelionis, Larry D. Getz, Russell Primrose, Terry G. Waltrip, Gerald Bauer, Ralph E. Palmer, James A. Hoeh, Gary J. Capone, John H. Throckmorton, Michael L. Keller, Dennis R. Parker, Kent W. Rogers, Lawrence A. Yates, and Steven W. Yates—brought the total number of Beta Delta actives to 47. The initiation banquet was held at the Houston House with Dr. W. H. Webb, the District Counselor, and Dr. E. L. Park, Jr., the chapter advisor, as special guests. Brother Mike Keller, who demonstrated the most initiative through pledge week and had the top score on the pledge examination, won the top pledge award, and Brother Larry Getz was named as the pledge with the best plaque.[50]

As in previous years, the chapter's pledge projects in 1965 benefited not only Beta Delta but also the Chemistry and Chemical Engineering departments as well. Examples of these projects included: replenishing safety kits in the laboratories; creating safety posters; writing safety essays; construction of a large "hexagon stand" which was placed outside of the Chemical Engineering building to announce chapter meetings; and planning exhibits for Engineer's Day.

According to the 1965 Rollamo, D. Clarida, Master Alchemist, W. Doll, Vice-Master Alchemist, D. Bugg, Recorder, and G. Breuer, Reporter, held their offices sometime during the year. Only G. Breuer's position as Reporter in the spring semester could be confirmed.[51]

First Row, Left to Right: G. Breuer (Reporter), Dr. Mayhan (Advisor), D. Bugg (Secretary), J. Roeseler, R. Montgomery, D. Clarida (Master Alchemist), W. Doll (Vice-Master Alchemist), T. Hrastich, C. Hanna. Second Row: P. Hodges, W. McCracken, M. Sims, K. Horner, J. Moore, H. Hickenbotham, M. Hardy, C. Tsimpris, J. Savage, R. Sagan. Third Row: S. Allen, J. Hunter, R. Kruep, M. Moran, G. Graham, D. Wolfersberger, L. Michael, O. Egemen, Dr. Webb (District Counselor). Fourth Row: A. Acosta, D. Schilling, D. John, F. Rudolph, G. Dreher, J. Beeson, G. Mizer, R. Porter.

Beta Delta Chapter 1965—Rollamo 1965

1966

In February, Jim Hunter, a Beta Delta brother, was selected by the members of Blue Key as "Man-of-the-Month" for December, 1965. Hunter, who graduated with a BS degree in Chemical Engineering in January, 1965, was currently working on a graduate degree in Chemical Engineering. He had previously received the Distinguished Military Graduate and Chicago Tribune awards for his work in ROTC (Reserved Officer Training Corp) as a second lieutenant in the Chemical Corps of the United States Army. As an undergraduate, he was a member of AIChE, Scabbard and Blade (a college military honor society), Kappa Alpha, Blue Key, and Kappa Kappa Phi. He also served as vice-president of Kappa Kappa Psi honorary service fraternity, vice-president of the Military Ball Board, and secretary of Kappa Alpha. His selection as December's "Man-of-the-Month," however, was probably eclipsed by another event that occurred that month: his marriage to Ms. Lee Delick.[52]

On March 25, the Miner reported that two more Beta Delta brothers, Constantine (Deno) Tsimpris and Gerald L. Bauer, received AIChE Scholarship Awards. Tsimpris received the Junior Scholastic Award for earning the highest scholastic rating during his freshman and sophomore years. He had also received the Sophomore Scholastic Award the previous year. In addition to his membership in Alpha Chi Sigma and AIChE, Tsimpris also belonged to Phi Eta Sigma honor society, the Independents, and the UMR ROTC Band. Bauer received the Sophomore Scholastic Award—based on his outstanding scholastic achievement during his freshman year; he was also a member of Phi Eta Sigma and Tau Kappa Epsilon social fraternity.[53]

On April 24, Beta Delta initiated 13 new members: Robert S. Sanders, Richard C. Carlson, Fred K. Vogt, Harold R. Lewis, James A. Youngman, James H. Jones, William J. McFadden, James L. Ziegenmier, James E. Thomas, Richard P. Bergsieker, Eric B. Rapp, James A. Latty, and Gerald R. Thiessen. Later that summer, Paul Griffin, Edward Schneider, Dr. William Webb, Lawrence Young, and Frank J. Zvanut attended the 28th Biennial Conclave held in Ann Arbor, Michigan, June 19-23.[54]

In September the following officers were elected: James W. Moore, MA; Michael L. Keller, VMA; Lawrence M. Young, Historian; James J. Beeson, MC; Harley D. Hickenbotham, Treasurer; Lawrence J. Mikelionis, Reporter; and Michael Savage, Alumni Secretary. On October 29, Delta chapter hosted the annual Missouri Valley District Jamboree. After the event, Beta Delta was still in possession of the Wiedemann Cup, though no account of the game was recorded.[55]

In November, Dennis Parker, a sophomore (initiated 1965), was awarded the Universal Oil Products Scholarship—a distinction presented annually to an outstanding chemical engineering student. A few weeks later, on December 4, 15 initiates—Edgar A. Ross, Gary A. Hoffman, J. K. Link, Lynn E. Zoellner, Sammie J. Hinchcliff, Steven C. Mueller, Michael C. Turco, Leonard F. Koederitz, George A. Smith, Nasiruddin Ahmed, Gerald W. McReynolds, Floyd W. Jennings, John G. Faes, Wouter Bosch, and Walter R. Eshbaugh—were inducted into the fraternity. The National Office records indicated January 1, 1967 as Wouter Bosch's initiation date. It was unclear why.[56]

Before the year ended, the issue of eligibility for membership regarding those academic disciplines considered within the scope of the chemical sciences—a question which had been smoldering in the by-laws since the 1940s, was finally resolved. On December 27, Dr. James F. Miller, Grand Master Alchemist, issued Constitutional Interpretation No. 50, Eligibility for membership with respect to 'allied professions in which chemistry predominates.' The Interpretation defined the "allied professions" as:

> a. Any course or field such as Biochemistry, Geochemistry, Paper Chemistry, etc., in which the word "chemistry" is part of the title.
>
> b. Any course or field which is derived from chemistry or is composed principally of a study of the composition, structure, reactions and properties of matter.
>
> c. Any field in which sufficient courses in the Chemistry Department are taken to constitute or be equivalent to the requirements for a minor...

The interpretation went on to list specific fields and curricula which would fall under the above definitions. Furthermore, a student wishing to initiate in his or her first year of college was "...to be completing or have completed a two-semester or equivalent course generally described as freshman college chemistry...." The precedent which set the stage for this Constitutional Interpretation was established on October 11, 1956, when Grand Master Alchemist, Ronald M. Warren, issued Constitutional Interpretation No. 49 which allowed students enrolled in the Science Engineering Program at the University of Michigan to be eligible for initiation into Alpha Chi Sigma.[57]

Front Row: J. Moore (Secretary), C. Tsimpris (Historian), F. Rudolph (Master of Ceremonies), R. Kruep (Master Alchemist), M. Hardy (Reporter), H. Hickenbotham (Treasurer), J. Savage (Alumni Secretary). Row 2: M. Keller, J. Schoeffel, D. Alt, C. Johler, J. Bennett, G. Wigginton, K. Rogers, J. Beeson. Row 3: J. Schlosser, R. Wenom, R. Montgomery, R. Brunson, L. Mikelionis, D. Parker, J. Throckmorton. Row 4: G. Graham, J. Hoeh, G. Cochran, R. Palmer, T. Waltrip.

Beta Delta Chapter 1966—Rollamo 1966

1967

The January 13 issue of the Missouri Miner reported that Gary Graham (Beta Delta '64) was named the November Man-of-the-Month by Blue Key. Graham was a member of Pi Kappa Alpha where he served as vice-president and treasurer. His other organizational involvements included the American Institute of Chemical Engineers (president and recorder), the Student Council, Alpha Phi Omega, Tau Beta Pi, Phi Kappa Phi, and Blue Key (secretary). Prior to the Man-of-the-Month honor, he had also been named the Outstanding Junior in Chemical Engineering and was listed in Who's Who in American Colleges and Universities.[58]

The honors kept coming in for Dr. Schrenk—long after his retirement in 1961. On February 22, UMR's venerable professor emeritus of Chemical Engineering was recognized once again. This time, he was presented a Fifty-Year Certificate by the American Chemical Society. "Doc" Schrenk, the first professor to receive such a distinction from the society, was given full membership in the society for the rest of his life—without dues. By this time Dr. Schrenk had been listed in *American Men of Science, Chemical*

Who's Who, Who's Who in Engineering and *Who's Who in the Midwest*, and was a registered professional engineer in the State of Missouri. In addition, he had worked as a consultant for the US Bureau of Mines, for the Mississippi Valley Research Station and for the Missouri Mining Experiment Station at UMR. He had also been published in the "Journal of the American Chemical Society" and the "Journal of the Electrochemical Society." (See also Chapter 1 Excursus, Chapter 2 Excursus, and Chapter 3 for further information on Dr. Schrenk.)[59]

On April 30, 1967, twelve new pledges were received into the fraternity: Terry L. Tolliver, John A. Oeffner, M. D. Braden, Marvin E. Fawks, Gary L. Lomax, Benny E. Divin, Robert H. Pahl, Donald L. Traut, Walter A. Edwards, William R. Bennett, William E. Rundle, and Kenneth J. Nissing.

In May, Beta Delta received a letter from Zeta chapter (University of Illinois at Urbana, IL) encouraging the members to contact their respective congressional representatives in regard to changes in the selective service law, which would be expiring at the end of the summer. One of the proposed changes was to eliminate graduate deferments. Zeta chapter had organized a committee to study this question, and the group urged others to voice their opinions. Zeta's letter argued that the graduate deferment should be retained because universities carried out much of the fundamental research for the country, and most of that research was conducted by graduate students. Moreover, in many fields, graduate students did much of the teaching of undergraduates as well as grading, tutoring and conducting labs. If substantial numbers of graduate students were drafted, the letter continued, the shortage of graduate students in the mid-sixties could become even more acute.[60]

Unfortunately, no record of Beta Delta's response exists. Zeta's pleas fell on deaf ears: the legislation renewing the draft eliminated the graduate student deferment entirely. Students became eligible for the draft once they had completed a four-year degree or turned 24, whichever came first. During this time the war in Vietnam had been escalating. The US had completed the building of its bases, and was poised, along with the South Vietnamese forces, to escalate its combat missions, which necessitated an increase in the number of draftees called up for service.

On December 3, Beta Delta welcomed a large group of new members. Twenty men—Gary L. Smith, Richard T. Divis, Donald L. Hovis, Gregory S. Allen, Donald L. Hornback, Larry D. Kennedy, David C. Mintner, Raymond C. Waggoner, Bradley W. Brice, Richard J. Fitzgerald, James L. Hull, Curtis A. Maune, John J. Zimmer, Paul E. Eckler, Charles J. Murray, David W. Hobelmann, Robert E. Kuhlmann, G. D. Freeman, Omar T. Stuenkel, and Darwyn E. Walker—were officially received at the initiation ceremony. For some unexplained reason, the chapter's own membership records listed three more—Bradley Brice, Keith LeRoy Gohlz, and Allen Smith.

Front Row: H. Hickenbotham (Treasurer), M. Hardy (Reporter), G. Thiessen, D. Parker (Treasurer), R. Sanders, G. McReynolds, E. Rapp. Row 2: F. Vogt, L. Mikelionis, W. Whelove, J. Latty, J. Throckmorton, G. Bauer, J. Link. Row 3: J. Youngman, H. Lewis, C. Johler, S. Hinchcliff, R. Palmer, E. Ross. Row 4: L. Koederitz, J. Jones, L. Zoellner, F. Jennings, R. Carlson, G. Mizer, J. Savage. Row 5: G. Wigginton, N. Ahmed, W. Eshbaugh, L. Young (Historian), G. Smith, J. Ziegenmier.

Beta Delta Chapter 1967—Rollamo 1967

1968

For several consecutive years Beta Delta members had earned Blue Key's highest award; 1968 would not be an exception. In February, Lenn Koederitz (Beta Delta '66) was named Blue Key's "January Man-of-the-Month." Koederitz's undergraduate work was in chemical engineering, and at the time of the award he was pursuing a Master's Degree in Petroleum Engineering. In addition to Alpha Chi Sigma, he was a member of Kappa Sigma (president), Circle K (Pledge Trainer and President), Blue Key (Alumni Secretary), Tau Beta Pi, M-Club, Scabbard & Blade, AIChE, and the Miner staff.[61]

Records for 1968 and 1969—presumed to have been discarded, but discovered recently—shed light on Beta Delta's everyday business during the final years of the decade. On April 28, 1968, the following were initiated into the fraternity: John M. Wilkins, Carl O. Schwanke, Stephen R. Close, Gregory K. Haseltine, Keith R. Troutman, Douglas M. Haseltine, Veo Peoples, Thomas H. Bell, Thomas J. Tate, Robert L. Vasquez, James H. Jones, Steven F. Lemasters, Ronald F. Scheff, Michael R. Hoff, Mark C B. Conrad, Harry

A. Burns, M. A. Mahrou, Robert M. Wellek, and William L. Tolle. Once again, national and local documents did not coincide perfectly. The National Office's records indicated that A. W. Smith and Keith L. Ashby were received into membership on January 1, 1968. And the Beta Delta Membership list included Keith R. Troutman among the April 28th inductees.

A few days later, on May 3, the Miner reported that two Beta Delta seniors achieved the highest grade point average of the semester—exactly the same average for both students. Perhaps this was not surprising since the students, Douglas and Gregory Haseltine, were twins. Both were also members of Tau Beta Pi and were studying chemical engineering at the time.[62]

Alpha Chi Sigma's 29th Biennial Conclave was held in Iowa City, Iowa, in the summer. Beta Delta was well represented. Benny Divin, Larry Kennedy, Edward Schneider, John Throckmorton, and Darwyn Walker—along with Dr. William Webb—attended. [63]

In the fall, Dr. Webb received especially good news on two fronts. On September 18, the Miner reported that he and two of his former students, Dr. Harry C. Hershey and Ronald D. Mitchell, were issued a United States patent for the separation of radioactive chemicals produced by nuclear fission. Dr. Webb, Chair of the UMR Department of Chemistry, explained, in the article, that the patent involved separating cesium and strontium, a process useful in medical research. The team's research was conducted at UMR under a contract with the United States Atomic Energy Commission. Dr. Hershey earned his PhD at UMR and was currently teaching chemical engineering at Ohio State University. Mitchell held an MS degree from UMR and was working in the nuclear reactor program of the US Army. A second patent was issued to Dr. Webb and another former student, Jerry Vie, at about the same time. It, too, involved the processing of radioactive materials. Vie (Beta Delta '55) earned his MS from UMR and was employed by the Mallinckrodt Chemical Works in St. Louis.[64]

Beta Delta held its first meeting of the fall on the same date as the Miner article, September 18. Master Alchemist Oeffner announced that committee chairs had been appointed and requested that members sign-up for the committees of their choice. In the meantime, Brother B. Divin summarized the Conclave he had attended in the summer. Each day of the Conclave, he explained, was divided into a morning session devoted to workshops on various topics and an afternoon session for business proceedings. He suggested that some of the ideas proposed during the workshops might be useful for Beta Delta members. He presented a long list of possible improvements: 1) Have slides of chapter activities to show at the Smoker, 2) Use faculty members as initiation participants when other faculty members were being initiated, 3) Sell safety glasses, 4) Publish a list of Alumni, 5) Achieve better relations between collegiate and professional chapters, 6) Look into the possibility of acquiring silver lapel pins for members, 7) Make it mandatory to have W. T. Schrenk's signature on pledge plaques, and 8) Keep graduate students on the collegiate rolls.

In addition, the members decided that the Regional Jamboree, which was also known as the Midwest Conclave, should be held on November 3 so all chapters would be able to attend and so pledges would be available to help. Brother D. Walker informed the group that the sweatshirts ordered the previous semester had arrived.[65] *(Note: it is interesting that the minutes of the meetings around this time began to use the title "Brother" more frequently and formally. This may just have been the personal preference of the Recorder at the time, but perhaps it reflected a more fundamental change in Beta Delta's culture.)*

The Smoker was held the following month. On October 16, 19 students were invited to pledge. However, by October 30, the date of the formal pledging, four candidates had declined the invitation for financial reasons. The first pledge project was cutting grass at Lions Park on the following Saturday morning (November 2) so the field would be ready for a Sunday football game.[66]

Throughout the month of November, Beta Delta, with Dr. Webb's authorization to utilize the necessary chemistry rooms and labs, worked with the Boy Scouts in their Chemistry Merit Badge Program. During this time, Beta Delta also initiated an investigation into the possibility of building a chapter house. Then, on November 24, 18 new initiates—Richard G. Chapman, James L. Diepenbrock, George Ban, Bizhan Binesh, Raymond W. Costello, John R. Turek, Victor J. Becker, Bruce T. Dreher, Keith D. Andersen, Richard K. Williams, Michael S. Sandella, Frank J. Doering,

Richard E. Morie, Lee E. Turpin, and Walter L. Conavay—were added to the membership roll. According to Beta Delta's membership records, three additional pledges—Robert W. Hill, Kenneth Moon, and Rodney Earl Jenkins—were also initiated. Beta Delta's ceremony took place in conjunction with Alpha Epsilon's reception; the combined banquet was held at Zeno's.[67]

Election of officers for the spring was held on December 4 to close out the semester. Those elected included: Benny Divin, Master Alchemist; Larry Kennedy, Vice-Master Alchemist; Tom Tate, Master of Ceremonies; Tom Bell, Recorder; Greg Allen, Reporter; Charles Murray, Treasurer; Keith Anderson, Alumni Secretary; and Lee Turpin, Historian. Also, during the meeting the following people volunteered to be on the Auditing committee: Terry Tolliver, Charles Murray, Lynn Zoellner, Darr Walker, Ron Scheff, Dave Mintner, and Vic Becker.[68]

Front Row: G. Smith, R. Fitzgerald, L. Zoellner, J. Faes (Vice-Master Alchemist), D. Parker (Master Alchemist), G. McReynolds (Historian), K. Nissing, E. Ross (Master of Ceremonies), J. Hull, B. Divin, (Reporter). Row 2: L. Kennedy, D. Braden, D. Freeman, G. Wigginton, T. Tolliver (Treasurer), T. Waltrip, W. Bennett, J. Zimmer, R. Divis, C. Murray. Row 3: K. Ashby, D. Minter, W. Edwards, (Alumni Secretary), I. Latty, R. Pahl, G. Thiessen, R. Palmer, A. Smith, G. Lomax. Row 4: J. Throckmorton (Recorder), D. Hornback, B. Brice, D. Hobelmann, R. Eshbaugh, J. Oeffner, G. Allen, D. Walker.

Beta Delta Chapter 1968—Rollamo 1968

1969

Installation of officers was the first order of business in the new year. At the January 7 meeting, Master Alchemist John Oeffner installed Benny Divin as the new Master Alchemist, who in turn installed the remaining officers. Dr. Webb then inducted the graduating seniors—Ali Mahrou, Bob Sanders, Bradley Brice, Jim Hull, Dave Hobelman, Bob Vasquez, Jack Zimmer, Richard Divis, Dave Mintner, and Don Hornback—into the Professional chapter. Committee assignments followed, and, with those, the chapter was set to execute its agenda for the semester.[69]

Spring 1969 Committees

Smoker	Refreshments	Membership	Outing
G. Ban (chair)	S. Lemasters (chair)	M. Turco (chair)	R. Costello (chair)
W. Conaway	K. Moon	R. Costello	R. Eshbaugh
K. Anderson		R. Williams	W. Conaway

Spring 1969 Committees Cont.

L. Turpin		K. Nissing	J. Oeffner
F. Doering		J. Wilkins	M. Conrad
B. Binesh		R. Turek	V. Becker

Initiation	Special Projects	Publicity	Banquet
T. Tate (chair)	J. Jones (chair)	C. Schwanke (chair)	K. Ashby (chair)
J. Oeffner	W. Edwards	R. Turek	W. Tolle
V. Becker	R. Morie	T. Tolliver	S. Close
G. Allen	L. Turpin		F. Doering
S. Close	J. Diepenbrock		T. Stuenkel
B. Fawks	T. Bell		

High Pressure*	Boy Scouts	Housing	Housing
J. Oeffner (chair)	P. Eckler (co-chair)	T. Dreher (chair)	J. Ziegenmier
T. Dreher	T. Tate (co-chair)	J. Oeffner	T. Bell
J. Wilkins	V. Becker	D. Walker	L. Zoellner
D. Walker	J. Ziegenmier	R. Pahl	
	L. Turpin	K. Anderson	
	D. Walker		

*created to follow-up on delinquent dues

The first notable event of the year was a regional meeting on March 1, hosted by the Rolla chapter, attended by chapters from Arkansas University, Washington University, and the University of Missouri at Columbia, honoring Douglas Haseltine, who had achieved academic excellence recognition the previous year and recently won first prize for a technical paper presented to the Rolla chapter of the American Institute of Chemical Engineers. That same week, the chapter finally voted to accept a petition of Alpha Rho colony at American University in Washington, D. C., for a charter—an issue it had not acted upon for several years. Later, on March 19 the Smoker was held. After a third vote on March 24—in an effort, perhaps, to follow up on brother Divin's suggestion the previous fall to get faculty members more involved in the local chapter—the members decided to approach Dr. Robertson, Dr. Nicholson, and Dr. Roach and offer them invitations to join.[70]

A meeting of the St. Louis Professional chapter took place that March as well—a meeting that would soon take on a great deal of significance for a fraternity like Beta Delta. Brother L. Zoellner, who attended the meeting in St. Louis, reported to the chapter on April 1 that the topic of sex discrimination had been discussed. Some delegates suggested that the constitution might have to be changed to remedy the issue, but the general consensus seemed to envision a sorority-like organization under the control of the National Chapter as a more feasible possibility. The issue of admitting women into the fraternity had very likely been raised in some places around the country, but this was the first record of the matter being discussed by Beta Delta members.

Formal Pledging took place on April 1, but before the ceremony, candidates for the "prestigious" Prof. Snarf award had to be chosen. The following professors were nominated from the Chemistry department: Raymond Venable, Prof. Stamfer, Robert Russell, James Stoffer, Hector McDonald, Prof. Hartke, Prof. Robertson, David Wulfman, and Prof. Carroll; from the Chemical Engineering department Russell Primrose, Gary Patterson, Orrin Crosser, Marshall Findley, Robert Wellek, Raymond Waggoner, Mailand Strunk, Carr, and Harvey Grice were nominated. (Apparently, all the chemistry and chemical engineering professors were equally "mean and nasty" toward their students.) With those selections out of the way, the following students were formally pledged: Vernon Alexander, Richard Bausell, Gerard Carron, Gerard Hoover, Anthony Mack, William Ott, Guy Robinson, Mike Thomas, and David Twellman. Evidently the professors who had been invited to pledge had declined.[71]

An important matter of establishing a chapter house, which the fraternity had discussed in late '68 came up again in the spring. At the April 16 business meeting, Brother Zoellner reported on the "housing" committee meeting which looked into the matter. Since the National organization would provide no financial support for a purchase, Zoellner explained that the possibility of renting a house was explored. Renting, he said, would require the commitment of at least 15 members each paying $32/month/person—a prospect that gained no traction at the time. (The issue re-surfaced in the early '70s, but it was considered infeasible then, too.)[72]

There would be one more honor bestowed on a Beta Delta affiliated faculty member before the end of the year. In April Dr. Wouter Bosch was honored for his meritorious service to UMR. On the 19th, the University of Missouri-Board of Curators approved the conferral of the emeritus degree on Bosch at their meeting in Columbia. Dr. Bosch (Beta Delta 1967) was appointed Director of the Graduate School in 1963 and became dean when the four schools at UMR were re-organized in 1965. He had joined the UMR faculty in 1958 as professor of paint and polymer chemistry.[73]

Chancellor Baker (right) confers the title of Dean Emeritus of the UMR Graduate School upon the venerable Dr. Wouter Bosch.

Rollamo 1969

The spring induction ceremony took place, as usual, at the end of April. Nine new members—Gerald L. Hoover, Guy M. Robinson, Vernon T. Alexander, David H. Twellman, William K. Ott, Gerard J. Carron, Anthony A. Mack, Michael B. Thomas, and Richard A. Bausell—were received into membership on April 27. The initiation banquet was held at Carney Manor in Rolla (Zeno's was not available).[74]

A week later, at a meeting on April 30, the new membership elected officers for the fall semester: Lynn Zoellner, Master Alchemist; Ray Costello, Vice-Master Alchemist; Mark Conrad, Master of Ceremonies; Keith Ashby, Recorder; and Tony Mack, Historian. A series of announcements followed—Brother J. Jones asked members to pick up their sweatshirts, Brother J. Oeffner called attention to the outing on May 17 at his home for the graduating seniors, and Brother Eshbaugh announced that the Senior Design Outing would be on May 12 at Lions Park.[75]

The spring semester ended with the installation of officers and the recognition of graduating seniors on May 7. K. Moon, G. Haseltine, D. Haseltine, J. Ziegenmier, D. Walker, T. Bell, T. Dreher, M. Fawks, R. Jenkins, L. Kennedy, J. Wilkins, T. Tate, J. Oeffner, T. Tolliver, V. Becker, W. Conaway, A. Smith, V. Alexander, W. Edwards, B. Divin, and R. Eshbaugh—an unusually large group of seniors—were installed into the Professional chapter.[76]

No activities were reported for the summer of 1969. And, for some reason, the first meeting of the fall semester was not held until October 1, at which the following committees were formed and chairs appointed: Smoker—F. Doering; Membership—K. Nissing; Initiation—S. Close; Banquet—W. Tolle; Outing—M. Hoff; Refreshments—G. Hoover; Safety—B. Binesh; Publicity—R. Bausell; Housing—D. Twellman; and Boy Scouts—M. Sandella. On October 15, special elections for VMA and Alumni Secretary were held. Carl Schwanke and Guy Robinson were elected to those positions respectively, but why a special election was necessary was not recorded in the minutes.

Earlier that fall, the Beta Delta leadership had taken stock of its service projects and decided to investigate other possibilities besides the usual Work Day activities, the Boy Scout Chemistry Merit Badge program, and the laboratory safety program. At the October 15 meeting, a special committee was appointed to explore a wider range of voluntary projects for future pledges. The committee—G. Hoover (chair), J. Jones, D. Twellman, L. Turpin, and M. Sandella—came up with a list of novel possibilities: paint the Phelps County Museum, present lab safety lectures for the high school, help the mentally disabled by taking them swimming at the Multi-Purpose building. Whether the chapter followed through on any of these suggestions is unclear, unfortunately, because of the paucity of records. One new project that the chapter did undertake, however, came from outside the fraternity. In mid-October, the UMR football coach requested that Beta Delta members conduct chemistry "help" sessions for students in the athletic department. Sadly, no record exists of any significant improvement in the grades of football players in their chemistry classes.[77]

On October 18, disaster struck on the UMR campus. Around 8pm, fire broke out in a basement storeroom of the Old Chemistry Building. Fire crews from Rolla and the neighboring St. James Fire Department were called in but were not able to control the fire until around 3:30am the following morning. The building was completely destroyed. The records of many research projects were lost, and documents and papers in professors' offices were burned. Beta Delta's office was in the building, but at the chapter's meeting a week after the fire, Brother M. Conrad reported that Beta Delta property was not damaged, and the chapter was able to continue with its "Work Day" and with the formal pledging of 28 prospective members on November 5.

At the end of the semester, on December 7, Beta Delta initiated one of the largest pledge classes in its history. Twenty-seven new members—Daniel C. Dugan, David R. Jones, Gordon D. Brannon, Bruce E. Varble, William W. Akin, Robert C. Reuter, K. D. Noel, , Stephen H. Hancock, Larry L. McCormick, Raymond J. Staebel, Lawrence U. Vidinha, James L. Gaddy, Neil L. Book, Jack R. Higgins, Mark E. Kaiser, Robert C. Meyer, Robert W. Boswell, Kenneth J. Tacchi, Richard J. Powell, Robert C. Haiducek, Lawrence J. Muskopf, Robert A. Zerbonia, Albert M. Lewis, Raymond H. Wildhaber, Edward A. Card, and Greg A. Janoch—were inducted. (Beta Delta's records also included Jeffrey Bushnell.) The banquet honoring the new initiates was held at Carney Manor in Rolla.[78]

Prior to the initiation, on December 3, volunteers were asked to form a committee to nominate Dr. Strunk for the Kuebler Award. Unfortunately, that effort was not successful. Two other committees were appointed at the meeting: Nominating—Costello, Turco, Twellman, Turpin, and Zoellner; and Audit—Costello, Jones, Becker, Sandella, and Bundle.[79]

On December 9, election of officers for the spring semester brought Beta Delta's business for 1969 to a close. Lynn Zoellner, the new Master Alchemist, would lead the chapter into the new decade. Keith Ashby as Vice-Master Alchemist, Steve Close as Master of Ceremonies, Benish Biszaha as Reporter, Guy Robinson as Treasurer, Frank Doering as Recorder, Robert Reuter as Alumni Secretary, and Jeffrey Bushnell as Historian, would round out the leadership team.[80]

By the end of the decade, several important membership issues had been resolved. The racial and ethnic discrimination of the 1950s and the expansion of the "chemical sciences" curriculum in the 1960s were no longer pressing matters as Bata Delta entered the 1970s. But one significant issue was waiting in the wings—the fraternity was still a "men's-only organization." Something would very soon have to be done about that.

Front Row: G. Allen, T. Bell (Recorder), B. Divin (Master Alchemist), L. Kennedy (Vice-Master Alchemist), C. Murray (Treasurer), D. Freeman. Row 2: S. Close, K. Ashby, R. Williams, K. Andersen, B. Binesh, R. Jenkins. Row 3: W. Tolle, A. Smith, G. Haseltine, R. Hill, D. Haseltine, W. Conway, R. Costello. Row 4: C. Schwanke, D. Walker, J. Oeffner, J. Jones, R. Eshbaugh, R. Turek.

Beta Delta Chapter 1969—Rollamo 1969

Excursus:

Dr. William H. Webb

See the Excursus for Chapter 6.

Dr. Mailand R. Strunk

Dr. M. R. Strunk, Chair, Department of Chemical Engineering

Rollamo-1966

Dr. Strunk joined the MSM faculty in 1957. He received his BS degree in chemical engineering in 1941 from Kansas State University, his MS degree in 1947 from MSM, and his Doctor of Science degree in 1957 from Washington University where he was an instructor of chemical engineering. Dr. Strunk was a member of the chemical engineering faculty at MSM-UMR for 22 years, 15 of which were spent as the Department Chair. He was the first Chair of the Chemical Engineering Department after its 1964 separation from the Chemistry Department.[81]

Strunk was a member of the American Institute of Chemical Engineers, the American Association for the Advancement of Science, and the Missouri and National Societies of Professional Engineers. He was also a member of many honorary and professional societies: Tau Beta Pi, Sigma Xi, AIChE, the American Society for Engineering Education, the National

Society of Professional Engineers, and Alpha Chi Sigma. He was listed in "Who's Who in Engineering Education," "Leaders in American Science," and "American Men of Science." In addition, he also served as president of the Rolla chapter of the Missouri Society of Professional Engineers. A Beta Delta member, he was initiated on December 18, 1942.[82]

Dr. Strunk passed away on June 2, 2008.

Dr. Dudley Thompson

Dr. Dudley Thompson-Missouri University of Science & Technology website.

Dr. Thompson joined the Missouri School of Mines Faculty in 1956 as a Chemical Engineering Professor and Chair of the combined departments of Chemistry and Chemical Engineering. From 1964-65, he was the Dean of Faculties and the Director for the School of Engineering and the Industrial Research Center. From 1973-74, he was Acting Chancellor, and in 1974 was named Vice Chancellor for the School of Engineering. He retired from that position in 1978. Dr. Thompson was initiated into Alpha Chi Sigma by Beta Delta in 1956.

His affiliations with other professional societies included a Fellowship with the American Association for the Advancement of Science and membership in the American Institute of Chemical Engineers, the American Chemical Society, the Acoustical Society of America, the American Institute of Mining, Metallurgical and Petroleum Engineers, the American Society for Engineering Education, the American Institute of Physics, the Institute of Electrical and Electronic Engineers, the American Association of University Professors, and the National Society of Professional Engineers.

Dr. Thompson also served a term as President of the Missouri Society of Professional Engineers. He was an American Society for Engineering Education Research Fellow, the Director of Applied Ultrasonic Research at Virginia Polytechnic Institute and at the University of Missouri-Rolla. He was a member of the Rolla Rotary Club, where he served as President. He was inducted into UMR's (Missouri S&T) academy for Chemical Engineering posthumously in 1996. In addition, he took an active role in the life of his church, serving as a Deacon and Chairman of the Board of Deacons. He and his wife, Le, became members of the Order of the Gold Shillelagh in 1996.[83]

Dr. Thompson passed away on July 27, 1996, at the age of 83.

Dr. Wouter Bosch

Dr. Wouter Bosch

Rollamo 1968

Before coming to UMR, Dr. Bosch served as chair of the Department of Paints, Varnishes and Lacquers at North Dakota State University, as Assistant Professor of analytical chemistry at Oklahoma State University, as a research chemist at Iowa State University, and as vice-president of H. Vettewinkel and Sons, Ltd. in Amsterdam, Holland. During his tenure at UMR he taught Polymer, Paint, and freshman chemistry courses, and the Summer Short Courses.

Dr. Bosch held a PhD degree in chemistry from the University of Minnesota and the State University, Utrecht, and BS and MS degrees from Utrecht. He was a member of the American Chemical Society, the American Chemical Society Division of Organic Coatings and Plastics Chemistry, the Royal Dutch Chemical Society, the Sigma Chi society, the Education Committee of the Federation of Societies for Paint Technology, the National Association of Corrosion Engineers, and the Arkansas Council of Painting and Decorating Contractors of America. He was also an honorary member of the St. Louis Society for Paint Technology and an honorary life member of the Missouri, Oklahoma, and Kansas State Councils of Painting and Decorating Contractors of America. In addition, Dr. Bosch was the Coordinator for the Corrosion Subcommittee for the Federation of Societies for Paint Technology.

Dr. Bosch was an author and co-author of numerous publications. He received the 1960 George Bauch Heckel Paint Industry Award and the 1964 service award of the St. Louis Coatings Society.

He retired near Puget Sound in Washington State, where he continued to be active in the community and in the lives of his wife, children and five grandchildren until his passing in 1988.[84]

Prof Snarf Award

The Prof. Snarf Award at UMR had its origin in the title character—Prof. Snarf—in the comic strip "Little Man on Campus," which was created by Dick Bibler, a fine arts student at the Univ. of Kansas. The strip first appeared in the Missouri Miner in 1952 and ran into the 1970s. Prof. Snarf, "the meanest, dirtiest, cruelest professor to ever live," was dedicated to making life as difficult as possible for his students.

According to the Miner's embellished version, the Prof. Snarf Award went to the UMR professor deemed to be the "meanest, cruelest, dirtiest Old Man to ever wield a shaft." Two of the earliest winners of this dubious honor were Dr. S. B. Hanna and Dr. "Ollie" Manual in 1965. According to the Miner, charitable "donations" were required to accompany student ballots to ensure that votes would be counted. Another recipient was Dr. Gary Patterson in 1973.[85]

Missouri Miner, January 15, 1965

Missouri Miner, October 1, 1965

Little Man on Campus-Missouri Miner, October 22, 1965

THE 1970s

...the King and Queen being begot togeathere
Being put presently in the Secret Prison,
Feed them with heavenly Dew; not Watry things

—*Thomas Rawlin, A Warning to the false Chymists
or the Philosophical Alphabet*

The Times

During the final years of the 1960s and the early years of the 1970s, life in America was viewed through the polarizing lens of the Vietnam War. For the first time in history Americans could see on a daily basis the toll of the conflict halfway across the world: firefights, body bags, casualty reports…. At home unrest manifested on the streets and campuses throughout the nation. Anti-war protests, riots, bombings of federal buildings, the resignation of a president, anxiety over the draft—all assaulted the consciousness of a war-torn people. But just as the United States was spared the ravages of WWII, Rolla did not experience any physical damages from the unrest. The toll on hearts and minds, however, was another matter. Fortunately, by 1975, with the evacuation of Saigon, the waging of the war was over, but the physical and psychological damage would be longer lasting.

University of Missouri-Rolla

In May of 1974, UMR dedicated the new Chemistry-Chemical Engineering Building on campus. Dignitaries who attended the ceremony included: Dr. Frank Conrad, Prof. Emeritus of the Department of Chemical Engineering; Dr. Mailand R. Strunk, Chair of the Chemical Engineering Building; Dr. J. Stuart Johnson, Dean of the School of Engineering; Dr. Walter T. Schrenk, Prof. Emeritus of both the Department of Chemistry and the Department of Chemical Engineering ; Dr. William H. Webb, Chair of the Chemistry Department; Dr. Adrian Daane, Dean of the College of Arts and Sciences; Dr. Dudley Thompson, former Chair of the Department of Chemical Engineering; Dr. C. Brice Ratchford and Dr. A. G. Unklesby, President and Vice-President of the University of Missouri; Mr. Irvin R. Fane, President of the Board of Curators; and Mr. Van O. Williams and Mr. John Sam Williamson, members of the Board of Curators. The keys of the building were presented to Dr. Ratchford who gave them to Dr. Thompson who, in turn, handed them over to Dr. Strunk and Dr. Webb.[1]

Alpha Chi Sigma

The beginning of the decade witnessed a sad historical moment for Alpha Chi Sigma. The last of the fraternity's founders, Joseph H. Mathews, passed away on April 15, 1970.[2]

For the most part, though, the Seventies were a time of hopeful changes and accomplishments for Alpha Chi Sigma. In the spring of 1976 the

Grand Recorder secured the services of Donald D. Dick and Associates to serve as the designer/architect for the new National Headquarters building in Indianapolis. That same year the Swedish Academy of Science announced that William N. Lipscomb was the recipient of the Nobel Prize in Chemistry. Dr. Lipscomb, an initiate of Alpha Gamma chapter (Kentucky), was recognized for his work with Borene compounds.[3]

Another positive occasion during the '70s was the first reactivation of a chapter since 1908 with Alpha Zeta of MIT returning to the fold in 1978. Alpha Zeta had withdrawn from the fraternity in the early '50s during the controversy over the discriminatory language in the Constitution and its members' dissatisfaction with the updated wording (see chapter 3).[4]

Later in the decade, in the fall of 1979, another brother would be the recipient of the Nobel Prize in Chemistry. Dr. Herbert C. Brown, honor initiate of the 25th Biennial Conclave held at Purdue in 1960, was named the winner of the coveted prize. Dr. Brown shared the award with Georg Wittig for their work using boron- and phosphorus-containing compounds in organic synthesis.[5]

Beta Delta: 1970

The most significant change, for Alpha Chi Sigma and for Beta Delta at the start of the decade—the change with the most lasting effects perhaps—was the admission of women to the fraternity. The late sixties were years of upheaval around the nation. During the protests and student activism on the country's campuses, the role of fraternities underwent serious examination. Were such organizations even necessary in the academic environment? Alpha Chi Sigma did not escape this scrutiny.

The routine business of the chapter continued as usual in the spring of 1970. The following committees and their respective chairs were appointed by Master Alchemist Lynn Zoellner at the February 18 meeting: Smoker (Greg Allen); Membership (Gerald Hoover); Initiation (Charles Murray, Mark Kaiser, and K. Noel); Banquet (James Diepenbrock); Refreshments (Raymond Wildhaber); Outing (Lawrence Vidinha); Special Projects (Raymond Staebel); Publicity (Gerard Carron); High Pressure (Victor Becker);

Safety (Ken Tacchi and Stephen Hancock); and Boy Scout (Mark Conrad). Zoellner also announced that the Conclave would be held August 16-20 at the University of Texas in Austin. In addition, a new reporter, Richard Fitzgerald, was elected. Other officers for the spring semester included: Keith Ashby, Vice-Master Alchemist; Frank J. Doering, Recorder; Guy Robinson, Treasurer; Stephen Close, Master of Ceremonies; Jeffrey Bushnell, Historian; and Robert Reuter, Alumni Secretary.[6]

A sign that Alpha Chi Sigma was still growing came to Beta Delta on March 4 when Master Alchemist Zoellner presented a petition for a charter from Eta chapter at the South Dakota School of Mines and Technology. Beta Delta voted in favor of accepting the petition. At the meeting, the chapter also decided to create a parliamentarian position, and MA Zoellner appointed Brother Lawrence Muskopf to that position. But the major focus of early March was the selection of pledges for the spring. In addition to the 19 potential candidates selected, professors Harvey Grice, Vincent Roach, and James Stoffer also passed the vote. The initiation date was set for April 26.[7]

Formal pledging, then, occurred on March 18. Professors Roach and Stoffer had declined to pledge, but Prof. Grice accepted. Before the formal pledging ceremony, however, business was conducted. During this meeting Brother Vic Becker reported that the Chemistry-Chemical Engineering help sessions were not going well; he requested that the chemistry professors post the help sessions in their classrooms. In addition, Brothers Gerald Hoover, Richard Fitzgerald, and Jeffrey Bushnell volunteered to be delegates to Conclave. Once again, there was no shortage of nominees for the Professor Snarf Award. Ray Waggoner, Orrin K. Crosser, J. Park, Gary Patterson, Robert Wellek, Samir Hanna, Robert Russell, David Wulfman, Donald Siere, and Ken Robertson—all made the list of mean, dastardly, professors. On April 1, Hoover was chosen as the delegate to Conclave with Bushnell and Robinson as first and second alternates, respectively.[8]

During the pledging period, what seemed to be a small matter at the time, but may have been a signal of a larger problem lying in the chapter's future, was the issue of hazing. The questioning of pledges by active members, when obtaining signatures for the pledge plaques, had become a matter of concern from the start of the semester. Some members felt that questioning pledges for longer than 30 minutes may have been perceived as a form of hazing, certainly not indicative of professionalism. In a meeting back on April 1, a motion had been made by Charles Murray that no active member other than the MA or VMA would be allowed to question pledges for longer than 30 minutes as a requirement for signing a plaque. That motion failed to pass, but it presaged changing attitudes toward pledging, and it foreshadowed actions that would be taken in the early 1980s.[9]

Leading up to the summer Conclave, the question of whether women should be included in the fraternity soon became the salient feature of discussions between Beta Delta members. If the fraternity was a professional fraternity, members started asking, why were women not included? If fraternities were losing legitimacy—and membership—as part of the anti-establishment mood running across college campuses, might not the admission of women accomplish a dual purpose? Not only did it seem to be the right thing to do, but it might also help address the membership decline. There were mixed feelings on the subject, of course.

The chapter reached a decision on the admittance of women at the April 15 meeting when it prepared the delegates for the upcoming Conclave. Before delving into that important issue, however, MA Zoellner read a letter from Grand Recorder James Miller, which congratulated Beta Delta for being the number one chapter in the fraternity. The members then approved a motion that Alpha Chi Sigma admit women into the fraternity as a sister organization. If the fraternity did not recommend a separate organization for women, however, the Beta Delta delegate was instructed to oppose the induction of women into the fraternity. It was ironic that despite members' opposition to the direct admission of women, an alumnus of Beta Delta (Ed Schneider) was the individual who orchestrated and won final approval for that very condition—a decision which ultimately convinced the Beta Delta delegate, and won the chapter's full endorsement. (See below.)[10]

As planned, the initiation ceremony for the spring was held on April 26 with the following new inductees: Gerald A. Nagel, Steven L. Walker, Phillip J. Tafra, Jonathan G. Beers, Stephen G. Majors, Kent R. Anderson,

Alan C. Van Deboe, Gary A. Schoenike, Harvey H. Grice, Michael L. Trancynger, Albert P. Cheng, Raymond O. Prenger, Michael R. McGath, and David E. Bachmann.

On April 29, when MA Zoellner shared the news with the full membership that Joseph H. Mathews, the last surviving member of the founders of Alpha Chi Sigma, had died on April 15, the chapter decided to donate $25 to the Mathews Education Foundation in his honor. The motion to do so was made by Keith Ashby.[11]

The spring semester closed with the installation of new officers and the Professional Recognition ceremony on May 6, an outing on May 9, and anticipation of the upcoming Conclave. The new officers for the fall included: Lee Hoover, Master Alchemist; Veo Peoples, Recorder; Guy Robinson, Treasurer; James Jones, Master of Ceremonies (Those elected to Vice-Master Alchemist, Reporter, Historian, and Alumni Secretary could not be determined).

When the issue of the admittance of women was addressed at the 1970 Biennial Conclave in the summer, the initial vote on the resolution failed. The champion who led the way through this controversy was GMA Edward P. Schneider, Jr. who worked out an agreement during the morning session that eventually secured the measure's passage. To win the votes of delegates from chapters which had objections, Schneider agreed to a concession which delayed the resolution's effective date until September 1, 1971. When the afternoon session was called to order, a Beta Delta delegate moved to reconsider motion 15 which admitted women into the fraternity with no strings attached. After considerable debate, the amended motion passed by a vote of 65 to 3 (with one abstention). (By September 1, 1971, nineteen women were recorded as full members of Alpha Chi Sigma. The last of the restrictive membership clauses was eliminated.)[12]

This momentous news from the Conclave was shared by MA Lee Hoover and Treasurer Guy Robinson at the first meeting of the fall semester on September 2. Other Conclave business reported to the chapter members included the sale of bound freshman chemistry exams, the dates for the upcoming Jamboree, the unlawful use of Alpha Chi Sigma letters and crest—which was apparently becoming a problem—and the announcement of the District Counselor's Efficiency Award winners: Beta Delta and Houston's Beta Omicron chapter. This was the highest honor that a non-house chapter could receive. But by far, the most significant news, of course, was the approval to initiate women into fraternity.

Before Beta Delta members had time to focus their attention on the ground-breaking decision by the delegates to the Conclave to accept women into the fraternity's membership, other semester-starting business had to be dealt with. First, the appointments of committee heads were made: Smoker—James Diepenbrock; Membership—Gerard Carron; Initiation—Stephen Hancock; Boy Scouts—Lynn Zoellner; Refreshments—Larry McCormick; Special Projects—Gary Schoenike; Publicity—Raymond Prenger; High Pressure—Jeffrey Bushnell; and Safety—Ken Tacchi. A special election for Master of Ceremonies was then held; James Jones was selected. It was also announced that the fall Jamboree would be hosted by the St. Louis chapter of Alpha Epsilon. With the consent of the Campus Book Store and the Chemistry Department Beta Delta was allowed to sell bound copies of past freshmen Chemistry exams. Dr. Kenneth Mayhan volunteered to discuss the matter of bound past exams with Dr. William Webb so they could be included with the books on the chemistry department faculty meeting agenda. Not only could these previous exam materials be helpful study guides for students, but they were also a reliable source of revenue for the chapter.[13]

At the month-end meeting on September 30, Beta Delta members decided to reinstate the chemistry help sessions, which had been suspended the previous April. Dr. Mayhan suggested that the sessions be organized by topics, but MA Lee Hoover explained that that would be difficult because three different texts were being used in the chemistry classes. Further, it was announced that the Boy Scouts would be meeting for the next three Saturdays, and that Lynn Zoellner and Vic Becker would assist them earn their chemistry merit badges. Unfortunately, the fraternity then made a decision which would have far-reaching, unintended consequences—a decision that would adversely affect the collective memory of the chapter in years to come. The group voted to destroy all chapter records over five years old and Conclave records over 6 years old.[14] (*This explains why there were no records from 1960-1965, and may also explain the dearth of records from the early 50s. Though the reason for the decision was not recorded, it may have been understandable if there were constraints on storage space.*)

On the same day of this meeting, the campus newspaper announced that preliminary plans were approved by the University of Missouri-Board of Curators for a new Chemistry-Chemical Engineering Building on the Rolla campus. This new structure would replace the Old Chemistry building which was destroyed by the fire in the fall of the previous year. The plans were to have the new facility built on the same site as the old one, and be attached to the existing Chemistry Building. The architect was Mantel, Steele and Teter Architects, Inc., of Kansas City, MO.[15]

On November 8, an additional 16 new members joined the fraternity: Jon L. Howell, George W. Cadwallader, Gary J. Fennewald, Jon L. Howell, Richard G. Kess, James C. Meng, Gary D. Bland, Albert R. Wampler, R. S. Kistler, Zebulun Nash, Craig L. Fadem, John T. Mason, William H. Burt, A. W. Cagle, Richard J. O'Hearn, and Ronald K. Dierolf. Gary Bland would later become the Missouri Valley District Counselor from 1974 to 1978. (The Missouri Valley District, of which Beta Delta was a member chapter, would later be renamed to the Midwest District.)

After the initiation ceremony, it was time to focus on preparations for the spring. Officers for the spring semester were elected on November 18: Guy Robinson, Master Alchemist; James Jones, Vice-Master Alchemist; Kenneth Tacchi, Reporter; Robert Haiducek, Recorder; Michael Trancynger, Treasurer; James Diepenbrock, Master of Ceremonies; Richard O'Hearn, Historian; and Zebulun Nash, Alumni Secretary.[16]

At the last meeting of the semester on December 2 several of the graduate students and faculty indicated they were willing to contribute to the loan fund for pledges (Evidently, a fund had been created earlier to help pledges with membership fees). The fund was controlled by the Master Alchemist, the Vice-Master Alchemist and the Master of Ceremonies, and could be used only for those pledges who pledged Alpha Chi Sigma. The meeting ended with the presentation of awards and installation into the professional chapter for the seniors, conducted by MA G. Robinson and

Dr. Webb. In addition, plaques were awarded to Brothers L. Zoellner and L. Hoover in recognition of their terms of office as Master Alchemists.[17]

Projects for the year once again included a campaign against laboratory accidents, the tutoring of underclassmen in chemistry and chemical engineering, and assistance to the local Boy Scout troop with their chemistry merit badge ventures.[18]

Front Row: B. Binesh, R. Fitzgerald, J. Bushnell, S. Close, K. Ashby, R. Reuter, Row 2: L. Muskopf, C. Murray, M. Sandella, R. Haiducek, G. Janoch, N. Book, D. Noel, Row 3: C. Schwanke, G. Allen, J. Diepenbrock, R. Meyer, K. Tacchi, L. McCormick, R. Staebel

Beta Delta Chapter 1970—Rollamo 1970

1971

Sometime near the dawn of the decade, Beta Delta was approached by a member like no other. While the prospective female pledges were still waiting in the wings, this lady's origins seem to have been lost in the fog of fading memories. One tradition had it that she was rescued (read stolen) from the Sigma Nu fraternity house across the street from the Chemical Engineering building. Her entry upon the stage of Beta Delta's historical drama was as if by some strange alchemical magic—as if Cagliostro, himself, were the conjurer. Ever since her misty beginnings, she has remained a permanent collegiate member of the chapter. Fondly known as Marsha, the AXΣ Sweetheart of "Pigma Nu," she was received into membership through what can be described only as an immaculate initiation perceived solely through the eyes of faithful alchemists. According to her lost "annals," Marsha has never missed a meeting or an initiation. For more than 50 years, she has been the perfect Beta Delta adept.

<<<< Marsha

So Marsha would have been present at Beta Delta's meeting on February 3. For years, UMR sponsored the annual science fair—the South Central Missouri Science Fair—an event aimed at aspiring high school students looking toward careers in the sciences or engineering. The fair invited students to develop and exhibit projects illustrating a particular scientific or engineering concept. At the meeting, Beta Delta decided to support the 1971 fair by contributing prize money to the first and second place awards. To carry out this decision and the other activities of the chapter, which included a resumption of tutoring services; development of a scrapbook of the chapter; provision of safety glasses and lab coats; assemblage of an organic exam book; and provision of cleaning services for the labs, an extensive system of committees was organized. The following officers headed up this arrangement: Guy M. Robinson, Master Alchemist; James Jones, Vice-Master Alchemist; Kenneth J. Tacchi, Reporter; Robert C. Haiducek, Recorder; Michael L. Trancynger, Treasurer; James Diepenbrock, Master of Ceremonies; Richard J. O'Hearn, Historian; Zebulun Nash, Alumni Secretary; and Kenneth Mayhan/Efton Park, Advisors.[19]

Spring 1971 Committees

Smoker	Membership	Initiation	Banquet
R. Wildhaber	D. Bachmann	J. Meng (chair)	A. Lewis (chair)
M. Kaiser (chair)		L. McCormick	G. Carron
J. Diepenbrock		G. Carron	K. Anderson
		R. O'Hearn	
		K. Anderson	
		K. Tacchi	

Boy Scouts	Refreshments & Outings	Special Projects and Safety
M. Sandella (co-chair)	S. Walker (co-chair)	D. Noel (chair)
V. Becker (co-chair)	W. Burt (co-chair)	N. Book
G. Fennewald	G. Cadwallader	J. Meng
R. O'Hearn	G. Bland	C. Fadem

Spring 1971 Committees Cont.

Publicity	High Pressure	Housing & Loan
G. Nagel (chair)	R. O'Hearn (chair)	J. Jones (chair)
G. Bland	V. Becker	G. Fennewald
		W. Cagle

Beta Delta Chapter of Alpha Chi Sigma, *Committees Spring 1971*, document. Beta Delta Archives.

On college campuses across the country during the late sixties and early seventies, students were becoming more socially aware of societal ills and more active in doing something about them. Members of Beta Delta became involved in some of those endeavors. Following the formal pledging of eight pledges, on March 17, for example, the chapter voted to join the inner city project in St. Louis on March 27. Unfortunately, the nature of this project was not recorded in the minutes, nor was the number of members who traveled to St. Louis to participate.[20]

On April 25, eight new members were initiated: Thomas D. Wichlinski, Thomas E. Burchfield, Roger E. Truitt, Dwight L. Deardeuff, Marvin T. Eaves, Ronald O. Bude, Robert E. Schwab, and Ronald W. Burkemper. Dr. Thomas Beveridge was the intended speaker; however, he was unable to attend due to an unspecified reason. In his place, Dr. Miller spoke at the banquet, which was held at Frederick's restaurant in Rolla.[21]

The election of officers for the fall was held on April 27 with the following results: Vic Becker, Master Alchemist; Richard O'Hearn, Vice-Master Alchemist; Raymond Wildhaber, Master of Ceremonies; Recorder, Robert Haiducek; and Tom Burchfield, Historian. The installation was held on May 5 along with the Senior Recognition ceremony conducted by Master Alchemist Vic Becker and Dr. William Webb.[22]

During the summer, Beta Delta members quietly laid plans to be the first chapter, or at least one of the first, to set an effective date for initiating women into the fraternity.

Consequently, Beta Delta was one of five chapters that sent—on the first day of eligibility in the fall of 1971—the first pledge election report with women on the list. When actual recording of membership roles were recorded on September 1, 1971, Beta Delta retained the distinction of being among the first chapters to initiate women for the first time. The three Beta Delta initiates—Carol (Langemach) Davies, Cecilia (Meyer) Freeman, and Patricia T. (Poertner) Deschler—became, along with 16 other women throughout the fraternity, the first women to join Alpha Chi Sigma. The other women initiated in 1971 were: Dr. Mary L. Willard, who had the distinction of being the first professional woman initiate (Nu-Penn State); Iris B. Ailin, Gloria Edwards, Elizabeth Fisher and Ellen Waldron (Alpha Rho -Maryland); Marian Kester and Mary Moore (Beta Eta-University of North Texas); and Alayne Adams, Beverly Alexander, Barbara Armstrong, Elizabeth Fisher, Milagros Madamba, Emily Palumbo, Lidia Roche, and Patricia Trzaskoma (Beta Upsilon-American University).[23]

The fruits of the ground-breaking legislation passed at the 1970 Conclave, then, were realized with incredible speed. And Beta Delta was at the forefront of this important movement. From this point on, women would play a prominent role in the workings of Beta Delta—whether as officers, as committee members and chairs, or through their individual contributions and achievements.

Looking back, Carol (Langemach) Davies reflected on her experience at that time:

> I was one of the first three women initiated into the Beta Delta Chapter of Alpha Chi Sigma on September 1, 1971. My recollections start about a year prior to that date.
>
> In the fall of 1970, I was invited to pledge Alpha Chi Sigma. I later learned about the role Beta Delta had played in allowing women to join the fraternity. The initial motion at the 30th Biennial Conclave in August, 1970, had failed. However, GMA Schneider (Beta Delta) was not ready to give up and he persuaded the Beta Delta delegates to reconsider. Gerald Hoover, Beta Delta's MA, made the motion to amend the measure to make it effective on September 1, 1971 and it finally passed.

The pledge class formed in the fall of 1970 with Victor Becker as the VMA and Pledge Master. Beta Delta sent the first pledge list to national with women listed, including Patricia Poertner, Celia Meyer, and Carol Langemach. Other members of the class included Gary Bland, William Burt, George Cadwallader, Gary Fennewald, Wayne Cagle, and others; I think there were about 15-18 of us.

I suspect that our pledging process was similar to those of the time. After the candidates were invited to pledge, we had about a month of weekly meetings to learn about the fraternity, both local and national. We had to learn the history of Alpha Chi Sigma and the Beta Delta Chapter, as well as other useless information that may or may not have been included in the final. We could be quizzed upon this information at any time by the actives. We created shingles (plaques) and were required to get signatures from the actives and some of them made it difficult. Initiation was a three-day event. On Friday, we met in the lecture hall in what was then the Chemical Engineering building and took the final.

After initiation, we all met at Zeno's Steakhouse for a celebration dinner. The three women completed the final station of initiation at 12:01 A.M. on September 1, 1971 and officially became full members of the Beta Delta Chapter of Alpha Chi Sigma. We always believed we were the first since it occurred at 12:01 but the national office only recorded the date and they list 19 women that were initiated on that date.[24]

Carol (Langemach) Davies — Rollamo 1973

Cecelia Meyer — Rollamo 1973

Pat (Poertner) Deschler — Rollamo 1972

In the fall, on October 31, ten additional initiates were received into membership: Neal A. Lewis, Thomas L. Ellison, Denis L. Stotler, Daniel L. Wallach, Gary A. Korzep, Andrew D. Simon, Michael B. Tibbits, Paul E. Erlandson, Jill E. (Senne) Giesick, and John E. Adams. (Adams would go on to serve as the Central District Counselor from 1993 to 1997 and then serve on the Supreme Council in 1998 as Grand Professional Alchemist from 1998 to 2000, as Grand Master Alchemist, from 2002-2004, and as Grand Parliamentarian from 2009 to 2022. He joined the faculty at the University of Missouri-Columbia in 1981 as Assistant Professor of Chemistry and became the advisor to the Delta chapter. He retired in 2015 as the Curator's Distinguished Teaching Professor Emeritus.)[25]

Front Row: C. Langemach; R. Morie, Historian; G. Robison, Treasurer; J. Jones, Master of Ceremonies; G. Hoover, Master Alchemist; V. Becker, Vice Master Alchemist; V. Peoples, Jr., Secretary; R. Reuter, Alumni Secretary; C. Meyer. Row 2: P. Poertner, J. Howell; G. Cadwallader; K. Anderson; M. Kaiser; M. McGath; R. Haiducek; G. Janoch; A. Wampler. Row 3: R. Dierolf; R. O'Hearn; A. Van Deboe; S. Majors; D. Bachmann; W. Cagle; L. Turpin; L. McCormick; K. Tacchi; D. Noel, Row 4: W. Burt, R. Kess; B. Varble; R. Wildhaber; J. Diepenbrock, Jr.; R. Prenger; M. Trancynger; Z. Nash; A. Lewis.

Beta Delta Chapter 1971—Rollamo 1971

1972

The search for Beta Delta's records for 1972 through 1974 was not successful. However, initiation records were readily available as well as an account of the bestowal of the John R. Kuebler award to Walter T. Schrenk. In addition, isolated records from diverse sources[26] revealed officer lists for the spring and fall, along with the spring committee assignments:

Spring 1972 Committees

Smoker	Membership	Initiation	Banquet
M. Kaiser	K. Tacchi	R. Dierolf	J. Senne
P. Erlandson	K. Noel	C. Langemach	P. Erlandson
N. Lewis	C. Fadem		

Boy Scout	Refreshments & Outings	Safety	Special Projects
V. Becker	R. Dierolf	M. Eaves	T. Burchfield
M. Tibbits	D. Wallach	T. Ellison	J. Howell
G. Fennewald		C. Meyer	C. Langemach
N. Lewis			

Spring 1972 Committees Cont.

High Pressure
S. Walker
M. Tibbits
M. Trancynger

Officers for the spring semester included: Dick O'Hearn, Master Alchemist; Ray Wildhaber, Vice-Master Alchemist; Gary Bland, Reporter; Carol Langemach, Recorder; Steven L. Walker, Treasurer; Jill Senne, Historian; and Mike Tibbits, Alumni Secretary. For the fall, the officers included: Victor Becker, Master Alchemist; Carol Langemach, Vice-Master Alchemist; Gary Bland, Reporter; Neal Lewis, Recorder; Steve Walker, Treasurer; Paul Erlandson, Master of Ceremonies; Andy Wilson, Historian; and Mike Tibbits, Alumni Secretary.

The first initiation of the year took place on April 23. Sixteen pledges—Robert L. Pike, Donald J. Siehr, Doug L. Bridges, Wayne R. Fischer, John M. Raley, Michael J. Kessler, Andrew J. Wilson, Charles W. Gehrke, Jerolyn M. Onstad-Wallach, David R. Evans, Jack C. Beers, Timothy T. Scruggs, Michael T. Moll, Patrick L. Mihalik, Alen F. Davidson, and Michael C. Greco—were inducted on that date.

By 1972, Dr. Schrenk had been retired for a decade, but he continued to be honored from all directions for his long and devoted service to the university. During the 31st Biennial Conclave, he was recognized as "Alpha Chi Sigma Man-of-the-Year" and presented with the John R. Kuebler Award for 1972. The Award ceremonies were held on June 14 in Bromley Hall in Champaign, Illinois. The award cited Dr. Schrenk's achievements both for the fraternity and throughout his professional career. Eighteen years earlier—in 1954—Schrenk had been elected to the highest post in the fraternity, Grand Master Alchemist. During his tenure in that position, the financial structure of the fraternity was strengthened and nine new chapters were installed. Upon completion of his term, he became the 20th member of the Order of Altotus. His extensive career of nearly 50 years in Chemistry and Chemical Engineering had established him as a prominent figure in his profession.

The last paragraph of the letter nominating Dr. Schrenk for the Kuebler Award best expressed the respect and fraternal love so many had extended to him:

> *Not nearly enough can be said for this man. In a sense, his record alone speaks very highly, but there must be something more than mere tangible attainments. You must give time to your fellow men. The little things, in which you do something for those who have need of man's help, something for which you get no pay and recognition, but the privilege of doing it, enriches your life and others. Dr. Schrenk remembered that he didn't live in a world all by himself. It is this altruistic attitude that he has carried with him throughout his life that has made him such a great man and earned the admiration and respect of countless people. For these reasons I so strongly nominate Dr. Schrenk, for this is the life he has lived for, worked for and achieved.*[27]

On November 12, another 17 were brought into the fold of Alpha Chi Sigma: Daniel L. Million, Stephen L. Patton, William J. McGranahan, Leo J. Scherrer, Robert F. Peterson, John S. DeGood, Keith J. Lissant, James J. Barbarito, Michael J. Quinn, Gary L. Declue, Raymond A. Freeman, Lindell E. Whaley, James R. Dollar, Gary D. Loud, David J. Suiter, Louis Biolsi, and Thomas K. Mills.

No additional women pledged in 1972, but two women held office during the year: Jill Senne was elected Historian, and Carol Langemach, Recorder. Carol would become the first female Vice-Master Alchemist and pledge master for the chapter the following spring semester.

The 1970s 253

Row1: R. Wildhaber, Vice-Master Alchemist; M. Tibbits, Alumni Sec.; J. Senne, Historian; R. O'Hearn, Master Alchemist; C. Langemach, Recorder; S. Walker, Treasurer; G. Bland, Reporter. Row 2: C. Meyer; J. Howell; P. Erlandson; D. Bachmann; K. Tacchi; J. Adams; D. Noel; C. Fadem. Row 3: K. Anderson; R. Kess; V. Becker; W. Cagle; M. Trancynger; N. Lewis; G. Fennewald

Beta Delta Chapter 1972—Rollamo 1972

1973

In the spring of 1973, Beta Delta was led by Gary Bland, Master Alchemist; Carol Langemach, Vice-Master Alchemist; John Adams, Reporter; Paul Erlandson/Jack Beers, Master of Ceremonies; David Suitor, Historian; Bob Dollar, Alumni Secretary; and Dr. Don Beistel, Advisor.

On April 1—all jokes aside—the following 15 pledges really were initiated: Joseph E. Connell, Robert T. Jackson, Ain Utt, Steven R. Felstein, Guy C. Rogers, Richard P. Yenzer, Robert L. Scharringhausen, John M. May, Charles A. Hillhouse, Douglas E. Ecoff, Mark D. Algaier, Anthony D. Messina, Laura W. (Webber) Blaser, Dennis M. Valentino, and Jon R. Townsend.

The officers for the fall semester included: Jack Beers, Master Alchemist; Andy Wilson, Vice-Master Alchemist; Tom Ellison, Master of Ceremonies; John Adams, Reporter; Dan Million, Recorder; Gary Korzep, Treasurer; John DeGood, Assistant Treasurer; Guy Rogers, Alumni Secretary; and Joe Connell, Historian.

One of the proposals from the fall of 1973 that survived the destruction of records at the time was to revive the idea of establishing a fund intended to provide loans for pledges who declined to join simply because of cost.[28] According to the plan, the loan would provide $25-$70 at a minimal interest rate. To ensure that no financial risk to the fraternity would be involved, pledges would be carefully screened on the basis of need and genuine interest in joining, and funds would be solicited only from alumni. The oversight committee would consist of the MA, VMA, Treasurer, Chapter Advisor and one professional member. Whether this idea was ever formally adopted—and actually put into practice—is, unfortunately not in the record.[29]

On November 11, 21 new members—Richard G. Schafermeyer, Steven J. Calvin, Shelley J. (Nugent) Claudin, David A. Barclay, Patricia A. Doyle, Gary A. Chappell, Roberta (Wilhelm) Treasurer, Thomas M. O'Connor, Robert P. Jansen, Gary L. Foutch, James D. Hauser, Terry R. Coffman, Judith L. Flebbe, Steven C. Peppers, Jerry L. Chancellor, Michael J. Wilhelm, Kathryn E. (Ogden) Payne, Stephen E. Hale, Lawrence S. Molina, Gary R. Fischer, and Stephen L. Chilton—were initiated into the fraternity. Five of them were women. Fischer would later become the District Counselor from 1984 to 1986 for the Midwest District, of which Beta Delta was a member.

Row 1: T. Jackson, P. Erlandson (MC), J. Adams (Reporter), C. Langemach (Vice-Master Alchemist), G. Bland (Master Alchemist), J. Beers (MC), D. Suiter (Historian), R. Dollar (Alumni Secretary), T. K. Mills. Row 2: R. Scharringhausen, R. Yenzer, L. Webber, J. De-Good, C. Meyer, L. Whaley, T. Ellison, K. Lissant, Mike Moll, T. Messina. Row 3: J. May, M. Quinn, G. Loud, A. Davidson, T. Burchfield, N. Lewis, D. Million, R. Pike, C. Hillhouse

Beta Delta Chapter 1973—Rollamo 1973

1974

1974 was a year when much was revealed. For some, the revelation was more information than desired; for others it was a welcome delight. Streaking became a favorite past-time all over the country—yes, even at UMR. In friskiness and utter abandonment, men and women ran across the campus in "full glory" to the surprise of any and all on-lookers—and to the consternation of the campus police. Records do not indicate the number of Beta Delta members who participated in this eye-opening fad, but it is likely that many of them—either as viewers or doers—did. Yes, 1974 was a memorable year.[30]

Despite such distractions, the fraternity went about its usual business. The following people stepped into leadership roles at the start of the year: Dan Million, Master Alchemist; Dave Suiter, Vice-Master Alchemist; Tom Ellison, Master of Ceremonies; Mike Quinn, Reporter; Tony Messina, Recorder; John DeGood, Treasurer; Tom Jackson, Alumni Secretary; and Jerry Chancellor, Historian. [31]

From 1974 on, women constituted a sizeable portion of the pledge classes, even if the classes were small. The group initiated on March 24 was a good example; half of the six initiates—Michelle A. Robeson, Keith A. Schuette, Debra M. (Kersting) Brzuchalski, Nicole L. Talbot, Timothy G. Bradley, and Douglas R. Powell—were women. Pledge master for this class was VMA Dave Suiter.

The lack of meeting minutes and coverage by the Miner prevented a recounting of the events of the spring and fall semesters.

In the fall, Beta Delta was placed in the capable hands of the following officers: Tony Messina, Master Alchemist; Gary Fischer, Vice-Master Alchemist; Mike Quinn, Reporter; Michelle Robeson, Recorder; Dave Barclay, Master of Ceremonies; John DeGood, Treasurer; Bob Jackson, Alumni Secretary; and Steve Chilton, Historian. The following committees were chosen:

Fall 1974 Committees

Advisory	Auditing	Membership	Scholarship
Dr. Beistel (Advisor)	G. Fischer (chair)	G. Fischer (chair)	T. Messina
T. Messina	D. Suiter	T. Ellison	D. Million
J. DeGood	R. Peterson	D. Suiter	M. Quinn
G. Bland	B. Pike	N. Talbot	

Safety	By-Laws	Budget	Smoker
T. Messina	J. Flebbe	T. Messina	D. Valentino (chair)
T. Ellison	G. Chappell	J. DeGood	P. Doyle
D. Powell	M. Quinn	R. Peterson	B. Jansen
N. Talbot	P. Doyle	T. Ellison	
T. Bradley		G. Fischer	
T. Mills		G. Bland	

Parliamentarians: J. Flebbe, D. Million, T. Mills

Fall 1974 Committees Cont.

Initiation	Banquet	Refreshment	Chapter Room
D. Million	L. Webber (chair)	D. Kersting	G. Fischer (chair)
T. Ellison	J. DeGood	S. Chilton	P. Doyle
G. Fischer	K. Ogden	T. Coffman	S. Chilton
T. Coffman		G. Foutch	K. Schuette
J. Flebbe		K. Schuette	R. Schafermeyer
T. Mills			
D. Kersting			
B. Pike			
K. Schuette			
N. Talbot			
D. Powell			

Note: Publicity Committee: G. Chappell, R. Schafermeyer, D. Ecoff, and M. Robeson. There also heads of the special projects, which included: G Chappell, Boy Scouts; B. Pike and T. Burchfield, Snarf Award; T. Bradley, Signs; and T. Messina, S. Chilton, and T. Burchfield, Alpha Chi Sigma Box [32]

The Biennial Conclave—the 32nd in the fraternity's history—was held late in 1974. Delegates convened on October 4-7 in College Park, Maryland. Dave Barclay, Beta Delta delegate, along with Gary Bland attended.

On October 12, during the Homecoming weekend, Dr. Schrenk had the honor of presenting two watercolor paintings of the Rolla Building and the old Chemistry Building to the Chemistry and Chemical Engineering Departments. The artist, Ms. S. Atkinson, had rendered the paintings from photographic reproductions of the buildings. The paintings were a donation from Mr. and Mrs. Hans E. Schmoldt of Bartlesville, OK. Schmoldt, president of Schmoldt Engineering, received a degree in Chemical Engineering from the Missouri School of Mines and Metallurgy in 1944.[33]

Dr. W.T. Schrenk presenting watercolors of the Rolla and Old Chemistry Buildings
Left to right: Mailand Strunk, Jimmy Schmoldt, Walter Schrenk,
Hans Schmoldt, William Webb

A month after Homecoming, on November 17, eleven men and women were inducted into the fraternity: Melanie M. (Miller) Naeger, James D. Wood, Steven D. McGinley, Bruce E. Poling, Charles F. Cooper, Rosa L. Herman, Patricia D. (Blankenship) Chilton, Steven F. Meyer, Karla K. Stephens, Suzanne E. (Duncan) Norberg, and Dean M. Anderson. Once again, almost half of the initiates were women.[34]

The 1970s

Row 1: D. Million (Master Alchemist), D. Suitor (Vice-Master Alchemist), J. DeGood (Treasurer), M. Quinn, T. Messina. Row 2: L. Molina, G. Loud, R. Pike, L. Webber, K. Ogden, W. McGranahan, J. Flebbe, Dr. Beistel (Advisor), D. Barclay. Row 3: G. Fischer, J. Beers, J. Adams, T. Coffman, C. Hillhouse, G. Foutch, G. Chappell, R. Jansen, S. Hale, R. Schafermeyer, S. Calvin, S. Chilton, T. Mills, N. Lewis, T. Jackson, R. Raley, A. Wilson, M. Kessler.

Beta Delta Chapter 1974—Rollamo 1974

1975

Much initial business was undertaken at the beginning of the year to start off the spring semester. Under the direction of the following officers—Dave Barclay, Master Alchemist; Tom Mills, Vice-Master Alchemist; Michelle Robeson, Reporter; Suzanne Duncan, Recorder; Mike Quinn, Master of Ceremonies; Bob Peterson, Treasurer; Steve Meyer, Historian; and Chip Cooper, Alumni Secretary, and Dan Million, Parliamentarian—a lengthy list of committee appointments was drawn up at the January 13 meeting to ensure that all the activities and events would be properly planned and successfully carried out.[35]

Spring 1975 Committees

Advisory	Auditing	Membership	Scholarship
Dr. Beistel (Advisor)	T. Mills (chair)	T. Mills (chair)	D. Barclay
D. Barclay	A. Messina	J. Flebbe	M. Quinn
R. Peterson	K. Schuette	G. Fischer	D. Million
G. Bland	P. Blankenship	D. Kersting	A. Messina
	L. Webber		P. Blankenship

Safety	By-Laws	Budget	Smoker
D. Barclay	D. Million (chair)	B. Peterson (chair)	J. Flebbe
Dr. Beistel	D. Powell	D. Barclay	G. Fischer
G. Fischer		G. Bland	S. Nugent
M. Miller		J. DeGood	R. Jackson
S. Duncan		S. Nugent	

Initation	Banquet	Refreshment	Chapter Room
D. Million (chair)	M. Quinn (chair)	N. Talbot	G. Fischer (chair)
N. Talbot		P. Blankenship	D. Kersting
J. Flebbe		G. Fischer	K. Schuette
S. Duncan			S. Nugent
D. Powell			R. Jackson
			D. Powell
			M. O'Conner
			D. Ecoff

In addition to these standing committees, several special projects committees were also set-up: Boy Scouts—Dave Suiter (chair), Joe Connell, Bob Jansen, and Mike Quinn; Snarf Award—Chip Cooper (chair), Patty Doyle, and Gary Chappell; Signs—Nicki Talbot; and Beta Delta Data—Doug Powell (editor), Chip Cooper, Steve Meyer, and Suzanne Duncan. With these officers and committees in place, Beta Delta finalized its schedule of activities for the semester: Boy Scout Program, Chemistry Help Sessions, Chapter Room improvements, Work Day (March 22), Science Fair (April 5), the initiation of pledges (April 20), and the Professional Recognition ceremony (April 30).[36]

By the end of January, the chemistry help sessions and the Boy Scout program were well underway. M. Quinn reported at the meeting on January 29 that the assistants at the chemistry help sessions were swamped and seeking additional volunteers. In addition, MA D. Barclay reported that the Boy Scout merit badge meetings had been scheduled. One final action taken by the members was the vote in favor of accepting the Arizona chapter's petition, despite reservations that the chemists outnumbered the chemical engineers in Arizona.[37]

One of the chapter room improvement projects, which was meant to be a stand-alone task, took on a life of its own. Like the ashtray project of the late 1930s and early 1940s, the decision to paint the room morphed into a much more complex adventure than anyone anticipated. On April 5, members painted the walls gold and the trim blue. Evidently, some of the painters thought themselves comparable to fine artists. At least that was Gary Fischer's assessment when he surveyed their work. There would definitely need to be further improvements in the chapter's meeting room.

By 1975, the impact of women on the chapter had significantly increased, not only in committee assignments, but in elected positions as well. In addition to the election of Mike Quinn as Master Alchemist and Keith Schuette as Vice-Master Alchemist, at the meeting on April 16, four women were chosen by the membership as officers: Debbie Kersting as Assistant Treasurer, Laura Webber as Master of Ceremonies, Melanie Miller as Recorder, and Shelley Nugent as Historian.[38]

On April 20 three new members—Robert J. Naeger, Rita M. (Webber) Stevens, and Theodore L. Beresik—were initiated into the fraternity. Dr. Don Beistel was the featured speaker at the banquet, which was held at Howard Johnson's on the Sunday evening following the induction ceremony.

Nine days later, on April 30, just before Beta Delta wrapped up its semester with a few final activities, Saigon, Vietnam, came under attack by North Vietnamese forces. Although the United States had withdrawn most of its forces in 1973 after signing the Paris Peace Accords, approximately 5000 Americans remained, including diplomats working at the U. S. Embassy. The North Vietnamese army had been steadily capturing towns and cities in South Vietnam throughout March and April, during which time U.S. forces had been evacuating thousands of Americans. On April 29, 1975, North Vietnamese troops shelled Saigon's Tan Son Nhut Air Base, which prevented planes from landing in Saigon and triggered the evacuation of the capitol. With the sea lanes also blocked, the only option for evacuation was a helicopter airlift. After the defense attaché compound was attacked, the U.S. embassy became the sole departure point for helicopters. From April 29th to April 30th, helicopters landed at 10-minute intervals at the embassy compound, including on the embassy roof. With some pilots flying for 19 hours straight, over 7,000 people were evacuated, including 5,500 Vietnamese, in less than 24 hours.[39]

Evacuation from the roof of the US Embassy-Saigon 1975

At the end of the spring semester Ed Schneider presided over the professional recognition ceremony on April 30 for the graduating seniors, a large group which included: Laura Webber, Doug Powell, Steve Meyer, Chuck Hillhouse, Bob Jackson, Dennis Valentino, Mike Quinn, and Doug Ecoff. Following the ceremony, District Counselor Gary Bland, in a state of concern because Mike Quinn would become MA, presented the chapter with a copy of the "Philosopher's Stone" in the hopes it would guide the members through the troubles that would be coming. Because Quinn was so dedicated to the chapter and took matters so seriously, he was a target of brotherly teasing.

This was also the time for final words and announcements before the semester ended. The chemistry help sessions were declared a success, and all the aides were congratulated. It was announced that Dr. Bruce Poling had won the "coveted" Prof. Snarf Award in the Chemical Engineering department. However, in the Chemistry department, the vote ended in a tie between Professors Hanna and Biolsi. Other humorous awards and titles were handed out. Immediately following the meeting, a special meeting—which by this time, had become a custom following the last meeting of the semester—was called to order at 8:02pm by newly elected MA Mike Quinn for the sole purpose of passing one motion. Judy Flebbe moved that "Rolla sucks." The motion passed unanimously, and the meeting adjourned at 8:04pm.[40]

In the summer interlude between the spring and fall semesters, the only recorded activity was the intramural softball tournament. The Alpha Chi Sigma team took second place, but the championship team was not recorded.

The fall semester of 1975 opened with a meeting on September 3, which began with a series of announcements signaling upcoming activities. Noteworthy was the announcement that Beta Delta alumnus John Adams had become Master Alchemist at Sigma chapter in Berkeley, CA. He transferred there after graduating from UMR in 1974 with a BS degree in Chemistry (Summa Cum Laude) to work on a doctorate degree, which he earned in 1979. His dissertation was titled, "Topics in Bound-State and Dynamical Processes: Semi-classical Eigenvalues, Reactive Scattering Kernels and Gas-Surface Scattering Models."[41] Another important announcement concerned two regional leadership conferences that would be held for the Central District—one in Indianapolis, IN, September 26-28 and another in Rolla, November 6-8. Since Grand Recorder James Miller would be attending, Dr. Beistel—with his customary sardonic sense of humor—urged everyone who would be attending to get sufficient training, particularly in the art of drinking, so they would be able to keep up with GR Miller's tippling skills. In fact, Miller had designed the conferences as training seminars for collegiate officers in order to bring the "Conclave Experience" to a larger audience. The first of these Leadership forums was held at State College, PA. All of Beta Delta's officers were required to attend one of the two conferences.[42]

Two major concerns dominated the discussion at Beta Delta's September 3 meeting—the chapter room paint job and the record-keeping issue. Even though the members appreciated the freshly painted walls, something more was needed for the chapter's comfortable "center of unity." The room required drapes, venetian blinds, a couch, and, as Dave Barclay pointed out emphatically, an Alpha Chi Sigma Flag.

The second problem that received an airing at the meeting was the fraternity's lack of an adequate method for recording and retaining its history. Gary Fischer moved that a filing system be started and that it be maintained at all times. But "what happens to files when students leave?" some members wanted to know. The motion was ultimately defeated—after a lengthy discussion—since no viable solutions were offered for specific unforeseen problems like space issues and the ownership of keys. These logistical issues surrounding record retention very likely contributed, at least in part, to the frequent gaps in the fraternity's archives. Eventually, the loss of the chapter room entirely, because of facility constraints imposed by the college, further complicated the storage of records.[43]

The fall activities were many and varied; they kept the following committee members, as well as others in the chapter, extremely busy.

Fall 1975 Committees

Advisory	Auditing	Membership	Scholarship
Dr. Beistel	K. Schuette (chair)	K. Schuette (chair)	D. Barclay (chair)
M. Quinn	M. Quinn	D. Suiter	M. Quinn
R. Peterson	D. Kersting		A. Messina
G. Bland	P. Blankenship		
R. Pohl			

Budget	Safety	Smoker	Initiation
R. Peterson (chair)	M. Miller (chair)	L. Webber	P. Blankenship (chair)
M. Quinn	T. Burchfield	S. Claudin (nee Nugent)	G. Fischer
G. Bland	C. Cooper	S. Duncan	M. Miller
D. Kersting		T. Beresik	T. Beresik

Fall 1975 Committees Cont.

Budget Cont.	Safety Cont.	Smoker Cont.	Initiation Cont.
R. Naeger			L. Blaser
G. Fischer			N. Talbot
			R. Naeger
			A. Messina
			M. O'Conner

Banquet	Refreshments	Chapter Room	Parliamentary Procedure & Constitution
M. Robeson (chair)	G. Fischer	G. Fischer (chair)	A. Messina (chair)
	S. Claudin	M. O'Conner	J. Flebbe
	D. Suiter		N. Talbot
			P. Blankenship
			T. Mills

Several events—the Smoker on September 25, a safety inspection on September 27, an outing at Lions Club Park on September 28, and the start of the chemistry help sessions—highlighted the rapid pace of Beta Delta activity that would not subside until the semester break for the Christmas holidays. And several other unplanned events required even more participation. Members responded to a request by the UMR Engineer magazine for an article about Alpha Chi Sigma and to the Counseling Office's need for tutors in addition to those in the chemistry help sessions. Ted Beresik, with the help of Mike Quinn, Chuck Hillhouse, Tom Burchfield and Steve Calvin, arranged an impromptu safety slide show. Amidst the plethora of activities, the pressing concern for a chapter room flag was not forgotten. Judy Flebbe, Michelle Robeson and Melanie Miller volunteered to make one.[44]

Formal Pledging took place on October 1. The new pledges included: William Campbell, Rita Stockhecker, Bradley Wyatt, David Levings, James Pucket, David Scharf, Michael Hardesty, DeWayne Gerber, Kent Sooter, Sherry Storer, and Lee Wehmeier. (Tram Dinh Hung, Yung Mi Yang and Gene Kerls also pledged but then de-pledged at a later date.) Kent Sooter was selected as the pledge captain.[45]

The pace of activities quickened even more in November. Beta Delta hosted the first of Jim Miller's (GMA 1966-68; Grand Recorder 1968-80, Grand Historian 1988-90) Leadership Conferences on November 6-8, a considerable undertaking for the local chapter. The entire Supreme Council and the Grand Recorder attended the sessions, affording the pledges the opportunity to have their plaques signed by the Grand Chapter Officers. Whether any Beta Delta members were able to keep up with Miller in the social activities which presumably followed the Leadership sessions—the records do not disclose. The result of Dr. Beistel's warning is lost to history.[46]

There was no pause for relaxation on the heels of the Conference. On the very next day, November 9, preparation of the pledge final examination was held at VMA Schuette's apartment. On November 13, the pledges sang for the Chemistry and Chemical Engineering secretaries. The pledge final was held on November 14, and the initiation followed on November 16. Also during the month, a lab inspection was performed (results were reported to Dr. Webb), Work Days and Mass Transfer events were held, Bob Jansen was married on November 15, and VMA Schuette threw a BYOB party after the basketball game on November 21—a spectacular party according to many of the attendees. Unfortunately, Brother Schuette swore he had no memory of it.[47]

On November 16, the following new members were initiated: H. Kent Sooter, Lee M. Wehmeier, William T. Campbell, Sherry L. (Storer) Vonklemen, David R. Scharf, Bradley J. Wyatt, James L. Puckett, Rita S. (Stockhecker) McMinn, Michael D. Hardesty, DeWayne C. Gerber, and D. Mitch Levings.[48] The banquet honoring the initiates was held at the Oak Meadows Country Club in Rolla. An interesting milestone in the history of Beta Delta was reached when one of the members of this pledge class was inducted into the fraternity. DeWayne Gerber was the 1000th member to join the Beta Delta family. He—and another member of the class, D. Mitch Levings—would advance to important positions on the Supreme Council in future years. Gerber joined the Council in 1986 as Grand Collegiate Alchemist, serving in that capacity until 1988. He then became Grand Master of Ceremonies in 1990 and held that office until 1992 when he became Grand Master Alchemist, a position he held until 1994. He also served as the District Counselor for the Texas Southern District—comprised of

Beta Eta, Beta Theta, Psi, and Beta Omega chapters—from 1984 to 1986. Levings first served on the Council as Grand Master of Ceremonies, 1984-1988, and then went on to serve as Grand Master Alchemist from 1988-1990. He is currently the Grand Historian for the fraternity, assuming that position in 1990. He was also District Counselor for the Texas Southern District from 1982 to 1984.[49]

Election of officers for the spring semester was held on November 19. Those elected were: Judy Flebbe, Master Alchemist; Terry Coffman, Vice-Master Alchemist; Keith Schuette, Master of Ceremonies; Debbie Kersting, Treasurer; Rita (Webber) Stevens, Reporter; Rita (Stockhecker) McMinn, Recorder; Suzanne (Duncan) Norberg, Alumni Secretary; and Brad Wyatt, Historian. This election demonstrated the profound impact women were having on the fraternity. Within only a few short years, female representation in the chapter increased from just a few active members in the fall of 1971 to a majority of office holders for the spring of 1976.[50]

At the final meeting of the semester on December 3, the Professional Recognition Ceremony was held to honor Gary Foutch. Dr. Webb conducted the ceremony. The result of the basketball game between the students and the faculty—a lopsided affair won handily by the students, 60-38—was also announced at this final meeting before the holidays. Terry Coffman, the hero for the student team, who scored 35 points in the victory, was extended special—well-deserved—accolades.

Of course, the very last meeting, as always, was the brief session held immediately after the final meeting of the year. This time, Chip Cooper made the brusque motion that "Rolla sucks." The motion carried and the meeting was adjourned. Beta Delta members took a welcomed respite; they'd be rested and ready for the next round of activities in the spring.[51]

Top row, l to r: T. Messina, G. Fischer, M. Quinn, D. Barclay, B. Jackson, M. Robeson, S. Chilton, J. Flebbe, T. K. Mills, Dr. D. Beistel, G. Foutch, S. Meyer, T. Bradley, B. Peterson, G. Chappell, C. Cooper, T. Coffman, D. Ecoff; Second Row: S. Calvin, N. Talbot, P. Blankeship, R. Schafermeyer, M. Miller, D. Anderson, B. Jansen, P. Doyle, S. McGinley, G. Loud; Third Row: R. Herman, L. Webber, T. Burchfield, J. Connell, K. Schuette, D. Powell, C. Hillhouse; Fourth Row: S. Duncan, D. Million, D. Suiter, T. Ellison.

Beta Delta Chapter 1975—Rollamo 1975

1976

Newly elected Master Alchemist Judy Flebbe, the first woman to hold that position for Beta Delta, presided over the chapter for the spring semester, which, like the previous semester, became a bustle of activity. The immediate focus, of course, was on the establishment of a pledge class. The Smoker was held on February 21 at Dave Barclay's home, followed by the third vote on February 23, at which 14 prospective pledges were approved. Formal pledging took place on February 26 with 11 pledges: Gary Cline, Teri Payne, Kay Thornton, Steve Lacy, Dave Mees, Gina Pruitt, Mary Mercer, Allen Erb, Mike Foley, Ronda Appleton, and Virendar Bakhshi. The pledge captain was Rhonda Appleton.[52]

Committee assignments for the spring semester were:

Spring 1976 Committees

Auditing	Membership	Scholarship & Boy Scouts	Budget
T. Coffman (chair)	T. Coffman (chair)	J. Flebbe (chair)	D. Kersting (chair)
A. Messina	M. Miller	D. Barclay	J. Flebbe
D. Suiter	R. Stockhecker	A. Messina	G. Bland
D. Gerber		M. Quinn	M. Quinn
		C. Cooper	

Safety	Smoker	Initation	Refreshments
J. Flebbe (chair)	D. Scharf (chair)	G. Fischer (chair)	G. Fischer (chair)
Dr. Beistel	M. Hardesty	M. Quinn	M. Hardesty
J. DeGood	K. Sooter	R. Naeger	
T. Burchfield	P. Blankenship	W. Campbell	
		J. May	
		D. Gerber	
		R. Stockhecker	
		S. Duncan	
		K. Sooter	

Chapter Room	By-Laws
M. Quinn (chair)	A. Messina (chair)
R. Storer	S. McGinley
J. May	T. Coffman
G. Fischer	W. Campbell

By early March, preparations were already underway for the Biennial Conclave scheduled to be held in Rapid City, SD, from August 8-12. Rita Webber was chosen to be the delegate with Jack May and Rita Stockhecker as first and second alternates, respectively. (K. Schuette had declined the nomination for delegate due to a summer job commitment.)[53] During March, the pledges sang at the AIChE meeting, and preparations were also made for the upcoming initiation on April 3 and the approaching Jamboree activities. District Counselor Gary Bland visited during St. Pat's weekend, March 12-14; and two other committees were re-established—one, the "High Pressure" committee (M. Quinn, G. Fischer, M. Hardesty and J. May), whose purpose was to "follow up" with members who were delinquent with their dues, and the other, the Snarf committee (M. Quinn, D. Gerber, and J. May) to conduct the annual "Snarf" nominations and voting. Also in March, the chemistry help sessions offered since the beginning of the semester were discontinued. Of course, the month could not be considered a success without additional improvements to the chapter room: new shelves were installed in the closet, and the files were cleaned out and organized.[54]

The chapter initiated eleven new members—Gary W. Cline, Gina R. (Pruitt) Nicholson, Steven L. Lacy, Rhonda L. (Appleton) Boles, Teri A. (Payne) Nunnally, Virendar S. Bakhshi, Michael L. Foley, David R. Mees, Allen J. Erb, Mary Mercer, and Kay E. (Thornton) Sooter—on April 3. The banquet, at which Dr. James spoke on South Africa, was held the following day, April 4.

Election of officers took place on April 7. The officers elected for the fall semester were: Terry Coffman, Master Alchemist; Rita Stockhecker, Vice-Master Alchemist; Bob Naeger, Master of Ceremonies; Kay Thornton, Recorder; DeWayne Gerber, Assistant Treasurer; and Jack May, Historian. Immediately following the election, MA Flebbe announced that the Professional Recognition Ceremony and officer installation would be held on April 21, and, in honor of Beta Delta's 40th anniversary, cake would be served in the Chemical Engineering office at the end of the week of May 2. On April 9, Grand Recorder James Miller paid a visit to the local chapter (The reason for the visit was not recorded).[55]

MC Keith Schuette presided over the Professional Recognition ceremony on April 21. The following graduating seniors—Judy Flebbe, Gary Chappell, Pat Blankeship, Melanie Miller, Leo Scherrer, Jim Wood, Terry Coffman, Steve McGinley, and Dave Barclay—were honored. District Counselor G. Bland and J. Becker briefly addressed the group. Other business conducted during the meeting involved a discussion of the possibility of an Alpha Chi Sigma colony at UMSL. DC Bland recommended further discussion in the future to determine how to organize such a project.[56] Of course, another meeting was called immediately afterward to affirm that "Rolla sucks."[57]

During the summer, the 33rd Biennial Conclave—at which Beta Delta was voted the outstanding chapter in the district—was held in Rapid City. V. Becker, R. Webber, G. Bland, M. O'Conner, and J. Adams attended the sessions.[58]

As students settled into campus life in September, Beta Delta established new committees, laid plans for recruiting new pledges, started up the chemistry help sessions again, and, together with Omega Chi Epsilon (Chemical Engineering Honor Society) and the W. T. Schrenk Society, organized a mixer.[59] It was the chapter room, however, that once again gained the most prominence on the chapter's "To-Do List." Brothers Fischer and Schuette tag-teamed—Fischer suggested the room be opened during the day, and Schuette recommended a soda machine. MA Coffman instructed them to come up with a plan. Fischer and Schuette took up the gauntlet in the days ahead.[60]

Fall 1976 Committees[61]

Advisory	Auditing	Membership	Scholarship
T. Coffman	R. Stockhecker (chair)	R. Stockhecker (chair)	T. Coffman (chair)
D. Kersting	T. Beresik	D. Gerber	D. Gerber
G. Bland	D. Gerber	L. Wehmeier	M. Quinn
Dr. Beistel			L. Blaser
			A. Messina
			D. Barclay
			J. Flebbe

Budget	Safety	Smoker	Banquet
D. Kersting (chair)	T. Beresik (chair)	S. Lacy (chair)	K. Sooter (chair)
T. Coffman	T. Coffman	B. Bakhshi	R. Appleton
G. Bland	Dr. Beistel	N. Talbot	
D. Gerber	M. Quinn	M. Mercer	
J. May	M. Foley	D. Levings	
	S. Calvin		

Fall 1976 Committees Cont.

Initation	Chapter Room	By-Laws	Beta Delta Data
G. Fischer (chair)	G. Fischer (chair)	A. Messina (chair)	S. Duncan (chair)
D. Levings	D. Levings	D. Suiter	J. May
K. Sooter	K. Schuette	J. Flebbe	G. Fischer
T. Beresik		D. Barclay	N. Talbot
N. Talbot		D. Mees	R. Herman
J. Flebbe		Dr. Beistel	
K. Schuette			
R. Herman			
R. Appleton			
M. Foley			
D. Scharf			
G. Pruitt			
A. Erb			
S. Duncan			
S. Claudin			
R. Stockhecker			

Immediately following the Smoker on September 23, to which 78 potential pledges were invited, Fischer and Schuette offered their response to MA Coffman's challenge regarding the chapter room. Fischer reported that there were no rules prohibiting a soda machine, but it would cost $40-$45 to rent one. At this point the engineer's training kicked in, and everyone got involved in the economics of the matter. Calculations indicated that the chapter would have to sell 78 bottles/month at $0.20/bottle to break even. Tony Messina suggested the chapter acquire an icebox and sell the soda for $0.12/bottle. After intense debate, Mike Quinn moved to buy a refrigerator and sell soda for $0.15/bottle. Because this proposal involved an appropriation of funds, however, the motion was tabled.[62]

The chapter room continued to be a focal point of discussion at subsequent business meetings, and increasingly, became the reincarnation of the ashtray project. Once the room had been painted, other ideas were suggested to improve the chapter's "resort." In previous meetings, issues concerning the curtains and blinds had been recurring. At the meeting on September 29, it was the matter of the couch. An appropriation of $30 was finally approved, and a couch was to be purchased for that amount at an auction. After the business meeting, formal pledging took place. The pledges included: Jana Trampe, Kathy Mullins, Mary Ann Mueller, Valarie Brenner, Mike Noble, Steve Smid, and Jim Bovarie. Afterward, everyone was invited to a party at Kent Sooter's place.[63]

The saga of the chapter room continued during the next meeting on October 6. Brother Fischer reported that the cost for Wulglass curtains would be $25 for lined and $15 for unlined. As to the couch, Fischer reported that the couches at the auction "were not in good shape," so he did not purchase one. On October 20, he announced that a couch had been purchased for $26.95, "under budget," and that a refrigerator had also been acquired, but it needed repairs for $6. Sherry Von Klemen gave a demonstration of the curtains she recommended for the room. The group approved the hefty $45 price-tag; they were to arrive, custom-cut, in November.

Another matter of vital importance was discussed at the meeting. Earlier, Bob Naeger had recommended that the chapter discontinue purchasing donuts at Foster's Bakery since "they screwed up the bill." Now, a contingent of members argued that Foster's still had the "best price in town" on donuts so it was likely—though the record does not indicate precisely how this perplexing problem was resolved—that Foster's retained the Beta Delta account.

The business meeting on October 20 took a more serious turn when Mike Quinn suggested that the chapter compile a book of old test questions and answers to sell to the chemical and chemical engineering students as an aid to their course work. Given the number of nominations for the Prof. Snarf award each semester, an exam book with questions and answers could potentially be a money-maker for the chapter. Dr. Beistel and DeWayne Gerber volunteered to follow up with professors, seeking their cooperation.[64]

On November 13, seven new members—Michael W. Noble, Jana L. (Trampe) Zigrye, Valarie A. (Brenner) Bagnell, Kathleen M. (Mullins) Alzos, Mary A. (Mueller) Ott, Stephen A. Smid, and James G. Boverie—were initiated. The banquet in honor of the new members was held at the Gashouse in Rolla.

Officers for the spring semester were elected on November 17. These included: Robert Naeger, Master Alchemist; Mike Hardesty, Vice-Master Alchemist; Ted Beresik, Master of Ceremonies; Kay Thornton, Reporter; Jana Trampe, Recorder; DeWayne Gerber, Treasurer; Mary Mueller, Alumni Secretary; and Steve Lacey, Historian.[65]

The chapter room escapades—though intriguing—did not overshadow the other important activities which occupied the time and effort of Beta Delta members in the fall of 1976. Nor did it diminish the impact of the Beta Delta women, who were becoming a crucial factor in the chapter's success. The traditional activities went on as usual. The Smokers, the pledging, the initiations, the help sessions, the assistance to the Boy Scout chemistry merit badge program—all continued to play important roles in the life of the fraternity. At the end of the semester, Beta Delta even found time to consider and approve the petition for membership from Alpha Rho Colony at John Hopkins University.

By this time, Beta Delta's women members were certainly very much in the forefront of all the chapter's activities—leading as officers, participating as committee members; directly involving themselves in all the decision-making at meetings. Examples of the significant contributions of women of the fraternity—while on campus and beyond—were ubiquitous: Valerie (Brenner) Bagnell along with her husband Charles (also a Beta Delta member) developed and conducted the Group and Resource Organizational Workshop (GROW) which replaced the Laboratory for Leadership Program for the fraternity. In addition, many of the women won achievements and recognitions outside of Beta Delta. For instance, Judy Flebbe and Michelle Robeson teamed up to place in intramural tennis tournaments. Nicole Talbot became active in the alumni organization becoming president of the Houston section for six years during the 1990s. She was also the Scholarship Chair from 2007 to 2013 and organizer of the high school recruiting efforts for the Houston area from 2006 to 2015. Gina Pruitt was nominated for Greek Week Queen. Judy Flebbe, Rita (Stockhecker) McMinn and Rita (Webber) Stevens achieved spectacular academic success during their years at UMR.

One anecdote, especially, demonstrated just how brilliant some of these women were. Rita Stockhecker had early on in the semester, earned the appellation of high achiever and "curve buster" in her Physical Chemistry class, amazing even the professor at the time—Dr. Bruce Poling (a Beta Delta member). According to sources, Dr. Poling wanted to put Stockhecker to the test, so he designed an exam he figured would stump her. It did, but only slightly. For once, Stockhecker scored less than 100% on a test, but the second-highest score on the curve was in the teens.[66]

First row, l to r: D. Mees, M. Hardesty, M. Levings, K. Thornton. Second row, l to r: S. Lacy, M. Foley, J. Puckett, M. Miller, R. Webber. Third row, l to r: M. Quinn, D. Gerber, J. De-Good, D. Kersting, K. Schuette, T. Beresik. Fourth row, l to r: J. Erb, G. Cline, Dr. J. Hufham, Dr. D. W. Beistel, L. Scherrer, N. Talbot, V. Bakhshi. Fifth row, l to r: J. Wool, D. Barclay, J. Flebbe, C. Cooper, G. Fischer, G. Chappell, P. Blankenship, R. Stockhecker. Sixth row, l to r: B. Naeger, S. Duncan, G. Foutch, T. Coffman, S. McGinley, D. Scharf, C. Hillhouse, G. Pruitt, L. Wehmeier. Seventh row, l to r: M. Robeson, D. Suiter, A. Messina, B. Wyatt.

Beta Delta Chapter 1976—Rollamo 1976

1977

The spring semester of 1977 began with—what else?—more discussion of chapter room decorating. Sherry Von Klemen reported, at the January 19 meeting, that one set of curtains for the room was ready to be hung while the others were still on order. This ended the Great Curtain Debate which had involved heated discussions; especially between brothers Gerber and Levings (Fortunately, they have remained close friends to this day).

After the usual officer and committee reports, the meeting focused on the appointment of committees to undertake the work of the upcoming semester. Plans were made—and dates set—for the usual events (the Smoker, the Formal Pledging, the Pledge Final, and the Initiation), but other projects were scheduled as well. The Boy Scout Merit Badge program would continue, a joint initiation with the Beta Psi chapter, Carbondale, MO, had to be organized, the Science Fair would be held April 1, and the Work Day would take place on March 26. A petition from another colony at C. W. Post Center of Long Island University for a chapter membership would also have to be considered before the end of the semester (Beta Delta voted in favor of the petition at the April 12 meeting).[67]

Spring 1977 Committees

Advisory	Auditing	Membership	Budget
R. Naeger (chair)	M. Hardesty	M. Hardesty	D. Gerber (chair)
D. Gerber	T. Beresik	L. Wehmeier	R. Naeger
G. Bland	B. Wyatt	G. Pruitt	G. Bland
		R. Stockhecker	R. Webber
		M. Foley	M. O'Conner
			J. Flebbe

Safety	Smoker	Scholarship	Initiation
R. Naeger	M. Hardesty	R. Naeger	K. Schuette (chair)
Dr. Beistel	D. Levings	J. May	D. Levings
R. Webber	R. Appleton		J. Flebbe
	J. Puckett		R. Appleton
	J. Trampe		A. Erb
	M. Foley		D. Scharf
			D. Mees
			R. Stockhecker

Banquet	Refreshments	Chapter Room	By-Laws
S. Von Klemen	S. Von Klemen (chair)	D. Levings	A. Messina (chair)
	D. Levings		C. Hillhouse
	R. Appleton		J. Flebbe
			D. Barclay
			T. Coffman
			K. Mullins

Spring 1977 Committees Cont.

Jamboree
M. O'Conner (chair)
R. Webber
T. Beresik
R. Stockhecker
J. May

The formal pledging ceremony took place immediately after the business meeting on February 16. Eleven students—Mike Haynes, John Hicks, Karen Ketterer, John King, Reyes Reinoso, Marjorie Riggins, Charlotte Pavelka, Mike Schmidt, Ed Webster, Steve Zigrye (pledge captain), and Steve Zuiss—were invited to pledge. Just before the formal pledging, the chapter room project reared its persistent head once again. More curtain issues had to be ironed out. Treasurer DeWayne Gerber reported that all of the curtains had been paid for, and Mitch Levings requested assistance in hanging them. Apparently, by this time the hatchet had been buried.[68]

The joint initiation with Beta Psi at Carbondale did not go as planned. MA Bob Naeger announced at the March 29 meeting that Beta Psi would bring eleven initiates, but he thought the actives of that chapter were not prepared to conduct the initiation, so Beta Delta would have to shoulder the responsibility. The pledge final was written on April 14 at Brother Schuette's residence, and the final preparations for the initiation were held on April 16 in the morning, followed by a picnic in the afternoon. The next day on April 17, the following pledges were initiated: Karen S. (Ketterer) Kulengowski, Stephen J. Zuiss, Charlotte S. Pavelka, John M. Hicks, Reyes Reinoso, Michael S. Schmidt, John W. King, Michael A. Haynes, Edward P. Webster, Marjorie Riggins, and Steve L. Zigrye. The banquet, organized by Sherry Von Klemen, to honor the new members was held at Zeno's.[69]

The election of officers and the Professional Recognition Ceremony rounded out the semester's activities. The election of the following officers took place on April 20: Mike Foley, Master Alchemist; Judy Flebbe, Vice-Master Alchemist; David Levings (Mitch), Master of Ceremonies; David Mees, Recorder; John King, Historian; and Edward Webster, Assistant Treasurer.[70]

The Professional Recognition ceremony was held on May 4. Those recognized were Bob Naeger, Keith Schuette, Suzanne Duncan, Debbie Kersting, Nicki Talbot, Chuck O'Conner, Brad Wyatt and Larry Molina. Mike Foley conducted the ceremony. The newly elected officers were then installed. Immediately following the ceremony the special meeting for the traditional declaration that "Rolla sucks" was called to order and, raucously, adjourned.[71]

A final note about the spring of 1977: in the spring semester, just two years before his death, Dr. Schrenk was honored as one of the founding members of the Order of the Golden Shillelagh. The Order of the Golden Shillelagh, founded in 1977, was designed exclusively to assist the campus in its fundraising effort. Any individual, alumnus or friend of the school, could become a member in one of three ways: donating a cash gift of $10,000, making a 10-year pledge of no less than $1,000 a year, or establishing an estate gift of $15,000. Membership was also possible by combining a bequest or trust with cash gifts totaling $12,500.[72]

James Grimm, Walter T. Schrenk and Bernard R. Sarchet (left to right)—three of the 27 founding members of the Order of the Golden Shillelagh

Records for the fall of 1977 were sparse, but it was likely that Beta Delta's routine for the fall semester was similar to the order of events in the spring. This much is known with certainty, however: the chemistry help sessions ran throughout the semester, formal pledging took place on October 5, and the Work Day happened on October 29. One other significant action was taken by Beta Delta on November 30: Beta Delta petitioned the UMR administration to name the Chemistry-Chemical Engineering building after Dr. Schrenk. Unfortunately, this undertaking would not be realized until two years later after Schrenk's death, when the chapter would once again raise the proposal.[73]

One of the few last events "Doc" Schrenk attended was the Alpha Chi Sigma/AIChE joint outing on October 1. Both organizations were honored by his presence which contributed to the success of the outing. The event was also a success for Beta Delta in particular, having defeated AIChE in a softball battle. The final score was not recorded; perhaps it was just too humiliating for the AIChE members.[74]

Fall 1977 Committees

Advisory	Auditing	Membership	Budget
Dr. Beistel	J. Flebbe	J. Flebbe	D. Gerber
M. Foley	T. Beresik	R Stockhecker	J. Boverie
	E. Webster	R. Appleton	E. Webster
	Dr. Beistel	J. May	J. Puckett
		S. Zigrye	M. Foley
			D. Levings

Safety	Smoker	Scholarship	Initiation
M. Foley	J. Erb	M. Foley	N. Talbot
R. Webber	J. Boverie	J. May	D. Levings
R. Appleton	J. Puckett		R. Stockhecker
M. Schmitt	R. Reinoso		J. King
Dr. Carrol	M. Mueller		D. Mees
	M. Hardesty		M. Riggins
			J. Erb
			S. Zigrye
			D. Scharf

Fall 1977 Committees Cont.

Banquet	Refreshments	Chapter Room	By-Laws
C. Pavelka	D. Mees	J. King	D. Barclay
R. Webber	N. Talbot	D. Levings	T. Beresik
	R. Reinoso		J. Puckett

On November 13, nine pledges were initiated: John A. Ederle, Kim E. Fleddermann, Terry F. Harvey, Kevin D. Wiese, Joseph M. Grana (pledge captain), Matthew F. Vogel, Stanley A. Heimburger, Steven C. Zinselmeyer, and Mark S. Ziobro. Two weeks later, on November 30, the following officers were elected: DeWayne Gerber, Master Alchemist; Jack May, Vice-Master Alchemist; Eddie Webster, Treasurer; Kim Fledderman, Reporter; Stan Heimburger, Recorder; Steve Zigrye, Master of Ceremonies; Charlotte Pavelka, Alumni Secretary; and John Ederle, Historian.[75]

The last meeting of the semester, on December 7, was the ceremony for Professional Recognition of Mary Ann Mueller, Jeff Erb, Kathy Mullins, and Lee Wehmeier. Once the new officers were installed, they announced that they had a beer keg waiting at the Mine Shaft after the meeting.[76]

First Row: R. Naeger, M. Miller, S. Duncan, D. Kersting, M. Foley, M. O'Connor; Second Row: M. Haynes, J. Boverie, D. Gerber, J. May, N. Talbot, Not identified; Third Row: J. Hicks, D. Levings, Not identified, C. Pavelka, T. Payne, K. Schuette, Not identified; Fourth Row: J. Flebbe, B. Wyatt, L. Weimer, S. Zigrye, E. Webster, T. Beresik, D. Mees, M. Hardesty; Fifth Row: Not identified, Not identified, S. Lacy, R. Stockhecker, J. Trampe, K. Thornton, Not identified

Beta Delta Chapter 1977-Rollamo 1977

1978

By the beginning of 1978, the chapter room deliberations seemed to have exhausted themselves. Apparently, interest in further improvements waned. Instead, the chapter turned its attention to a problem that had been developing for several years. In either late 1973 or early 1974, during a joint pledge final and initiation ceremony, which was hosted by the Delta chapter in Columbia, differences occurred between the two chapters over specifics in their practices, which led to a cessation of activities between Delta and Beta Delta until 1978. Now, Beta Delta members made the decision to try to heal the broken relationship by accepting Delta's invitation to a softball game on April 29. This resulted in the restoration of good relations with Delta Chapter in Columbia, and the annual Beta Delta vs. Delta football and softball games were reinstated. (Beta Delta also established relations with Beta Psi in Carbondale around this time, and the two chapters held joint initiations on several occasions.)[77]

Once committees were formed on January 18, Beta Delta launched its Smoker on February 7, which resulted in invitations to 18 potential pledges. Of those invited, only seven formally pledged on February 15: Dr. James Halligan, Chris Miranti, Bob Meredith, Ron Fischer, John Hesse, Vicky Bradham, and Charles Bagnell.[78]

Spring 1978 Committees

Auditing	Scholarship	By-Laws	Membership
J. May	D. Gerber	D. Barclay	J. May
R. Herman	J. May	J. Boverie	J. Grana
J. Flebbe	J. Hicks	J. Puckett	T. Harvey
	M. Ziobro		

Safety	Budget	Banquet	Snarf
D. Gerber	E. Webster	C. Pavelka	S. Calvin
Dr. Beistel	D. Gerber	K. Thornton	S. Heimburger
J. King	G. Roberts		
	M. Foley		
	S. Zigyre		

Smoker	Refreshments	Initiation	Initation Cont.
V. Brenner	T. Beresik	T. Beresik	K. Thornton
K. Fledderman	S. Heimburger	D. Levings	L. Blaser
M. Haynes	R. Reinoso	M. Riggins	M. Ziobro
	J. Boverie	G. Pruitt	T. Harvey

Note: Later on March 1 two additional committees were formed: Beta Delta Data—R. Appleton, Hicks, R. Herman, and C. Pavelka (chair), and Schrenk Committee—J. Flebbe, S. Zigrye, J. May, and M. Foley.[79]

Early in the semester, the chapter rose to a couple of challenges. On February 10, Beta Delta trounced the faculty 62 to 48 in basketball. Then, for the St. Pat's games, Beta Delta entered a team consisting of DeWayne Gerber, Jack May, Jim Boverie, Mitch Levings, John Hicks, Matt Vogel, Bruce Poling, Mark Ziobro, and alternates Rosa Herman and Steve Zigrye in the quarter barrel chug. There is no record of how the team fared (probably because no one would have been in any condition to record the event).[80] With the adrenaline rush over, the chapter initiated nine new members into Alpha Chi Sigma on April 15: Charles R. Bagnell, Ronald J. Fisher, Thomas B. Shilling, Chris A. Miranti, James E. Halligan, John C. Hesse, Vicki E. Bradham, Terry (Dixon) Brandt, and Garry S. Tobin. Once again, the initiation banquet was held at Zeno's.

Three days later, at the April 18 meeting, officers were elected for the fall semester: Steve Zigrye, Master Alchemist; Jana Trampe, Vice-Master Alchemist; Mike Haynes, Reporter; Gary Tobin, Recorder; Mark Ziobro, Master of Ceremonies; Eddie Webster, Treasurer; Vicki Bradham, Assistant Treasurer; Charlotte Pavelka, Alumni Secretary; and Tom Shilling, Historian. In addition, Conclave delegates were selected—Mark Ziobro with Steve Zigrye and DeWayne Gerber as first and second alternates, respectively. The Conclave would be held in the summer in Denton, TX. (At the first meeting in the fall, Mike Haynes would be moved into the Reporter position and an election would be held to select a new Recorder.)[81]

During the March 18 meeting, it was announced that Beta Gamma, UCLA, would become a new chapter of Alpha Chi Sigma on March 29.

The newly elected officers were installed on April 30, and the Professional Recognition for Rita Stockhecker, Mike Hardesty, Rosa Herman, Rita Webber, Ted Beresik, Jim Boverie, Mike Foley, Steve Smid, Dave Scharf, Gina Pruitt, Kent Sooter, and Steve Lacey was conducted during the same meeting. Mark Ziobro, the Conclave delegate (34th Biennial Conclave held in Denton, TX) was then instructed that the chapter was not in favor of any major changes to the initiation ceremony. This position was taken as a consequence of the extent to which the revised pledge manual had been trimmed down, which resulted in a significant loss of material. The chapter did not want to see the same thing happen to the ritual.[82]

The Ritual Revision Committee, chaired by Missouri Valley District[83] Counselor Greg Roberts, was created by the action of the previous Conclave, largely in response to the inclusion of women into its ranks. The committee, charged specifically with modifying the initiation ceremony, spent two years researching rituals, alchemy, heraldry, and secret societies, in detail. The final result would be the most significant change to the fraternity's initiation ritual since 1924. But getting to language that was acceptable to all the delegates was not an easy task. [84]

Mitch Levings (Beta Delta '75) and DeWayne Gerber (Beta Delta '75), were members of the working group studying the issue for the past two years. They, like Beta Delta's delegate Ziobro, were aware of the chapter's aversion to any major changes in the initiation rite. When the delegates convened in Denton, however, a thorough review of the history of the ritual and a clarification of the meaning of each part were undertaken. The awkwardness of the current language—given that women were now an integral part of the fraternity—became clearly objectionable. After long discussion, the Beta Delta delegation realized that major change, especially the incorporation of more inclusive language, was warranted. A serious lobbying effort to explain the revisions to Beta Delta members—and members of other chapters, who were opposed to any significant changes in the ritual—was necessary. Ultimately, the Conclave resolution to revise the ritual passed unanimously.

Beta Delta was fortunate to have Levings and Gerber on the committee-not only because they were able to work out language that was acceptable to everyone, but also because they had the final revisions in hand and were able to bring the new document back to the chapter immediately. Consequently, Beta Delta had the privilege—with the approval of the Supreme Council—of being the first chapter to use the new ritual in the fall of '78-even before it was reprinted and distributed by the National Office.[85]

Also that April, one of Beta Delta's own members, Gina Pruitt, was nominated for Greek Week Queen. Like Carol Langemach, Judith Flebbe, and Rita Stockhecker before her, Pruitt was one of many Beta Delta women who made notable contributions to the college community outside of the chapter. Pruitt was also a member of Alpha Phi Alpha—the intercollegiate fraternity for African-Americans founded in December, 1906, at Cornell University—which nominated her for the Greek Week honor. Unfortunately, she was not elected queen, but her other achievements were stellar. Originally from Florissant, MO, Pruitt was a senior majoring in Chemical Engineering in 1978. She had served as parliamentarian for the Association for Black Students (ABS), and was a member of the organizing committee for the National Society of Black Engineers. She sang with the University Chamber Choir and was on the cheerleading squad.[86]

Gina Pruitt, Beta Delta '76—Rollamo 1978

The fall semester began in August for Beta Delta. Committees were appointed at its first meeting on August 30, and they wasted no time getting things started. By September 5, less than a week later, the Smoker was held, and, after the third vote on September 18, twelve prospective new members were invited to pledge. [87]

Fall 1978 Committees[88]

Auditing	Scholarship	Parliamentary	Beta Delta Data
J. Trampe	S. Zigrye	S. Zuiss	C. Pavelka
V. Bradham	J. Hicks	K. (Thornton) Sooter	D. Gerber
S. Heimburger	M. Ziobro	T. Shilling	C. Miranti
Dr. Beistel	D. Gerber		
	J. May		
	G. Tobin		

Safety	Smoker	Banquet	Refreshment
D. Gerber	E. Webster	V. Brenner	M. Vogel
S. Zigrye	J. Puckett		J. Ederle
V. Brenner	V. Bradham		
Dr. Beistel	J. Hicks		

Fall 1978 Committees Cont.

Social	Initation	Chapter Room
M. Vogel	Kent Sooter	M. Ziobro
K. Weiss	M. Ziobro	D. Gerber
V. Bagnell	T. Shilling	G. Fischer
C. Pavelka	D. Gerber	
	S. Heimburger	

Note: the Membership Committee consisted only of J. Trampe. The Snarf Committee consisted of: J. May, J. Ederle, G. Tobin and C. Miranti.

For the most part, the fall semester of 1978 progressed in the usual and customary way. On Parents' Day, September 21, volunteers gave tours of the Chemical Engineering-Chemistry building. Formal pledging was held on September 20. The special election for Recorder was held at the same meeting. (Gary Tobin was elected, but because of his illness in November, Valerie Brenner and Anne Fulton finished out his duties.) A special formal pledging ceremony was held for Rapeepong Pisilpong on September 21 at the Boles residence. The chemistry help sessions continued throughout the semester, Beta Delta lost (again) to Delta, 14-7, in the football game on September 30, and work days were held on October 24 and 28; Beta Delta members raked leaves, painted, and cleaned out gutters.[89]

On November 11, seven pledges had the distinction of being the first to be initiated under the newly revised initiation ritual: Burton K. Walker, Peter C. Scholtes, Yeh F. Wang, and Anne F. (Fulton) McIntyre. Beta Delta Membership records also list Raymond Furlong, Ralph Morgan, and Rapeepong Pisilpong. GMA R. Pflaum attended the ceremony, and he commented later, in a letter to Beta Delta that he thought the new initiation ceremony was excellent. He did offer several suggestions for improvement, but what they were, the records did not disclose. The customary banquet to honor the new members was held at Zeno's.[90]

At the November 29 meeting, the chapter—ever mindful of future needs—decided to join Delta in co-hosting the 1980 Conclave. Members also decided to hold a Jamboree for the Missouri Valley district chapters in the spring. Election of officers then followed, with these results: Jana

Trampe, Master Alchemist; Kay (Thornton) Sooter, Vice-Master Alchemist; Vicki Bradham, Treasurer; Kent Sooter, Master of Ceremonies; Peter Scholtes, Alumni Secretary; Raymond (Chip) Furlong, Reporter; Anne (Fulton) McIntyre, Recorder; and Steve Zigrye, Historian. The installation of officers and the Professional Recognition ceremony, which honored Joe Grana, Eddie Webster, and Kay (Thornton) Sooter, were held a week later, on December 6. Dr. Bruce Poling was the guest speaker.[91]

During the fall of 1978, important changes occurred in the chemical engineering faculty. Dr. Neil L. Book (Beta Delta '69) had returned to Rolla to join the Chemical Engineering faculty. He had received his BS degree from UMR and his MS and PhD degrees at Colorado. Before returning, he had been teaching at Tulane University in New Orleans. More significantly, perhaps, was Dr. Harvey H. Grice's announcement that he was retiring. He had been teaching at UMR since 1965, and, though he was no longer working in the classroom, he would continue his research in the field of dialysis.[92]

First Row: L. Webber, R. Webber, J. Hicks; Second Row: M. Haynes, D. Gerber, T. Brandt, J. May, Not identified, C. Meranti; Third Row: J. Boverie, S. Zigrye, K. Fledderman, M. Ziobro, R. Herman, J. King; Fourth Row: M. Hardesty, D. Levings, R. Stockhecker, J. Trampe, R. Appleton, Not identified, E. Webster; Fifth Row: B. Campbell, C. Bagnell, V. Brenner, J. Puckett, T. Beresik; C. Pavelka, Not identified, Not identified; Sixth Row: Not identified, Not identified, J. Flebbe, K. Thornton, K. Sooter

Beta Delta Chapter 1978—Rollamo 1978

1979

Once again, Beta Delta got down to business as soon as the new semester got underway. At the first meeting of the year, on January 17, the usual task of establishing standing committees was handled efficiently with MA Trampe in charge. Vicki Bradham was installed as Treasurer, and Rita (Webber) Stevens was selected to be Beta Delta's nominee for the Alpha Chi Sigma Scholar. A week later, on January 23, the Smoker was held. On January 31, 15 potential pledges were invited to formally pledge. Of that group, Michael Carr, Tom Mack, Beth McVey, Jane Riolo, Ernie Smoot,

Brent Sparks, and Peggy Taylor pledged immediately. Formal pledging for Dr. X. B. Reed, Kevin Todd and Cynthia Williams would be held February 1, and Dr. Vincent Roach would formally pledge on February 7.[93]

Spring 1979 Committees

Auditing	Scholarship	Social	Beta Delta Data
K. Sooter	J. Trampe	D. Gerber	J. Hesse
V. Bradham	A. Fulton	R. Morgan	P. Scholtes
Dr. Beistel	M. Ziobro	P. Scholtes	B. Walker
S. Zigrye	C. Furlong		R. Boles
	R. Pisilpong		

Safety	Budget	Chapter Room	Refreshment
D. Gerber	V. Bradham	S. Zigrye	Kay Sooter
S. Zigrye	J. Trampe	Kent Sooter	Kent Sooter
M. Schmidt	D. Gerber	P. Scholtes	P. Scholtes

Smoker	Initation	By-Laws
S. Heimburger	Kent Sooter	V. Brenner
C. Furlong	S. Zigrye	Kay Sooter
C. Bagnell	P. Scholtes	R. Pisilpong
R. Morgan	C. Furlong	
	R. Morgan	
	C. Bagnell	
	B. Walker	
	R. Pisilpong	
	Kay Sooter	

Note: The Membership Committee consisted only of K. Sooter, and the Banquet Committee consisted only of A. Fulton. The Snarf Committee consisted of: M. Ziobro, M. Schmidt, S. Heimburger and A. Fulton.[94]

Activity continued apace through the months of February and March. On March 6, Mass Transfer took place. Pledges sang for the Chemistry-Chemical Engineering secretaries on March 23. The pledge final was given on March 23. Also, during the semester: an invitation was received by the chapter to Charles Bagnell and Valerie Brenner's wedding, and the chapter donated $100 to the Strunk-Grice Scholarship Fund, which offered scholarships to entering freshmen, transfer students, or current chemical engineering students in good academic standing who were chosen by a department chair or the scholarship committee.[95]

On March 24, the following women and men were initiated: Dr. D. Vincent Roach, Cynthia M. Williams, Elizabeth A. (McVey) Thurman, Peggy A. (Taylor) Scholtes, Jane A. Riolo, Brent G. Sparks, Thomas G. Mack, Robert E. Stevens, Dr. X. B. Reed, Michael J. Carr, and Ernest A. Smoot. Stevens would go on to be the current Assistant Treasurer of the Alpha Chi Sigma Educational Foundation. (He was one of the primary actors in the restart of the St. Louis Professional Chapter which was inactive from 1987 through June 1996.)[96]

Dr. Kenneth Edwards of the Nuclear Engineering department spoke on "Political Engineering" (Chapter records did not explain what this title entailed) at the banquet held at one the chapter's favorite restaurants—Zeno's. At the conclusion of the banquet, the celebration was adjourned to the apartment of DeWayne Gerber and Mark Ziobro whereupon the revelry was re-ignited and continued until the champagne was completely drained.[97]

After the initiation, Beta Delta's activities continued at a relentless pace. On March 28, a new communique was published by the chapter—The AXΣ Bulletin. The short publication was printed bi-monthly and contained such information as a calendar of events and other reminders for the members. During April, the active members also took on the faculty in a basketball game, which—in a shocker—the faculty won 52-49. On April 21, a work day was held at the country club and a week later, on April 28, Kevin Todd was initiated at Washington University, for which Beta Delta provided the regalia.[98]

For some time, Beta Delta membership qualifications had not been seriously reviewed. But during the April 18 meeting they were revised significantly. The grade point average minimum was set at 2.0 out of a possible 4.0, and the curriculum requirement was changed to read "…chemistry and related curricula…," which brought the chapter's by-laws into better alignment with the interpretation of disciplines qualifying as chemical sciences set in the 1960s. The other major business on the 18th was the election of officers. The new leadership included: Mark Ziobro, Master Alchemist; Charles Bagnell, Vice-Master Alchemist; Mike Schmidt, Master of Ceremonies; Kevin Wiese, Recorder; Jane Riolo, Assistant Treasurer; and Peggy Taylor and Brent Sparks, Historians. The meeting closed with two announcements, one disappointing and one celebratory. News was received that Alpha Epsilon would not be reactivated that semester. The joyous news was the announcement that a reception in honor of Charles and Valerie Bagnell's wedding would be held on Saturday, April 21.[99]

Beta Delta's busy spring semester ended on May 2 with the Professional Recognition ceremony for 14 seniors: Jana Trampe, Anne Fulton, Ronda Boles, Valerie Brenner-Bagnell, Mike Noble, Kim Fledderman, DeWayne Gerber, Stan Heimburger, John King, Chris Miranti, Yeh Fin Wang, Mark Ziobro, Kevin Todd, and Cynthia Williams. The newly elected officers were also installed. The meeting ended with more wonderful news: Gary Fischer and Nancy Brown would be married on May 19. The summer would be a welcome quiet interlude.[100]

In the fall, the semester began early again. The chapter met for the first time on August 22, which meant organizational matters and the first round of selecting pledges came before Labor Day on September 5. Several award winners were recognized early on in the semester: Rita Webber was selected as the Outstanding Senior for her remarkable academic accomplishments as an undergraduate, and Dr. Wilbur Tappmeyer and Dr. Ray Waggoner of the Chemistry and Chemical Engineering departments, respectively, shared the notorious Prof. Snarf award.

Fall 1979 Committees [101]

Scholarship	Initation	Safety	Budget
M. Ziobro	M. Schmidt	R. Freeman	V. Bradham
J. Trampe		D. Gerber	M. Ziobro
V. Bagnell		S. Zigrye	J. Riolo
E. Smoot			D. Gerber

Fall 1979 Committees Cont.

Membership	Smoker	Chapter Room	Social
V. Bagnell	C. Bagnell	M. Schmidt	J. Trampe
J. Trampe	M. Schmidt	B. Sparks	
	C. Furlong	R. Morgan	
	R. Morgan	E. Smoot	

Banquet	Beta Delta Data
Dixon	P. Scholtes
	J. Hesse
	M. Schmidt
	S. Zigrye

Note: D. Gerber was Parliamentarian.

The result of the Smoker and the subsequent pledge activities—Formal Pledging on September 26, pledge class sessions, and the customary pledge sing for the Chemistry and Chemical Engineering department secretaries on Wednesday, November 14—was the initiation of a large pledge class on Sunday, November 18. Nineteen of the pledges—David M. Price, Matthew C. Song, Bill D. Bockelman, John Wang, Janet L. Thornton, William A. Brooks, Steven R. Block, Nancy E. (Brown) Fischer, Edward A. Kyser, Kevin J. Hagan, Shelley S. Heigert, Richard D. Purgason, Stephanie M. Tanaka, Anthony S. Petruska, Dale A. Abrahams, Teresa A. (Gaddy) Adams, Laura A. (Pfautsch) Kramer, James C. Roberts, and Steven D. Brooks—were inducted into the fraternity.[102]

At the final meeting of the year, on December 5, the election of officers for the spring semester took place as usual. Those elected, and the offices for which they were chosen, were: Steve Zuiss, Master Alchemist; Peggy Taylor, Vice-Master Alchemist; Brent Sparks, Master of Ceremonies; Jane Riolo, Treasurer; Kevin Hagan, Recorder; Rich Purgason, Reporter; Steve Zigyre, Alumni Secretary; and Tony Petruska, Historian. Dr. Beistel conducted the Professional Recognition ceremony for Charles Bagnell and Steve Zigrye. Charlotte Pavelka, Marjorie Riggins, Ralph Morgan, Rap Pisilpong, and Burton Walker were not present for the traditional event.[103]

The year ended sadly for Beta Delta and for the entire UMR community.

Walter T. Schrenk passed away on December 8 in Rolla. In honor of Dr. Schrenk, the Alumni Association immediately established the Walter T. Schrenk Memorial. But Beta Delta felt the loss especially deeply. Even in his retirement years "Doc" had maintained close ties with the members of the chapter, often welcoming them to his home for luncheons or just casual "meet and greets." Dr. Schrenk's legacy would be remembered and honored for years.[104]

The day after Schrenk died, several Beta Delta members met in the mailroom between the Chemical Engineering and Chemistry sections of the building and decided to write a letter requesting the building be renamed in his memory. The letter was sent to the Chair of the Board of Curators, the System President, and the Rolla Chancellor. Copies were also mailed to the two deans and the Chemistry and Chemical Engineering department chairs. The name change was formally requested by the UMR Departments of Chemistry and Chemical Engineering and approved by the Board of Curators. In 1980 the Chemistry-Chemical Engineering Building was renamed Walter T. Schrenk Hall.[105]

In 1982, Dr. Schrenk's wife, Irene, and businessman and artist, George Carney, donated a portrait of Schrenk to UMR's Departments of Chemistry and Chemical Engineering in his honor. What "Doc" meant to all who knew him was summed up best by the title of an article by Thomas J. Stewart, ChE '34, that appeared in the 1996 winter issue of the MSM Alumnus Magazine: "'Doc' Schrenk's Lessons Last a Lifetime."[106]

Walter T. Schrenk--1979

First Row: Not identified, M. Schmidt, J. Trampe, J. King, E. Smoot

Second Row: K. Weiss, S. Zigrye, P. Scholte, P. Taylor, Not identified

Third Row: K. Todd, C. Bagnell, V. Brenner, R. Weber, R. Pissilpong

Fourth Row: Not identified, D. Gerber, J. Nobel, Not identified, C. Miranti
Fifth Row: R. Stevens, K. Fledderman, Not identified, G. Pruitt, M. Ziobro

Sixth Row: Dr. Beistel, Not identified, C. Bennett, A. Fulton, Not identified, R. Appleton
Beta Delta Chapter 1979-Rollamo 1979

Probably the hallmark of the decade for Beta Delta was the contribution of its women members. The 1970s saw the admission of women into the fraternity for the first time, and within just a few short years they were becoming foundational, setting a professional tone, providing leadership and guidance, striving for excellence, enhancing the vitality of the chapter. These contributions would extend far into Beta Delta's future.

Excursus:
Edward P. Schneider

Brother Schneider was Grand Collegiate Alchemist from 1966 to 1968 and Grand Master Alchemist from 1968 to 1970. He was also president of the Alpha Chi Sigma Education Foundation and was recognized for his service with the conferral of the John R. Kuebler Award by the fraternity. Schneider initiated in 1942 and graduated with a bachelor's degree in Chemical Engineering that same year.[107] He then went on to work for Monsanto Company in the Chemical Warfare Service. In 1946 he moved to the Foreign Sales Division in Springfield, Massachusetts. In 2004 he acquired a position with the Wagner Electric Corporation where he was plant manager for the Brake Fluid Plant. From 1964 through 2009, Schneider was the Founder and President of the Lark Engineering Corp. He also earned a JD degree from Washington University.[108]

Edward P. Schneider

Outside of Alpha Chi Sigma, Brother Schneider was a member of AIChE, Alpha Phi Omega (a service fraternity), the Masonic Order 32nd degree, President of the St. Louis Air Pollution Control Association, and a member of an amateur radio club. In 2010, he was inducted into the Academy of Chemical Engineers. Schneider passed away on October 1, 2011. He was preceded in death by his wife, Virginia Belville Schneider.[109]

Judith L. Flebbe

Upon completion of her doctoral dissertation, "Vapor pressures of some C_4 hydrocarbons and their mixtures," under the guidance of Dr. Dave Manley, and her subsequently awarded PhD in 1980, Judith Flebbe became the first woman to earn a doctorate in Chemical Engineering at the University of Missouri-Rolla.[110]

Judy Flebbe—Missouri Miner 1979

Flebbe, a graduate of Ruskin High School in Kansas City where she excelled in math and science, began her college career at UMR in 1972, enrolling in Chemical Engineering. Her father, George Flebbe, a mechanical engineer, suggested she consider engineering as a career. Though she was a National Merit Scholar, she admitted she was "scared stiff" when she first set foot on the UMR campus in the fall of 1972. But Flebbe proved to be a remarkable student. She received the Outstanding Chemical Engineering Freshman award and was at the top of her class every year as an undergraduate. She received every academic honor for her field, including the American Institute of Chemical Engineers (AIChE) Award for superior academic achievement for her freshman and sophomore years, and she was named in UMR's Who's Who her senior year.

She was also elected to Tau Beta Pi, Omega Chi Epsilon, and Phi Kappa Phi honorary fraternities.[111]

Flebbe was not one to simply have "her nose in the books," however. As an undergraduate, she was involved in a wide range of other organizations and activities. She was a member of the American Institute of Chemical Engineers, PiKA Little Sister, and Alpha Chi Sigma, pledging in the Fall of '73 (11/11/73). She also participated in the Association of Women Students, Chamber Choir and the Concert Band, for which she performed flute solos. An avid tennis player, she won the Women's Singles, and—along with Michelle Robeson (Beta Delta '74)—won the Women's Doubles in the 1976 Intramurals.[112]

In addition to her school work, she worked three summers in the chemical industry. Two summers were spent with DuPont, working in Elastomers Research and Development in the Beaumont, TX, facility and in the Pigments Department in the New Johnsonville, TN plant. She worked the other summer in the Synthetic Fuels Research Labs of Exxon Research and Development in Baytown, TX.[113]

During an interview with the Miner (December 6, 1979), Flebbe was asked what it was like to be one of the first female engineers. Her reply was, "The only pressure I felt was my own. I felt, as one of the first female engineers, I should do a little better than average." On campus and at work she found women engineers were not considered that unusual. Away from the technological sphere, however, she found people did consider her differently. She shared moments when people wanted to know how she would handle a career and a family. Her reply to such inquiries: "Right now, the career comes first. I'll work on it awhile. Then, if and when marriage comes, I'll consider that part of my life. Just like any other woman who works, I'll figure out how to manage it."[114]

Flebbe also had an insightful wit. When a group of active members were trying to come up with trivia questions for the pledges, she offered the following question: "How many bricks are there in the smokestack of the power plant?" The power plant referenced no longer exists, but it was very tall and everyone was stumped about how to arrive at the correct answer. Flebbe had it all figured out: "One less than too many, and one more than too few."[115]

Unfortunately, after being awarded her doctorate (Spring 1980), Flebbe met an untimely death in September of that year. In her honor, Beta Delta members came together to establish a scholarship fund to memorialize her. In the spring of 1981, Dave Barclay (Beta Delta '73) was recruiting for Conoco on campus when he contacted the MA of Beta Delta to discuss setting up a scholarship. "It started right then with several donations from her Beta Delta brothers, and I think from the chapter also," Barclay explained, "Beta Delta initiated the idea and got the scholarship set up."[116]

The award is known as the Judith L. Flebbe Memorial Scholarship Award. Originally reserved for women in chemical engineering, it soon became available to both men and women. The recipient must be a junior and in the upper 25% of his or her class in Chemical Engineering. The amount awarded is dependent on the account balance.[117]

Harvey Grice

Dr. Harvey Grice, Prof. Emeritus Chemical Engineering –Rollamo 1972

Dr. Grice began teaching at UMR (now Missouri S&T) in 1964 as a professor of Chemical Engineering. He earned his BS ChE in 1937, his MS ChE in 1938, and his PhD ChE in 1941 at Ohio State University. His professional career took him to General Foods where for 13 years he held positions ranging from Project Engineer to Plant Manager and Manufacturing & Engineering Manager. In addition to his industrial experience, he spent six years as president of Graceland College in Lamoni, Iowa, before coming to the University of Missouri-Rolla. During his 14 years at UMR, he influenced students far beyond the classroom. He was the chemical engineering Freshmen Advisor, the Co-op Student Advisor, the Transfer Student Advisor, and Faculty Advisor to the Student Chapter of AIChE. In recognition of his devotion to UMR, Grice was an Alumni Association Award recipient. He and his wife Ruth became members of the Order of the Golden Shillelagh in 1992.

Dr. Grice's professional affiliations included membership in Alpha Chi Sigma (Beta Delta '70), Tau Beta Pi, Sigma Xi, AIChE, the American Society for Engineering Education, the American Chemical Society, and the Missouri Society of Professional Engineers. He received the Distinguished Alumnus Award from Ohio State University in 1978 and the Outstanding Counselor Award from the American Institute of Chemical Engineers for dedicated service as advisor to the student chapter of AIChE in 1972 and 1978. His talents as an advisor also extended to his church where he held many positions of ministerial leadership over the years. The Harvey H. Grice Endowment Fund was established in his honor for the support of the Chemical Engineering Department.

Grice passed away on October 1, 1993. After his death, he was inducted into the Academy of Chemical Engineers at Missouri S&T posthumously in 1996. Ruth Grice passed away on October 4, 2001.[118]

THE 1980s AND 1990s

The aspirant should study this thoughtfully and thoroughly...
Careful study will open the door to the secrets...

—*Wei Po Yang, Ts'an T'ung Ch'i*

Parenthetical

Recovered records for the years 1980 to 2014 were scant, consisting only of membership lists and a few news clippings from the Missouri Miner, the Alumni magazine, and the Hexagon. Fortunately, it was possible to conduct interviews with several alumni; these provided an overview of the major events described in the chapter. Since only summaries of the decades are presented, the names of those who initiated along with pictures of the members have been placed in the excursus. Where more details of persons and events were available, these have been presented in separate sections.

The Times

The 1980s were the final decade of the Cold War between the two superpowers, the US and the Soviet Union. During the first half of the decade, President Reagan scrapped the policy of détente and adopted a more aggressive stance, escalating tensions between the two countries. The second half of the decade, however, saw a dramatic easing of tensions and ultimately the collapse of the Soviet Union. Nationalism was making a comeback in the eastern European countries, and a desire for democracy in communist-led socialist states, combined with economic recession, led to changes in the Soviet Union and its eventual downfall. As a result, the Berlin Wall was torn down in 1989.

Other major conflicts—the Iran-Iraq War, the Soviet-Afghan War, the 1982 Lebanon War, and the first Intifada in the Gaza Strip and the West Bank (an area bordering Israel which was under Israeli occupation)—also disturbed the world's peace in the 1980s. As if these conflicts did not provide enough suffering for people across the globe, the decade also witnessed the outbreak of the AIDS epidemic.

Not all was bad news, however. The 1980s were a time of great advances in genetic and digital technology. Gene-tagging led to the first gene therapy implementation in 1990. The global internet took shape in the latter half of the decade and by 1989 the Internet, and the networks linked to it, were an extensive system including satellite links.

Conflicts and technological advances continued into the 1990s. After Iraq invaded Kuwait in 1990, the US launched Operation Desert Shield to end Iraq's occupation, and then, in 1991, followed up with an invasion of Iraq, known as Operation Desert Storm. Later, in 1993 the United States became aware of the threat of international terrorism with the first bombing of the World Trade Center. In 1995, the Oklahoma City bombing occurred, and the issue of domestic terrorism became a major concern for the public.

In the realm of gene technology, cloning emerged, gene therapy advanced, and DNA identification led to significant applications in criminal law. The decade was also an exciting time for space exploration: the Galileo space probe reached Jupiter, the first extrasolar planets were discovered, the Pathfinder spacecraft landed on Mars, black holes were confirmed, and the Hubble Space Telescope was launched in 1990. And for those who desired to be emancipated from folding maps, the Global Positioning System (GPS) became operational.

University of Missouri-Rolla

In 1980, the request to change the name of the Chemistry-Chemical Engineering building to the Walter T. Schrenk Hall, first proposed by the Beta Delta members shortly after Dr. Schrenk's death in 1979, was approved by the University of Missouri-Board of Curators.[1]

During this period, major renovations to the Chemical Engineering building were undertaken. In the spring of 1980, work centered on updating physical aspects of the 40-year-old building. New utilities and plumbing were installed, along with an HVAC system for the entire building. These renovations were completed in 1982, and after that Beta Delta was able to once again use the facilities for the initiation ceremonies. Additional renovations were made to Walter T. Schrenk Hall in 1994, when once again, the heating, ventilation and air conditioning systems were updated.[2]

In the spring of 1990 the Chemistry Department received computer equipment and software from IBM worth about $70,000. This new system made it possible for Chemical Engineering students to do molecular modeling graphically for the first time.[3]

Alpha Chi Sigma

In the first half of the decade, two Beta Delta alumni were appointed district counselors: Mitch Levings (Beta Delta '75) was named Texas-Southern District Counselor (1983-1984) to succeed Dr. Robert Desiderato, Jr. (Beta Eta '73) who resigned, and Howard Mizuki (Beta Delta '80) was appointed Michigan District Counselor (1984-1986). Also, in 1983, the new headquarters of Alpha Chi Sigma in Indianapolis was completed.[4]

In 1985, Alpha Chi Sigma brothers were recognized for their significant achievements in the chemical sciences. Dr. R. Bruce Merrifield, Beta Gamma (UCLA), earned the Nobel Prize in Chemistry for his work with solid-phase peptide synthesis, while Dr. H. C. Brown, Beta Nu (Purdue), won the Gold Medal of the American Institute for Chemists for his service to the science of chemistry. Dr. Kenneth Pitzer, Sigma (CA-Berkeley), received the Welch Award from the Welch Foundation, a private funding source for fundamental chemistry research at educational institutions, for his achievements in quantum mechanics, statistical mechanics and thermodynamics. A few years later, in 1988, Dr. George H. Hitchings, Omicron (Harvard), was awarded the Nobel Prize in Medicine for his work in the development of drugs like AZT which were used in the treatment of AIDS.[5]

In 1991 the Supreme Council established a new award, named after Order of Altotus brother Ronald T. Pflaum, which would recognize the Outstanding Chapter Advisor and would be given at the Conclaves. That year the Supreme Council also added the finishing touches to the Risk Management Policy, the comprehensive statement which defined the fraternity's position on substance abuse, hazing and sexual harassment.

Another significant advancement was made in 1995. Several chapters expanded their Boy Scout program to include Girl Scouts. Working through Albert Holler, Chair of the Scout Activities Committee, the fraternity assisted in developing the new chemistry program for girls and young women across the country.[6]

Beta Delta

Throughout the late 1960s and early 1970s the nation's collegiate population developed a deeper consciousness of what was happening in society beyond the confines of the campuses. Strong sentiment against the Vietnam War led to anti-establishment attitudes—not only toward government institutions but toward many other traditional organizations as well. Fraternities and sororities were among the suspect institutions. Many students began to see them as elitist organizations—with their secret rituals and forced discipline—and begun to shun them. Membership in all Greek letter societies, including Alpha Chi Sigma, dropped, and chapters closed all over the country. Though Beta Delta had fewer successful activities, it did not shut down. It did experience a decline in membership, which began in the mid-1980s and extended through the 1990s. Moreover, in the 1990s, the chapter compounded the membership decline with its failure to build on its strengths—still present in the 1980s—and to execute requirements vital to its continuation.[7]

In addition to the social bias against fraternities, an abhorrence and intolerance of hazing and drinking on college campuses was growing, which precipitated an evaluation by fraternities of their behavior and implementation of policies to protect their members and allay public concerns. Alpha Chi Sigma was no exception, and Beta Delta adopted the measures set forth by the national fraternity. Though anti-hazing rules had always been part of Alpha Chi Sigma's constitution and by-laws, alcohol and sexual abuse on college campuses became a significant issue in the early 1980s. The Professional Fraternity Association (PFA) became much more concerned about these issues and began pressuring the professional fraternities to take a closer look at managing their risks.

The issues raised by the PFA were first brought to the Supreme Council by Paul Jones (later to be Grand Master Alchemist 1990-1992) in the 1988-1990 Biennium, and by 1992 the fraternity decided to take action. The next two years, 1993-1994, were spent developing policies and reviewing the implications with the chapters. The first Risk Management Policy was approved at the 1994 Conclave in Minneapolis, MN. It addressed the issues of hazing, alcohol and drug abuse, and sexual assault. At the time, members were expected to read the policies and sign an agreement to abide by them. (These policies remained in effect until they were updated in 2020.)

Though the societal bias against fraternities, in general, may have been a contributing factor in the decline of Beta Delta, in particular, there may have been earlier signs that forewarned of the downturn. As early as the fall of 1983, the MA Report in the Beta Delta Data expressed concern over the chapter's diminishing numbers. The following year (1984) the chapter room was lost to a professor who persuasively argued that he needed more room in which to conduct his research. The Chemistry-Chemical Engineering departments obliged, forcing Beta Delta to relinquish a crucial area on campus which allowed members to congregate and socialize. That same year, MA Pat Van Ryckeghem noted in the Beta Delta Data that the chapter had diminished not only in size but in the scope of its activities as well. At the beginning of the spring semester, no activities—other than the usual pledge functions—were planned. In the fall, the members made an attempt to recover, however, pledging 17 that semester, which doubled the membership. Activities—including the reactivation of the chapter's safety program—started up once again.[8]

But beginning in 1986, the submission of chapter reports to the district counselor and the national office became sporadic. After the Risk Management Policy was implemented in 1994, customs—such as the pledge final and mass transfer—had to be modified or discontinued because of the potential perception that hazing might be involved. Alterations like these almost certainly had a negative effect on the chapter's membership. Ironically, changes intended to remove factors contributing to the decrease in membership—societal bias against fraternities and the allegations of alcohol abuse and sexual abuse—effectively disrupted the opportunities for the shared experiences and friendship-building activities necessary for any successful social organization. Whether this was causally true or not, a precipitous decline occurred immediately after the changes were implemented. The chapter did not initiate any new members in spring or fall of 1995, nor in the spring of 1996. Furthermore, no delegate was sent to Conclave in 1996. This immediately placed the chapter on probation, threatening Beta Delta's status as an active chapter.[9]

Though membership increased slightly toward the end of the decade, the downward trend continued into the 1990s. This decline, coupled with loss of membership from graduations, placed the chapter in a precarious situation. Moreover, smaller numbers meant fewer members willing to step into leadership roles, and—suddenly—Beta Delta was floundering.[10]

Though Beta Delta alumni, Charles and Valerie Bagnell, led a team in the development of the fraternity's Group and Resource Organizational Workshop (GROW) in 1992, which replaced the Laboratory for Leadership Program created by Don Coyne, by 1988 there was little interest in participating in such leadership-building projects. In the few cases in which there was attendance at these workshops, there was no follow-up to ensure that what was learned was applied to the chapter. No reports of short-term or long-term planning were submitted to the district counselor.[11]

District activities were seldom attended; travel and interaction with other chapters in the district declined sharply. According to the DC's report in 1998, Beta Delta was encouraged to strengthen relationships within the district, especially attending the 2000 district conclave in St. Louis; resume Professional Recognition ceremonies, which had not been conducted for several years; and reconnect with alumni, but, for the most part, these obligations were not met. Other contributing factors plaguing the fraternity included the initiation of people who did not meet the membership qualifications and a seeming lack of enthusiasm and seriousness among the members, which did not reflect favorably on prospective pledges. There may also have been a lack of support from the national fraternity. Nevertheless initiations resumed in the fall of 1996, and a delegate, Mozow Yusof, was sent to the 1998 Conclave held in Atlanta, GA, staving off the inactivation of the chapter. Beta Delta would not reverse the decline and place itself on a path of recovery until early in the next decade.[12]

Chapter Activities—1980s

Despite declining numbers, available records indicate that during the 1980s and into the first few years of the 1990s the chapter engaged in the usual activities: conducting chemistry help sessions, pledging, holding initiations and officer elections (see tables below), organizing Mass Transfer and the Boy Scouts Merit Badge program, attending the Biennial Conclaves (See appendix Beta Delta Conclave Attendance), and sponsoring various social activities.[13]

In the spring of 1980 a new tactic for guiding pledges was tested out by VMA Peggy Taylor. The program entailed having one member from the chapter assigned for each pledge. The active member was to remind pledges of Alpha Chi Sigma activities and motivate them in their study of the fraternity. The intent of Taylor's plan was not only to increase participation of the actives; it was to instill a sense of unity and brotherhood among the pledges as well. At the fall Smoker (no date given), the pledge class heard Dr. Harvey Grice speak about the professional chapter and had the supplemental text, *Alchemy*—published by the Grand Chapter—added to their educational arsenal. The trivia contest following Dr. Grice's talk, should logically have been won by the table at which Grice sat with Drs. Crosser and Johnson, but, for some reason, that astute team did not come away with the win, proving that the profs were not infallible. Formal pledging was held on October 2; Julie O'Connell was selected as the pledge captain.[14]

In addition to instruction of pledges, the chapter also engaged in other activities of an educational nature during the 1980s. In the spring of 1985, a display on Alchemy and the history of distillation was created and installed in the Chemical Engineering building, and a chemistry magic show was presented on University Day (date could not be determined) and Parents' Day (April 16). Reactions used in the magic show included: Tollen's Test (silver on the inside of a one-liter flask), ammonia fountain (ammonia dissolving in water pulls water into a flask), colored flares, iodine clock, liquid nitrogen, and the making of Prussian blue and chrome yellow. The magic show was also used at the annual Boy Scout Chemistry Merit Badge Day (February 23). That 1985 event was one of the biggest in the history of the chapter, with 22 scouts from five different troops participating.[15]

The chapter engaged not only in activities to improve the minds of others and stimulate interest in the chemical sciences, but the members also worked diligently at upgrading safety practices in the labs. In 1986, the reactivated safety committee, chaired by Carol Kenesey, organized a slide show for the chemistry lab classes and reviewed the location and use of the safety shower, the fire extinguisher, and the eye wash stations with chemistry students. In addition, the committee presented a long-range plan to the Chemical and Chemical Engineering faculty that would improve hood ventilation and air circulation in the labs.[16]

Many of the socially oriented customs were still undertaken in the 1980s. In the spring of 1982 the Weidemann Cup was wrested from Beta Delta's grasp after a valiant struggle. Beta Delta lost by only one touchdown, but neither the score nor the opposing team—presumably Delta chapter—were reported). The Cup would find its way back home, however, in the fall of 1983. Since the game that year ended in a 14-14 tie, the winner was determined in a chugging contest between the Master Alchemists of the competing chapters. The MA who drank beer from the cup the fastest would win the prized Weidemann Cup for the chapter. Beta Delta's MA, Pat Van Ryckeghem, downed the contents of the Cup in 38 seconds. The Delta MA took so long, the team did not even report her time. The heroic efforts of one stalwart Beta Delta carried the day. But not for long. By the fall 1987, the Weidemann Cup was in the possession of Gamma Theta in Kirksville, MO, 185 miles to the north.[17]

Concerns over the chapter room continued throughout the first half of the 1980s. During the spring of 1982, the room had to be moved to a temporary location because of the renovation of the chemistry building. The following spring, it returned to its original location. By the fall of 1984, however, the space had been snatched away altogether.[18]

Officers 1980s[19]					
Office	1980		1981	1982	
	Spring	Fall	Spring	Spring	Fall
Master Alchemist	Steve Zuiss	Mike Schmidt	Eddie Kyser	Dave Sextro	Dale Abrahams
Vice-Master Alchemist	Peggy Taylor	Peter Scholtes	Christopher Wood	Mike Schmidt	Pat VanRyckeghem
Reporter	Rich Purgason		Dave Sextro	Karen Penny	Karen Penny
Recorder	Kevin Hagan	James Roberts	Jeff Hunninghake	Betty Weinhold	Julie Deles
Treasurer	Jane Riolo		Christopher Thomas	Lisa Baganoff	Lisa Baganoff
Master of Ceremonies	Brent Sparks		Rex Stammerjohn	Dale Kyser	Howard Mizuki
Historian	Tony Petruska		Janet Thornton	Cindy Knapstein	Chris Lancaster
Alumni Secretary	Steve Zigrye		Bruce Fortune	Jeff Hunninghake	Jeff Hunninghake
Chapter Advisor	Dr. Beistel	Dr. Beistel	Dr. Beistel	Dr. Don Beistel	Dr. Beistel

Note: The fall of 1982 also saw the return of the office of historian which had been dormant for many semesters.[20]

Officers 1980s[21]						
Office	1983		1984		1985	
	Spring	Fall	Spring	Fall	Spring	Fall
Master Alchemist	Howard Mizuki	Pat Van Ryckeghem	Christie Lakeman	Tom Kreek	Greg Mattingly	Jeff Huber
Vice-Master Alchemist	Karen Penny	Chris Lakeman	Mark Santschi	Eva Freund	Joyce Weinhold	Mark Hall
Reporter	Mark Santschi	Mark Santschi	Theresa Ney	Theresa Ney	Steve Shinn	Steven Shinn
Recorder	Joyce Weinhold	Diane Clements	John Hume	Dawn Dupler	Sue Manda	Nora Tochtrop
Treasurer	Julie Deles	Julie Deles	Greg Mattingly	Greg Mattingly	Jerry Jenkins	Jerry Jenkins
Master of Ceremonies	Chris Lancaster	Thomas Kreek	Carol Maxeiner/ Andrew Hall (Assist.)	Andrew Hall/ John Hume (Assist.)	John Hume/ Ken Curtis (Assist.)	John Hume/ Bill Carr (Assist.)
Historian	Pat Van Ryckeghem	Jim Hays	Val Johnson	Tom Burns	Ed Harris	Jonna Cole
Alumni Secretary	Eva Freund	Eva Freund	Joyce Weinhold	Joyce Weinhold	Stephen Guck	Stephen Guck
Chapter Advisor	Dr. Beistel	Dr. Beistel	Dr. Beistel	Dr. Beistel	Dr. Beistel	Dr. Beistel

	Officers 1980s					
Office	1986		1987		1989	
	Spring	Fall	Spring	Fall	Spring	Fall
Master Alchemist	John Hume	John Denzel	Dave Schlotzhauer	Laura Oehlert	Laura Spencer	Fred Roe
Vice-Master Alchemist	Jerry Jenkins	Dave Schlotzhauer	Laura Oehlert	Rob Holt	Fred Roe	Anne Chmelir
Reporter	Jody Mawhorter	Jody Mawhorter	Yvonne Paris	Yvonne Paris	Michael Miller	
Recorder	Yvonne Paris	Maureen Flick	Julie Minzey	Susan Mullins	Dave Platt	Clara Edwards
Treasurer	Steve Shinn	Steve Shinn	Eric Steutemann	Eric Steutemann	Tracy Perkins	Chip Divin, Assist. Treas.
Master of Ceremonies	Bill Carr/ John Denzel (Assist.)	Andrew Hall/Mike Fredholm (Assist.)	Mike Fredholm/ Maureen Flick (Assist.)	Rich Schuth/ Mark Hewlett (Assist.)	Teresa Sears/ Keith Belville, Assist. MC	Keith Belville/ Dan Carey, Assist. MC
Historian	Mike Fredholm	Eric Steutemann	Mark Biznek	Don McGowan	Allen Brown	Allen Brown
Alumni Secretary	Lisa Schipper	Lisa Schipper		Peggy Kolodziej	Mike Drury	
Chapter Advisor	Dr. Beistel	Dr. Beistel	Dr. Beistel	Dr. Beistel	Dr. Ybarra	Dr. Ybarra

At the start of the decade, Beta Delta received an interesting honor. During the 1980 Conclave, the chapter won a cash award for having the most collegiate members in attendance. The delegation decided not to accept the money, however, and returned the award to the fraternity to be used for a traveling plaque instead. In the future, the Beta Delta delegates stipulated, the plaque should be presented to the chapter with the most collegiate members at Conclave. The award was to include a distance weighting—so the distance traveled by each delegation would play into the equation—and it would be named, of course, after W. T. Schrenk.[22]

Though the professional recognition ceremonies were not always accurately recorded, honoring the graduating seniors continued to be one of the important threads holding chapter members together. Seniors recognized in the spring of 1983 included: Dale Abrahams, Lisa Baganoff, Jan Keutzer, Cindy Knapstein, Chris Lancaster, Mike Luke, Howard Mizuki, Bruce Spinzig, Rex Stammerjohnn, Jon Treat, and John Draper. In 1984, Jim Hays, Christie Lakeman, and Pat Van Ryckeghem—who stayed on for graduate school and also became the Editor-in-Chief for the Missouri Miner—were recognized. The graduates honored in the fall of 1985 included: Jeff Huber, Mark Hall, Joyce Weinhold, Valerie Johnson, Kenneth Curtis, Diane Clements, Scott Mayes, and Eva Freund.[23]

The Prof. Snarf award also hung on into the 1980s. Two lucky professors won the award for the spring of 1982. Dr. Neil Book received the greatest number of votes from the ChE Department, while Dr. Don Siehr won the award from the Chemistry Department. Both graciously acknowledged the honor that fall at the September 16 AIChE Smoker.[24]

Members also received recognition for their activities outside of their involvement with Beta Delta. Several of the chapter's women, for example, were nominated for Homecoming Queen: Natalie Betz in 1986, Susan Schumacher in 1986, and Maureen Flick in 1988 (Unfortunately they were not selected for the royal position).[25] Receiving honors, however, was not restricted to women. GDI (The organization of Independents) named Bob Linke, ChE, initiated in 1985, as that organization's St. Pat's Student Knight in 1989.[26]

Natalie Betz-Missouri Miner | Susan Schumacher-Missouri Miner | Maureen Flick Rollamo 1988

Robert Linke—Rollamo 1989

Though Beta Delta's central concern during the 1980s was the establishment of risk management policies and ensuring that the chapter had adequate liability coverage, the decade was framed by more serious events of grief. In September 1980, Judy Flebbe passed away after a tragic accident. Immediately after her death, the Judith L. Flebbe Scholarship award was established by alumni and active members of

Beta Delta. By the spring of 1981, the fund was off to a good start, having received $1500 in donations plus another $1000 from Beta Delta. A committee of ChE faculty had also been formed by this time to select recipients of the award.[27] (For a list of some of the recipients and the initial donors see Appendix D.)

At the close of the decade the chapter received news of two other deaths. Dr. William Webb passed away in May of 1989, and Mary Kay O'Conner, wife of Mike O'Conner (Beta Delta '73), was killed in the Phillips petroleum plant explosion in Pasadena, TX, in October of 1989 (see the Excursus below).

Chapter Activities—1990s

Only a few notable events and recognitions for Alpha Chi Sigma and Beta Delta members were recorded in the Hexagon, the Missouri Miner, and the Meeting Minutes from 1990 through 1999.

\multicolumn{6}{c}{Officers 1990s[28]}					
Office	1990		1991		1992
	Spring	Fall	Spring	Fall	Spring
Master Alchemist	Tony Rouse	Clara Edwards	Doug Rivard	Mark McCoy	Rachel Wiggins
Vice-Master Alchemist	Clara Edwards	Shawn Sitton	Sean Dingman	Rachel Wiggins	Robert Randolph
Reporter	Susan Shefchyk		Lori Sticker	Lori Stricker	Brian Mangonia
Recorder	Shawn Sitton		Rebecca Lema	Charles Buttry	Deanne Valentino
Treasurer	Chip Divin	Chip Divin/Darren Rosenbaum, Assist.	Darren Rosenbaum	Darren Rosenbaum/ Marcus Bahr, Assist. Treas.	Mark Bahr/ Wayne Greene, Assist Treas.
Master of Ceremonies	Dan Carey/ Doug Rivard, Assist. MC	Doug Rivard/ Brian Lawrence, Assist. MC	Mike Halbach/ Mark McCoy, Assist. MC	Mike Halbach/ Shawn Edwards, Assist. MC	Larry Dechent/ Kevin Robertson, Assist. MC
Historian	Mark McCoy	Mark McCoy	Dave Cramer	Steve Ford	Lena Tsoulfanidis
Alumni Secretary	Carrie Sachs		Barbra Halpin		Mike Smith
Chapter Advisor	Dr. Ybarra	Dr. Ybarra	Dr. Ybarra	Dr. Ybarra	Dr. Ybarra

In 1990, Jill Goetges, a metallurgical engineering student and a 1989 Beta Delta initiate, was nominated by Sigma Tau Gamma as a St. Pat's Queen candidate. Unfortunately, even the sobriquet "metallurgical engineer in Alpha Chi Sigma" could not guarantee the coveted crown.[29]

Jill Goetges—Rollamo 1992

Also, in 1990, Beta Delta was touched by the war in Iraq. Brian Lawrence had left the campus and joined the armed forces to fight in Kuwait as part of Operation Desert Storm. Since he was the Assistant Master of Ceremonies at the time, a special election for his replacement was held on August 29, 1990. Mike Halbach was elected.[30]

In 1994, Beta Delta achieved a remarkable milestone for the fraternity. Anica Elaine Winkle, initiated Nov. 5, 1994, won the distinction of being Alpha Chi Sigma's 50,000th member.[31]

Excursus

Dr. William H. Webb

Dr. Webb, who passed away on May 6, 1989, was arguably Beta Delta's most prominent alumnus—second only to his mentor and friend, Dr. W.T. Schrenk.

Dr. William H. Webb 1977

Dr. Webb first came to Rolla in 1936 with a BS degree from Mississippi State College to do graduate work with Schrenk, who was then head of the Chemistry-Chemical Engineering Department. Webb liked what he found in the Department and its Chair. His original intention was to do graduate work at the School of Mines and Metallurgy and then move on. However, those plans did not work out: he was a graduate assistant for one year, but then stayed on to become a full-time instructor. He received his MS degree in 1939.[32]

Webb was initiated into Alpha Chi Sigma in 1938. Three years later, in January 1941, he was elected Alumni Secretary[33] and held that position until 1942. He would go on to be Chapter Advisor for almost twenty years (1947 to 1964) and Missouri Valley District Counselor from 1964 to 1967.[34] Because of his workload, Dr. Webb found it necessary to resign his position of District Counselor in the spring of '68:

> *May 8, 1968, Dear Brother Miller: It is with regret that I must submit my resignation as District Counselor for the Mid-West District*

of Alpha Chi Sigma. My duties have piled up so much that I feel that a younger person should take over and give more assistance to these chapters. I have mailed Ed Schneider my copies of the Chapter Survey Reports for Delta and Alpha Epsilon. I will visit Delta on May 9 and 10 and complete these reports. The effective date of my resignation is May 15, 1968. This should enable my replacement to attend the Conclave which I consider very important. I am still holding the travel check and will return it if a replacement is found. I could attend the Conclave, but in the interest of economy for the Fraternity, I feel that the new Counselor should attend. If I can continue to be of service to the organization in any other way, don't hesitate to call. Yours in the double bond, William H. Webb, District Counselor[35]

Though there were very few women students on the campus at the time, many came to the Summer School sessions, then run by University of Missouri-Columbia's School of Education. One of them was Ruby Fogleman, a teacher from Eldon, to whom Webb took a liking. They were married in 1942, just one month before Webb was called to active duty with the army. He served four years as a commissioned officer in an anti-aircraft artillery unit with duties in England, France, Belgium, Holland, and Germany. He returned in November, 1945, and began teaching again at MSM in January of 1946.

After the war, Webb was away from Rolla only one time. He was granted a sabbatical leave of absence by the Board of Curators in May of 1948 for the following academic year to work on his PhD at the University of Wisconsin. With his PhD in hand, he continued teaching and doing research in his special fields—analytical chemistry and radiochemistry. Webb also worked five summers during the fifties as research chemist and physicist at the Oak Ridge National Laboratory. He also did contract work with the US Atomic Energy Commission on separation of fission products, held two patents on separation of fission elements by electrodialysis, and was listed in "Who's Who in Engineering," "Leaders of American Science," and "Who's Who in Atoms," in Great Britain. On September 1, 1957, he was promoted to full professorship.[36]

Dr. Webb was involved in another significant project conducted by MSM for the US Air Force in the 1950s. The project concerned the methods of plating titanium onto other metals and was completed—after three and a half years—in 1956. Titanium, at the time, was a relatively new metal and was noted for its resistance to corrosion. The Air Force was interested in finding ways to plate titanium coating onto a base metal such as iron or copper. Contracts for research were made with the Metallurgy Department of MSM, the US Bureau of Standards, and the College Park, Maryland, Station of the US Bureau of Mines. All the studies indicated that the metal could not be plated from aqueous solutions as was the case with nickel or chromium. The final solution was determined by the team at MSM: a bath of molten salts maintained at high temperature and protected by an atmosphere of helium gas.[37]

An advisory board, on which Dr. Webb served, was the impetus for the establishment of a mineral research lab in Rolla. Webb and other members of the board served as part-time consultants to the lab which, as a division of Geomar Minerals Corp., was incorporated under the laws of the State of Missouri to provide commercial testing and analysis facilities in the Midwest. The laboratories provided petrographic and mineral analysis, and X-Ray, spectrographic, chemical, and radiometric analysis. Webb also served on the Advisory Committee which oversaw the Nuclear Reactor project which was constructed at MSM in the early 1960s.[38]

An especially meaningful recognition for Dr. Webb was the invitation he received to be the principal speaker at the American Chemical Society's Gold Anniversary on Wednesday, September 30, 1959. The University of Missouri section of the American Chemical Society launched the Anniversary celebration of its 50 years of activity on the Columbia campus. The occasion allowed Dr. Webb to focus his address on his favorite topic—the nuclear studies at MSM—and his speech included an explanation of the characteristics of the reactor: its type, core, and thermal flux.[39]

In 1963, MSM hosted an institute for High School Science Teachers. This was the sixth consecutive summer in which the eight-week course was offered. The institute was sponsored by the National Science Foundation. The summer of '63 saw 75 teachers—who could apply completed Institute work toward the degree of Master of Science for Teachers—in attendance. Courses offered included: Intermediate Chemistry, General Physics, Advanced Modern Physics for High School Teachers, Modern Mathematics for Secondary School Teachers, Review of Analytic Geometry and Calculus, Advanced Algebra for Secondary School Teachers, and a special one credit hour course in Introduction to Operating Principles of Nuclear Reactors for High School Teachers. Dr. Webb was a member of the faculty for the Institute.[40]

Dr. Webb became chair of the department in 1964, the year the Chemistry-Chemical Engineering department was separated into two departments. By the time of his appointment as Chair, Webb had been published in the Analytic Chemistry, Review of Scientific Instruments, Physical Review, and Industrial and Engineering Chemistry. Another accomplishment was achieved in 1968, when Dr. Webb, along with two of his former students—Dr. Harry C. Hershey and Ronald D. Mitchell—was issued a United States Patent. The patent involved the separation of radioactive chemicals produced by nuclear fission—specifically radioactive cesium and strontium, which are used in medical work and research.[41]

Besides his duties during the academic year, Webb was the Director of a Summer Institute (during the summers of 1964, '65, and '66) in Nuclear Science and Engineering for College Teachers, which was sponsored jointly by the Atomic Energy Commission and the National Science Foundation.

Throughout his career, Webb was affiliated with many professional organizations, including Sigma Xi, American Society for Engineering Education, Alpha Chi Sigma, and the American Chemical Society, which he served as Vice-President. In 1966, he was also elected as Counselor for the South Central Missouri Section of the American Society for Chemistry, which had received its charter that year.[42]

Webb retired in 1977, at which time he was honored with the title of Professor Emeritus (A professor emeritus remains as a non-voting member of the campus faculty whose name appears in the list of Officers of Instruction and Administration in the university catalog). At the Alumni Awards Banquet, the closing event of Homecoming '77, Webb was recognized by the Alumni Association and honored with these words from Alumni Association President Bauer:

> We recognize him not only for his outstanding ability as a teacher, researcher, and administrator, but for the frank, wise and thoughtful counsel which he was always willing to bring to the concerns of the campus.[43]

In 1988, Webb was honored once again when the William H. Webb Reading Room in Schrenk Hall was dedicated to him. (This room no longer exists).

After retiring in 1977, the Webbs moved to Louisville, Mississippi, within 9 miles of the farm on which Webb grew up. He and his wife, Ruby, had four children and four grandchildren. As an alumnus, Webb continued to support the school he loved; he was a long-time member of the Century Club, (donors who contributed more than $100 yearly).[44]

After his illustrious career in chemistry, and his raising of a successful family, Webb died on May 6, 1989, at the age of 77. He was buried at Noxapater Methodist Cemetery in Noxapater, Winston County, Mississippi, his boyhood home. Webb was born on February 11, 1912 to John Foster Webb and Lula Mae (Burrage) Webb.[45]

Webb's wife would live another 20 years. She passed away on 9 June, 2019, in Kansas City, MO, at the age of 102. She taught several years in the Missouri public school system, teaching at Eugene, Valley Park, and Rolla. After she and Webb were married (May 22, 1942), she remained active in the First United Methodist Church of Rolla, the Coterie—a society of university faculty wives—and the League of Women Voters. After her husband's death, she traveled extensively around the world with her sisters and friends.

In 2000, she moved to Kansas City, MO, and, in 2006, to the Kingswood Retirement Community. While at Kingswood, she volunteered in the library and joined a knitting group, making hundreds of knitted caps for newborns for several area hospitals. Over the years she kept in touch with her friends and family through letters, an activity which gave her great pleasure.[46]

Mary Kay O'Connor

Though Mary Kay (b. 1955) was not a member of Alpha Chi Sigma, she was the wife of Mike O'Connor (Beta Delta '73) and a chemical engineering graduate of the University of Missouri in Columbia, with an MBA from the University of Houston-Clear Lake. As such, she was very much a part of the Beta Delta family.[47]

In October of 1989, Mary Kay, an Operations Superintendent, along with 22 others, lost their lives in an explosion at the Phillips Petroleum Complex in Pasadena, TX. The explosion injured an additional 314 people.

The facility produced approximately 6.8 million tons per year of high-density polyethylene, a plastic used to make milk bottles and other containers. The accident involved a series of explosions initiated by the release of flammable process gases that occurred during regular maintenance operations in one of the plant's polyethylene reactors. The initial explosion registered 3.5 on the Richter Scale.[48]

Mary Kay's death led to a call for a greater emphasis on process safety in chemical engineering all across the country. After the incident, Mike O'Connor sent a proposal to 10 different universities to have process safety included at the academic level before engineers joined the workforce and entered other facilities.

Brother O'Connor envisioned a 'Process Safety Center,' not just to memorialize his wife, but to address the problem that took her life and to integrate process safety into the curriculum at the education, research, and service levels.[49]

The Mary Kay O'Connor Process Safety Center was established in 1995 as part of the Texas A&M Engineering Experiment Station (TEES) in her memory. The Center's mission is to promote safety as second nature in industry with the goal of preventing future accidents like the one that took her life.[50]

Members-1980s

First Row: Not identified

Second Row: Not identified, Not identified, H. Mizuki, Not identified, Not identified, Not identified

Third Row: Not identified, N. (Brown) Fischer, P. Scholte, P. (Taylor) Scholte, K. Todd, Not identified

Fourth Row: Not identified, D. Gerber, Not identified, J. Riolo, Not identified, Not identified

Fifth Row: S. Zigrye, J. (Trampe) Zigrye, D. Parks, Not identified, Not identified, E. Smoot

Sixth Row: M. Ziobro, Not identified, Not identified, Not identified, Not identified, S. Zuiss

(Identifications were not given in the Rollamo)

Beta Delta 1980—Rollamo 1980

Above: E. Kyser, C. Maxeiner, J. Hume, V. Johnson, J. Weinhold; Second Row: D. Clements, S. Breeden, T. Kreek, J. Deles, A. Hall, D. Dupler, T. Ney, S. Manda; Third Row: P. Reddy, S. Guck, D. Schlotzhauer, M. Laudenschlager, D. Lucas, J. Wakeman, R. Burns; Fourth Row: C. Mans, M. Hall, J. Brandel, J. Jenkins, M. Santschi, T. Buelter, C. Lakeman, J. Huber, J. Hayes.

Beta Delta-1984—Rollamo 1984

First Row: J. Jenkins, C. Manns, S. Breedan, D. Schlotzhaver, K. Blankenship, T. Buelter; Second Row: V. Johnson, D. Lucas, D. Hurt, J. Huber, E. Harris, B. Lashley, E. Keyser; Third Row: T. Burns, T. Ney, D. Dupler, J. Weinhold, J. Hume, G. Mattingley, T. Kreck, A. Hall, E. Freund, B. Steven

Beta Delta 1985—Rollamo 1985

First Row: J. Denzel, R. Horn, L. Schipper, D. Schlotzhauer, T. Kreek; Second Row: J. Cole, L. Camp, Y. Paris, K. McCoy, J. Weinhold, N. Tochtrop; Third Row: C. Koller, S. Donze, A. Hall, S. Meyer, J. Wakeman; Fourth Row: C. Mans, E. Carr, C. Keran, S. Guck, P. Wall, J. Jenkins; Fifth Row: M. Hall, M. Loudenslager, E. Bussen, J. Hume, E. Kyser, B. Stevens

Beta Delta 1986-Rollamo 1986

The 1980s and 1990s

First Row: M. Fredholm, J. Robinson, S. Shinn, A. Hall, J. Minzey, D. Backer; Second Row: G. Steutemann, L. Snelson, L. Oehlert; Third Row: L. Schipper, D. Scholtzhauer, M. Flick, J. Denzel; Fourth Row: M Armstrong, L. Camp, V. Paris, R. Holt, D. Draheim, S. Donze, N. Betz; Fifth Row: E. Bussen, B. Linke, C. Kenesay, J. Mawhorter, P. Gripka

Beta Delta 1987—Rollamo 1987

(The membership is listed in alphabetical order and does not align with the photograph) M. Barnett, J. Barr, H. Barstad, K. Bellville, B. Bethel, M. Biznek, T. Blue, C. Bough, D. Brandt, A. Brown, N. Butler, E. Bussen, D. Carey, A. Chmelir, S. Clark, D. Clifton, A. Cohen, D. Cramer, M. DeBarr, S. Depriest, C. Divin, M. Drury, C. Edwards, G. Elphingstone, J. Fabella, D. Fitzgibbons, M. Flick, G. Flieg, J. Frank, K. Ford, J. Goetges, A. Hall, S. Hattikudar, C. Hayes, B. Hearn, M. Hilton, B. Linke, L. Luther, D. McClellan, M. Miller, D. Molli, T. Neaf, T. Perkins, D. Platt, S. Risbeck, F. Roe, L. Ross, T. Rouse, S. Ruggeri, L. Samaie, R. Schuth, T. Sears, L. Snelson, A. Spears, L. Spencer, L. Stricker, A. Voyles, B. Watson, Ge. Weible, D. Weible, D. Weidman, G. Wilkening, B. Ybarra

Beta Delta 1989-Rollamo 1989

Initiates-1980s

1980		
Spring (March 30)	Spring (March 30)	Fall (Nov 23)
Jon W. Treat	Dale A. Kyser	Loree A. (Gahen) Rowe
Jason L. Behm	Michael W. McMenus	Bruce D. Spinzig
Rebecca L. (Pickens) Siscel	Bruce R. Fortune	James L. Schoen
Howard T. Mizuki	George D. Havalias	Paul J. Dolan
Cynthia S. (Mette) Gross	Charles L. Meyer	Edward J. Nobus
Alan L. Fox	Cynthia A. Lackner	David C. Sextro
Marjorie R. (Adler) Green	Christine M. (O'Neil) Dashti	Joseph H. Holli (Nov 17)
Christopher J. Thomas	Rex W. Stammerjohn	Betty C. (Weinhold) Baggett
Christopher L. Wood	Larry D. Wayman	Julie A. (O'Connell) Yerigan
Bart H. Mild	Jeffery J. Hunninghake	Susan A. (Sharp) Murphy
Donna K. Parks	Cindy Locke	Cynthia M. (Knapstein) Henneberger

1981	
Spring (March 29)	Fall (Nov 22)
Kammie R. (Akers) Settle	Connie A. Myers
Janice M. Keutzer	Scott D. Lemmons
Michael E. Luke	John B. Draper
Janel G. Davidson	Lorraine L. Gochanour
Jeffrey R. Ramberg	Chris E. Lancaster
Roger K. Dougherty	Karen C. (Penny) White
Lisa K. (Baganoff) Gaynor	Patrick J. Van Ryckeghem
James W. Rieck	
Paul W. Kramer	
Janel G. Rundlett	

The 1980s and 1990s

1982	
Spring (March 28)	Fall (Nov 7)
Rae A. Kelly	Brent M. Babyak
Eva R. (Freund) Miranda	Thomas W. Kreek
Julie A. (Deles) Stansfield	Mark E. Santschi
James J. Bogan	Joyce S. (Weinhold) Hume
	Christie A. Lakeman
	Jean-Christophe J. Hajduk (Nat'l)
	Kenneth J. McNeely

Note: In 1982 two others had pledged but, apparently, did not initiate—Ellen Westerman, Chem. and Joan Maruske, ChE. Also, Howard Mizuki would become District Counselor for the Michigan District in 1984.[51]

1983	
Spring (March 27)	Fall (Nov 20)
Jerry J. Brandel	Christopher B. Mongillo
James P. Hays	John A. Hume
Juan M. Ayala	David S. Schlotzhauer
Carol E. (Maxine) Edwards	Susan M. (Breden) Nichols
Marjorie D. (Clements) Gilbert	Valerie A. (Johnson) O'Keefe
Greg W. Mattingly	Dawn A. Dupler
John Collins	Theresa A. (Ney) Ziegelmeyer
Laura A. (Duet?) Ford	Kris L. Kyser (Blankenship)
	Andrew F. Hall
	James MacElroy

Note: According to the fall, 1983, issue of the Beta Delta Data, Dr. Jean Hadjuk was initiated at Beta chapter. Neither the Beta Delta Membership Register nor the National Office records list Dr. Hadjuk as having initiated as a Beta Delta member.

1984	
Spring (April 15)	Fall (Nov 4)
Cary D. Mans	Kenneth I. Curtis
David J. Hurt	Stephen D. Hancock
William A. Lashley	John S. Claudius
Thomas W. Burns	Patrick J. Gripka
James Stoffer	Jonna L. (Cole) Horn
Suzanne M. (Mande) Alexander	Andrew D. Kazanas
Mark R. Hall	Deborah L. (Manley) Yarnell
James C. Wakeman	Chris M. Keran
Mai H. Nguyen	Richard L. Clegg
Diane C. (Lucas) Millikin	Donghwi S. Shinn
Jerry B. Jenkins	Linda L. Camp
Edward S. Harris	John C. Denzel (pledge captain)
Stephen M. Guck	Paul F. Isakson
Thomas R. Buelter	Cynthia A. (Keller) Chapman
Anthony T. Kaczmarek	William C. Carr
Jeffrey A. Huber	Philip M. Wall
Mark D. Loudenslager	

1985	
Spring (April 14)	Fall (Nov 17)
Richard G. Horn	Jody K. (Mawhorter) Baughman (best pledge)
Louis C. Brueggeman	Denis A. Backer
Nora C. Tochtrop	Mikael R. Fredholm
Suzanne M. McMeyer	Denise L. Draheim
Michelle (Donye) Gaither	Laura A. (Oehlert) Clegg
Gayle M. (Behr) Schlotzhauer	Eric G. Steutermann
Yvonne S. (Paris) Prevallet	John M. Kelly
Lisa K. (Shipper) Mayberry	Scott E. Mayes (pledge captain)
James L. Baker	Robert C. Linke
Todd J. Newsom	Robert V. Tokar
Eric W. Bussen	Maureen M. Flick (best plaque)
Kimberly A. Curran	

1986	
Spring (April 20)	Fall (Nov 16)
Lori Snelson	Karla J. Bier
Donald E. McGowan Jr.	Craig S. Prevallet
Susan R. (Mullins) Tibbits	Mark E. Biznek
Carol K. Kenesey	Elizabeth A. Ross
Sharon A. (Brauch) Palmer	Peggy E. Kolodziej
Juliet A. (Murzny) Snook	Andrew R. Thomson
Steven E. Ederle	Lisa C. (Mueller) Kroutil
Joshua H. Robinson	Gary A. Wilkening
Robert G. Holt	Richard A. Schuth
Martin J. Armstrong	
Susan E. Schumacher	

1987	
Spring (May 3)	Fall (Nov 15)
Mark A. Hewlett	Scott A. DePriest
Tommy Tam	Sonuel L. Ivery
William A. Heineken	Lee F. Samaie
David W. McClellan	Rock A. Stevens
Andre T. Spears (pledge captain)	Robert D. Dobson
Robert M. Ybarra	Sumant M. Hattikudur
Stephen E. Ruggeri	Daniel P. Weidman
Kristine M. Ilstrup	William D. Clifton
Farhad Adib	Martha L. Hilton
	Michael C. Preston
	Teresa L. Sears
	William M. Stolte
	David A. Cramer
	Regina Washington
	Robert W. Richmann
	Don K. Howard
	Laura I. (Spencer) Brewer
	Gerald M. Elphingstone

1988	
Spring (April 24)	Fall (Nov 20)
Joyce A. Smith	David B. Platt
Bryan E. Gilliam	Brenda K. Bethel
Tracy S. Perkins	Nancy E. (Butler) Barr
Mark T. Rosebrough	Dennis L. Molli
John M. Barr	Allen L. Brown
Michael E. Miller	Lori A. (Stricker) Divin
Barbara J. Hearn	Kimberly L. (Ford) Richmann
Fred L. Roe	Denise C. Brandt
Anne L. Voyles	Heather L. Barstad
Anne M. Chmelir	Jason C. Frank
Albert D. Cohen	Sara A. Risbeck
	Daniel A. Carey
	Keith R. Bellville
	Michael D. Drury

1989	
Spring (March 12)	Fall (Oct 29)
David P. Fitzgibbons (best pledge)	Brian K. Osborne
William B. Divin	John Concannon
Jill A. Goetges	Christopher S. Sitton
William H. Watson	David L. Maschler
Teresa M. Blue	Edward Casleton
Michael J. DeBarr	Joyce S. Meyer
Michael L. Barnett	Darren F. Rosenbaum
Virgilio C. Fabella	Christina A. Pruett
Shawn D. Clark	Carrie Sachs
Thomas P. Neaf	Douglas C. Rivard
Gregory L. Flieg	Mark A. McCoy
Clara M. (Edwards) Rouse (best pledge)	Renee A. (Proctor) Groenemann
Anthony L. Rouse	Jeff Van Fassan
	Christina M. (Hayes) Schmidt
	Thomas C. Rogers
	Dominic G. Greene
	Susan L. Shefchyk

Note: Best Pledge and Pledge Captain information was gleaned from the Beta Delta Datas for those years.

Members-1990s

First Row: S. Shefchyk, C. Edwards, V. Fabella, S. Sitton, D. MacGrianna; Second Row: C. Sachs, D. Maschler, J. Vanfossen, D. Carey, M. Miller; Third Row: B. Lawrence, A. Brady, D. Rivard, D. Rosenbaum, R. Wiggins, J. Starkey, T. Miller, M. Halbach; Fourth Row: M. McCoy, C. Divin, Z. Beeblebrox, T. Pruett, A. Cohen, D. Platt, J. Kocktosinosin, M. DeBarr

Beta Delta 1990-Rollamo 1990

First Row: A. Wilkins, Jr., L. Wood, L. Stricker, B. Cordts, S. Dingman, D. Rivard; Second Row: D. Rosenbaum, B. Mangogna, B. Clemson, M. Halback, E. O'Hare, R. Randolph; Third Row: M. Bahr, A. Mische, K. Robertson, S. Ford, R. Wiggins, B. Suvagia, M. McCoy; Fourth Row: C. Buttry, F. Simon, R. Proctor

Beta Delta 1991-Rollamo 1991

(Identifications were not given)

Beta Delta 1992-Rollamo 1992

(Identifications were not given)

Beta Delta 1995-Rollamo 1995

The 1980s and 1990s

(Identifications were not given)

Beta Delta 1998-Rollamo 1998

Initiates-1990s

1990	
Spring (March 4)	Fall (Nov 4)
Rachel Wiggins	Chris E. Aufdembrink
Sean D. Dingman	Brian H. Hunnius
Shawn Edwards	Jeffrey T. Alvarez
Brian E. Lawrence	Chad A. Dunnegan
Thomas M. Miller	Rebecca L. Lema
Jodi M. Starkey	Steven J. Ford
Guy A. Brady	Marcus J. Bahr
Michael R. Halbach	Steven J. Renick
	Barbara A. Halpin

1991	
Spring (April 14)	Fall (Nov 3)
Brian Clemson	Michael D. Smith
Lori D. Wood	Deanna DeLacerda
Frank Simon	Michael J. Clemmons
Kevin K. Harrison	George S. Stewart
H. A. Wilkins	Wayne T. Greene
Charles R. Buttry	Lena Tsoulfanidis
Amy C. (Mische) Whorton	John E. Fitzsimmons
Erik O'Hare	
Bob Randolph	
Brian Mangogna	
Brandon L. Cordts	
Erol Baskurt	
Bharat Suvagia	
Melissa Mesko	
Kevin M. Robertson	

1992	
Spring (March 22)	Fall
Joseph F. Skerik	Kirk W. Oehlert
Douglas F. Schieszer	Michael Arbini
James E. Davis	Tarsha Gregory
Christopher D. Krull	Tina Faughn
Michael Wilkins	Michael S. McClellan
Lamar K. Gerber	Jeffrey C. Bruns
Cathleen A. (McMillan) Irvin	Diane K. Faulkner
Mike Koenigstein	Thaweechai Kungwankrai
Mary E. (Nussbaum) Smith	
Sandra B. Todd	

1993	
Spring (March 21)	Fall (Nov 21)
Deena R. (Chapman) Kountz	Brian E. Howard
Christine M. Peterson	Kirk D. Narzinski
Stephen T. Hunnius	Jeffrey W. Mockaitis
	Stephen J. Bennett
	Michael Matthews
	Melissa Mesko

1994	
Spring (March 27)	Fall (Nov 6)
Angela (Redington) Singer	Anica (Winkler) Addison
Gary L. Haas	Brian Gibson
Sean Teitelbaum	Chris Pundmann
Traci D. Morgan	Lance A. Callaway
Michael C. Smith	Ramon B. Miraflores
Thomas J. Wagner	Amy Bremer
Brent W. Ramsey	
Daniel M. Storey	

Note: No one was initiated from the spring 1995 through the spring 1996

1996	
Spring	Fall (Nov 24)
	Brooke L. Beville
	Robert Kossina
	Andrew H. Sharp
	Kelly M. Fuge
	Melissa McGuire
	Jeffrey W. Aubuchon
	Craig C. Tyhurst
	Kelly M. Morris
	Dominic Purpura
	Jason Doyle
	Tara Kruep
	Julie Youngren

1997	
Spring (April 27)	Fall (Nov 23)
Jennifer (Ward) Whalen	Eric Buchanan
Andy Carr	Kari Troyer
Bridget Cannon	Christopher T. Brannan
Marisa McGregor	Mark W. Walburg
Colleen N. Stucker	Elisabeth Maguire
Ellen Holthaus	Ranee Bowers
John R. Schroeder	Francisco J. Garza
	Eric J. Breitenbach
	Nicholas R. Cook
	Mozow Yusof
	Lesley A. Schmid
	Robert B. Unzicker

1998	
Spring (April 19)	Fall (Nov 22)
Andrea Collazo	Michelle R. Hedrick
Charity R. (Baxter) Frederick	Amanda L. Brown
Brye C. Mitchell	Eric Fryatt
Matthew D. Fries	Andrew Blase
Damion Frederick	Cynthia Rabbitt
Craig L. Sebaugh	Geoffrey M. Floro
Tommy L. McCoy	
Arthur Buesch	
Scott A. Moll	
Lucie Johannes	
Michael Beardsley	
Andrea Bone	

1999	
Spring (April 18)	Fall (Nov. 21)
Stephen Pickardt	Stacy L. Davis
Kris Schumacher	Jared L. Gregory
Julia A. Kuseski	Joshua Gross
Mark Daffron	Jake Gross
Douglas W. Randall	Ryan Rzadca
Milton P. Hadinoto	Brian P. Holley
Amanda M. Wilson	Brian A. Grimes
Megan M. Jekel	Kerry E. Wehner
Amanda B. Modlin	Jason Abbott
Adam Steimel	Kurtis G. Vogler
Otto Rajtora	

THE 2000s

> For I am every dead thing,
>
> In whom love wrought new Alchimie.
>
> For his love did expresses
>
> A quintessence even from nothingness,
>
> From dull privations, and leane emptiness
>
> He ruine'd mee, and I am re-begot
>
> Of absence, darkness, death; things which are not.
>
> —*John Donne*, Nocturnall upon S. Lucies Day

The Times

In America, the first two decades of the new millennium were bracketed by the events surrounding 9/11 in 2001—which ultimately led to the invasion of Afghanistan—and the final withdrawal from that country in August, 2021. Within this timeframe, Barak Obama was elected the first Black president of the United States, Osama bin Laden was killed by US forces in 2011, and the Covid-19 pandemic emerged on the world scene in 2020.

Missouri S&T

On April 6, 2007, the University of Missouri-Board of Curators approved the college's proposal to change its name to Missouri University of Science and Technology (Missouri S&T). The new name took effect on January 1, 2008. The name change was promoted as part of UMR's goal to become one of the top five technological research universities in the United States, and, consequently, distinguish itself from the other four campuses of the University of Missouri. The University of Missouri-Rolla no longer seemed to reflect the distinctive nature of the college and often led to the misunderstanding that the school was just a branch campus of the University of Missouri-Columbia, which was commonly referred to as the University of Missouri.[1]

In 2020, Missouri S&T received the largest single gift in the history of Missouri higher education. Fred Kummer and his wife, June, donated $300 million to a foundation intended to support Missouri S&T programs far into the future. The unprecedented gift enabled the university to establish a new college of innovation and entrepreneurship, the Kummer College; to develop new areas for research—infrastructure, advanced manufacturing, artificial intelligence and autonomous systems, and environmental and resource sustainability—and to provide numerous scholarships and fellowships for students.

Fred Kummer, 91, was the founder and chair of the St. Louis-based HBE Corp., which he established in 1960. The company became the leading 'design to build' health care firm in the world. Though Kummer was not a member of Alpha Chi Sigma or Beta Delta, he was a 1955 civil engineering graduate of the Missouri School of Mines and Metallurgy.[2]

Chemistry and Chemical Engineering

In April of 2013, ground was broken for the construction of Bertelsmeyer Hall. Several years earlier, in 2011, Chancellor Jack Carney decided that instead of making major renovations to the aging Schrenk Hall, a more cost effective remedy would be building a new facility for the chemical and biochemical engineering department. This decision was facilitated by a significant contribution to the school from Jim Bertelsmeyer (ChE '66). The new building was dedicated on October 17, 2014.[3]

Alpha Chi Sigma

The big event of the 2000s for Alpha Chi Sigma was the Centennial Celebration of the fraternity's founding in the summer of 2002 in Madison, Wisconsin, where the first chapter was founded in 1902. The Centennial Celebration actually started with a banquet in Madison on Dec. 11, 2001. That was followed by a symposium at the American Chemical Society meeting in Orlando in April, 2002—co-sponsored by Alpha Chi Sigma and the Division of the History of Chemistry—which focused on the Alpha Chi Sigma Hall of Fame and on how its members influenced the development of chemistry.[4]

One of Beta Delta's sister chapters within the Central District, the St. Louis Chapter, Alpha Epsilon, had been providing chemistry outreach to the St. Louis community since the chapter's reactivation in 1996. For more than ten years, the chapter had been visiting classrooms, science fairs, and workplace family events to give demonstrations and talks on a variety of chemistry topics. But then, in 2008, Alpha Epsilon did something unique. The members acquired an apothecary shop which provided an eclectic setting and a different approach for their demonstrations.[5]

In the fall of 2010, Richard F. Heck, Beta Gamma (UCLA), was awarded the Nobel Prize in Chemistry. He was recognized along with Ei-ichi Negishi and Akira Suzuki for the discovery and development of the Heck Reaction, which used palladium to catalyze organic chemical reactions that coupled aryl halides with alkenes. (The analgesic Naproxen is an example of a compound prepared by using the Heck Reaction.)[6]

In 2018, two Alpha Chi Sigma brothers were inducted into the Alpha Chi Sigma Hall of Fame: M. Frederick Hawthorne, Beta Delta 1946, and William Frank Libby, Sigma 1941, deceased. The inductees or their representatives were invited by the GPA to participate in the ceremony at the 54th Biennial Conclave. While seeking a PhD in organic chemistry, Hawthorne worked under Donald Cram who shared the 1987 Nobel Prize in Chemistry with Jean-Marie Lehn and Charles J. Pedersen for the development and use of molecules with structure-specific interactions of high selectivity. He also conducted post-doctoral research in physical-organic chemistry at Iowa State University and authored or co-authored more than 560 research papers, 30 patents, and 10 book chapters that reflected the joint efforts of approximately 200 PhD students and post-doctoral associates and 11 PhD co-workers at Rohm and Haas Research Laboratories in Redstone, Alabama.[7]

From 1945 to 1954, Libby was Professor of Chemistry in the Department of Chemistry and Institute for Nuclear Studies (now the Enrico Fermi Institute) at the University of Chicago. He was appointed in 1954 to the US Atomic Energy Commission by President Eisenhower. He was best-known for his work on natural carbon-14 and its use in dating archaeological artifacts, research for which he was awarded the Nobel Prize in Chemistry in 1960.

The Alpha Chi Sigma Hall of Fame was established in 1982 to recognize outstanding members of the fraternity and to publicize their contributions to the science of chemistry and its related professions. (Nominations to the Hall of Fame may be made by any member of the fraternity.)

In 2018, two colonies petitioned the fraternity to become chapters: Northern Illinois University and Kettering University. Both were accepted.[8]

Legislatively, a significant development was the establishment of the Health & Safety Program for the fraternity at the 55th Biennial Conclave which was held virtually because of the Covid pandemic, July 6-9, 2020. This addition to the by-laws was an update to the Risk Management Policy which had been adopted on July 12, 2003.[9]

Beta Delta

In 1996, the chapter pulled itself back from the brink of inactive status by sending a delegate to Conclave in the summer and re-igniting a pledging and initiation program in the fall. From 1996 through 2000, the reception of new members held fairly steady. But then—as a sign that the life of the chapter was still sputtering—no one was initiated in the fall of 2000, nor in the spring of 2001. Initiations resumed in the fall of 2001 and continued into the spring of 2006. There was a pledge class in the fall of 2006, but the initiation was not held until January of 2007.

Another indication that the chapter's fire still flickered was its participation in 2000 in hosting the 45th Biennial Conclave—the Millennium Conclave—held at the Henry VIII Hotel in St. Louis. Beta Delta members, along with members from the St. Louis Professional chapter and the other Missouri collegiate chapters—Delta and Gamma Theta—played an important role in organizing the activities. During this Conclave, Harvest Collier was an honors initiate received into membership on August 12.[10]

However, even though Beta Delta initiated new members and participated in the Conclaves, that did not mean the chapter was suddenly into recovery mode. Actual recovery would not begin until 2002, and signs of a fully revitalized chapter would not emerge until the end of the first decade of the new millennium. The first two decades of the 21st century for Beta Delta were a long journey, which ultimately brought new life and vigor to the chapter.

When Jon Wenzel (Delta '96, Grand Professional Alchemist 2014-2016, Currently Assistant Grand Recorder and Associate Professor of Chemical Engineering at Kettering University in Flint, MI), stepped into the Central District Counselor position in 2002, Beta Delta was still treading water. Though the numbers of new members had been slowly increasing, the chapter had lost significant knowledge of its history and customary activities. Even its day-to-day operations were largely neglected or forgotten. Wenzel decided that something had to be done to revitalize the chapter. He first took the approach of working with the members as though they were a colony seeking admission into the fraternity. He applied basic team-building concepts and ensured that chapter rules were being followed (only qualified candidates could be initiated, for example). He elicited support from other chapters in the district; cultivated leaders through officer training; had the chapter host a district conclave; and—most importantly, perhaps—provided attention and support to build enthusiastic members. Working with a sensitive touch—not with a heavy hand—Wenzel employed a management philosophy of introducing a request and then negotiating a compromise that all members could agree upon.[11]

Let to Right: First Row: A. Steimel, M. Kelly, J. Grindel. Second Row: S. Zuckerman, S. Sansing, L Davies, B. Heiting. Third Row: R. Losson, T. Elyan, J. Gregory, M. Terryberry.

Beta Delta 2002-Rollamo 2002

One of the early signs of Wenzel's positive influence was his enthusiastic promotion of a gratuitous project undertaken in 2004 in response to an issue raised by the first year chemistry students. Their complaint disparaged the periodic table hanging at the front of Schrenk Hall's G-3 lecture room. The table was much too small and out of date, they observed, and it did not even include, element 106, Seaborgium, which was discovered by Glenn Seaborg, an Alpha Chi Sigma member who was initiated at Sigma Chapter in Berkeley. Beta Delta's solution, spear-headed by Trini King, was to design a periodic table that covered the entire wall. Work began on April 23, and the final flourish of the brush took place nine days later.[12]

Beta Delta brothers take on the Table...and the Wall

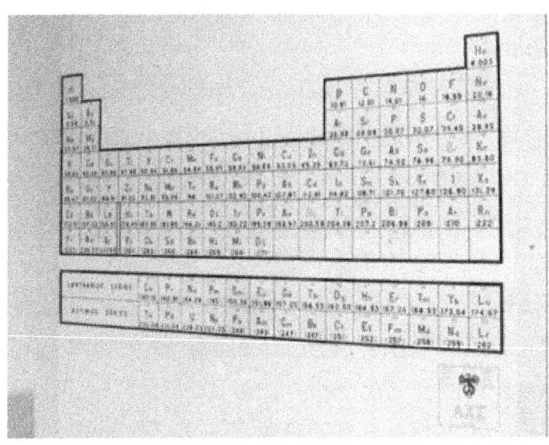

Beta Delta brothers unveil the finished product!

The proud signature!

Pictures from the Fall 2016 Issue of the Hexagon

Of special note in 2004: one of Beta Delta's founders, Dr. Frank J. Zvanut, passed away on May 2 at the age of 92. Zvanut (Beta Delta 1936, Order of Altotus) was born in St. Louis, Missouri, on August 30, 1911. He earned his

BS degree in 1932 and a PhD in Ceramic Engineering from the University of Missouri School of Mines and Metallurgy in 1937. He was instrumental in the establishment of Beta Delta Chapter and he became a charter member of the chapter at the May 2, 1936, installation. He served the Cleveland Professional Chapter as its secretary in 1940-41 and was the Hexagon Correspondent in 1941 and its president in 1946-47. He also served as the East Central District Counselor from 1941 to 1954, Grand Master of Ceremonies from 1954-58, Grand Collegiate Alchemist from 1958-60, and Grand Master Alchemist from 1960-62 (See also Chapter 1 Excursus).[13]

In 2006, Beta Delta initiated an innovative program which played a significant role in revitalizing the fraternity. The Bigs-Littles Program helped mightily to restore the chapter's legendary culture. The concept originated in the Zeta Chapter at the University of Illinois-Urbana and was introduced to Beta Delta when graduate student, Jennifer Bingham, transferred from there to UMR. In the program, each pledge (the "little") was paired to an active member (the "big") who became the pledge's mentor. In the pairing, the pledge was allowed a voice throughout the selection process. (At the time of this writing, the program is still in practice.)

Another sign that Beta Delta was on the road to recovery was the increasing frequency at which members began stepping into positions in the wider fraternity. Rachel Palasky was a good example. She was initiated in 2007 and became the District Counselor for the Gateway district from 2016-2018. When the district was renamed the Central District, she continued to hold the position until 2020. (The Gateway District consisted of Beta Psi, Psi, Delta Delta, Alpha Epsilon and Alpha Sigma. The Central District consisted of Beta Psi, Delta Delta, Alpha Epsilon, Alpha Sigma, Delta, Beta Delta, and the Westminster Group, an unsuccessful expansion attempt at Westminster College in Fulton, MO.) Another Beta Delta initiate, Matthew Senter (2012) became Central District Counselor in 2020.

More telling that the chapter was recovering was the re-establishment of customs that had been discontinued and the beginning of new ones. In 2009, Beta Delta instituted an annual banquet held at the end of the school year for the first time. Organized by Rachel Palasky, who was Master of Ceremonies at the time, this event was held in lieu of the banquet which previously honored the new initiates but had been discontinued during the chapter's lean years. (When this occurred specifically, could not be determined.) The purpose of this annual banquet was to close out the school year in a celebratory manner and to honor the chapter at the same time. By 2014, the banquet appears to have transformed into a function called the Formal, which was held at the end of each semester. In 2014, the Formal was held in Schrenk Hall and included a potluck style dinner. After that year, the dinners were held at restaurants around Rolla.[14]

Another activity that was lost over the years and re-introduced by the chapter in 2009 was the high school math and science program. This project fell by the wayside in 2014 but rebounded in 2016 when the chapter once again offered math tutoring—primarily in Algebra I and Geometry—for Rolla high school students.

Front row: Dan Palasky, Kendrick Callaway, Jessie Cates, Not identified, Kristy Geltz, Tom Mills; Middle row: Amber McFadden, Sandra Smith, Jenn Bingham, Sean Mickey; Back row: Chad Smith, Tim Lee, John Bartow

Beta Delta 2008-Rollamo 2008

First Row: S. Mickey, R. Thurman, D. Palasky, J. Bingham. Second Row: M. Brosnahan, B. Lindsay, H. Baldwin, T. Mills. S. Judd, S. Smith, B. Basler, J. Bartow. Third Row: R. Rader, I. Bond, T. Lee, J. Campbell, A. Windhausen, M. Wallace, A. Heinzke.

Beta Delta 2009-Rollamo 2009

The advent of the internet provided another opportunity for the chapter to continue its comeback. As early as 2006, Beta Delta established its own website, and, with it, a new position—Webmaster—was created. Though the position was not officially required by the fraternity's constitution, the National Office requested the Webmaster's name on the Officer List that chapters were required to complete. Between 2007 and 2009, another new position—Pledge Education Training Assistant (PETA)—was inaugurated. The purpose of the PETA was to assist the Vice-Master Alchemist in the education of the pledges.[15]

Two additional positions were established during the latter half of the decade—the Outreach coordinator and Social officer. The growth of the chapter's activities necessitated an officer to organize and schedule the increasing number of social events—game nights with other organizations, for example, like those with Triangle in the spring of 2016, and intramural sports—bowling, inner tubing, water polo, 4v4 volleyball and soccer. The Social officer planned and directed Beta Delta's participation in all these events and—more importantly, perhaps—made all the arrangements for the Formal at the end of each semester.

The Social Officer, then, was charged with promoting the fraternity's first objective—providing opportunities for creating bonds of friendship between members. The Outreach position, on the other hand, was concerned with the chapter's philanthropy. Its purpose was to advance the chapter's second objective—touting the chemical sciences. Contributing to the surrounding community became an important mission for Beta Delta. Many members donated time at GRACE, the Greater Rolla Area Charitable Enterprise—a non-profit in Rolla that sponsored a food pantry and provided other services for disadvantaged people. Other members volunteered to foster the Boy Scout Merit Badge program or to work at the "Introduce a Girl to Engineering" events—activities meant to encourage elementary and middle school girls to take more STEM (Science, Technology, Engineering and Math) courses in high school.[16]

The Outreach Officer also oversaw the High School Math Tutoring program (primarily Algebra I and Geometry) and saw to Beta Delta's participation in the Science Olympiad Regionals hosted by Missouri S&T. The Science Olympiad was a national, non-profit organization dedicated to improving the quality of science education, increasing student interest in science, and providing recognition for outstanding achievement in science education by both students and teachers. These goals were accomplished through classroom activities, research, training workshops, and the sponsorship of intramural, district, regional, state and national tournaments. Beta Delta members participated as graders and judges, assessing the merits of the projects presented or assisted with other tasks assigned by the faculty member involved. Most recently, Dr. Cynthia Bolon, Associate Teaching Professor, and a member of Beta Delta, held this position. Unfortunately, the Science Olympiad regional has not been held since the beginning of the pandemic in the spring of 2020.[17]

Front Row: E. Kirk, R. Thurman, S. Judd, B. Brown, T. Huynh, M. Brosnahan. Second Row: D. Caligiuri, J. Sapphire, N. Potje, J. Jeffryes, K. Baldwin, A. Schott. Third Row: T. Lee, S. Li, G. Obeldobel, B. Linsey, I. Bond, J. Bartow. Fourth Row: T. Mills, S. Mickey, S. Richardt, A. Pearson, M. Niehoff, A. Creasy, A. Mann

Beta Delta 2010—Rollamo 2010

Back to front, left to right: A. Creasy, L. Jones, S. Richardt, A. Mann, G. Obeldobel, T. Mills, A. Pearson, Dr. D. Ludlow, A. Liu, M. Gill, M. Dahl, D. Dasani, S. Sutterer, M. Jones, J. Bartow, A. Collin, M. Brosnahan, B. Brown, M. Elliott, N. Potje, A. Schott, R. Naeger, S. Acar, S. Li, E. Kirk, B. Basler, S. Judd, A. Schlender, A. Sloan.

Beta Delta 2011-Rollamo 2011

Recent Years

2015

By 2015, Beta Delta had fully recovered from its turn-of-the century doldrums. It was now a successfully functioning organization, with regular, periodic initiations of sizable pledge classes, enthusiastic leaders in new positions, restored traditions, and some novel practices as well. A sign that a renewed seriousness infused the chapter's culture involved the pledge final. Prior to 2015, the test was often taken as a joke, used only light-heartedly to assess the pledges' knowledge. Rejecting this approach, the members gave the final a more thoughtful format in the spring of 2015. Other chapters in the district—which also encountered this problem—soon followed suit. The district counselor at the time, Sarah Pickett, devoted a good deal of effort during her term working to ensure that the pledge final became a more meaningful part of the initiation process.[18]

In the spring Beta Delta was governed by a full slate of officers and committees, who orchestrated the activities for the semester. Maria Vega-Westhoff was Master Alchemist; Courtney Mandeville, Vice-Master Alchemist; Brady Campbell, Master of Ceremonies; Kenny Domann, Treasurer; Sean Tennyson, Recorder; Justin Chisco, Alumni Secretary; Spencer Norman, Social; Aaron Latal, PETA; Alex Capalupo, Historian; Amanda Koebbe, Outreach; and Abigail Buchheit, Webmaster. The committees and their chairs were: Auditing—C. Mandeville; Budgeting—C. Mandeville; and Membership—C. Mandeville, M. Senter, E. Tuxbury, and J. Schletzbaum.

The activities were many and varied. There were numerous social and business events, including an ice cream social (February 9), a bowling party (February 17), pizza at Alex's (a local pizzeria, which had been around since 1964) on February 25, and a game night with Triangle (February 28). Also on the calendar were the traditional membership events: Pinning (formal pledging) the week of March 2, Mass Transfer (April 17), the Formal (May 1), Initiation (May 2), and the Professional Initiation Ceremony (May 3). In addition, the chapter was invited to initiations of other chapters in the Tri-District, including: Delta on April 18; Delta Delta on April 11; and Beta Rho on April 25.

The highlight event of 2015 was the Tri-District Conclave held on February 21, which was hosted by Delta in Columbia, MO. This conference was a very large gathering of fraternity representatives from a wide geographical area. From 2014 to 2016 the Tri-District consisted of the Central District (Delta, Beta Delta, Gamma Theta, the Mid-Missouri Professional group, and the Kansas City Professional chapter), the Gateway District (Alpha Epsilon, Beta Psi, Delta Delta, and the St. Louis Professional chapter), and the Great Plains District (Beta Eta, Beta Rho, Beta Phi, and Kappa Colony). After 2016, the chapters held conclaves within their own districts.[19]

An interesting innovation which the chapter adopted during the spring was a feature in the chapter's meeting minutes that shared special events and personages from the chemistry world. Below are a few examples;

> *Swiss Chemist Jean-Charles-Galinard de Marignac died on this day, April 15, in 1894. He was one of the first to suggest the existence of isotopes. He also discovered the element ytterbium (Yb) and co-discovered gadolinium (Gd).*
>
> *American chemist Melvin Calvin was born on this day, April 8, in 1911. He is most famous for discovering the Calvin cycle, the pathway for carbon dioxide (CO_2) assimilation in plants. He was awarded the Nobel Prize in Chemistry in 1961 for this work.*
>
> *On This day in Chemistry—April 29: American chemist Harold Urey was born on this day in 1893. Urey co-discovered deuterium (2H) with Ferdinand Brickwedde and George Murphy. They produced the first measurable samples of the isotope from liquefied hydrogen.*[20]

Officers for the fall semester were elected on May 6: Michael DeVoss, Master Alchemist; Robert Leach Clark, Vice-Master Alchemist; Kenny Domann, Master of Ceremonies; Justin Schletzbaum, Treasurer; Amanda Sebelski, Recorder; Matt Senter, Reporter; Abby Buchheit, Historian; Paige Eckert, Alumni Secretary; Valentine Hollingsworth, Outreach; Spencer Norman, Social; Alex Capalupo, Webmaster; Erin Wharton, PETA; and Ian Schroen, Laura Shaffer, and Brady Campbell, ChemE Liaison.[21]

When the fall semester began in September, the following committees were established: By-Laws—M. DeVoss, S. Norman, I. Schroen; Membership—R. Clark, Matt, B. Campbell, Brandon; Budget—R. Clark, J. Schletzbaum; and Audit—R. Clark, K. Domann. Committee members were kept very busy organizing the events on the fall schedule: MinerRama (August 28), Tri-District Conclave (September 26), Bowling (September 9), Alex's Pizza (September 17), Pinning (September 24), Mass Transfer (October 30), Pledge test (November 12), Delta's Initiation (November 8), Delta Delta's Initiation (November 14), Initiation (December 5), and The Formal (December 4) at Sybil's.

2016

In the spring semester, Beta Delta was led by the following officers: Kenneth A. Domann, Master Alchemist; Brandon M. Haugabrook, Vice-Master Alchemist; Matthew B. Senter, Reporter; Justin J. Schletzbaum, Treasurer; Michael L. DeVoss, Master of Ceremonies; Ellen Tuxbury, Historian; Alexander R. Capalupo, Webmaster; Abby (Buchheit) Stevens, Anniversary; Rachel Pyszka, Outreach; and Robert Leach Clark, Social. The most important business for the semester, which began at the first meeting on January 20, was the preparation for Beta Delta's 80th anniversary. Abby Stevens headed this effort which would require several additional committees—Decorations, Catering, Location, and Fundraising. The pre-existing standing committees—Budgeting, Auditing, Membership, and By-Laws—would play an important role as well.

An interesting new custom—the Harem Game—got its start about this time. In an effort to honor a Delta brother, Glenn Kuhlman, who had died in an automobile accident, the game was designed to promote interchapter travel within the district. Each chapter was given a small gargoyle as part of "Glenn's Harem." Beta Delta named its gargoyle Brittany Danielle (the origin of the name was not recorded). Beta Delta members who traveled to another chapter could steal that chapter's gargoyle, and the chapter with the most gargoyles at the district Conclave won the event. At the 2016 Conclave at Southeastern Missouri State, Beta Delta tied with Delta Delta for the Harem Game Championship.[22]

A custom that had existed in various forms since the dawn of Beta Delta's history continued into 2016. Over the decades, Mass Transfer came to mean different things to different members at different times, but the core of the activity had remained intact. The intent of the activity had always been—and continued to be—the creation of a shared experience meant to bind the members together. In the spring of 2016 Mass Transfer was held on Friday, March 3, at Schuman Park. BBQ and fried fish were the fare of the day.[23]

A tri-district meeting was held on March 19 in Rolla. Six of the nine chapters attended, but which six, and other details, of the meeting were not recorded.

While members engaged in the various social and outreach activities, they continued to practice the functions at the core of the chapter's existence. Formal pledging was held on February 11, and pledge meetings were held in Bertelsmeyer Hall on Wednesday evenings. These preliminaries led to the initiation of eight new members on April 16: Roxanne M. Feliciano, Alexandra R. Bueltmann, Andreaunna Hawkins, Tucker S. Shoup, Joshua K. Lanz, Victoria N. Kramer, Caleb Z. Trecazzi, and Michael S. McMahon.

The big event of the year—Beta Delta's 80th anniversary—finally arrived on the weekend of April 30. The event kicked off on Friday evening with trivia at Dr. Ludlow's house. On Saturday, members and their guests went go-kart racing and played mini-golf at Kokomo Joe's "Go Karts and Putt-Putt Golf," starting at noon. That evening, the formal celebration and banquet were held at the Comfort Suites Banquet Hall in Rolla. Alpha Chi Sigma Grand Historian D. Mitch Levings, Central District Counselor Sarah Pickett, and Chapter Advisor Dr. Ludlow were the chapter's honored guests. Brothers from Alpha, Beta Rho, and Delta Delta joined the festivities.[24]

Beta Delta 80th Anniversary Banquet—April 30, 2016 (Photo provided by D. Mitch Levings, Grand Historian)

In May, during the officer nominations, the ChemE liaison position was created at the request of the Chemical Engineering department chair, Dr. Al-Dahhan who had established the Student Advisory Council (SAC). The SAC acted—not only as a communication link with other organizations—but it also provided mentor training in which alumni from industry assisted students with their resumes, and shared job experience and expectations to assist graduates who planned to enter professional careers.[25]

The 2016 Biennial Conclave in Atlanta (July 25-30) was well attended by Beta Delta actives—Abbie Braden, Julie M. Breckenridge-Briski (initiated 2002), Matthew Senter, and Abigail Buchheit—and alumni—DeWayne C. Gerber, D. Mitch Levings, John Adams, Spencer Norman, Daniel Palasky, Rachel Palasky, Sandy A. Sansing, and Robert E. Stevens. In the course of this Conclave, Beta Delta won an award that proved just how far the chapter had advanced over the past few years. Winning the One Star Award meant that Beta Delta members had successfully met every one of the following requirements set by the national fraternity:

- Submission of the Pledge Report form four weeks prior to the initiation ceremony;
- Submission of all pledge and lifetime membership fees two weeks prior to the initiation ceremony;
- Submission of the Initiation Confirmation Report within 10 days after the ceremony;
- Initiation of a minimum of 8 or 1/3 of the number of current active collegiate members;
- Conducting at least two major service or professional activities;
- Submission of an officer list within two weeks of each election;
- Completion of alcohol awareness training; and
- Submission of various reports by June 15 (Annual Report of Collegiate Chapter Activities; Audit and Financial Statement; Charter, Ritual and Regalia Inspection; Active Collegiate Member Register; and IRS 990-N form).

Moreover, the chapter had to be in good standing with the fraternity. Accomplishing all these prerequisites was obviously no small task. Winning the prestigious "One Star" in 2016 indicated that Beta Delta was diligently engaged in its own affairs and was genuinely concerned about its relations with the wider community.[26]

A week later, on August 9, Rachel Palasky (Beta Delta 2007) was appointed District Counselor for the Gateway District which consisted of Beta Psi, Delta Delta, Alpha Epsilon, and Alpha Sigma chapters.[27]

After the "high" of the Atlanta Conclave, the fall semester began with the following leadership team in place: Courtney Mandeville, Master Alchemist; Erin Wharton, Vice-Master Alchemist; Abby Buchheit, Master of Ceremonies; Tim Avery, Treasurer; Roxanne Feliciano, Historian; Andreaunna Hawkins, Alumni Secretary; Tucker Shoup, Reporter; Rachel Pyszka, Recorder; Ben House, Outreach; Michael DeVoss, Webmaster; Brady Campbell, Social; and Dr. Ludlow, Advisor.

At the first meeting of the fall semester, on August 23, the committees organized to assist the officers were announced: Membership—Erin Wharton, Brady Campbell, and Ellen Tuxbury; By-Laws—Courtney Mandeville, Abby Buchheit, and Rachel Pyszka; Auditing—Erin Wharton; Budgeting—Erin Wharton, and Tim Avery. The minutes of the meeting indicated that the chairs requested additional members, so it's likely that other members were added to some of the committees at a later date. MA Mandeville then had the pleasure of announcing Beta Delta's receiving the One Star Award at Conclave.

During the meeting on August 23, the remainder of the chapter's fall schedule was announced. Members were first asked to put the "Miner-Rama" on November 2 on their calendars. Like the Spring O'Rama, this event was an informational fair at which various organizations distributed information about themselves. Other outreach events included a tie-dyeing service project on the evening of September 14 at Dr. Ludlow's church, a bowling party on Aug. 31, Formal Pledging (Pinning) on Sept. 12; Mass Transfer on Oct. 21, the Formal on Nov. 11, and Initiation on Nov. 12. Members were asked once again to sign up for the math tutoring sessions to help high school students in their Algebra 1 and Geometry classes.[28]

On August 30, two positions, not filled earlier, were mentioned in the meeting minutes: Ellen Tuxbury was named Pledge Education Teaching Assistant (PETA), and Ben House, Aaron Latal, and Ellen Tuxbury were named ChemE Liaisons. The position of Student Council Representative (StuCo) first appeared in the September 6 meeting minutes; Abbie Braden was the first Beta Delta member to hold that job.[29]

At the September 20 meeting, Beta Delta revised the Big/Little tradition. The VMA at the time the policy was enacted, Erin (Wharton) Fors, thought input should come not just from the brothers but from the pledges as well. Matthew Senter and Michael DeVoss came up with a system that incorporated the names of several alchemical metal families. The plan was debated and, after a vote of the membership, implemented. The chapter was split into 7 families: Tin, Mercury, Copper, Iron, and Lead. Gold and Silver were reserved for past Master Alchemists, past Vice Master Alchemists, and past Master of Ceremonies. All past MAs became members of the Gold Family, and, upon leaving office, future MA's would also become members of the Gold Family. This same approach was used for the Silver family. Since there were not enough active members in the chapter to support six families, Silver was reserved for VMAs and MCs. These alterations to the original plan were accepted at the following meeting on October 4. The alchemical families have been in use—along with the Big-Little tradition—ever since (see Appendix E).[30]

Two days later on September 22, Alpha Chi Sigma, Omega Chi Epsilon, the Chemical Engineering Honor Society, AIChE and iGem Foundation, an independent, non-profit organization dedicated to the advancement of synthetic biology, held a joint social from 5 to 7 pm. Beta Delta provided cookies and other deserts.[31]

Besides the initiation of new members the other big event of the fall was the Tri-District conclave held September 24 in Kansas City, MO, hosted by the Kansas City Professional chapter. Several interesting ideas that were debated at the Tri-District and discussed at Beta Delta's October 4 meeting dealt with outreach suggestions: Chemistry demonstrations were proposed, for example, as an activity during national chemistry week, and a safety box to include safety supplies was also suggested. Ben House made a successful argument for this project. Also, during this meeting, Michael DeVoss and Rachel Pyszka were nominated to represent Alpha Chi Sigma as Homecoming King and Queen for the Homecoming event, which was held the week of October 10-15.[32]

The Formal was held on November 11 at Sybil's in Rolla, and the initiation of 15 new members—Jasmin L. Hill, Jennifer M. Frasch, Breanon L. Dowling, Parker S. Schellenberg, Samantha M. Oelklaus, Dale J. Wright, Taylor E. Tarter, Elizabeth Sotolongo, Alex L. Lodholz, Austin L. Vaughn, Daniel T. Rosner, Brian J. Baumgartner, Daniel T. Rosner, Nathan E. Boys, and Christina J. Hamilton—took place the next day. Instead of the traditional initiation banquet after the ceremony like those in the past, a potluck, provided by the members themselves, was arranged afterwards.

According to the Beta Delta Membership list, Joseph Gresick was initiated on December 10 at Alpha Epsilon's initiation. Beta Delta actives Matt Liberson, Erin Wharton, and Abby Buchheit accompanied Gresick to the Alpha Epsilon event.

New officers were elected for the spring semester on December 6. Beta Delta's new leaders included: Rachel Pyszka, Master Alchemist; Ellen Tuxbury, Vice-Master Alchemist; Justin Schletzbaum, Master of Ceremonies; Will Whelan, Recorder; Mary Carey, Alumni Secretary; Jean Hamilton, Historian; Alex Lodholz, Outreach; Abbie Braden, Social; Austin Vaughn, Webmaster; Roxanne Feliciano, Pledge Education Teaching Assistant (PETA); Austin Vaughn and Ryan Delahanty, ChemE Liaisons; and Justin Wright, Student Council Representative.[33]

Members: B. House, C. Mandeville, Dr. Ludlow, M. Liberson, L. Chaiwong, M. Senter, C. Cripps, L. Casey, J. Hernandez, V. Hollingsworth, B. Haugabrook, I. Schroen, E. Wharton, M. DeVoss, K. Domann, E. Tuxbury, J. Schletzbaum, A. Stroup, A. Koebbe, A. Capalupo, A.Braden, A. Buchheit, R. Delahanty, A. Sebelski, R. Pyszka, W. Whelan, K. O'Brien, A. Latal, R. Clark, T. Avary, M. Smith. Not Pictured: S. Norman, D. May, M. Marsh, B. Campbell.

Beta Delta 2016—Rollamo 2016

2017

The spring semester of 2017 continued with the same gusto the chapter demonstrated the previous term but with new officers at the helm.

The first meeting of the spring semester was held on January 25; committee appointments topped the list of new business. MA Pyszka reminded the officers that they were required to read the By-Laws and complete a quiz covering that material by February 1. Then the schedule for the semester was laid out, affirming the established routine and consistency of the chapter's life:

- January 30: Informational (Informational sessions took the place of the Smokers from previous decades)
- February 1: Bowling
- February 2: Informational
- Week of February 6: Pinning/Pledging (Also known as Formal Pledging)

- February 10: Russell House Round-Up (a family crisis service providing shelter, counseling, and care for victims of domestic and sexual violence)[34]

- February 11: Introduce a Girl to Engineering Day and Merit Badge University

- February 18: Science Olympiad

- April 7: Mass Transfer

- April 29: Initiation

- April 30: Professional Initiation Ceremony

Spring 2017 Committees

Membership	By-Laws	Auditing
E. Tuxbury (chair)	A. Buchheit (chair)	E. Tuxbury (chair)
R. Feliciano	R. Pyszka	R. Pyszka
R. Pyszka	J. Schletzbaum	
J. Schletzbaum	M. Marsh	

Budgeting	Risk Management	Fund Raising
A. Koebbe (chair)	R. Pyszka	
E. Wharton	A. Vaughn	
T. Avery	A. Braden	
A. Braden		
R. Pyszka		
D. Rosner		
Jean Hamilton		

There were plenty of other activities as well: Trivia nights, Ice Skating, Pretzel Making, and Green Fridays (a series of events held every Friday from the beginning of the spring semester to St. Pat's Day, designed to get the students and faculty fired up for the best St. Pat's ever!)[35]

The chapter's Outreach activities were, in fact, much more extensive than outlined in the original schedule. The full slate of Outreach projects included: a Blood Drive, a Canned Food Drive, Russell House Round-Up, Merit Badge University (a program which assisted Scouts who were working to earn their chemistry merit badges) on February 11, the 'Introduce a Girl to Engineering Day' on February 11, the Science Olympiad on February 18, and the Rolla High School Tutoring (Algebra I and Geometry). To encourage more involvement with the off-campus community, the Outreach chair planned numerous service events each semester, which could be counted toward the three hours of service required for each member.[36]

In addition, members of the chapter could report hours from other service activities not planned by Beta Delta. Examples of service projects of this kind included: park clean-ups, the Graduate Student Spooky festival (a celebration around Halloween with games, treats, and music), and the Celebration of Nations (an annual event that increased awareness of the vibrant cultural diversity of Rolla). Beta Delta members who fulfilled the service-hour requirements were eligible for various recognition awards such as the Wyvern pins the fraternity presented for participation in science outreach programs.[37]

Beta Delta members were not just focused internally or on the local community, however. Members stayed abreast of the activities of the other collegiate chapters in the Central District and were encouraged to attend as many of these as they could. At the first meeting of the semester, for example, the actives were made aware of the upcoming initiations at Beta Psi (SIUC) on January 28, Delta Delta (SEMO) on April 8, Beta Rho (Kansas State) on April 8, and Gamma Theta (Truman) on April 22. The chapter did more than simply maintain an awareness of what was happening with other chapters in the district; it actually engaged with them. Visiting other chapters became common practice; Beta Delta members visited Delta Delta on April 8, Beta Psi on April 22, and Delta (no date was given for the Delta visit).[38]

The spring semester closed with the Professional Initiation Ceremony on April 30. The event honored nine graduating seniors: Mike Marsh, Michael DeVoss, Aaron Latal, Cheyenne Cripps, Will Whelan, Jasmin Hill, Leelaya Chaiwong, Abby Buchheit, and Rachel Pyszka.

At the end of the fall semester in 2017, the office of Chapter Historian was combined with the position of Webmaster. Initially this was not an official designation, but since the Webmaster was responsible for maintaining a digital record of the chapter and the chapter's website, the Webmaster, essentially became responsible for recording the chapter's history as well.[39]

Back Row: R. Delahanty, T. Avery, M. Marsh, M. Senter, J. Schletzbaum. Third Row: P. Weakley, A. Capalupo, V. Kramer, A. Buchheit. Second Row: J. Lanz, M. DeVoss, Dr. D. Ludlow, E. Tuxbury, M. Carey, A. Stoup. Front Row: L. Chaiwong, C. Mandeville, T. Shoup, A. Bueltmann, R. Feliciano, R. Pyszka, A. Braden.

Beta Delta 2017—Rollamo 2017

2018

The officers elected for the spring of 2018 were: Erin Wharton, Master Alchemist; Dan Rosner, Vice-Master Alchemist; Samantha Oelklaus, Master of Ceremonies; Maddie Hines, Recorder; Alex Bueltmann, Treasurer; Kaytee Bailey, Outreach; Taylor Tarter, Social/PETA (the two positions were combined); Nathan Boys, Webmaster/Historian; Brian Baumgartner, Alumni Secretary; Nathan Boys and Josh Lanz, ChemE Liaisons; and Logan Hansen, StuCo Rep.[40]

Spring 2018 Committees

Membership	By-Laws	Auditing
D. Rosner	D. Rosner	E. Wharton
T. Tarter	E. Wharton	
E. Wharton	A. Braden	

Spring 2018 Committees Cont.

Budgeting	Risk Management	Fund Raising
A. Bueltmann	E. Wharton	A. Bueltmann
D. Rosner	M. Carey	J. Lanz
J. Hamilton		S. Oelklaus
J. Lanz		V. Kramer
E. Wharton		E. Wharton

The leadership's first role, as in prior semesters was to announce the schedule for the chapter's core activities—Informational, February 2; Pinning, February 29; Mass Transfer, April 13; Initiation, April 21—and the social and outreach activities chosen for the semester, which included the Spring O'Rama (the same event as the MinerRama except that it was held in the spring semester) on January 26; the Russell House Round Up on February 23; Game Night on February 27; and the Alpaca Social (a workday dedicated to shearing alpacas at a local Alpaca farm) on April 14.[41]

The Outreach activities continued unabated, as well. The Merit Badge University (MBU), which now included seven divisions—Chemistry Introduction; Separating chemistry and classical divisions; Cartesian Diver and Job Descriptions; Onion Activities; Pollution and Agencies; and Lab Tour—was held on February 10 at Schrenk Hall. The Math Lab tutoring for the Rolla High School and participation in the Science Olympiad Regionals (held February 17) also remained on the spring schedule.[42]

The day after the initiation ceremony, April 22, the Professional Initiation Ceremony recognized seven graduating seniors: Justin Schletzbaum, Ellen Tuxbury, Alex Bueltmann, Michael McMahon, Nathan Boys, Tim Avery, and Erin Wharton.

During the summer, at the 54th Biennial Conclave at Duquense University in Pittsburgh, which was hosted by Gamma Upsilon chapter, Rachel Palasky, Beta Delta '07, was appointed Central District (Beta Psi, Delta Delta, Alpha Epsilon, Alpha Sigma, Delta, Beta Delta, and the Westminster group) counselor for the 55th Biennium. Abbie Braden and Kelly Pachowicz, current chapter members, attended the Conclave along with Beta Delta alumni—Mitch Levings, Dan Palasky, John Adams (Grand Parliamentarian), Sandy Sansing, and Matt Senter. During the Conclave, John Adams received the Kuebler Award.[43]

54th Biennial Conclave Beta Delta Attendees

Back Row, Left to Right: Mitch Levings, Bob Stevens, Dan Palasky, John Adams, Sandy Sansing, Matt Senter. Front Row, Left to Right: Rachel Palasky, Kelly Pachowicz, Julie Breckenridge-Briski, Josh Lanz.

Picture provided by Matt Senter

The officers elected for the fall semester were: Samantha Oelklaus, Master Alchemist; Josh Lanz, Vice-Master Alchemist; Anna Schneider, Recorder; Tucker Shoup, Master of Ceremonies; Bryn Guthrie, Treasurer; Erik Gull, Reporter; Dale Wright, Historian; Emily Quist, Alumni Secretary; Kelly Pachowicz, Outreach; Elliot Sutalski, Social/PETA; Elliot Sutalski, ChemE Liaison; and Jean Hamilton, StuCo Rep. The first action of the opening meeting of the fall was to appoint committees.[44]

Fall 2018 Committees

Membership	By-Laws	Auditing
J. Lanz	S. Oelklaus	J. Lanz
E. Sutalski	A. Braden	E. Gull
A. Braden	J. Lanz	M. Snarzyk

Budgeting	Risk Management	Fund Raising
B. Guthrie		B. Guthrie
S. Oelklaus		V. Kramer
M. Jean		J. Hamilton

The fall semester activities essentially repeated those of the spring semester. The scheduled chapter activities included the Informational, August 27 and 29; the Pledging Ceremony, September 13; Mass Transfer, September 28; District Conclave, September 15; and Initiation, November 10. The social activities reflected the past fall season: MinerRama, August 24; BBQ at Schuman Park, August 31; and a Halloween Party, October 31. The Outreach activities appeared to have been drastically scaled back (though this may have been the result of inadequate reporting). Only the canned food drive held November 12-15 was recorded. In addition, Beta Delta threw its hat in the ring for Homecoming, nominating Brian Baumgartner and Josh Lanz for King and Abbie Braden for Queen.

At some point during the semester, a moratorium on chemistry demonstrations, applying to chapter, rush, and outreach events was imposed. The fraternity's insurance provider dropped the coverage because its policy did not include protection from chemistry demonstrations gone wrong. The moratorium lasted almost a year until the Supreme Council put in place new demonstration guidelines and obtained a new insurance policy.[45]

2019

2019 proved once again that the years since the chapter's recovery were destined to get better and better. The core activities—officer elections, pledge recruitment, Mass Transfers, Formals, Pinnings, and Initiations—continued as usual. And the social and outreach events—including the Alpaca shearing, the Blue Key Service Social, the Pumpkin Carving Contest, and the Canned Food Drive—all went off without a hitch.

The officers for the spring semester, 2019, were: Kelly Pachowicz Master Alchemist; Elliot Sutalski, Vice-Master Alchemist; Erik P. Gull, Reporter; Jacob Brownfield, Recorder; Bryn Guthrie, Treasurer; Abbie M. Braden, Master of Ceremonies; Garrett Ward, Webmaster/Historian; Emily Quist, Alumni Secretary; Logan Hansen, Outreach; Austin Scheer, Social/PETA; Bryn Guthrie & Sami Smith, ChemE Liaison; and Matt Snarzyk, StuCo Rep.[46]

For the fall semester, the officers elected included: Matt Snarzyk, Master Alchemist; Taylor Tarter, Vice-Master Alchemist; Kari Knobbe, Recorder; Kyle Newport, Master of Ceremonies; Rae Boillat, Treasurer; Chrysalin Martin, Reporter; Chris Coronado, Webmaster/Historian; Nicole Moon, Alumni Secretary; Adam McTigue, Social; Taishi Higuchi-Roos, Outreach; Rae Boillat, StuCo Rep; and Chris Coronado, ChemE Liaison.

The fall of 2019 also saw the establishment of a new Beta Delta officer. According to the meeting minutes of September 11, the Health and Safety officer position was created in anticipation of it becoming a required position for all fraternity chapters (This requirement was not officially adopted until the 2020 Biennial Conclave. See the discussion below). The new Health and Safety officer would be responsible for risk management at all chapter events. The position could not be held by the MA, VMA or MC, and the preference was that it not overlap with any other positions. The person filling the position was required to have been a chapter member for at least one year and have observed and understood all chapter events and ceremonies. MA Matt Snarzyk reported that, for Alpha Chi Sigma to remain a recognized school organization, a Risk Management Policy would have to be in place by 2020. Consequently, Derek Dillinger was elected Beta Delta's first Health & Safety Officer on October 9.[47]

Back Row, Left to Right: L. Hansen, K. Guthrie, M. Snarzyk, B. Baumgartner, V. Kramer, A. Scheer, S. Oelklaus, A. Douglas, N. Moon, C. Coronado, T. Shoup, M. Senter, M. St. Amour. Middle Row, Left to Right: D. Dillinger, G. Ward, K. Newport, D. Rosner, E. Gull, T. Stevens, C. Martin, B. Guthrie, J. Brownfield, A. McTigue, M. Smith. Front Row, Left to Right: R. Boillat, J. Caswell, B. Dowling, A. Braden, E. Sutalski, D. Neely, K. Pachowicz, T. Higuchi-Roos

Picture provided by the Chapter--2019

2020

Covid-19 changed everything. The pandemic brought on restrictions that altered all of Beta Delta's plans for 2020. In March, during the St. Pat's break, Missouri S&T announced that classes would be conducted remotely for the next two weeks. Within a day, the school had modified that requirement, extending the duration of virtual instruction through the end of the semester in May. No summer courses would be offered either. To continue functioning, the chapter had to get creative and devise virtual methods to carry on its activities. In the general confusion that characterized the onset of the pandemic, the spring initiation ceremony had to be canceled, a decision that had a significant impact on the life of the chapter. An attempt was made to salvage Mass Transfer, however, but that event, which previously involved a scavenger hunt in which the pledges would have hunted for items associated with Alpha Chi Sigma, and which then would have been followed by a social gathering at Schuman Park, was reduced to a simplified virtual game night (a version of Family Feud) and on-line conversation. The formal pledging ceremony was also conducted virtually, but the initiation had to be put off until the fall semester.

This disruption in the normal pledging and initiation procedure led to the suspension of the Pledge Final in the spring. At this time, the practice of offering the Pledge Final one to two weeks in advance of the initiation ceremony came into question (When this practice began could not be determined). Giving the Pledge Final early allowed any pledge who failed the test to have an opportunity to re-take it. This contributed, once again, to the sense that the Pledge Final was not being taken as seriously as it should have been and that it was designed to ensure a pass. (The cause of the problem this time was a different concern than that raised fraternity-wide in regard to pledge finals prior to 2015)[48] Beta Delta members debated the issue. If the Pledge Final was not a serious event, some argued, then just how seriously would new members regard the fraternity? At the same time, the purpose of studying for and taking the Final was to ensure that new members had a firm grasp of knowledge concerning the fraternity, but its difficulty ought not prevent a prospective pledge from being initiated. In practice, however, the Final Exam was not significantly changed. Only minor revisions were made in the fall so it could be taken online.[49]

In addition to these difficulties, many other activities had to be suspended. The annual spring canned food drive, in which Beta Delta partnered with the General Chemistry classes, and the Alpaca-shearing Day at the Sutton Home Alpacas farm were scratched. Members anticipated that these activities would start up again once the restrictions due to the Covid-19 pandemic were lifted, but no one knew when that might be. At the same time, the Boy Scout Chemistry Merit Badge involvement was also interrupted. The chapter's participation had been dropping off over the past couple of years, and the pandemic restrictions quietly led to its discontinuation in 2020. Nevertheless, there was still a desire among some members to fully revive the chapter's involvement when the restrictions were lifted. The chapter's involvement in tutoring first year college Chemistry students also met its demise when Missouri S&T took over the activity and encouraged all tutoring to be done through its program.[50]

But not everything came to a halt. A new initiative, the Pledge Scholarship, started in the fall. The reward provided monetary assistance to a deserving pledge to defray the expenses involved in joining the chapter. Recipients were chosen by a committee of the Master Alchemist, the Vice-Master Alchemist, and the Master of Ceremonies.

The establishment of the Health & Safety Officer position (see above) was another new issue that occupied a great portion of the chapter's virtual time. By the 55th Biennial Conclave which was hosted on Zoom from July 6-9, 2020, this position had already become a requirement. The Health & Safety Officer was charged with staying abreast of policy changes of the fraternity regarding health and safety issues and communicating these changes and associated requirements to the members. The individual who held this position was expected to monitor all outreach activities to ensure that health and safety policy regulations were met during both the planning and the execution of the events. The Health & Safety Officer, along with the Chapter Advisor and another elected member, comprised the Conduct Committee, which was responsible for handling all cases of misconduct.[51]

Known as 3P2E (Philosophy, Policy, Procedure, Education and Enforcement), the Health & Safety Program replaced the Risk Management policies that had been in place. Whereas the Risk Management policies—developed in the early '90s—arose out of internal investigations and were the offshoot of the previous Anti-Hazing Policy, the impetus for the Health & Safety Program emerged primarily because of insurance concerns. 3P2E, developed under the guidance of Dr. Lori Hart and Holmes Murphy and Associates Fraternal Insurance Practice, was an extremely extensive program. It covered issues related to alcohol and drugs, bullying, hazing, sexual misconduct, firearms, explosives and incendiary devices, and retaliation.[52]

The first semester officers who guided the chapter through the initial months of the pandemic were: Chris Coronado, Master Alchemist; Kari Knobbe, Vice-Master Alchemist; Whitney Sheffield, Recorder; Adam McTigue, Master of Ceremonies; Rae Boillat, Treasurer; Chrysalin Martin, Reporter; Rae Boillat, Webmaster and Historian; Nicole Moon, Alumni Secretary; Kayla Shy, Social/PETA; Loki Cortner, Outreach; Whitney Sheffield, StuCo Rep; Taishi Higuchi-Roos, ChemE Liaison; and Derek Dillinger, Health & Safety. Their jobs were not easy. A few activities such as

Spring O'Rama (January 24), an Alcohol Risk Management Presentation (February 2), and Mass Transfer (February 28) took place before the lockdowns, but other activities—the District Conclave hosted by Beta Delta on April 4, for example, and regular business meetings had to be conducted virtually. The members ultimately made the decision to initiate both the spring and fall pledge classes at separate ceremonies in the fall so the top pledge for each class could still be determined.[53]

Officer elections for the fall semester were held at the end of the spring semester and conducted via Zoom. The following were elected: Derek Dillinger, Master Alchemist; Kari Knobbe, Vice-Master Alchemist; Elliot Sutalski, Master of Ceremonies; Nicole Moon, Recorder; Whitney Sheffield, Treasurer; Taishi Higuchi-Roos, Reporter; Rae Boillat, Webmaster and Historian; Kayla Shy, Alumni Secretary; Chrysalin Martin, Social; Kinder Guthrie, Outreach; Whitney Sheffield, StuCo Rep; Adam McTigue, ChemE Liaison; and Loki Cortner, Health & Safety.

In the fall, academic classes took place in a "hybrid" arrangement—those that could be held online were administered in that manner while hands-on classes such as labs were allowed to be conducted in person. At first, class size could not exceed one third of the room capacity, which required additional lab sections or limited the number of students who could register for labs in the first place. Campus organizations were allowed to reserve rooms only for events with less than 10 people. Since almost all of Beta Delta's activities exceeded this limit, the chapter found itself in an isolated, virtual world.

Nevertheless, Mass Transfer was still held on Friday, September 11, but only the pledges, their mentors (Bigs and Littles), and essential officers were allowed to attend. Most social events—such as game night on September 19—were still conducted online, as were the chapter's business meetings, at which important business still got done. At the September 3 meeting, for instance, MA Dillinger announced that Matthew Senter (Beta Delta '12) was the new district counselor, and during the September 10 meeting, two proposals regarding dues were entertained and passed. One was to increase dues by $5 to be used toward a pledge scholarship fund and the other was a $5 increase for general operating expenses.[54]

2021

As a Missouri S&T—sanctioned organization, Beta Delta was still required to follow the college's pandemic restrictions in the spring of 2021. Conditions were similar to the previous fall, but gradually the restrictions became less onerous. Smaller classes returned to in-person sessions, but the lecture halls remained unoccupied. In March, around St. Pat's, the college opened-up in-person events slightly, allowing up to 25 people to gather at a single location. For Beta Delta this allowed the initiation to be held, though the number of actives attending still had to be limited.[55]

Officers were still elected virtually, however, and the chapter found ways to ensure that its business was addressed. The officers for the spring semester were: Derek Dillinger, Master Alchemist; Adam McTigue, Vice-Master Alchemist; Nicole Moon, Master of Ceremonies; Vaughn Foreman, Recorder; Whitney Sheffield, Treasurer; Taishi Higuchi-Roos, Reporter; Rae Boillat, Webmastorian; Kayla Shy/Sarah West, Alumni Secretaries (Early in the semester, however, at the February 3 meeting, West was nominated and elected to the position in her own right; presumably, Shy had to withdraw, for some reason.); Chrystel Hillier, Social/PETA; William Bump, Outreach; Whitney Sheffield, StuCo Rep; William Bump, ChemE Liaison; Loki Cortner, Health & Safety; and Dr. Douglas Ludlow, Chapter Advisor.

With the activities still restricted, chapter meetings continued to be conducted on Zoom, while other events were limited to only necessary members. Formal Pinning on February 13, for example, was done in person with only the pledges and the top officers (MA, VMA, and MC) in attendance. Everyone else, including alumni and actives, could participate, but only virtually. To make matters worse, a major snowstorm hit Rolla on the night before the Pinning. The entire campus shut down, preventing the use of the room reserved for the event. Thanks to some quick thinking by Nicole Moon, the Master of Ceremonies, the materials needed for the ceremony were retrieved from the chapter's storage location on campus just before the storm descended, and the ritual proceeded virtually while the snow piled up.[56]

Other social events like Mass Transfer, on February 26, and the virtual visit of the Grand Collegiate Alchemist, Merryn Cole, on April 21, still took place online. Some projects, such as Rae Boillat's recipe book, actually worked well virtually and through email. One event—the sale of beakers as a fund raiser, held November 8-12 in Havener Hall—was deemed a small-group affair since only three members worked the table at any one time and was allowed to proceed in-person. According to Treasurer W. Sheffield, in spite of the pandemic, the sale was a success.

By April, the school had relaxed even more restrictions, allowing groups of 25 or less to attend events. Fortunately, this was in time for the spring initiation on April 10, a picnic and movie night on April 24, and the Formal (potluck) on April 25, at Lions Club Park.[57]

By the fall of 2021, life—for the most part—returned to normal. Some classes were still offered online, but most had returned to meeting in-person. A limitation of two-thirds or three-fourths room capacity still existed, but the mask mandate had been lifted by mid-semester. The Alpha Chi Sigma National office, however, continued to require masks during chapter events. Chapter meetings were held primarily in-person, but for those who preferred, attending virtually could easily be arranged.

Most of Beta Delta's activities resumed as normal. The Schuman Park clean-up was held on September 2, and recruitment of potential new members started on September 3. Formal Pinning occurred on September 14, Mass Transfer on October 15, and Initiation on November 13. Other activities included the Bonfire social at Rae and Kyle Boillat's home on September 24, the Pumpkin Carving Contest on October 23, the Friendsgiving Potluck/BBQ held at MA Kari Knobbe's house on November 16, the Formal on December 4, the National Chemistry Week beginning on October 18, (A picnic was planned during this week, but was canceled due to a conflict with the ACS conference, which many Beta Delta members attended), and the Food Drive from November 29 through December 3.[58]

Two campus-wide events were also held in the fall of 2021. Beta Delta members participated in both of them. The Celebration of Nations took place on September 25, and STEMfest, an annual, family-friendly event that celebrated the disciplines of STEM — science, technology, engineering and math—was held on October 2. STEMfest showcased STEM-related activities and research that took place at Missouri S&T during the year and included a variety of interactive demonstrations, exhibits and hands-on activities organized by at least a dozen student organizations, including several S&T student design teams.[59]

The officers for the fall semester included: Kari Knobbe, Master Alchemist; Vaughn Foreman, Vice-Master Alchemist; Loki Cortner, Master of Ceremonies; Chrystal Hillier, Reporter; Caroline Williams, Recorder; Sarah West, Treasurer; Christina Arens, Alumni Secretary; Nicole Moon, Outreach; Megan Hutchcraft, Social/PETA; Rae Boillat, Webmastorian; Whitney Sheffield, StuCo Rep; Sarah West, ChemE Liaison; Taishi Higuchi-Roos, Health & Safety. Dr. Douglas K. Ludlow was chapter advisor.[60]

Top row: A. McTigue, N. Moon, C. Martin, L. Cortner, M. Hutchcraft, D. Bugarin, A. Lewis. Middle row: V. Foreman, T. Higuchi-Roos, J. Christensen, S. West, E. Hay, C. Arens. Bottom row: C. Hillier, M. Strickland, R. Boillat, K. Newport, W. Sheffield, K. Heimburger.

And on a more humorous parting:

Top row: A. McTigue, N. Moon, C. Martin, L. Cortner, M. Hutchcraft, D. Bugarin, A. Lewis. Middle row: V. Foreman, T. Higuchi-Roos, J. Christensen, S. West, E. Hay, C. Arens. Bottom row: C. Hillier, M. Strickland, K. Knobbe, K. Newport, W. Sheffield, K. Heimburger.

Actives not pictured in either: W. Bump, I. Clubb, E. Pitz, C. Williams, S. Coin

Inactive members not pictured: D. Dillinger (co-op), E. Sutalski, A. Hawkins, J. Gloriod, N. Wheeler, S. Sahoo

Pictures provided by Beta Delta

Excursus

Officers 2006-2014 (The names of officers for these years were taken from the records provided by the National Office of Alpha Chi Sigma and from a few minutes from the fall of 2014. No chapter records for this time period were recovered.)

Office	2006	2007	
	Fall	Spring	Fall
Master Alchemist	Elizabeth Abram	Elizabeth Abram	Jessie A. Cates
Vice-Master Alchemist	Wesley A. Glick	Wesley A. Glick	Elizabeth Abram
Reporter	Adam Martin	Adam Martin	Kristy Geltz
Recorder	Amber R. Kirkpatrick	Amber R. Kirkpatrick	Brandi Clark
Treasurer	Kelly Arrington	Kelley Arrington	Amber R. Kirkpatrick
Master of Ceremonies	Jessie A. Cates	Jessie A. Cates	Elizabeth Abram
Webmaster	Katherine Durham	Katherine Durham	Thuydung Huynh
Alumni Secretary/ Historian			Sean Mickey
Chapter Advisor	Douglas K. Ludlow	Douglas K. Ludlow	Douglas K. Ludlow

Office	2008		2009	
	Spring	Fall	Spring	Fall
Master Alchemist	Daniel Palasky	Daniel Palasky	John Bartow	John Bartow
Vice-Master Alchemist	John Bartow	Jennifer Bingham	April E. Sloan	April E. Sloan
Reporter	Brandi Clark	David D. Gorham	David D. Gorham	Scott M. Richardt
Recorder	Jennifer A. Wolf	Ryan K. Rader	Ryan K. Rader	Mitchell J. Niehoff
Treasurer	Amber R. Kirkpatrick	Andrew B. Mann	Andrew B. Mann	Daniel A. Caligiuri
Master of Ceremonies	Timothy S. Lee	Rachel K. Palasky	Rachel K. Palasky	Sean Micky

Webmaster	Sean Mickey	Megan Oldroyd	Megan Oldroyd	Ellen M. Kirk
Alumni Secretary/Historian	Thuydung Huynh	Kristy Geltz	George E. Obeldobel	George E. Obeldobel
Chapter Advisor	Douglas K. Ludlow	Douglas K. Ludlow	Douglas K. Ludlow	Douglas K. Ludlow

Office	2010		2011	
	Spring	Fall	Spring	Fall
Master Alchemist	Rachel K. Palasky	April E. Sloan	Brandon J. Basler	Jonathon D. Stocker
Vice-Master Alchemist	Aline L. Collin	Blair R. Brown	Arch D. Creasy	Megan M. Schuller
Reporter	Scott M. Richardt	Scott M. Richardt	Scott M. Richardt	Elise A. Breitweiser
Recorder	Meghan J. Ray	Amanda R. Wilson	Blair R. Brown	Jennifer A. Drost
Treasurer	April E. Sloan	Matthew E. Jones	Matthew E. Jones	Ashley C. Upschulte
Master of Ceremonies	Jeremy A. Sapphire	Stephanie R. Judd	Blythe W. Ferriere	Blythe W. Ferriere
Webmaster/Historian	Amanda R. Wilson	James C. Moore	James C. Moore	Joshua M. Grobe
Alumni Secretary	Ellen M. Kirk	Ellen M. Kirk	Ellen M. Kirk	April E. Sloan
Chapter Advisor	Douglas K. Ludlow	Douglas K. Ludlow	Douglas K. Ludlow	David A. May

Office	2012		2013	
	Spring	Fall	Spring	Fall
Master Alchemist	Blythe W. Ferriere	Rachael A. Naeger	Megan M. Heath (Schuller)	David M. DeVoss
Vice-Master Alchemist	Joshua A. Weeks	Margaret M. Adams	Clayton T. Buback	Clayton T. Buback
Reporter	Elise A. Breitweiser	Maria T. Vega-Westhoff	Maria T. Vega-Westhoff	Frederic S. Bush

Recorder	Kevin L. Clark	Kevin L. Clark	Richard H. Gorski	Jose A. Morales/ Frederic S. Bush
Treasurer	Elise A. Breit-weiser	Maria T. Vega-Westhoff	Ashley C. Upschulte	Ashley C. Upschulte
Master of Ceremonies	Kelsey K. Bass	Megan M. Schuller	Matthew B. Senter	Matthew B. Senter
Webmaster/Historian	Joshua M. Grobe	Ariel C. Mollhagen	Kevin L. Clark	Blake M. Hiza
Alumni Secretary	April E. Sloan	Joseph R. Hoing	Joseph R. Hoing	Maria T. Vega-Westhoff
Chapter Advisor	Douglas K. Ludlow	Douglas K. Ludlow	Douglas K. Ludlow	Douglas K. Ludlow

Office	2014	
	Spring	Fall
Master Alchemist	Matthew B. Senter	Sean G. Kilgore
Vice-Master Alchemist	Jessica K. Randall (Pisarik)	Lauren M. Walkup (Casey)
Reporter	Jose A. Morales	Matthew B. Senter
Recorder	Joseph D. Kramer	Sean Tennyson
Treasurer	Ashley C. Upschulte	Joseph D. Kramer
Master of Ceremonies	Cheyenne M. Morrissette	Alan T. Landers
Webmaster/Historian	Blake M. Hiza	Piero G. Burzio-Roca/ Paige Eckert
Alumni Secretary	Spencer G. Norman	Justin M. Chrisco
Social		Maria T. Vega-Westhoff
Outreach		Kyle Norris
Chapter Advisor	Douglas K. Ludlow	Douglas K. Ludlow

Committees for fall, 2014: Auditing—L. Casey, Maria; Membership—Lauren; By-Laws—S. Kilgore, S. Norman, M. Vega-Westoff, Cheyenne; Budget—S.Kilgore, Alan, Maria.[61]

Initiates:

2000		2001
April 9	Aug 12	November 10
Jay Verhoff	Harvest L. Collier	Laney Fritz
Laura E. Davies		John A. Grindel
Timothy Lottmann		Darcy Denner
Sean Zuckerman		Joshua G. Lawalin
Robert Mooshegian		Amala Dass
Robert Leerssen		Antony Samy
Matt Terryberry		Stephen M. Handley
Matthew Kelly		Brian Heiting
		Thomas O. Glynn
		Nicole M. Brossier

2002	
April 27	November 16
Ryan M. Losson	Julie M. Breckenridge-Briski
Oliver K. Manuel	Jeffrey D. Smith
Sandy A. Sansang	Erin M. Hayden
Jacob Barrows	Tim Robert
	Jessica M. McCord
	Tonya Trudgeon

2003			
May 2	May 2	November 21	November 21
Ethan Buckmier	James Reck	Parisa Khosraviani	Matthew M. Holmes
Joshua Heil	Daniel Regenhardt	Lauren G. Sisel	Erin Miller
Rebecca Wayman	Michael B. Johnson	Wesley R. Street	Joshua Sneller
John V. Simpson	Kristin Beckmeyer	Ramin Herati	Dawn Walker
Caleb Allen	Stephanie L. Maiden	Eric Theiss	
Trini King	Meghan Donnellan	Brian Schwegal	
Rachel L. Grodsky	Jessica M. Wilson	Alana E. Housman	
Zachary Best	Matthew J. Lenzner	Katherine Durham	
Christopher Ramsay		Paul A. Becker	

Note: Antony Samy was listed only in the records of the National Office of Alpha Chi Sigma for the 2001 initiates. For the 2003 initiates, Matthew Holmes was listed in the National Records but not in the Beta Delta Membership List.

Initiates:

2004	
April 16	November 13
Stephen Taylor	Craig Began
Jacob Pupillo	Kevin Day
Travis McKindra	James Moynihan
Latisha M. Poulard	Elizabeth Abram
Matthew Holmes	Douglas K. Ludlow
	Kelley Arrington
	William F. Ruzicka
	Toua Lipperd

2005		2006
April 29	December 2	April 28
Wesley A. Glick	Emily J. Speorl	Brandi Clark
Jessie A. Cates	Michael McNamee	Amber R. (McFadden) Kirkpatrick
Michael D. Schroer	Jessica (Mueller) Blair	Agatha Dwilewicz
Kendrick Callaway	Lindsay A. Epstein	Danielle Lyman
Melissa Leek	Chad M. Winkler	Nicole M. Dierking
Johnathan Nguyen	Loren Moody	
Christopher Buterbaugh	Adam Martin	
Emily M. Hackworth		

2007		
January 12	April 27	November 30
Kelsie Van Hoose	Sean Mickey	Anita B. Heinzke
Tyler Fears	John Bartow	Matthew S. Wallace
Bryan Rapp	Kristy Geltz	Michelle R. Brosnahan
Thuydung Huynh	Timothy S. Lee	Rachel K. (Thurman) Palasky
	Megan Oldroyd	Isaac C. Bond
	Brooke Burroughs	Jennifer A. Wolf
	Austin H. Shaw	Alan B. Windhausen
	Sandra J. Smith	Brooke A. Lindsey
	Chad C. Smith	

Note: Douglas K. Ludlow would go on to be the current Chapter Advisor (2006-2021). Of the 2005 initiates, Jessica Cates, and of the 2006 initiates, Agatha Dwilewicz were listed in the National records but not in Beta Delta's.

Initiates:

2008		2009	
May 2	November 8	April 18	November 14
Stephanie R. Judd	Jenna M. Jeffryes	Nicholas J. Potje	Blythe W. Ferriere
David D. Gorham	Jared S. Bouquet	Margret C. Powell	Aline L. Collin
Andrew B. Mann	Andrew W. Naida	Ellen M. Kirk	Meghan J. Ray
Ryan K. Rader	Charles A. Pearson	Blair R. Brown	Martin R. McPhail
Brandon J. Basler	Jonathan E. Tuttle	Daniel A. Caligiuri	Amanda R. Schlender
Katie J. Baldwin	Andrew N. Schott	Mitchell J. Niehoff	
Devang A. Dasani	Jonathon D. Stocker	Arch D. Creasy	
Angela M. Gugliano	April E. Sloan	Ying Chau A. Liu	
John T. Campbell	George E. Obeldobel	Josh A. Wilmes	
	Scott M. Richardt	Zheng Li	
	Jeremy A. Sapphire	Matthew D. Gill	
	Aditya Ghosh		

2010		2011	
April 24	December 4	April 16	December 3
Selin Acar	Emily R. Menkes	Kevin L. Clark	Zachary C. Brooks
Emitt C. Witt	Adam M. Mikulus	Joshua A. Weeks	Andrew J. Naeger
James C. Moore	Nicole D. French	Spencer G. Norman	Joey A. Silhavy
Matthew E. Jones	Rebecca G. Nelson	Joshua M. Grobe	Easton I. Mann
Rachael A. Naeger	Megan M. Schuller	Elise A. Breitwieser	Kristina L. Sevy
Matthew S. Dahl	Kelsey K. Bass	Margaret M. Adams	Brian P. Shepard
Nathan C. Decker	Alyssa L. (Steinert) Blackson	Joseph R. Hoing	Patrick M. McCarver
Melissa K. Elliott	Ashley C. Upschulte	Charles L. Dewsnup	Kyle J. Stocker
Sarah M. Sutterer	Jennifer A. Drost	David A. May	David A. May
Ryan T. Morse		Tiffany C. Edwards	Jialun Li
Karl J. Dachroeden		Rachel E. Downen	Amanda K. O'Dell
Luke R. Jones		Caleb D. Richardson	Maria T. Vega-Westhoff
Kelsey Richard		Chris M. Terry	Ariel C. Mollhagen
Jason W. Picou		Jessica Walker	Clayton T. Buback
		Catherine M. Bohanon	Justin M. Chrisco
			Blake M. Hiza
			David M. DeVoss
			Casey J. Zimmerman

Note: According to the Beta Delta Records for 2010, Kelsey Richard and Matthew Jones were initiated on Friday, April 23.[62]

Initiates:

2012		2013	
April 21	November 10	April 20	November 16
Seth A. Molenhour	Angela V. Swyers	Jose A. Morales	Thaddeus J. Stepniewski
Matthew B. Senter	Meagan R. Schneier	Paige K. Eckert	Lauren B. Weil
Cheyenne M. Morrissette	Joshua Moyers	Zachary T. Woolsey	Amanda A. Sebelski
Joseph D. Kramer	Chelsea R. Winkelmann	John A. Armstrong	Caitlyn M. Schottel
Sean G. Kilgore	Kenneth J. Castellano	Kathleen M. Fowler	Michael L. DeVoss
Justin A. Cobb	Jordan W. England	Andrew M. Clum	Kenneth A. Domann
Zachary A. Hume	Mike W. Marsh	Breanna M. Stumpe	Brandon M. Haugabrook
Peter E. Daniels	Ashleigh N. Eady	Andrew Smith	Courtney L. Mandeville
Erica Ann Ronchetto	Laura R. Shaffer		Brady M. Campbell
	Hannah E. Frye		Mary E. (Putnam) Carey
	Alan T. Landers		Lauren M. Casey
	Jessica K. Randall		Kaley S. Short
	Frederic S. Bush		Sean M. Tennyson
	Richard H. Gorski		
	Kyle C. Crane		
	Rachel L. Kurrelmeyer		

Note: The Beta Delta Membership records for 2012, but not the records of the National Office, list Erica Ann Ronchetto. Also, Matthew Senter would become Central District counselor from 2020 to 2022.

Initiates:

2014		2015	
April 26	December 6	May 2	December 5
Jamie C. Bader	Alexander D. Ayres	Dana Q. Lawson	Joshua A. Hernandez
Ian P. Schroen	Erin F. Wharton	Matthew S. Liberson	Ryan F. Delahanty
Aaron J. Latal	Ellen A. Tuxbury	Cheyenne R. Cripps	Benjamin E. House
Sunghee B. Choi	William B. Whelan	Michael B. Smith	Kevin G. O'Brien
Piero G. Burzio-Roca	Justin J. Schletzbaum	Valentine A. Hollingsworth	Abbie M. Braden
Kyle T. Norris	Abigail A. Buchheit	Leelaya Chaiwong	Rachel N. Pyszka
Amanda J. McDuffee	Robert H. Leach Clark		Tim M. Avery
	Alexander R. Capalupo		
	Tammy L. Martin		
	Allison C. Stroup		
	Amanda A. Koebbe		
	Price K. Weakley		

Note: The National Office records for 2014 also included Jamie C. Bader, who was not listed in Beta Delta's membership records.

Initiates:

2016		2017	
April 16	November 11	April 29	November 11
Roxanne M. Feliciano	Jasmin L. Hill	Ivan S. Sedlacek	Marc P. St. Amour
Alexandra R. Bueltmann	Jennifer M. Frasch	Rachel Sciaroni	Kaytee N. Bailey
Andreaunna Hawkins	Breanon L. Dowling	Eric W. Fors	Samantha K. Smith
Tucker S. Shoup	Parker S. Schellenberg	Logan Hansen	Erik P. Gull
Joshua K. Lanz	Samantha M. Oelklaus	Alexia N. Douglas	Bayleigh E. Mitchell
Victoria N. Kramer	Dale J. Wright	Mason J. Carey	Madeline R. Hines
Caleb Z. Trecazzi	Taylor E. Tarter	Michael A. Clemons	
Michael S. McMahon	Elizabeth Sotolongo		
	Alex L. Lodholz		
	Austin L. Vaughn		
	Daniel T. Rosner		
	Brian J. Baumgartner		
	Nathan E. Boys		
	Christina J. Hamilton		
	Joseph Gresick		

Note: According to the Beta Delta Membership List for 2016, Joseph Gresick was initiated on December 10 at Alpha Epsilon's initiation.

Initiates:

2018		2019	
April 21	November 10	April 27	November 2
Meghan Sutalski	Austin D. Scheer	Derek Dillinger	Samuel Alexander
Emily Quist	Jessica Caswell	Taishi Higuchi-Roos	Mikayla Shy
Bryn Guthrie	William K. Guthrie	Adam McTigue	Loki Cortner
Anna Schneider	Garett Ward	Kari Knobbe (April 13)	Whitney Sheffield
Christopher Coronado	Samuel S. Ross	Chrysalin Martin	Andrew Holloway
Kelly Pachowicz (April 14)	Nicole Moon	Rachel Boillat	Nicole Wheeler
Michael Donley	Jacob Brownfield	Taylor Stevens	
Ashish Zore	Sam Ross	Delaney Neely	
Kyle Newport	Lefatshe Lefatshe		
Jacob Whanger			
Dr. Cynthia Bolon			
Matt Snarzyk			
Dr. Peter J. Ryan			
Michael Ferguson			
Nathan Thyparambi			

Note: Jessica Caswell was not listed in the Beta Delta Membership records doe 2018, but she was included in the National Office records, while Lefatshe Lefatshe appears only in the Beta Delta Membership records for 2018.

Note: Even though the official Beta Delta Membership records indicate that Kelly Pachowicz was initiated on April 21, 2018, she was actually initiated on April 14 when MA Erin Wharton took her to Beta Rho (Kansas State) to be initiated at their ceremony.

Note: The Beta Delta Membership records for 2019 have Kari Knobbe initiated on April 13 at Beta Rho.[63]

Initiates:

	2020	2021	
---	November 7	April 10	November 13
	William Bump	Megan Hutchcraft	Justin Christensen
	Sarah West	Alex Hawkins	Isabela Clubb
	Kyle Boillat	Dan Bugarin	Saige Coin
	Chrystel Hillier		Ethan Hay
	Christina Arens		Karli Heimburger
	Caroline Williams		Andrew Lewis
	Megan Brandt		Emily Pitz
	Suraj Sahoo		Kristen (Mallory) Strickland
	Vaughn Foreman		

Note: There was a pledge class in the spring of 2020, but due to the pandemic no initiation was held in the spring. Instead the initiation in the fall was for both pledge classes.

CONCLUSION—AUREUM OPUS

In Projection it shall be proved if our practice be profitable…

—*George Ripley, The Twelfth Gate*

Histories have been described as stories, as journeys, or with other related imagery. These metaphors hold true for Beta Delta as well. But a more appropriate comparison, perhaps, in the case of a group centered on the chemical sciences, may be an analogy to an alchemical process. In this scenario, Beta Delta acts as a retort which accepts the *prima materia* and transmutes it into gold. The resultant gold is the influence the chapter's members have on the fraternity, on the college, on the community, and on all the chemically-related industries around the world.

Striking about this history of Beta Delta is the significant role its members have played beyond the local chapter. Beta Delta brothers have been involved at all levels of the national fraternity. At the collegiate level, Charles and Valerie Bagnell reached out to the members, providing leadership development through their GROW conferences. At the district level, many Beta Delta brothers served as district counselors: Walter Schrenk, William H. Webb, Edward Schneider, Gary Bland, Gary Fischer, John Adams, DeWayne Gerber, D. Mitch Levings, Rachel K. Palasky, and Matthew Senter. All held the position of district counselor at some point in the chapter's nine-decade existence.

Beta Delta's contributions to the fraternity went even higher, however—all the way to positions on the Supreme Council: Walter Schrenk, Grand Master of Ceremonies (1948-1950), Grand Collegiate Alchemist (1950-1952), and Grand Master Alchemist (1954-1956); Frank J. Zvanut, Grand Master of Ceremonies (1954-1956), Grand Collegiate Alchemist (1958-1960), and Grand Master Alchemist (1960-1962); Edward P. Schneider, Grand Collegiate Alchemist (1964-1966) and Grand Master Alchemist (1968-1970); DeWayne Gerber, Grand Collegiate Alchemist (1986-1988), Grand Master of Ceremonies (1990-1992), and Grand Master Alchemist (1992-1994); John Adams, Grand Professional Alchemist (1998-2000) and Grand Master Alchemist (2002-2004); and D. Mitch Levings, Grand Master of Ceremonies (1984-1986), Grand Master Alchemist (1988-1990), and Grand Historian (1990 to date). These brothers played significant roles at crucial moments in the fraternity's history. They presided over the admission of women into the fraternity, the elimination of restrictive language in the by-laws, and the significant changes in the Ritual.

Beyond the fraternity, members of the chapter were significant contributors to the faculty and the academic standing of the college, whether it was at MSM, at UMR, or now at Missouri S&T. Members such as Walter Schrenk, William Webb, Mailand Strunk, Wouter Bosch, and Harvey Grice became department chairs and deans; their research and professional writings elevated the college. Many Beta Delta brothers also became faculty members at other educational institutions, including Neil Book at Tulane and John Adams at the University of Missouri-Columbia. The most important contribution of all these teachers, however, was their genuine dedication to the education of their students. As faculty, they provided the necessary ingredients to transform their students, who were under the sign of the Wyvern (i.e., lacking certain knowledge), into competent engineers and scientists prepared for careers in scientific fields beyond the university. These professors and instructors were the catalysts, enabling the transformative processes of education to accomplish its great work.

The graduates of the chemical sciences went forth along various industrial and research avenues to make contributions, individually, both great and small. Collectively their efforts can be described as a *magnus opus*. Reflecting on the sheer numbers of students who have applied their chemical knowledge in such industries as agriculture, petroleum, pharmaceutical, energy production, food processing, and even beer-making, we must stand in awe of the immensity of their accomplishments.

Though not all who studied under the chemical sciences became members of Alpha Chi Sigma, they were still shaped by the faculty who had been members of Beta Delta. For those who initiated into the fraternity, however, Beta Delta was both the retort and the flame that heated the material contained within. The chapter provided the warmth of friendship, which supported and encouraged the members' endeavors, and the energy to initiate and sustain the intellectual and imaginative reactions involved in the acquisition of knowledge. During the students' college careers, the chapter offered tutoring in first-year chemistry, awarded materials such as handbooks, supported events, and assisted students struggling in courses like Mass Transfer, Thermodynamics and the dreaded Physical Chemistry. But the vessel and its contents and reactions were not a closed system, something unto itself. A product was brought forth. Even before the members were initiated into the professional world to add their knowledge and talent to that realm, they were contributing to the surrounding community through high school math tutoring, service projects, and events encouraging interest in science and engineering among middle and high school students.

The impact Beta Delta brothers have had on society at large clearly reflects their loyalty to the fraternity's last two objectives: "To strive for the advancement of chemistry both as a science and as a profession," and "To aid its members by every honorable means in the attainment of their ambitions as chemists throughout their mortal lives." In the process of achieving these two goals, the fraternity's first objective was, and, indeed, must continue to be, fulfilled: "To bind its members with a tie of true and lasting friendship."

Beta Delta, then, has been the retort in which the elements of the *prima materia* were admixed. Out of that admixture came forth a work of gold—the *Aureum Opus*.

Appendix A—Epsilon Pi Omicron Members, Initiates, and Officers

1932[1]

Charter Members		Elected Members	Initiates
T. G. Day, Pres.	R. L. Cunningham	Dr. W. T. Schrenk	T. J. Stewart
G. Hale, Vice-Pres.	M. Larwood	Dr. H. L. Dunlap	H. A. Brisch
M. L. Herzog, Secretary	C. R. Maise	Dr. C. J. Monroe	W. B. Danforth
P. C. McDonald, Treas.	J. H. Tobin	Prof. K. K. Kershner	W. A. Howe
T. Donahue, Historian	A. H. Walther		H. F. Lange
J. S. Sabine	T. Burnham		J. I. McCaskill
C. S. Abshier	R. A. Parker		B. A. Menke
L. Merchie	W. A. Westerfeld		N. R. Pulley
H. E. Boyd	G. S. Richardson		J. Smith

1933[2]

Initiates

Al Howe, Jim Stewart, Ned Pulley, and Bert Menke

1934[3]

Officers	
President	G. A. Hale
Vice-President	H. E. Boyd
Secretary	C. R. Maise
Treasurer	P. C. McDonald

Members			
Active Student Members		Faculty Members	Initiates
C. S. Abshier	C. R. Maise	Dr. H. L. Dunlap	Frank J. Zvanut
J. G. Burham	B. A. Menke	Prof. K. K. Kershner	L. Poese
H. E. Boyd	J. S. Sabine	Dr. C.H. Monroe	H. Haffner,
R. L. Cunningham	T. J. Stewart	Dr. W. T. Schrenk	H. Mortland
T. G. Day	J. H. Tobin		W. Neel
T. S. Donahue	A. H Walther		O. Fager
G. A. Hale	W. W. Westerfeld		E. Fiss
W. A. Howe	W. B. Danforth		
M. B. Larwood	H. B. Lange		
P. C. McDonald			

1935[4]

Officers	
President	H.F. Lange
Vice-President	F. J. Zvanut
Secretary	E.C. Fiss
Treasurer	C.R. Maise
Historian	H.S. Sabine

Members			
Active Student Members		Faculty Members	Initiates
J.S. Sabine	H.G. Mortland	Dr. H. L. Dunlap	H.G. Thompson
T.G. Day	R. H. Striker	Prof. K. K. Kershner	R.A. Macke
C.S. Abshier	H.H. Haffner	Dr. C.J. Monroe	E.L. Smith
W.A. Howe	H.A. Brisch	Dr. W. T. Schrenk	E.C. Meckfessel
B.A. Menke	L.A. Bay		E.W. Volz
W.B. Danforth	R.H. Cardetti		R.C. Lange
W.O. Neel	H.C. Berger		H.G. Thompson

1936[5]

Officers	
President	Frank J. Zvanut
Vice-President	Richard J. Cardetti
Secretary	Harry C. Berger
Treasurer	Clemens R. Maise

Members			
Active Student Members		Faculty Members	Initiates
Leroy A. Bay	Hoyt G. Thompson	Thomas G. Day	Roger C. Tittel
Herman A. Brish	Harry C. Berger	Howard L. Dunlap	Leo M. O'Hara
Clemens R. Maise	Richard J. Cardetti	Clarence J. Monroe	John F. Campbell
John S. Sabine	Arthur P. Hausmann	Walter T. Schrenk	Eugene F. Hill
Frank J. Zvanut	Peter A. Jenni		Edward A. Ballman
Oscar H. Fager	Robert C. Lange		
Edward C. Fiss	Grant W. Schaumburg		
Elmer L. Smith	Elmer W. Volvz		
Ralph H. Striker			

Appendix B—Beta Delta Conclave Attendance

(Information provided by D. Mitch Levings, Grand Historian)

Con-clave	Year	Location/Dates	Beta Delta Member		
1	1908	Madison, Wisconsin, June 25-27			
2	1910	Madison, Wisconsin, June 23-25			
3	1912	Madison, Wisconsin, June 20-22			
4	1914	Madison, Wisconsin, June 18-20			
5	1916	Evanston, Illinois June 22-24			
6	1919	Columbus, Ohio December 29-31			
7	1922	Saint Louis, Missouri June 22-24			
8	1924	Pittsburgh, Pennsylvania June 16-19			
9	1926	Ann Arbor, Michigan June 16-19			
10	1928	Chapel Hill, North Carolina June 16-20			
11	1930	Minneapolis, Minnesota June 17-19			
12	1932	Washington, D. C. June 13-17			

13	1934	Bloomington, Indiana June 13-17			
14	1936	Cincinnati, Ohio June 16-20	C. R. Maise		
15	1938	New Orleans, Louisiana June 21-25	W. T. Pearl		
16	1940	Berkeley, California June 21-25	H. J. Nicholas		
17	1942	Chicago, Illinois June 19-22	James C. Johnson	Frank J. Zvanut	
18	1946	Saint Louis, Missouri June 12-16	Virgil A. Johnson	Edward P. Schneider	Frank J. Zvanut
19	1948	Cleveland, Ohio June 15-19	Robert C. Booth	Frank J. Zvanut	
20	1950	Washington, D. C June 21-25	Jack Venarde	Frank J. Zvanut	
21	1952	Madison, Wisconsin June 22-26	Edward L. Creamer	Frank J. Zvanut	
22	1954	East Lansing, Michigan June 21-25	John Max Brawley	Paul D. Griffin	Frank J. Zvanut
23	1956	State College, Pennsylvania June 25-29	Jim E. Fick	Frank J. Zvanut	
24	1958	Houston, Texas June 23-27	J. W. Donaldson Frank J. Zvanut	William A. Enderson	Edward P. Schneider
25	1960	West Lafayette, Indiana June 27-July 1	Gary D. Achenbach	Edward P. Schneider	Frank J. Zvanut
26	1962	Cincinnati, Ohio August 26-30	Daniel Middleton	Edward P. Schneider	Frank J. Zvanut

27	1964	Long Island, New York June 14-19	Paul D. Griffin	Edward P. Schneider	
28	1966	Ann Arbor, Michigan June 19-23	Paul D. Griffin	Edward P. Schneider	William H. Webb
			Lawrence M. Young	Frank J. Zvanut	
29	1968	Iowa City, Iowa June 16-20	Benny E. Divin	Larry Kennedy	Edward P. Schneider
			John Throckmorton	Darwyn Walker	William H. Webb
30	1970	Austin, Texas August 16-20	Gerald L. Hoover	Robert Reuter	Guy Robinson
			Edward P. Schneider	Frank J. Zvanut	
31	1972	Urbana, Illinois June 11-16	Victor J. Becker	Robert L. Pike	Edward P. Schneider
			William H. Webb		
32	1974	College Park, Maryland October 4-7	David Barclay	Garrett Bland	
33	1976	Rapid City, South Dakota August 8-12	John E. Adams	Victor J. Becker	Garrett Bland
			Mike O'Conner	Michael Quinn	Rita Webber
34	1978	Denton, Texas August 13-17	Charles R. Bagnell	Valarie A. Bagnell	Kim Fledderman
			DeWayne C. Gerber	Joseph Granna	D. Mitch Levings
			Steve Zigrye	Mark Ziobro	
35	1980	Ithaca, New York August 10-14	Charles R. Bagnell	Valarie A. Bagnell	DeWayne C. Gerber
			D. Mitch Levings	Peggy Ann Scholtes	Jana Zigrye
			Steve Zigrye	Cindy Ziobro	Mark Ziobro

36	1982	Columbia, Missouri August 10-15	John E. Adams	Valarie A. Bagnell	DeWayne C. Gerber
			D. Mitch Levings	Howard Mizuki	Edward P. Schneider
			Peggy Ann Scholtes	Peter C. Scholtes	Robert E. Stevens
			Frank J. Zvanut		
37	1984	Syracuse, New York July 31-August 5	Charles R. Bagnell	Valarie A. Bagnell	DeWayne C. Gerber
			John A. Hume	Joyce (Weinhold) Hume (delegate)	Tom Kreek
			D. Mitch Levings	Howard Mizuki	
38	1986	Chapel Hill, North Carolina July 30-August 3	Charles R. Bagnell	Valarie A. Bagnell	Mike R. Fredholm
			DeWayne C. Gerber	John A. Hume	Tom Kreek
			D. Mitch Levings	Eric Steutermann	
39	1988	Berkeley, California July 27-31	Valarie A. Bagnell	Scott DePriest	DeWayne C. Gerber
			Joyce Hume	Tom Kreek	D. Mitch Levings
			Robert E. Stevens	Daniel Weidman	
40	1990	Tallahassee, Florida August 14-19	Charles R. Bagnell	Valarie A. Bagnell	DeWayne C. Gerber
			D. Mitch Levings	Shawn Sitton	
41	1992	Indianapolis, Indiana August 4-9	Charles R. Bagnell	Valarie A. Bagnell	DeWayne C. Gerber
			D. Mitch Levings	Lamar K. Gerber	
42	1994	Minneapolis, Minnesota August 2-7	John E. Adams	Charles R. Bagnell	Valarie A. Bagnell
			DeWayne C. Gerber	Lamar K. Gerber	D. Mitch Levings

Appendix B

43	1996	Fayetteville, Arkansas August 6-11	John E. Adams	Charles R. Bagnell	Valarie A. Bagnell
			DeWayne C. Gerber	D. Mitch Levings	Edward P. Schneider
44	1998	Atlanta, Georgia August 11-15	John E. Adams	Charles R. Bagnell	DeWayne C. Gerber
			D. Mitch Levings	Mozow Yusof	
45	2000	Saint Louis, Missouri August 8-13	John E. Adams	Andrea Collazo	Harvest L. Collier
			DeWayne C. Gerber	Milton P. Hadinoto	Robert T. Jackson
			James C. Johnson	D. Mitch Levings	Edward P. Schneider
			Robert E. Stevens	Kurtis G. Vogler	
46	2002	Madison, Wisconsin August 5-11	John E. Adams	DeWayne C. Gerber	D. Mitch Levings
			Jeffrey R. Ramberg	Sandy A. Sansing	Robert E. Stevens
47	2004	Blacksburg, Virginia August 3-7	John E. Adams	Julie M. Breckenridge-Briski	DeWayne C. Gerber
			D. Mitch Levings	Jeffrey R. Ramberg	Sandy A. Sansing
			Robert E. Stevens		
48	2006	Los Angles, California August 8-13	John E. Adams	Kendrick Callaway	DeWayne C. Gerber
			D. Mitch Levings	Robert E. Stevens	
49	2008	Bloomington, Indiana July 22-27	John E. Adams	Michelle R. Brosnahan	DeWayne C. Gerber
			D. Mitch Levings	Douglas K. Ludlow	Daniel Palasky
			Jeffrey R. Ramberg	Robert E. Stevens	Matthew S. Wallace

50	2010	Athens, Ohio August 3-8	John E. Adams	Julie M. Breckenridge-Briski	Aline L. Collin
			DeWayne C. Gerber	D. Mitch Levings	Douglas K. Ludlow
			Sandy A. Sansing	Edward P. Schneider	April E. Sloan
			Robert E. Stevens		
51	2012	Iowa City, Iowa July 24-29	John E. Adams	Julie M. Breckenridge-Briski	Blythe W. Ferriere
			DeWayne C. Gerber	D. Mitch Levings	Sandy A. Sansing
			Megan M. Schuller	Robert E. Stevens	
52	2014	Charlottesville, Virginia July 27-August 1	John E. Adams	Julie M. Breckenridge-Briski	DeWayne C. Gerber
			D. Mitch Levings	Spencer Norman	Daniel Palasky
			Rachel Palasky	Sandy A. Sansing	Matthew Senter
			Robert E. Stevens		
53	2016	Atlanta, Georgia July 25-30	John E. Adams	Abbie Braden	Julie M. Breckenridge-Briski
			Abigail Buchheit	DeWayne C. Gerber	D. Mitch Levings
			Spencer Norman	Daniel Palasky	Rachel Palasky
			Sandy A. Sansing	Matthew Senter	Robert E. Stevens

Appendix B

54	2018	Pittsburgh, Pennsylvania July 23-28	John E. Adams	Abbie Braden	Julie M. Breckenridge-Briski
			Joshua Lanz	D. Mitch Levings	Kelly Pachowicz
			Daniel Palasky	Rachel Palasky	Sandy A. Sansing
			Matthew Senter	Robert E. Stevens	
55	2020	Zoom Conference July 6-9	John E. Adams	Michael DeVoss	Derek Dillinger
			DeWayne C. Gerber	D. Mitch Levings	Kelly Pachowicz
			Rachel Palasky	Sandy A. Sansing	Matthew Senter
			Robert E. Stevens		

Appendix C—Beta Delta Kuebler Award Recipients and Order of Altotus Members

Kuebler Award

The highest award Alpha Chi Sigma can bestow on one of its members is the John R. Kuebler Award. This award is presented for outstanding service to the Fraternity and outstanding service to the profession or accomplishment in the science of chemistry. Established in 1961, it honors John R. Kuebler, Epsilon 1910, who served Alpha Chi Sigma for 33 years as Grand Recorder (1926 to 1959), 37 years as Grand Editor of The HEXAGON (1922 to 1959) and 10 years as Grand Historian (1957 to 1967). The award, consisting of a hand-lettered scroll, was presented annually until 1978 and since then biennially in Conclave years. It is customary to present the award at the Conclave banquet and for the recipient to deliver an award address.

--Taken from *John R. Kuebler Award,* Membership Awards and Programs, Alpha Chi Sigma--Kuebler.pdf (alphachisigma.org).

John R. Kuebler, Epsilon 1910

The Beta Delta recipients of this award included: Dr. Walter T. Schrenk, Alpha '17, Edward Schneider, '42, and David Mitch Levings, '75.

Order of Altotus

The Order of Altotus, originated in 1932, is an organization whose membership is restricted to past Grand Master Alchemists. The Order was created by Supreme Council Proposition 623 with the intent of legitimizing the advisory relationship between the Supreme Council and the former leaders. The duties of the Order are to keep in touch with the fraternity through the Chrome and Blue; advise the GMA in all matters pertaining to the welfare of the fraternity, and inspect petitioners at the request of the GMA.[1]

The following are the Beta Delta brothers who belong to the Order of Altotus. Dr. Walter T. Schrenk is included in the list, even though he pledged Alpha Chapter, since he was one of the founders of Beta Delta and a significant presence for the chapter throughout his career and life.

Beta Delta Members of the Order of Altotus	Year Initiated	Year(s) Served as GMA
Walter T. Schrenk	Alpha 1917	1954-1956
Frank J. Zvanut	1936	1960-1962
Edward P. Schneider	1942	1968-1970
D. Mitch Levings	1975	1988-1990
DeWayne Gerber	1975	1992-1994
John E. Adams	1971	2002-2004

Appendix D—Judith L. Flebbe Memorial Scholarship Recipients and Initial Donors

The recipients of the Judith L. Flebbe Memorial Scholarship listed below are for the years 2007 through 2021. Records from 1982—the inception of the scholarship—to 2006 could not be accessed. However, three of the early recipients were determined from the Spring, 1984, issue of the Beta Delta Data and the August, 1986, issue of the Alumni Magazine, now known as the Missouri S&T Magazine: Theresa Ney (Beta Delta '83), Judith Anderson, (Chem. Eng. 1986), and Frederick Kielhorn, (Chem. Eng. 1986).[1]

Recipients			
Name	Year	Name	Year
Katherine Scanlon	2006-2007	Brianne Claspill	2013-2014
Angela Reinholdt	2007-2008	Kirstin Bier	2013-2014
Sarah Perdue	2007-2008	Andrew Naeger	2013-2014
Katherine Scanlon	2007-2008	Angela Swyers	2013-2014
Stacy Bradfield	2008-2009	Nathan Krenning	2013-2014
Amy Krugeel	2008-2009	Brianne Claspill	2014-2015
Nichole Hurd	2009-2010	Amanda Sebelski	2014-2015
Kristy Geltz	2009-2010	Angela Swyers	2014-2015
Devang Dasani	2009-2010	Lauren Casey	2014-2015
Abigail Asher	2010-2011	Amanda Sebelski	2015-2016
Angela Schneider	2010-2011	Thomas Roustio	2015-2016
Emily Menkes	2010-2011	Deanna Hyde	2015-2016
Michelle Kropf	2011-2012	Tyler Howe	2015-2016
Derek Schloemann	2011-2012	Sarah Morris	2016-2017
Jennifer Costello	2011-2012	Chase Herman	2016-2017
Kevin Benedict	2011-2012	Lee Torack	2016-2017
Elise Breitweiser	2011-2012	Jakeb Baldridge	2016-2017
Adeline Hellebusch	2012-2013		2016-2017*
Andrea Colson	2012-2013	Alexander Higinbotham	2016-2017
Ann Torack	2012-2013		2017-2018*
Kathleen McKinley	2012-2013	Jacob Johannigmeier	2017-2018

Name	Year
Jeffrey Reid	2017-2018
Kimberly Henry	2017-2018
Zachary Compton	2018-2019
Holly Coleman	2018-2019
Corinne Stulce	2018-2019
Elizabeth Pomerenke	2019-2020
Adam Gordon	2019-2020
Chloe Dorst	2019-2020
Jimmie Washington	2019-2020
Emily Rapp	2019-2020
Avery English	2020-2021
Peyton Bradley	2020-2021
Joseph Schultz	2020-2021
Wyatt Spiker	2020-2021
Brianna Pfeiffer	2020-2021
Ethan Drake	2020-2021
Trevor Anthony	2020-2021
Spencer Runzo	2020-2021
Mackenzie Mills	2020-2021
Tyler Dye	2020-2021

*The students had requested that their names not be published.

Initial Donors (1981)[2]		
Michael Noble	David Barclay	Douglas Powell
Bradley Wyatt	W. J. James	Dr. H. H. Grice
James Wood	Michael Foley	James Puckett
Dr. G. K. Patterson	Kay & Kent Sooter	Tony Messina
Dr. Wouter Bosch, Sr.	Michael Quinn	Gary Bland

Dr. A. Daane	Douglas Ecoff	DeWayne Gerber
G. J. Fennwald	Dr. J. W. Johnson	John Adams
Alen Davidson	C. N. Hudson	Helen Hatleid-Hester
Shelly Claudin	Richard Schaefermyer	Rita McMinn

The Judith L. Flebbe Memorial Scholarship is still active as of this writing. Contributions may be made to the fund supporting the scholarship. Contact the Financial Aid Department of Missouri S&T.

Appendix E—Bigs and Littles

The members listed between Fall, 2008, and Fall, 2011, are incomplete lists; lists from Spring, 2012, to date are complete (Information provided by Derek Dillinger, Matthew Senter, and Christina Arens).

Fall 2008	
Pledge	Big
April Sloan	

Fall 2009	
Pledge	Big
Blythe Ferriere	

Spring 2010	
Pledge	Big
S Acar	

Fall 2010	
Pledge	Big
Ashley Upschulte	April Sloan
Megan Schuller	Scott Richardt

Spring 2011	
Pledge (18?)	Big
Spencer Norman	Ashley Upschulte
Kevin Clark	
Margaret (Maggie) Adams	
Josh Weeks	No one knows (except perhaps the unknown big)
Charles Dewsnup	

Fall 2011	
Pledge	Big
David DeVoss	Josh Weeks
Maria Vega-Westhoff	Megan Schuller
Justin Chrisco	April Sloan
David May	

Spring 2012	
Pledge (9)	Big
Sean Kilgore	Casey Zimmerman
Erica Ronchetto	Rachel Naeger
Cheyenne Morrissette	Maria Vega-Westhoff
Joe Kramer	Josh Weeks
Peter Daniels	
Zachary Hume	Kevin Clark?
Justin Cobb	
Seth Molenhour	
Matthew Senter	Spencer Norman

Fall 2012	
Pledge (16)	Big
Jessica Pisarik (Randall at the time)	Blythe Ferriere
Rachel Kurrelmeyer	Cheyenne Morrissette
Angela (Tori) Swyers	Matthew Senter
Ashleigh Eady	Ashley Upschulte
Chelsea Winkelmann	
Hannah Frye	Kelsey Bass
Laura Shaffer	
Meagan Schneier	Justin Chrisco
Mike Marsh	Megan Schuller
Jordan England	Kevin Clark
Kyle Crane	Kevin Clark

Appendix E

Fall 2012	
Pledge (16)	Big
Richard Gorski	Kevin Clark
Josh Moyers	Patrick McCarver
Fred Bush	David DeVoss?
Kenneth Castellano	
Alan Landers	

Spring 2013	
Pledge (8)	Big
Paige Eckert	Megan Schuller
Breanna Stumpe	Hannah Frye
John Armstrong	
Zachary Woolsey	Alan Landers
Jose Morales	Josh Moyers
Andrew Smith	Matthew Senter
Andrew Clum	Spencer Norman
Katie Fowler	Meagan Schneier

Fall 2013	
Pledge (13)	Big
Courtney Mandeville	Matthew Senter
Lauren Casey	Jessica Pisarik
Brady Campbell	Spencer Norman
Amanda Sebelski	Mike Marsh
Lauren Weil	Breanna Stumpe
Michael DeVoss	Joe Kramer
Sean Tennyson	David DeVoss
Brandon Haugabrook	David DeVoss?
Kenneth Domann	Zachary Woolsey
Mary Carey (Putman at the time)	Hannah Frye
Caitlyn Schottel	Cheyenne Morrissette

Fall 2013	
Pledge (13)	Big
Kaley Short	
Thaddeus Stepniewski	Sean Kilgore

Spring 2014	
Pledge (7)	Big
Ian Schroen	Lauren Casey
Briana Choi	
Aaron Latal	Kenneth Domann
Piero Burzio-Roca	
Jamie Bader	Courtney Mandeville
Kyle Norris	Josh Weeks
Amanda McDuffee	

*Jamie Bader was initiated at Delta Chapter. As of November 2, 2016, she had not signed our plaque or record book.

Fall 2014	
Pledge (12)	Big
Erin Wharton	Amanda Sebelski
Robert Leach Clark	Brady Campbell
Justin Schletzbaum	Ian Schroen
Will Whelan	Kenneth Domann
Tammy Martin	Justin Chrisco
Alex Capalupo	Courtney Mandeville
Alex Ayres	Matthew Senter
Amanda Koebbe	Maria Vega-Westhoff
Price Weakly	Aaron Latal
Allison Stroup	Paige Eckert
Ellen Tuxbury	Spencer Norman
Abigail Buchheit	Lauren Casey

*Martyn Henry from Beta Rho was initiated at Beta Delta that semester.

Spring 2015	
Pledge (6)	Big
Michael Smith	Robert Leach Clark
Valentine Hollingsworth	Kenneth Domann
Dana Lawson	Abigail Buchheit
Cheyenne Cripps	Amanda Koebbe
Leelaya Chaiwong	Allison Stroup
Matt Liberson	Brady Campbell

Fall 2015	
Pledge (7)	Big
Abbie Braden	Abigail Buchheit
Tim Avery	
Ben House	Robert Leach Clark
Rachel Pyszka	Erin Wharton
Josh Hernandez	Spencer Norman
Kevin O'Brien	Brandon Haugabrook
Ryan Delahanty	Michael DeVoss

Spring 2016	
Pledge (8)	Big
Roxanne Feliciano	
Josh Lanz	Ryan Delahanty
Tucker Shoup	
Michael McMahon	Aaron Latal
Alex Bueltmann	Kenneth Domann
Andreaunna Hawkins	Ellen Tuxbury
Victoria Kramer	Michael Smith
Caleb Trecazzi	Michael DeVoss

Fall 2016				
Founding Members of New Alchemical Families				
Tin	Mercury	Copper	Iron	Lead
Brady Campbell	Matthew Senter	Lauren Casey	Mike Marsh	Aaron Latal
Matthew Liberson	Courtney Mandeville	Abby Buchheit	Mary Carey	Amanda Koebbe
Ben House	Jamie Bader	Justin Schletzbaum	Michael DeVoss	Price Weakley
Ellen Tuxbury	Alex Ayres	Tim Avery	Erin Wharton	Will Whelan
Michael Smith	Alex Capalupo	Abbie Braden	Ryan Delahanty	Cheyenne Cripps
Andreaunna Hawkins	Allison Stroup	Tucker Shoup	Rachel Pyszka	Roxanne Feliciano
Victoria Kramer	Leelaya Chaiwong	--	Alex Bueltmann	Michael McMahon
--	--	--	Josh Lanz	--

From the Fall of 2016 to date, the Bigs and Littles have been assigned to an alchemical family.

Fall 2016		
Pledge (15)	Big	Family
Samantha Oelklaus	Ben House	Tin
Brian Baumgartner	Mary Carey	Iron
Christina (Jean) Hamilton	Erin Wharton	Iron
Breanon (Bre) Dowling	Mike Marsh	Iron
Taylor Tarter	Roxanne Feliciano	Lead
Alex Lodholz	Ellen Tuxbury	Tin
Austin Vaughn	Justin Schletzbaum	Copper
Joe Gresik	Rachel Pyszka	Iron
Dale (Justin) Wright	Tim Avery	Copper
Nathan Boys	Tucker Shoup	Copper
Elizabeth Sotolongo	Matthew Senter	Mercury
Jasmin Hill	Alex Bueltmann	Iron
Jennifer Frasch	Mary Carey	Iron

Fall 2016

Pledge (15)	Big	Family
Daniel Rosner	Michael DeVoss	Iron
Parker Schellenberg	Michael Smith	Tin
	Amanda Koebbe	Lead
	Abbie Braden	Copper

Spring 2017

Pledge	Big	Family
Mason Carey	Ellen Tuxbury	Tin
Michael Clemons	Dale (Justin) Wright	Copper
Rachel Sciaroni	Taylor Tarter	Lead
Logan Hansen	Alex Bueltman	Iron
Eric Fors	Alex Capalupo	Mercury
Ivan Sedlacek	Josh Lanz	Iron
Alexia Douglas	Samantha (Sam) Oelklaus	Tin

Fall 2017

Pledge	Big	Family
Kaytee Bailey	Daniel Rosner	Tin
Bayleigh Mitchell	Samantha Oelklaus	Tin
Erik Gull	Eric Fors	Mercury
Marc St. Amour	Logan Hansen	Iron
Maddie Hines	Mary Carey	Iron

Spring 2018

Pledge	Big	Family
Jacob Whanger	Alex Bueltmann	Iron
Kelly Pachowicz	Abbie Braden	Copper
Ashish Zore	Bayleigh Mitchell	Tin
Chris Coronado	Tucker Shoup	Copper
Emily Quist	Erin Wharton	Iron

Spring 2018		
Pledge	Big	Family
Anna Schneider	Samantha Oelklaus	Tin
Bryn Guthrie	Taylor Tarter	Lead
Elliot Sutalski	Parker Schellenberg	Lead
Matt Snarzyk	Jean Hamilton	Iron
Kyle Newport	Mason Carey	Tin
Michael Donley	Bre Dowling	Iron
Michael Ferguson	Erik Gull	Mercury
Dr. Ryan	Brian Baumgartner	Iron

Fall 2018		
Pledge	Big	Family
Adam McTigue	Tucker Shoup	Copper
Nicole Moon	Bayleigh Mitchell	Tin
Kinder Guthrie	Bryn Guthrie	Lead
Austin Scheer	Erik Gull	Mercury
Jessica Caswell	Anna Schneider	Tin
Sam Ross	Josh Lanz	Iron
Jacob Brownfield	Elliot Sutlaski	Lead

Spring 2019		
Pledge	Big	Family
Taishi Higuchi-Roos	Jacob Brownfield	Lead
Derek Dillinger	Jessica Caswell	Tin
Rae Boillat	Erik Gull	Mercury
Kari Knobbe	Austin Scheer	Mercury
Delaney Neely	Chris Coronado	Copper
Taylor Stevens	Abbie Braden	Copper
Chrysalin Martin	Elliot Sutlaski	Lead

Appendix E

Fall 2019		
Pledge	Big	Family
Andrew Holloway	Matt Snarzyk	Iron
Samuel Alexander	Kyle Newport	Tin
Whitney Sheffield	Kari Knobbe	Mercury
Kayla Shy	Chrysalin Martin	Lead
Nicole Wheeler	Nicole Moon	Tin
Loki Cortner	Adam McTigue	Copper

Spring 2020		
Pledge	Big	Family
Kyle Boillat	Loki Cortner	Copper
Suraj Sahoo	Whitney Sheffield	Mercury
Christina Arens	Nicole Wheeler	Tin
Joey Gloriod	Chris Coronado	Copper
Megan Brandt	Kinder Guthrie	Lead
William Bump	Derek Dillinger	Tin

Fall 2020		
Pledge	Big	Family
Vaughn Foreman	Kari Knobbe	Mercury
Sarah West	Taishi Higuchi-Roos	Lead
Carrie Williams	Elliot Sutalski	Lead
Chrystel Hillier	Kayla Shy	Lead

Spring 2021		
Pledge	Big	Family
Megan Hutchcraft	Rae Boillat	Mercury
Dan Bugarin	Kyle Newport	Iron
Alex Hawkins	Vaughn Foreman	Mercury

Notes

Chapter 1: Beginnings

1. The Great Work signifies the process and result of the alchemical arts.

2. Gragg, Dr. Larry, *Forged in Gold: Missouri S&T's First 150 Years,* (Missouri University of Science & Technology, 2020), 5-12; Clarence N. Roberts, *History of the University of Missouri School of Mines and Metallurgy, 1871-1946,*(1946) 43-76; Lawrence O. Christensen, and Jack Ridley, *UM-Rolla: A History of MSM/UMR,* (Columbia, MO: University of Missouri, 1983), 5-76; and *To The Supreme Council of Alpha Chi Sigma from Epsilon Pi Omicron,* School of Mines and Metallurgy, 1936, document.

3. Gragg, 13.

4. Roberts, 77-79.

5. Harry A. Curtis, *History of Alpha Chi Sigma Fraternity: 1902-1927*, 40.

6. *The Alpha Chi Sigma Fraternity Pledge Manual 1968,* (Issued by the Office of the Grand Master of Ceremonies, 1969), 29-30.

7. The reason could not be discovered, but from pictures it does not seem to have anything to do with physical stature.

8. A social fraternity founded in 1869 at the University of Virginia in Charlottesville Kappa Sigma website: www.kappasigma.org. (Accessed January 7, 2021).

9. "Satyr Pledges," *The Missouri Miner,* December 17, 1929.

10. *The Rollamo 1921*, 42, 152, 170; and "The Faculty Increases," *Missouri Miner.* September 9, 1921.

11. "Ira Remsen Society Holds First Meeting of the Year," *The Missouri Miner,* October 13, 1924.

12. Ira Remsen - Wikipedia. (Accessed January 28, 2021).

13. Ira Remsen (nasonline.org). (Accessed February 7, 2021).

14. *To The Supreme Council of Alpha Chi Sigma from Epsilon Pi Omicron,* School of Mines and Metallurgy, 1936.

15. Curtis, 167.

16. *To The Supreme Council of Alpha Chi Sigma from Epsilon Pi Omicron*, School of Mines and Metallurgy, 1936.

17. David M. Levings, Grand Historian, Alpha Chi Sigma, *Timeline Book of Alpha Chi Sigma*, document.

18. Kuechler was also a member of the Grubster's Club, which was installed as a Chapter of Triangle, a national collegiate fraternity of engineers. "Grubsters Become Chapter of Triangle Fraternity," *The Missouri Miner,* December 12, 1927.

19. Adolf Harmon Kuechler, "The Properties of the Fire Clays Used for the Manufacture of Zinc Reto" (master's thesis, Missouri School of Mines and Metallurgy, 1925).

20. "Alumni News," *The Missouri Miner,* December 3, 1929; and "Eastern Section Alumni Association Meeting" and "General Alumni News," *MSM Alumnus, Vol. 2 No. 3,* March 15, 1928, 4, 10.

21. "New Society is Organized," *The Missouri Miner,* January 31, 1933.

22. *Epsilon Pi Omicron Pledge Ceremony.* Beta Delta Chapter Records.

23. Ibid.

24. Grading Scale E 95-100; S 85-95; M 75-85; I 65-75; F below 65. Roberts, 84.

25. *To the Supreme Council and Chapters of Alpha Chi Sigma from Epsilon Pi Omicron,* School of Mines and Metallurgy. University of Missouri, 1936.

26. H. H. Armsby, Student Advisor, MSM, letter to Mr. T. G. Day, President, Epsilon Pi Omicron, May 17, 1933; and Thomas G. Day, Letter to Mr. H. H. Armsby, Student Advisor, MSM, September 27, 1933.

27. George Hale, President, Epsilon Pi Omicron, letter to MSM Faculty, September 27, 1933.

28. *The Rollamo 1936,* (The University of Missouri School of Mines and Metallurgy, 1936).

29. E. J. Schrader, Grand Scribe, Theta Tau, letter to Mr. Alex Gow, Theta Tau Chapter, MSM, February 23, 1933.

30. Levings, email to author, March 24, 2021.

31. L. S. Gaston, National President, Triangle, letter to Mr. James P. Sloss, President, MSM Chapter of Triangle, December 15, 1934. Beta Delta Archives.

32. H. E. Wiedemann, Grand Master Alchemist, Alpha Chi Sigma, letter to Dr. W. T. Schrenk, Epsilon Pi Omicron, December 22, 1934. Beta Delta Archives.

33. H. E. Wiedemann, Grand Master Alchemist, Alpha Chi Sigma, letter to Beta Delta, January 4, 1935. Beta Delta Archives.

34. "Chem Fraternity Initiates," *The Missouri Miner,* May 9, 1933; and "Eight Initiated by Epsilon Pi Omicron," *The Missouri Miner,* May 1, 1934.

35. *The Rollamo 1935,* (The University of Missouri School of Mines and Metallurgy, 1935), 72. Also, "8 Chemists Pledged," *The Missouri Miner,* November 13, 1935.

36. "Chem Fraternity Holds Business Meet," *The Missouri Miner,* October 10, 1933.

37. "Epsilon Pi Omicron Honors Dr. Wiedemann," *The Missouri Miner,* November 28, 1934.

38. A process for extracting sulphur from elemental deposits and was the primary means for recovering sulphur until the late 20th century. Wolfgang Nehb, Karel Vydra. "Sulfur", *Ullmann's Encyclopedia of Industrial Chemistry.* Weinheim: Wiley-VCH. https://doi.org/10.1002/14356007.a25_507.pub2.

39. "Ninety-Second Chemical Element Also Universal," *The Missouri Miner,* April 8, 1936.

40. "8 Chemists Pledged," *The Missouri Miner,* November 13, 1935.

41. For a list of members, initiates and officers see Appendix: Epsilon Pi Omicron Members, Initiates and Officers

42. *The Rollamo 1934,* (The University of Missouri School of Mines and Metallurgy, 1934).

43. *The Rollamo 1935,* (The University of Missouri School of Mines and Metallurgy, 1935).

44. *The Rollamo 1936,* (The University of Missouri School of Mines and Metallurgy, 1936).

45. *To the Supreme Council and Chapters of Alpha Chi Sigma from Epsilon Pi Omicron. 1936.* School of Mines and Metallurgy. University of Missouri. 1936.

46. Missouri S&T, "Walter T. Schrenk (1891-1979)," https//www.chem.mst.edu/people/facultyinmemoriam/Schrenk/.– Chemical and Biochemical Engineering | Missouri S&T (mst.edu). Missouri S&T.

47. *To the Supreme Council and Chapters of Alpha Chi Sigma from Epsilon Pi Omicron.* 1936. (School of Mines and Metallurgy. University of Missouri, 1936).

48. Roberts, 88.

49. Levings, *Timeline Book of Alpha Chi Sigma.*

50. "Epsilon Pi Omicron Begins Year's Work," *The Missouri Miner,* September 25, 1935.

51. Alpha Chi Sigma Supreme Council Proposition 713, September 15, 1934, and Proposition 726, January 26, 1935.

52. *To the Supreme Council and Chapters of Alpha Chi Sigma from Epsilon Pi Omicron.* 1936. (School of Mines and Metallurgy. University of Missouri, 1936); and John R. Kuebler, Grand Recorder, Alpha Chi Sigma, letter to Mr. Charles H. Fulton, Director, School of Mines and Metallurgy, University of Missouri, December 24, 1935, acknowledging receipt of Fulton's letter of recommendation. Beta Delta Archive.

53. Alpha Chi Sigma, May 2, 1936, *Report of Installation Meeting. Missouri School of Mines and Metallurgy, Rolla, Mo. May 2, 1936.*document.

54. Alpha Chi Sigma, May 2, 1936, *Report of Installation Meeting. Missouri School of Mines and Metallurgy, Rolla, Mo. May 2, 1936; and* Harry Burger, Chapter Recorder, *Initial Meeting of the Beta Delta Chapter of Alpha Sigma, Saturday, May 2, 1936,* meeting minutes, Beta Delta Archives.

55. Information provided by the National Office of Alpha Chi Sigma. Also Beta Delta members list.

56. Alpha Chi Sigma Supreme Council Proposition 781, May 22, 1936. Information provided by D. Mitch Levings, Grand Historian, to the author. See also Harry Burger, Chapter Recorder, *Meeting Minutes of May 8, 1936 of the Beta Delta Chapter,* meeting minutes. Beta Delta Archives.

57. Harry Burger, Chapter Recorder, *Meeting Minutes of May 8, 1936 of the Beta Delta Chapter,* meeting minutes. Beta Delta Archives.

58. Harry Burger, Chapter Recorder, September 18, 1936, *Meeting Minutes of September 18, 1936*, meeting minutes. Beta Delta Archives.

59. Burger, Chapter Recorder, October 7, 1936, *Meeting Minutes of October 7, 1936*, meeting minutes. Beta Delta Archives.

60. Burger, Chapter Recorder, October 21, 1936, *Meeting Minutes of October 21, 1936*, meeting minutes. Beta Delta Archives.

61. Burger, Chapter Recorder, November 4, 1936, *Meeting Minutes of November 4, 1936*, meeting minutes. Beta Delta Archives.

62. Burger, Chapter Recorder, November 23, 1936, *Meeting Minutes of November 23, 1936*, meeting minutes. Beta Delta Archives.

63. Burger, Chapter Recorder, December 6, 1936, *Meeting Minutes of December 6, 1936*, meeting minutes. Beta Delta Archives.

64. Burger, Chapter Recorder, December 16, 1936, *Meeting Minutes of December 16, 1936*, meeting minutes. Beta Delta Archives.

65. Levings, *Beta Delta Timeline.*

66. Ibid.

67. Burger, Chapter Recorder, January 6, 1937, *Meeting Minutes of January 6, 1937*, meeting minutes. Beta Delta Archives.

68. John R. Kuebler, Grand Recorder, letters to A. P. Hausmann, R. L. Yungbluth and the Chapter in general, January 5, January 7, January 12, February 12, February 24, April 24, May 6, May 8, and May 13, 1937. Beta Delta Archives.

69. Berger, Chapter Recorder, January 20, 1937, *Meeting Minutes of January 20, 1937*, meeting minutes. Beta Delta Archives.

70. Thomas G. Day letter to Houston Taylor, February 22, 1937. Beta Delta Archives; and Houston Taylor letter to Thomas G. Day, December 20, 1936. Beta Delta Archives.

71. Burger, Chapter Recorder, March 4, 1937, *Meeting Minutes of March 4, 1937*, meeting minutes. Beta Delta Archives.

72. Volkening, MA Delta Chapter, letter to Mr. R. L. Yungbluth, March 30, 1937. Beta Delta Archives.

73. John R. Kuebler, Grand Recorder letters to A. P. Hausmann, R. L. Yungbluth and the Chapter in general January 5, January 7, January 12,

February 12, February 24, April 24, May 6, May 8, and May 13, 1937. Beta Delta Archives.

74. John R. Kuebler letter to Mr. R. L. Yungbluth dated April 24, 1937. Beta Delta Archives.

75. Herbert F. Crecelius, May 20, 1937, *Meeting Minutes of May 20, 1937*, meeting minutes. Beta Delta Archives.

76. H. H. Armsby letter to Mr. Clemens R. Maise, Pres., Alpha Chi Sigma Fraternity May 24, 1937. Beta Delta Archives.

77. Crecelius, September 15, 1937, *Meeting Minutes of September 15, 1937*, meeting minutes. Beta Delta Archives.

78. Crecelius, October 6, 1937, *Meeting Minutes of October 6, 1937*, meeting minutes. Beta Delta Archives.

79. This information was added to the end of the Meeting Minutes of November 16, 1937.

80. Crecelius, November 10, 1937, *Meeting Minutes of November 10, 1937*, meeting minutes. Beta Delta Archives.

81. Crecelius, November 16, 1937, *Meeting Minutes of November 16, 1937*, meeting minutes. Beta Delta Archives.

82. This information was added to the end of the Meeting Minutes of November 16, 1937.

83. Crecelius, December 15, 1937, *Meeting Minutes of December 15, 1937*, meeting minutes. Beta Delta Archives.

84. *The Rollamo 1937*, (The University of Missouri School of Mines and Metallurgy, 1937).

85. Crecelius, January 5, 1938, *Meeting Minutes of January 5, 1938*, meeting minutes. Beta Delta Archives.

86. "Alpha Chi Sigma Elects Officers," *The Missouri Miner, February 2, 1938*; and Information provided by the National Office of Alpha Chi Sigma. The National Office record indicates that Webb was initiated on January 1. The practice of recording the initiation date as January 1 of the following year was common and was a result of when records were officially completed.

87. Crecelius, January 19, 1938, *Meeting Minutes of January 19, 1938*, meeting minutes, and February 2, 1938, *Meeting Minutes of February 2, 1938*, meeting minutes. Beta Delta Archives.

88. Crecelius, February 16, 1938, *Meeting Minutes of February 16, 1938*, meeting minutes. Beta Delta Archives.

89. Harold P. Gaw, Grand Master of Ceremonies, letter to Counselors, Master Alchemists, and Masters of Ceremonies, February 24, 1938. Beta Delta Archives.

90. Crecelius, *Meeting Minutes of March 2, 1938*. Beta Delta Archives; and "1200 Expected for Engineer's Day," *The Missouri Miner,* April 20, 1938.

91. Crecelius, March 8, 1938, *Meeting Minutes of March 8, 1938*, meeting minutes. Beta Delta Archives.

92. Paul Bender, Chi Chapter, Yale, letter to Brother Yungbluth, Beta Delta, March 17, 1938. It is unclear who Prof. Graine was. No records could be found of a Professor Graine.

93. *The Rollamo 1938.*

94. Crecelius, March 30, 1938, *Meeting Minutes of March 30, 1938*, meeting minutes. Beta Delta Archives.

95. Crecelius, April 13, 1938, *Meeting Minutes of April 13, 1938*, meeting minutes. Beta Delta Archives.

96. Crecelius, April 20, 1938, *Meeting Minutes of April 20, 1938,* meeting minutes. Beta Delta Archives.

97. The National Records indicate Clyde Cowan as active in April 1938 since those records have January 1, 1938 as his initiation date. Beta Delta records, however, would indicate Cowan was still pledging since those records have May 6, 1938 as his initiation date.

98. "Alpha Chi Sigma," *The Missouri Miner,* May 11, 1938. Actual name was Theophrastus von Hohenheim which later became styled Pilippus Aureolis Theophrastus "Paracelsus" Bombastus von Hohenheim, The Alpha Chi Sigma Fraternity Pledge Manual. August 1969. 51.

99. *Paracelsus,* The Alpha Chi Sigma Fraternity Pledge Manual, August 1969. 52.

100. "Alpha Chi Sigma Pledge Meeting," *The Missouri Miner,* April 27, 1938.

101. "Alpha Chi Sigma," *The Missouri Miner,* May 11, 1938.

102. R. A. Carter, Recorder, May 4, 1938, *Meeting Minutes of May 4, 1938,* meeting minutes. Beta Delta Archives.

103. John R. Kuebler, Grand Recorder, Alpha Chi Sigma, letter to Mr. Jack Moore, Reporter, Beta Delta, May 12, 1938. Beta Delta Archives.

104. Certificate of Death. Missouri State Board of Health. Bureau of Vital Statistics. Certificate # 22864. See also, Rollamo 1937, and John R. Kuebler, Grand Recorder, Alpha Chi Sigma, letter to Jack Moore, Beta Delta October 12, 1938. Beta Delta Archives.

105. Carter, Recorder, September 21, 1938, *Meeting Minutes of September 21, 1938,* meeting minutes. Beta Delta Archives.

106. "Rush Smoker Given by Alpha Chi Sigma," *The Missouri Miner,* October 5, 1938. Also, "Pledges Selected by Alpha Chi Sigma," *The Missouri Miner,* October 12, 1938.

107. Levings, "Looking Back," *The Hexagon*, Fall 2013, 70.

108. Kenneth Hancock, Secretary, Alpha Epsilon Chapter, *Mid-West District Meeting of Alpha Chi Sigma (Held October 30, 1938, Edwin Long Hotel, Rolla, Missouri),* meeting minutes. See also "Report of the First Mid-West District Meeting." Beta Delta Chapter. Beta Delta Archives.

109. Carter, Recorder, November 16, 1938, *Meeting Minutes of November 16, 1938,* meeting minutes. Beta Delta Archives.

110. Rampacek is not listed in the Beta Delta membership list provided by the National Office of Alpha Chi Sigma. He is, however, mentioned in the 1939 Rollamo Yearbook as a member of the Mining and Metallurgy Society, and in the Jan. 11, 1939 issue of the Miner as an initiate of Alpha Chi Sigma. "Blue Key, Alpha Chi Sigma, Initiate Men," *The Missouri Miner,* January 11, 1939. Outside of these two references no other references to C. Rampacek could be found.

111. "Officers are Elected by Alpha Chi Sigma," *The Missouri Miner,* February 8, 1939. The National Office List does not agree with the report from the Miner. The Miner lists four which omits Parker and Boltz but has H. A. Hayden. "Four Men Initiated by Alpha Chi Sigma," *The Missouri Miner,* March 1, 1939.

112. Robert L. Robins, District Area Committee, letter to Mr. Jack W. Moore, January 24, 1939.

113. L. R. Johnson, February 1, 1939, *Meeting Minutes of February 1, 1939*, meeting minutes. Beta Delta Archives.

114. Johnson, February 15, 1939, *Meeting Minutes of February 15, 1939*, meeting minutes. Beta Delta Archives.

115. Beta Delta Membership Records. Beta Delta Archives. The National Office records have January 1, 1939 as an initiation date for Crecelius and Elliott, and no record of Hayden. The National Office and Beta Delta are in agreement on Cramer's initiation date. See also National Office of Alpha Chi Sigma's records.

116. Johnson, March 1, 1939, *Meeting Minutes of March 1, 1939*, meeting minutes. Beta Delta Archives.

117. "Dr. Schrenk to Lecture on Liquid Air," *The Missouri Miner*, March 8, 1939.

118. Submission to "Polymorphisms," Alpha Chi Sigma from J. Marvin Coon, Reporter, Beta Delta. Beta Delta Archives. "Polymorphisms" was a communique for chapters to share their news. See also "Social Column," *Missouri Miner*, April 5, 1939.

119. Information provided by the National Office of Alpha Chi Sigma and Beta Delta Membership List. There is a discrepancy between the records of the National Office and Beta Delta regarding David Boltz. The National Office records indicate his initiation date was January 1, 1939. Another pledge, Leonard E. Henson, was initiated on May 19, 1939 according to both the Beta Delta Membership List and the National Office records.

120. Lawrence Johnston, Reporter, Delta Chapter, letter to Marvin Coon, Reporter, Beta Delta, April 30, 1939; and Marvin Coon, Reporter, Beta Delta, letter to Lawrence Johnston, Reporter, Delta, May 1, 1939. Beta Delta Archives.

121. "Alpha Chi Sigma Initiates" and Plays Water Polo in Columbia," *The Missouri Miner*, May 12, 1939.

122. Marvin Coon, Reporter, Beta Delta, letter to Lawrence Johnston, Reporter, Delta, May 9, 1939. Also Letter from, Lawrence Johnston to Marvin Coon May 15, 1939. Beta Delta Archives. "Alpha Chi Sigma Holds Meeting," *The Missouri Miner*, May 19, 1939.

123. Hayden was missing in the Beta Delta member list provided by the National Office of Alpha Chi Sigma. However, he is listed as a member of Alpha Chi Sigma and as Master Alchemist in the 1940 Rollamo Year Book. Also, he is listed as one of the initiates in the May 19, 1939 issue of the Miner.

124. Levings, *Beta Delta Timeline*.

125. Romine Elected Treasurer of Alpha Chi Sigma," *The Missouri Miner*, October 11, 1939; and Letter from J. Marvin Coon, Reporter, Beta Delta to Mr. John R. Kuebler, Grand Recorder, dated October 16, 1939.

126. D. G. Crecelius, Recorder, October 5, 1939, *Meeting Minutes of October 5, 1939*, meeting minutes. Beta Delta Archives.

127. "Three Initiated by Alpha Chi Sigma," *The Missouri Miner*, October 18, 1939. Also Information provided by the National Office of Alpha Chi Sigma.

128. C. Leslie, Chapter Recorder, October 14, 1939, *Initiation Meeting of Beta Delta of Alpha Chi Sigma*, Saturday, meeting minutes; Harold Smith, Reporter, Kappa, letter to Reporter, Beta Delta, September 29, 1939; and "Polymorphisms," dated October 31, 1939. Submitted by Marvin Coon, Reporter, Beta Delta. Beta Delta Archives

129. "Smoker Held by Alpha Chi Sigma," *The Missouri Miner*, November 1, 1939.

130. D. G. Crecelius, Chapter Recorder, November 1, 1939, *Meeting Minutes of November 1, 1939*, meeting minutes. Beta Delta Archives.

131. "Alpha Chi Sigma Host at Jamboree," *The Missouri Miner*, November 8, 1939; J. C. Leslie, Chapter Recorder, November 5, 1939, *Minutes of the Jamboree Meeting of Beta Delta Chapter of Alpha Chi Sigma, Sunday, November 5, 1939*, meeting minutes; and Marvin Coon, Reporter, *News of the Beta Delta Chapter for the Month Ending Nov. 30, 1939*, report. Beta Delta Archives.

132. D. G. Crecelius, November 15, 1939, *Meeting Minutes of the Beta Delta Chapter of Alpha Chi Sigma*, meeting minutes. Beta Delta Archives.

133. John R. Kuebler, Grand Recorder, Alpha Chi Sigma, letter to Professional Chapter and Group Secretaries and Reporters of the Collegiate Chapters, December 1, 1939. Beta Delta Archives.

134. D. G. Crecelius, chapter Recorder, December 6, 1939, *Meeting Minutes of Beta Delta Chapter of Alpha Chi Sigma, December 6, 1939,* meeting minutes. Beta Delta Archives.

135. "Alpha Chi Sigma Initiates Four," *The Missouri Miner,* December 20, 1939; and J. C. Leslie, Chapter Recorder, December 16, 1939, *Initiation Meeting of Beta Delta Chapter of Alpha Chi Sigma, Saturday, December 16, 1939*, meeting minutes. Beta Delta Archives.

136. "Play Rehearsals are in Full Swing," *The Missouri Miner,* November 16. 1938; "Coffer-Miller Plays," *The Missouri Miner,* March 04, 1930; and "Play Rehearsals are in Full Swing," *The Missouri Miner,* November 16, 1938.

137. University of Wisconsin-Madison, Dissertations & Theses, Library, University of Wisconsin, https://www.search.library.wisc.edu/catalog/9910035427302121. Dissertations & Theses | UW-Madison Libraries (wisc.edu).

138. "Dr. Schrenk Has Been Prominent in Science and Service," *The Missouri Miner,* November 19, 1941; "Dr. W.T. Schrenk to Teach Chemistry Here," *The Missouri Miner,* September 3, 1923; and Missouri S&T, "Walter T. Schrenk (1891-1979)," https//www.chem.mst.edu/people/facultyinmemoriam/Schrenk/.– Chemical and Biochemical Engineering | Missouri S&T (mst.edu).

139. "Ira Remsen Society Meeting," *The Missouri Miner,* November 5, 1923.

140. "Ira Remsen Society," *The Missouri Miner,* February 7, 1927; "Dr. Schrenk to Talk to the Missouri Public Health Association," *The Missouri Miner,* April 25, 1927; and "Dr. Schrenk Lectures," *The Missouri Miner.* June 1, 1925.

141. "Knights of St. Patrick," *The Missouri Miner,* March 30, 1925.

142. "Summer Session at MSM," *The Missouri Miner,* April 29, 1930.

143. *To the Supreme Council and Chapters of Alpha Chi Sigma from Epsilon Pi Omicron.* 1936. (School of Mines and Metallurgy. University of Missouri, 1936); *The Rollamo 1925,* (The University of Missouri School of Mines and Metallurgy, 1925); *The Rollamo 1935,* (The University of Missouri School of Mines and Metallurgy, 1935); and *The Rollamo 1933,* (The University of Missouri School of Mines and Metallurgy, 1933).

144. *To the Supreme Council and Chapters of Alpha Chi Sigma from Epsilon Pi Omicron,* 1936, (School of Mines and Metallurgy. University of Missouri, 1936).

145. "Changes in Faculty and Administrative Offices, Fall 1936," *MSM Alumnus,* October 30, 1936. 4.

146. *To The Supreme Council and Chapters of Alpha Chi Sigma from Epsilon Pi Omicron, 1936; The Rollamo 1935,* (The University of Missouri School of Mines and Metallurgy, 1935); "Met and Chem Society," *The Missouri Miner,* November 21, 1919; *The Rollamo 1928,* (The University of Missouri School of Mines and Metallurgy, 1928); and *The Rollamo 1920,* (The University of Missouri School of Mines and Metallurgy, 1920).

147. *To The Supreme Council and Chapters of Alpha Chi Sigma from Epsilon Pi Omicron, 1936.*

148. "Prof. and Mrs. Dunlap Entertain," *The Missouri Miner,* November 30, 1917.

149. "Freshman Column," *The Missouri Miner,* November 30, 1917.

150. www.findagrave.com.

151. "The Faculty Increases," *The Missouri Miner,* September 9, 1921.

152. *To The Supreme Council and Chapters of Alpha Chi Sigma from Epsilon Pi Omicron, 1936.*

153. "Drs. Monroe, Schrenk Attend A.C.S. Meet," *The Missouri Miner,* December 13, 1932.

154. "Five Faculty Members Transferred to MU," *MSM Alumnus,* May-June 1948, 2.

155. Karl K. Kershner, "The preparation and physical properties of benzene- and toluene-sulphonamides," (master's thesis, The University of Missouri School of Mines and Metallurgy, 1920).

156. *To The Supreme Council and Chapters of Alpha Chi Sigma from Epsilon Pi Omicron, 1936.*

157. "Five Faculty Members Transferred to MU," *MSM Alumnus,* May-June 1948, 2.

158. Thomas Gordon Day, "Factors affecting the electrolytic deposition of small amounts of lead as lead dioxide and the composition of the deposit," (master's thesis, The University of Missouri School of Mines and Metallurgy, 1932).

159. *To The Supreme Council and Chapters of Alpha Chi Sigma from Epsilon Pi Omicron, 1936.*

160. *To The Supreme Council and Chapters of Alpha Chi Sigma from Epsilon Pi Omicron, 1936;* and Frank Joseph Zvanut, "Pyrochemical changes in Missouri halloysite," (doctoral dissertation, The University of Missouri School of Mines and Metallurgy, 1937). Advisors: Dr. W.T. Schrenk and Dr. C.M. Dodd.

161. Frank Joseph Zvanut, "The effect of different rates of ram movement on the transmission of pressure in dry pressed bodies," (bachelor's thesis, The University of Missouri School of Mines and Metallurgy, 1932) and "Pyrochemical changes in Missouri halloysite," (doctoral dissertation, University of Missouri School of Mines and Metallurgy, 1937).

162. Levings, "Looking Back," *The Hexagon,* Winter 2016. 93.

163. Alumni Section News," *MSM Alumnus,* February 1986. 54-55.

164. "1968 Annual Alumni Fund Roster of Contributors," *MSM Alumnus,* August 1968, 13; "Honor Roll 1972 Annual Alumni Fund Roster of Contributor," *MSM Alumnus,* August 1972, 9; "Annual Alumni Fund 1979 Century Club," *MSM Alumnus,* February 1980, 3; "Century Club," *MSM Alumnus,* February, 1981. 12-13; "Homecoming 1982 Century Club," *MSM Alumnus,* December, 1982, 2; "Century Club," *MSM Alumnus,* February, 1988, 5-9; "Homecoming 1986," *MSM Alumnus,* December, 1986, 6; "Homecoming 1985," *MSM Alumnus,* December, 1985, 4; "Alumni Donors to Association and University," *MSM Alumnus,* February, 1985, 2; and "Century Club," *MSM Alumnus,* February, 1984, 15.

165. "Alumni Personals," *MSM Alumnus,* December 1984, 23; and "Alumni Notes," *MSM Alumnus,* February 1989, 49.

166. *The Rollamo 1931.* (The University of Missouri School of Mines and Metallurgy, 1931; *The Rollamo 1932.* (The University of Missouri School of Mines and Metallurgy, 1932); and Frank J Zvanut 1911-2004 – Ancestry (accessed January 28, 2021).

167. Class of '32, 50-Year Anniversary Reunion," *MSM Alumnus,* June 1982. 1-5.

168. John Shaw Sabine, "A study of methods for separating the elements that interfere in the electrolytic deposition of lead as lead oxide," (master's thesis. The University of Missouri School of Mines and Metallurgy, 1933).

169. *To The Supreme Council and Chapters of Alpha Chi Sigma from Epsilon Pi Omicron, 1936.*

170. LeRoy Augustave Bay, "A study of methods for the recovery of silver, bromine, iodine, and sodium thiosulfate from used photographic fixing baths," (master's thesis. The University of Missouri School of Mines and Metallurgy, 1937).

171. Clemens Raebel Maise, "The catalytic vapor-phase hydrolysis of benzene and toluene," (master's thesis. The University of Missouri School of Mines and Metallurgy, 1938).

172. *To The Supreme Council and Chapters of Alpha Chi Sigma from Epsilon Pi Omicron, 1936.*

173. Ibid.

Chapter 2: 1940s

1. Roberts, 105-106.

2. "Half of Chemistry Building to be Completed Soon," *The Missouri Miner,* December 17, 1940.

3. Clarence, 112.

4. An initiation conducted during Conclave usually for the purpose of demonstrating how an initiation is meant to be conducted, but may also be used at Conclave to conduct a special initiation. Levings, "Looking Back," *The Hexagon,* Summer 2015, 34; and *Pledging and Business Meeting of Beta Delta Chapter of Alpha Chi Sigma,* meeting minutes, March 6, 1940. Beta Delta Archives.

5. Alpha Chi Sigma Fraternity Pledge Manual, August 1969, 20.

6. A nonprofit organization promoting health and safety in the United States, founded in 1913.

7. National Safety Council. Wikipedia, (accessed May 13, 2021); Levings, "Looking Back," *The Hexagon,* Fall 2016, 56-57; and Levings, "Looking Back," *The Hexagon,* Winter 2018, 62.

8. Levings, Grand Historian, "Looking Back," *The Hexagon,* Spring 2021. 14.

9. D. G. Crecelius, Chapter Recorder, January 11, 1940, *Business Meeting of Beta Delta Chapter of Alpha Chi Sigma,* meeting minutes; and J. C. Leslie, Chapter Recorder, January 24, 1940, *Business Meeting of the Beta Delta Chapter of Alpha Chi Sigma,* meeting minutes. Beta Delta Archives.

10. J. C. Leslie, Chapter Recorder, February 7, 1940, *Business Meeting of Beta Delta Chapter of Alpha Chi Sigma*, meeting minutes; Levings, Grand Historian, Email to author. August 8, 2021; and J. C. Leslie, Chapter Recorder, February 21, 1940, *Business Meeting of Beta Delta Chapter of Alpha Chi Sigma*, meeting minutes. Beta Delta Archives.

11. National Office of Alpha Chi Sigma's records and Beta Delta Membership list. See also J.C. Leslie, Chapter Recorder, February 24, 1940, *Initiation Meeting of Beta Delta Chapter of Alpha Chi Sigma*, meeting minutes. Beta Delta Archives.

12. Beta Delta Chapter of Alpha Chi Sigma, March 6, 1940, *Pledging and Business Meeting of Beta Delta Chapter of Alpha Chi Sigma,* meeting Minutes.

13. Leslie, Chapter Recorder, March 20, 1940, *Business Meeting of Beta Delta Chapter of Alpha Chi Sigma*, meeting minutes. Beta Delta Archives.

14. Leslie, Chapter Recorder, April 3, 1940, *Business Meeting of Beta Delta Chapter of Alpha Chi Sigma*, meeting minutes. Beta Delta Archives.

15. Leslie, Chapter Recorder, April 17, 1940, *Business Meeting of Beta Delta Chapter of Alpha Chi Sigma*, meeting minutes. Beta Delta Archives.

16. Leslie, Chapter Recorder, May 1, 1940, *Business Meeting of Beta Delta Chapter of Alpha Chi Sigma*, meeting minutes. Beta Delta Archives.

17. Leroy Kuhn, Reporter, Alpha Epsilon, letter to H. H. Nicholas, Reporter, Beta Delta, April 18, 1940. Beta Delta Archives. Also, Levings, *Beta Delta Timeline.* Names of Beta Delta pledges and dates provided by the National Office of Alpha Chi Sigma.

18. Leslie, Chapter Recorder, May 4-5, 1940, *Founder's Day Meeting of Beta Delta Chapter of Alpha Chi Sigma*, meeting minutes. Beta Delta Archives.

19. Leslie, Chapter Recorder, May 9, 1940, *Business Meeting of Beta Delta Chapter of Alpha Chi Sigma*, meeting minutes. Beta Delta Archives.

20. R. A. Pohl, Chapter Recorder, September 11, 1940, *Business Meeting of Beta Delta Chapter of Alpha Chi Sigma*, meeting minutes; Pohl, Chapter Recorder, September 18, 1940, *Business Meeting of Beta Delta Chapter of Alpha Chi Sigma*, meeting minutes; and Pohl, Chapter Recorder, September 25, 1940, *Business Meeting of Beta Delta Chapter of Alpha Chi Sigma*, meeting minutes. Beta Delta Archives.

21. Pohl, Chapter Recorder, October 9, 1940, *Business Meeting of Beta Delta Chapter of Alpha Chi Sigma*, meeting minutes; Pohl, Chapter Record-

er, October 23, 1940, *Business Meeting of Beta Delta Chapter of Alpha Chi Sigma*, meeting minutes. Beta Delta Archives; and Alpha Chi Sigma Holds Gay Party," *The Missouri Miner,* October 15, 1940.

22. "Pearl Speaks at Alpha Chi Sigma," *The Missouri Miner,* September 28, 1940.

23. For Schrenk's enthusiasm for baseball see the sports sections of the following issues of *The Missouri Miner*: May 5, 1924; March 30, 1925; April 13, 1925; May 3, 1926; April 4, 1927; and April 11, 1927.

24. "Alpha Chi Sigma Holds Jamboree," *The Missouri Miner,* October 29, 1940.

25. Pohl, Chapter Recorder, October 26, 1940, *Special Meeting of Beta Delta Chapter of Alpha Chi Sigma*, meeting minutes. Beta Delta Archives.

26. Pohl, Chapter Recorder, November 13, 1940, *Business Meeting of Beta Delta Chapter of Alpha Chi Sigma*, meeting minutes. Beta Delta Archives.

27. Pohl, Chapter Recorder, November 27, 1940, *Business Meeting of Beta Delta Chapter of Alpha Chi Sigma*, meeting minutes. Beta Delta Archives.

28. "Alpha Chi Sigma Pledges Eleven," *The Missouri Miner,* November 16, 1940; and "Alpha Chi Sigma Initiation Today," *The Missouri Miner,* November 30, 1940.

29. Pohl, Chapter Recorder, December 11, 1940, *Business Meeting of Beta Delta Chapter of Alpha Chi Sigma*, meeting minutes. Beta Delta Archives.

30. "Eleven Alpha Chi Sigma's Visit Mo U," *The Missouri Miner,* December 14, 1940.

31. "1226 Treatments by MSM Hospital From Jan 7 to 18," *The Missouri Miner*, January 28, 1941.

32. "Influenza on Campus Fewer," *The Missouri Miner*, January 18, 1941.

33. Pohl, Chapter Recorder, January 8, 1941, *Business Meeting of the Beta Delta Chapter of Alpha Chi Sigma*, meeting minutes; and Pohl, Chapter Recorder, January 22, 1941, *Business Meeting of the Beta Delta Chapter of Alpha Chi Sigma*, meeting minutes. Beta Delta Archives.

34. Levings, *Beta Delta Timeline*. Also, "Four Initiated to Chem Frat at Joint Meeting," *The Missouri Miner,* January 14, 1941.

35. Pohl, Chapter Recorder, January 22, 1941, *Business Meeting of the Beta Delta Chapter of Alpha Chi Sigma*, meeting minutes. Beta Delta Archives.

36. NL Industries. Wikipedia.

37. "Doc Maise Leaves," *The Missouri Miner,* January 18, 1941; and David Ferdinand Boltz, "The volumetric determination of alumina in clays and related materials" (master's thesis, The University of Missouri School of Mines and Metallurgy, 1940).

38. C. A. Schaeffer, Chapter Recorder, February 15, 1941, *Business Meeting of the Beta Delta Chapter of Alpha Chi Sigma*, meeting minutes. Beta Delta Archives.

39. Schaeffer, Chapter Recorder, February 26, 1941, *Business Meeting of the Beta Delta Chapter of Alpha Chi Sigma*, meeting minutes; and Schaeffer, Chapter Recorder, March 11, 1941, *Business Meeting of the Beta Delta Chapter of Alpha Chi Sigma*, meeting minutes. Beta Delta Archives.

40. "Mr. E.C. Hunze to Address Alpha Chi Sigma," *The Missouri Miner,* March 22, 1941; "Alpha Chi Sigma Hears Krueger Tomorrow Night," *The Missouri Miner,* April 22, 1941; and "P.A. Krueger, Chemist, Talks on Illumination," *The Missouri Miner,* April 26, 1941.

41. "Dedication to be April 11," *The Missouri Miner,* March 22, 1941; *The Hexagon*, May 1941, 414; "Chemical Engineering Building Dedicated Yesterday," *The Missouri Miner,* April 12, 1941; and Schaeffer, Chapter Recorder, April 16, 1941, *Business Meeting of the Beta Delta Chapter of Alpha Chi Sigma*, meeting minutes. Beta Delta Archives.

42. Information provided by the National Office of Alpha Chi Sigma and the Rollamo, 1942. See also, "Alpha Chi Sigma Initiates Twelve," *The Missouri Miner,* May 6, 1941.

43. Schaeffer, Chapter Recorder, May 7, 1941, *Business Meeting of the Beta Delta Chapter of Alpha Chi Sigma*, meeting minutes; and the Beta Delta Membership List. Beta Delta Archive. According to the Beta Delta Membership records, Charles Koch was initiated on May 23, and not on May 3 as reported by the National Office.

44. "Pohl Elected Master Alchemist," *The Missouri Miner,* May 17, 1941; "Muskopf Vice-President of Student Council," *The Missouri Miner,* May 17, 1941; and Schaeffer, Chapter Recorder, May 14, 1941, *Business Meeting of the Beta Delta Chapter of Alpha Chi Sigma*, Meeting minutes. Beta Delta Archives.

45. Levings, *Beta Delta Timeline*.

46. Harold P. Gaw, Grand Collegiate Alchemist letter to Dr. T. G. Day, Beta Delta., August 26, 1941. Beta Delta Archives.

47. E. C. Conary, Chapter Recorder, September 17, 1941, *Business Meeting of the Beta Delta Chapter of Alpha Chi Sigma*, meeting minutes; and Conary, Chapter Recorder, October 1, 1941, *Business Meeting of the Beta Delta Chapter of Alpha Chi Sigma*, meeting minutes. Beta Delta Archives.

48. "Alpha Chi Sigma Holds Smoker," *The Missouri Miner*, October 11, 1941.

49. "Alpha Chi Sigma Holds Jamboree," *The Missouri Miner*, October 22, 1941.

50. "Alpha Chi Sigma Pledges Ten," *The Missouri Miner*, November 12, 1941; and Conary, Chapter Recorder, November 4, 1941, *Business Meeting of the Beta Delta Chapter of Alpha Chi Sigma*, meeting minutes. Beta Delta Archives.

51. "Dr. Bent Speaks to Sigma Xi and Alpha Chi Sigma," *The Missouri Miner*, November 15, 1941.

52. George Richardson letter to Thomas Day, October 4, 1941; Thomas Day letter to John R. Kuebler, Grand Recorder, November 17, 1941; John R. Kuebler letter to Thomas Day, November 19, 1941; and Thomas Day letter to George Richardson from Thomas Day, November 26, 1941. Beta Delta Archives.

53. Conary, Chapter Recorder, November 4, 1941, *Business Meeting of the Beta Delta Chapter of Alpha Chi Sigma*, meeting minutes. Beta Delta Archives.

54. Conary, Chapter Recorder, January 6, 1942, *Business Meeting of the Beta Delta Chapter of Alpha Chi Sigma*, meeting minutes. Beta Delta Archives.

55. Ryan Reed, "106 North Oliver, the Heimberger House," Rolla Preservation Alliance: 106 North Olive - The Heimberger House, (https://rolla-preservationblogspot.com), November 20, 2014. Also, USGenWeb Archives. Phelps Burials (usgwarchives.net).

56. "Mrs. W.T. Schrenk Dies January 22," *The Missouri Miner*, January 28, 1942; and "Mrs. W.T. Schrenk Dies January 22," *MSM Alumnus*, Winter 1941-1942.

57. Beta Delta Chapter of Alpha Chi Sigma, January 27, 1942, *Business Meeting of the Beta Delta Chapter of Alpha Chi Sigma*, meeting minutes; "Alpha Chi Sigma Installs Officers," *The Missouri Miner*, January 31, 1942; and Warren Kadera, Chapter Recorder, February 18, 1942, *Business Meeting of the Beta Delta Chapter of Alpha Chi Sigma*, meeting

minutes. Beta Delta Archives; and "Alpha Chi Sigma Working on Safety Program," *The Missouri Miner,* February 21, 1942.

58. John W. Cross, Chair, Professional Activities Committee, Alpha Iota Chapter, letter to H. W. Flood, Beta Delta, March 23, 1942.

59. Warren Kadera, Chapter Recorder, March 5, 1942, *Business Meeting of the Beta Delta Chapter*, meeting minutes. Beta Delta Archives; and "Muskopf Voted Best Alpha Chi Sigma Reporter," *The Missouri Miner,* March 7, 1942.

60. Warren Kadera, Chapter Recorder, March 17, 1942, *Business Meeting of the Beta Delta Chapter*, meeting minutes. Beta Delta Archives; and "Grand Master Alchemist Will Speak at Alpha Chi Sigma Meeting," *The Missouri Miner,* March 14, 1942.

61. "Alpha Chi Sigma Pledges Six," *The Missouri Miner,* March 20, 1942; Kadera, Chapter Recorder, March 31, 1942, *Business Meeting of the Beta Delta Chapter,* meeting minutes. Beta Delta Archives; "Johnson to Head Alpha Chi Sigma," *The Missouri Miner,* April 18, 1942; and Beta Delta Membership Records.

62. Warren Kadera, Chapter Recorder, April 14, 1942, *Business Meeting of the Beta Delta Chapter,* meeting minutes. Beta Delta Archives; and "Johnson to Head Alpha Chi Sigma," *The Missouri Miner,* April 18, 1942.

63. "Alpha Chi Sigma to Develop New Flag," *The Missouri Miner,* May 1, 1942; *The Alpha Chi Sigma Fraternity Pledge Manual. August 1969.* 39; and "Johnson Represents AXE at Chicago," *The Missouri Miner,* June 18, 1942.

64. Kadera, Chapter Recorder, April 27, 1942, *Business Meeting of the Beta Delta Chapter*, meeting minutes. Beta Delta Archives.

65. Kadera, Chapter Recorder, May 12, 1942, *Business Meeting of the Beta Delta Chapter,* meeting minutes. Beta Delta Archives.

66. Standard Certificate of Death. File No. 29143. Missouri State Board of Health.

67. "Seb Hertling Talks to AXE on Safety," *The Missouri Miner,* July 1, 1942.

68. Kadera, Chapter Recorder, September 9, 1942, *Business Meeting of the Beta Delta Chapter,* meeting minutes. Beta Delta Archives.

69. AIChE. Student Design Competition. 1942-StudentDesignContent-Problem_0.pdf (aiche.org), (accessed July 1, 2021).

70. "AXE Jamboree Well Attended," *The Missouri Miner*, September 23, 1942; and "Alpha Chi Sigma Plans Dance and Jamboree," *The Missouri Miner*, September 19, 1942.

71. "Alpha Chi Sigma Holds Smoker for Pledges," *The Missouri Miner*, October 17, 1942; and "Alpha Chi Sigma Plans Safety Program," *The Missouri Miner*, October 24, 1942.

72. "In the Campus Spotlight," *The Missouri Miner*, October 24, 1942.

73. Kadera, Chapter Recorder, November 18, 1942, *Business Meeting of the Beta Delta Chapter*, meeting minutes; and Kadera, Chapter Recorder, November 4, 1942, *Business Meeting of the Beta Delta Chapter*, meeting minutes. Beta Delta Archives.

74. Kadera, Chapter Recorder, September 9, 1942, *Business Meeting of the Beta Delta Chapter*, meeting minutes. Beta Delta Archives.

75. "Dr. Schrenk Weds During Holidays," *The Missouri Miner*, January 13, 1943.

76. "St. Pat's Ruled Out Because of War," *The Missouri Miner*, February 17, 1943.

77. "Alpha Chi Sigma to Hold Smoker March 7," *The Missouri Miner*, February 20, 1943. Also, Kadera, Chapter Recorder, January 5, 1943, *Business Meeting of the Beta Delta Chapter of Alpha Chi Sigma*, meeting minutes. Beta Delta Archives.

78. Kadera, Chapter Recorder, February 2, 1943, *Business Meeting of the Beta Delta Chapter of Alpha Chi Sigma,* meeting minutes; and James R. Miller, Chapter Recorder, February 16, 1943, *Business Meeting of the Beta Delta Chapter of Alpha Chi Sigma*, meeting minutes. Beta Delta Archives.

79. James R. Miller, Chapter Recorder, March 30, 1943, *Business Meeting of the Beta Delta Chapter of Alpha Chi Sigma*, meeting minutes; and Miller, Chapter Recorder, April 6, 1943, *Business Meeting of the Beta Delta Chapter of Alpha Chi Sigma*, meeting minutes. Beta Delta Archives.

80. "Alpha Chi Sigma Plans Activities," *The Missouri Miner*, April 2, 1943.

81. "Alpha Chi Sigma Pledges 7 Men," *The Missouri Miner*, April 23, 1943; and Miller, Chapter Recorder, April 12, 1943, *Business Meeting of the Beta Delta Chapter of Alpha Chi Sigma*, meeting minutes. Beta Delta Archives.

82. Miller, Chapter Recorder, April 27, 1943, *Business Meeting of the Beta Delta Chapter of Alpha Chi Sigma*, meeting minutes. Beta Delta Archives; "Faulty Flue is Cause of Fire at Tech Club," and "Blue Key to Aid Tech Club," *The Missouri Miner,* April 9, 1943; and *Rollamo* 1943.

83. "Alpha Chi Sigma Holds Initiation Banquet for 11," *Missouri Miner,* May 7, 1943.

84. Miller, Chapter Recorder, May 11, 1943, *Business Meeting of the Beta Delta Chapter of Alpha Chi Sigma*, meeting minutes. Beta Delta Archives; and "Alpha Chi Sigma Elects Officers," *The Missouri Miner,* May 14, 1943.

85. Miller, Chapter Recorder, June 22, 1943 and July 20, 1943, *Business Meeting of the Beta Delta Chapter of Alpha Chi Sigma*, meeting minutes. Beta Delta Archives.

86. Miller, Chapter Recorder, September 21, 1943, *Business Meeting of the Beta Delta Chapter of Alpha Chi Sigma*, meeting minutes; and Miller, Chapter Recorder, September 27, 1943, *Business Meeting of the Beta Delta Chapter of Alpha Chi Sigma*, meeting minutes. Beta Delta Archives.

87. Miller, Chapter Recorder, October 6, 1943, Business Meeting of the Beta Delta Chapter of Alpha Chi Sigma, meeting minutes. Beta Delta Archives.

88. "Dance Dates," *The Missouri Miner,* October 19, 1943.

89. Information provided by the National Office of Alpha Chi Sigma. Also, Miller, Chapter Recorder, November 3, 1943, *Business Meeting of the Beta Delta Chapter of Alpha Chi Sigma*, meeting minutes. Beta Delta Archives; and "Alpha Chi Sigma Elects Schmitz as President," *The Missouri Miner,* November 9, 1943.

90. Wayne Hoerth, Chapter Recorder, November 17, 1943, *Business Meeting of the Beta Delta Chapter of Alpha Chi Sigma*, meeting minutes; and Hoerth, Chapter Recorder, December 1, 1943, *Business Meeting of the Beta Delta Chapter of Alpha Chi Sigma*, meeting minutes. Beta Delta Archives.

91. The Nobel Prize. Org, "Edward Doisy," The Noble Prize, Edward A. Doisy - Facts (nobelprize.org).

92. "Nine Initiated at Alpha Chi Sigma Banquet," *The Missouri Miner,* December 14, 1943.

93. Hoerth, Chapter Recorder, January 5, pril 7, 1944.Sigma to John W. sjst fly right out the brothers'entation of an alumni charm. covered in the curriculum. 1944, *Business Meeting of the Beta Delta Chapter of Alpha Chi Sigma*, meeting minutes. Beta Delta Archives.

94. John W. Sjoberg, Beta Delta, letter to John R. Kuebler, Grand Record, Alpha Chi Sigma, January 20, 1944; John R. Kuebler, letter to Dr. Thomas G. Day, January 21, 1944; John R. Kuebler, letter to John W. Sjoberg, January 21, 1944. Beta Delta Archives; Sjoberg, Beta Delta, letter to John R. Kuebler, Grand Recorder, Alpha Chi Sigma, February 8, 1944; and John R. Kuebler, Grand Recorder, Alpha Chi Sigma, letter to John W. Sjoberg, Beta Delta, February 11, 1944.

95. "Alpha Chi Sigma Forms Program for Semester," *The Missouri Miner,* February 8, 1944.

96. Hoerth, Chapter Recorder, February 16, 1944, *Business Meeting of the Beta Delta Chapter of Alpha Chi Sigma,* meeting minutes. Beta Delta Archives.

97. Bart Yoder, Chapter Recorder, March 2, 1944, *Business Meeting of the Beta Delta Chapter of Alpha Chi Sigma*, meeting minutes. Beta Delta Archives.

98. Yoder, Chapter Recorder, March 16, 1944, *Business Meeting of the Beta Delta Chapter of Alpha Chi Sigma*, meeting minutes. Beta Delta Archives.

99. Yoder, Chapter Recorder, April 6, 1944, *Business Meeting of the Beta Delta Chapter of Alpha Chi Sigma*, meeting minutes. Beta Delta Archives; and "Alpha Chi Sigma Pledges Chems," *The Missouri Miner,* April 4, 1944. For Custis's initials see *The Rollamo 1944.*

100. "Corrosion to be Topic of AXE Lecture," *The Missouri Miner,* April 25, 1944.; and John R. Kuebler, Grand Record, Alpha Chi Sigma, letter to John W. Sjoberg, Beta Delta, April 7, 1944.

101. "Theta Tau Leads MSM in G.P. Average," *The Missouri Miner,* April 4, 1944.

102. Yoder, Chapter Recorder, May 18, 1944, *Business Meeting of the Beta Delta Chapter of Alpha Chi Sigma*, meeting minutes. Beta Delta Archives.

103. "Enrollment Shows General and Chemical Engineering Most Popular Courses," and "Alpha Chi Sigma," *The Missouri Miner,* September 26, 1944.

104. James McKelvey, Chapter Recorder, September 21, 1944, *Business Meeting of the Beta Delta Chapter of Alpha Chi Sigma*, meeting minutes. Beta Delta Archives.

105. Yoder, Chapter Recorder, October 12, 1944, *Business Meeting of the Beta Delta Chapter of Alpha Chi Sigma*, meeting minutes. Also, Nils Nelson, Collegiate Chapter News for the Hexagon, document, May 30, 1945. Beta Delta Archives.

106. Beta Delta Membership Record. Beta Delta Archives and National Office of Alpha Chi Sigma's Records. See also "Alpha Chi Sigma Initiates Five Chems," *The Missouri Miner*, December 12, 1944.

107. Nelson, Chapter Recorder, December 2, 1944, *Meeting Minutes,* meeting minutes. Beta Delta Archives.

108. Alpha Chi Sigma, Chem Frat Wins Scholastic Crown," *The Missouri Miner*, February 20, 1945; and Roberts, 84; and Christensen, 151.

109. Nelson, Reporter, News for the Month Ending March 31, 1945, Beta Delta Chapter, document, March 31, 1945. Beta Delta Archives.

110. AXE Honor Frat Initiates Six," *The Missouri Miner,* May 8, 1945.

111. "Committee for 75th Anniversary Celebration Appointed," *MSM Alumnus,* June-July 1945, 1.

112. Bill Break, Recorder, September 21, 1945, *Business Meeting of the Beta Delta Chapter of Alpha Chi Sigma, meeting minutes*. Beta Delta Archives.

113. Break, Recorder, October 18, 1945, *Business Meeting of the Beta Delta Chapter of Alpha Chi Sigma*, meeting minutes. Beta Delta Archives.

114. Break, Recorder, November 1 and November 15, 1945, *Business Meetings of the Beta Delta Chapter of Alpha Chi Sigma*, meeting minutes. Beta Delta Archives.

115. Levings, "Looking Back," *The Hexagon*, Winter 2020 61.

116. Break, Recorder, January 3, 1946, *Meeting of the Beta Delta Chapter of Alpha Chi Sigma*, meeting minutes. Beta Delta Archives; and "Daniels to Head AXE in Spring," *The Missouri Miner,* January 15, 1946.

117. Break, Recorder, January 16, 1946, *Meeting of the Beta Delta Chapter of Alpha Chi Sigma*, meeting minutes. Beta Delta Archives; and Break, Recorder, February 7, 1946, *Meeting of the Beta Delta Chapter of Alpha Chi Sigma*, meeting minutes. Beta Delta Archives.

118. "AXE to Send Virgil Johnson to National Conclave," *The Missouri Miner,* March 13, 1946; Break, Recorder, March 7, 1946, *Meeting of the Beta Delta Chapter of Alpha Chi Sigma*, meeting minutes; and Break, Recorder, March 21, 1946, *Meeting of the Beta Delta Chapter of Alpha Chi Sigma*, meeting minutes. Beta Delta Archives.

119. Break, Recorder, April 4, 1946, *Meeting of the Beta Delta Chapter of Alpha Chi Sigma*, meeting minutes. Beta Delta Archives; and "AXE Pledges Eleven Men," *The Missouri Miner,* April 23, 1946.

120. Break, Recorder, April 25, 1946, *Meeting of the Beta Delta Chapter of Alpha Chi Sigma*, meeting minutes. Beta Delta Archives; and "Johnson to Head Alpha Chi Sigma," *The Missouri Miner,* April 30, 1946.

121. Break, Recorder, May 8, 1946, *Meeting of the Beta Delta Chapter of Alpha Chi Sigma*, meeting minutes. Beta Delta Archives.

122. "Triangle Wins Scholastic Cup for Spring Semester," *The Missouri Miner,* June 26, 1946.

123. "Campus Group Discuss Atoms with Local Men," *The Missouri Miner,* June 26, 1946; and "Dr. W.T. Schrenk Talks to Jeff City Group Monday," *The Missouri Miner.* June 12, 1946.

124. "Alpha Chi Sigma Annual Conclave to be Held in Rolla, Oct. 13," *The Missouri Miner,* October 09, 1946; and Albert Malone, Chapter Recorder, October 3, 1946, *Meeting of Beta Delta Chapter of Alpha Chi Sigma*, meeting minutes. Beta Delta Archives.

125. Levings, *Beta Delta Timeline.*

126. "Men of Chemistry Frat Average Highest in Grade Pt. and Cuts," *The Missouri Miner,* November 20, 1946.

127. Albert Malone, Chapter Recorder, October 17, 1946, *Meeting of Beta Delta Chapter of Alpha Chi Sigma*, meeting minutes. See also *Rollamo* 1947.

128. Malone, Chapter Recorder, November 21, 1946, *Meeting of Beta Delta Chapter of Alpha Chi Sigma*, meeting minutes. Beta Delta Archives.

129. "Earl Jackson to Play for Tri-Tech Dance," *The Missouri Miner,* November 14, 1946.

130. Malone, Chapter Recorder, December 5, 1946, *Meeting of Beta Delta Chapter of Alpha Chi Sigma,* meeting minutes; and Malone, Chapter Recorder, December 19, 1946, *Meeting of Beta Delta Chapter of Alpha Chi Sigma*, meeting minutes.

131. Malone, Chapter Recorder, January 2, 1947, *Meeting of the Beta Delta Chapter of Alpha Chi Sigma,* meeting minutes. Beta Delta Archives.

132. "Strunk to Head Alpha Chi Sigma: 15 Men Initiated," *The Missouri Miner,* January 8, 1947. Also, the National Office of Alpha Chi Sigma, however, had the initiation date of January 1 for A. L. Van Amburg, Robert A. Stahl and Roderique. Also, the Beta Delta Membership record indicated that Robert A. Stahl was not initiated until May.

133. Levings, Grand Historian, *Beta Delta Conclave Attendance*, document; F. Hawthorne, Chapter Recorder, January 16, 1947, *Meeting of the Beta Delta Chapter of Alpha Chi Sigma*, meeting minutes. Beta Delta Archives; and David M. Levings, Grand Historian, email to author, August 15, 2021.

134. F. Hawthorne, Chapter Recorder, February 6, 1947, April 3, 1947, April 16, 1947, and April 22, 1947, *Meeting of the Beta Delta Chapter of Alpha Chi Sigma*, meeting minutes; and Hawthorne, Chapter Recorder, February 20, 1947 and March 7, 1947, *Meeting of the Beta Delta Chapter of Alpha Chi Sigma*, meeting minutes. Beta Delta Archives.

135. "Alpha Chi Sigma and AIChE to Hold Joint Meeting," *The Missouri Miner,* April 16, 1947.

136. Hawthorne, Chapter Recorder, May 1, 1947, *Meeting of the Beta Delta Chapter of Alpha Chi Sigma*, meeting minutes. Beta Delta Archives. See also "Armstrong Elected Head of Honorary Chem Fraternity," *The Missouri Miner,* May 7, 1947.

137. Charles Hudson, Chapter Recorder, May 15, 1947, *Meeting of the Beta Delta Chapter of Alpha Chi Sigma*, meeting minutes. Beta Delta Archives.

138. "Van Amburg to Receive Scholarship Award," *The Missouri Miner,* July 2, 1947.

139. "Off the Campus," *The Missouri Miner,* July 30, 1947.

140. "Chem Building Fund, New Dorm Approved," *The Missouri Miner,* July 2, 1947.

141. Charles Hudson, Chapter Recorder, September 18, 1947, *Meeting of the Beta Delta Chapter of Alpha Chi Sigma*, meeting minutes; and Hudson, Chapter Recorder, November 6, 1947, *Meeting of the Beta Delta Chapter of Alpha Chi Sigma*, meeting minutes. Beta Delta Archives.

142. Hudson, Chapter Recorder, October 2, 1947 and October 16, 1947,

Meeting of the Beta Delta Chapter of Alpha Chi Sigma, meeting minutes; and Hudson, Chapter Recorder, November 20, 1947, *Meeting of the Beta Delta Chapter of Alpha Chi Sigma*, meeting minutes. Beta Delta Archives.

143. Hudson, Chapter Recorder, December 4, 1947, *Meeting of the Beta Delta Chapter of Alpha Chi Sigma*, meeting minutes; and Hudson, Chapter Recorder, November 6, 1947, *Meeting of the Beta Delta Chapter of Alpha Chi Sigma*, meeting minutes. Beta Delta Archives.

144. Hudson, Chapter Recorder, December 18, 1947, *Meeting of the Beta Delta Chapter of Alpha Chi Sigma*, meeting minutes; and Hudson. Chapter Recorder, November 6, 1947, *Meeting of the Beta Delta Chapter of Alpha Chi Sigma*, meeting minutes. Beta Delta Archives.

145. "Ode to a Chemist," *The Missouri Miner*, September 24, 1947.

146. Robert A. Stahl, Chapter Recorder, February 5, 1948, *Meeting of the Beta Delta Chapter of Alpha Chi Sigma*, meeting minutes; and Stahl, Chapter Recorder, January 15, 1948, *Meeting of the Beta Delta Chapter of Alpha Chi Sigma,* meeting minutes. Beta Delta Archives. Also, Griessen is listed in the February 5, 1948 meeting minutes, but his name could not be found in either the Beta Delta Membership records or the National Office records.

147. Beta Delta Membership Records also indicated Emory D. Fisher was initiated on January 11, 1948. Beta Delta records did not list Robert S. Ferry, C. J. Hyslop and Donald F. Carney. These records indicated C. J. Hyslop, Donald Carnay, and Robert Ferry were not initiated until May 2. Also, Harry Kuhn and Raymond Lieb were listed by Beta Delta but not by the National Office. Also, the records of the National Office indicated Paul Shatto, Michael Ditore, Donald Carney, J. Middeler, Robert Ferry, and C. J. Hyslop were initiated on January 1, 1948.

148. Stahl, Chapter Recorder, February 18, 1948, *Meeting of the Beta Delta Chapter of Alpha Chi Sigma*, meeting minutes. Beta Delta Archives.

149. Stahl, Chapter Recorder, March 4, 1948, *Meeting of the Beta Delta Chapter of Alpha Chi Sigma*, meeting minutes. Beta Delta Archives.

150. "Television Reception Provided in Rolla by Two MSM Students," *The Missouri Miner,* February 18, 1948; and Stahl, March 4, 1948, *Meeting of the Beta Delta Chapter of Alpha Chi Sigma*, meeting minutes. Beta Delta Archives.

151. Stahl, Chapter Recorder, April 15, 1948, *Meeting of the Beta Delta Chapter of Alpha Chi Sigma*, meeting minutes. Beta Delta Archives; and

"Crime Detection Expert to Speak at A.C.S-AIChE. Meeting," and "Alpha Chi Sigma's Pledge New Men and Make Plans for Outing," *The Missouri Miner,* April 9, 1948.

152. Stahl, Chapter Recorder, April 29, 1948 and May 6, 1948, *Meeting of the Beta Delta Chapter of Alpha Chi Sigma*, meeting minutes. Beta Delta Archives.

153. J. W. Ehrler, Chapter Recorder, May 20, 1948, *Meeting of the Beta Delta Chapter of Alpha Chi Sigma*, meeting minutes. Beta Delta Archives.

154. Stahl, Chapter Recorder, March 25, 1948, *Meeting of the Beta Delta Chapter of Alpha Chi Sigma*, meeting minutes. Beta Delta Archives.

155. "Alpha Chi Sigma Initiates 25 New Men," *The Missouri Miner,* May 7, 1948. Also, information provided by the National Office of Alpha Chi Sigma. The list provided by the Missouri Miner does not match the official record provided by the National Office of Alpha Chi Sigma. No further information was found concerning the nature of Dr. Schrenk's accident.

156. See note 147.

157. "New Buildings and Improvements on MSM Campus," *The Missouri Miner,* September 17, 1948.

158. Ehrler, Chapter Recorder, October 7, 1948, *Meeting of the Beta Delta Chapter of Alpha Chi Sigma*, meeting minutes. Also meeting minutes from September 16, 1948. Beta Delta Archives.

159. Ehrler, Chapter Recorder, December 2, 1948, *Meeting of the Beta Delta Chapter of Alpha Chi Sigma*, meeting minutes. Beta Delta Archives.

160. Levings, Grand Historian, letter to Robin Robinett. Re: Alpha Zeta, February 15, 1991.

161. Ehrler, Chapter Recorder, January 6, 1949, *Meeting of the Beta Delta Chapter of Alpha Chi Sigma*, meeting minutes. Beta Delta Archives.

162. National records did not show Donald Peterson initiated on January 9. According to the National records Thurston B. Howard, Loren Lafferty, John T. Hilgenbrink, and Richard B. Miller had an initiation date of January 1, 1949. Also, The Beta Delta records did not have Don L. Honerkamp and Roland J. Niederstadt listed.

163. E. C. Breidert, Chapter Recorder, February 4, 1949, *Meeting of the Beta Delta Chapter of Alpha Chi Sigma*, meeting minutes., and minutes from February 17, 1949. See also, "Process Development Topic of Mr.

Hullette at AIChE Meeting," *The Missouri Miner,* February 18, 1949; and the *Rollamo* 1949.

164. "ACS and AICHE Hear Dr. Odin Knight at Joint Meeting Mar 12," *The Missouri Miner,* May 20, 1949.

165. Breidert, Chapter Recorder, April 21, 1949, *Meeting of the Beta Delta Chapter of Alpha Chi Sigma,* meeting minutes; Breidert, Chapter Recorder, May 5, 1949, *Meeting of the Beta Delta Chapter of Alpha Chi Sigma,* meeting minutes. Beta Delta Archives; and "Edwin Long Site of Alpha Chi Sigma Initiation Banquet," *The Missouri Miner.* May 6, 1949. Again there is a discrepancy between the list of the Missouri and that of the National Office of Alpha Chi Sigma.

166. W. W. Campbell, Chapter Recorder, May 17, 1949, and May 19, 1949, *Meeting of the Beta Delta Chapter of Alpha Chi Sigma,* meeting minutes. Beta Delta Archives.

167. "St. Louis Chapter Sends Three Speakers to Alpha Chi Sigma," *The Missouri Miner,* September 23, 1949; and Campbell, Chapter Recorder, September 15, 1949, *Meeting of the Beta Delta Chapter of Alpha Chi Sigma,* meeting minutes. Beta Delta Archives.

168. "Alpha Chi Sigma in Readiness for Inspection," *The Missouri Miner,* September 30, 1949. After he received his PhD at Minnesota, Dr. Chamberlain went into industry for several years before his teaching position at Washington University.

169. Campbell, Chapter Recorder, October 6, 1949, *Meeting of the Beta Delta Chapter of Alpha Chi Sigma,* meeting minutes. Beta Delta Archives.

170. Levings, *Beta Delta Timeline*; and "St. Louis Chapter Sends Three Speakers to Alpha Chi Sigma," *The Missouri Miner,* September 23, 1949.

171. "Local AXE Stars Take Wiedeman Cup From Tired Professionals," *The Missouri Miner,* October 21, 1949; and "Alpha Chi Sigma to be Host to Chapters from Midwest Sunday," *The Missouri Miner,* October 14, 1949.

172. Corkball uses a 1.6-ounce (45 g) ball, which is stitched and resembles a baseball. The bat has a barrel that measures up to 1.5 inches (3.8 cm) in diameter and a maximum of 38 inches (97 cm) in length. Runners advance as many bases as the batter gets on the hit. If a runner is on first and the batter hits a double, then the resulting runners will be on second and third. If a runner is on first and the batter hits a single,

then it will be first and second. Corkball. Wikipedia.

173. Campbell, Chapter Recorder, October 20, 1949, *Meeting of the Beta Delta Chapter of Alpha Chi Sigma*, meeting minutes. Beta Delta Archive.

174. "Alpha Chi Sigma Initiates Thirteen Into Fraternity," *The Missouri Miner,* November 11, 1949.

175. "Doc Olson Stumped by AXE Smoker Quiz," *The Missouri Miner,* November 18, 1949; Campbell, Chapter Recorder, November 17, 1949, *Meeting of the Beta Delta Chapter of Alpha Chi Sigma*, meeting minutes; and meeting minutes of December 1, 1949. Beta Delta Archives.

176. See the Rollamo Yearbooks for 1942, 1943, 1944, 1945, 1946, 1947, and 1948.

177. "1963 Engineering Honor Awards," *The Missouri Alumnus*, May 1963. 2-3.

178. "Dr. Harry Curtis, Ex—TVA Director; Appointee of Truman Who Opposed Dixon-Yates Dies," *New York Times*, July 2, 1963.

179. Ryan Reed, "106 North Oliver, the Heimberger House," Rolla Preservation Alliance: 106 North Olive - The Heimberger House, (https://rolla-preservationblogspot.com), November 20, 2014.

180. Ibid.

181. "Putting Hubby Through is Motto of University Dames," *The Missouri Miner,* May 23, 1958; and "University Dames to Elect Officers," *The Missouri Miner,* March 23, 1962.

Chapter 3: The 1950s

1. "Chemical Engineering Building Completed," *MSM Alumnus,* July-August 1953, 5.

2. "Dr. Eppelsheimer Announces Future Plans for Building of Nuclear Reactor," *The Missouri Miner,* September 26, 1958; "New Electrical Engineering Building to Provide More Adequate Facilities," *The Missouri Miner,* February 27, 1959; and, "Campus Expansion in Full Swing; Civil Building Opens Next Fall," *The Missouri Miner,* March 6, 1959.

3. "New Chemical Engineering Building," *MSM Alumnus,* November-December 1951, 1.

4. Levings, "Looking Back," *The Hexagon*, Spring 2005, 22.

5. Levings, "Looking Back," *The Hexagon*, Spring 2002, 14.

6. Levings, "Looking Back," *The Hexagon*, Summer 2002, 30.

7. Levings, "Looking Back," *The Hexagon*, Summer 2007, 38.

8. Levings, "Looking Back," *The Hexagon*, Winter 2009, 78.

9. "Initiates and New Officers Feted by Alpha Chi Sigma," *The Missouri Miner,* January 13, 1950.

10. Paul Manocchio and LaPatina were present in the Beta Delta Records. Later LaPatina was expelled from the fraternity. National indicates a January 1, 1950 initiation date for George Palmer. William Vose was initiated in November 1949, but the National Office records indicated January 1, 1950. Also, National has George T. Palmer initiated January 1, 1950 but Beta Delta records did not have him initiated in January 1950.

11. W. W. Campbell, Chapter Recorder, January 5, 1950, *Meeting of the Beta Delta Chapter of Alpha Chi Sigma*, meeting minutes; and Norman Vaniman, Chapter Recorder, Sigma February 2, 1950, *Meeting of the Beta Delta Chapter of Alpha Chi Sigma*, meeting minutes. Beta Delta Archives.

12. Norman Vaniman, Chapter Recorder, January 17, 1950, *Meeting of the Beta Delta Chapter of Alpha Chi Sigma*, meeting minutes.

13. Vaniman, Chapter Recorder, February 2, 1950, *Meeting of the Beta Delta Chapter of Alpha Chi Sigma*, meeting minutes.

14. Vaniman, Chapter Recorder, March 30, 1950, April 6, 1950 and April 30, 1950, *Meeting of the Beta Delta Chapter of Alpha Chi Sigma*, meeting minutes. Beta Delta Archives.

15. Vaniman, Chapter Recorder, May 4, 1950, Meeting of the Beta Delta Chapter of Alpha Chi Sigma, meeting minutes. Beta Delta Archives.

16. "Mauer and Boushka to Lead Alpha Chi Sigma Next Semester," *The Missouri Miner,* May 12, 1950.

17. Beta Delta Membership list also records a George P... but the last name was not clear.

18. Warren Keller, Chapter Recorder, September 21, 1950, *Meeting of the Beta Delta Chapter of Alpha Chi Sigma*, meeting minutes. Beta Delta Archives.

19. Warren Keller, Chapter Recorder, October 5, 1950, *Meeting of the Beta Delta Chapter of Alpha Chi Sigma*, meeting minutes. Beta Delta Archives.

20. Keller, October 19, 1950, *Meeting of the Beta Delta Chapter of Alpha Chi Sigma*, meeting minutes. Beta Delta Archives.

21. Keller, November 2, 1950, and November 16, 1950, *Meeting of the Beta Delta Chapter of Alpha Chi Sigma*, meeting minutes. Beta Delta Archives.

22. Barker and McDonald were not found in the Beta Delta Membership List or the National Office records.

23. "Fifteen Men Initiated to Alpha Chi Sigma," *The Missouri Miner*, January 12, 1951.

24. *Rollamo,* 1951, 132.

25. Levings, *Beta Delta Timeline*; and *Rollamo*, 1951, 132.

26. Walter Schrenk, "W.T. Dr. Schrenk Reviews History and Progress of Chemical Engineering Department at M.S.M," *The Missouri Miner,* February 15, 1952.

27. Chemistry Building Completion Stalled for Lack of Funds," *The Missouri Miner,* March 7, 1952.

28. "Dr. W.T. Schrenk Honored by Alpha Chi Sigma," *MSM Alumnus,* July-August 1952.

29. "Alpha Chi Sigma Hold Convention; Lose Cup to St. Louis Chapter," *The Missouri Miner,* November 7, 1952.

30. "Smoker Held by Alpha Chi Sigma to Welcome New Pledge Class," *The Missouri Miner,* November 21, 1952.

31. "Event Highlighted by Honor and Scholastic Awards to Students," *The Missouri Miner,* May 1, 1953.

32. "Annual Jamboree and Picnic of Alpha Chi Sigma Held Sunday," *The Missouri Miner,* October 23, 1953.

33. "Eight Men Pledged by Alpha Chi Sigma," *The Missouri Miner,* December 18, 1953.

34. Rollamo, 1953, 99; and "Officers Elected for Forthcoming Semester by Alpha Chi Sigma," *The Missouri Miner,* December 12, 1952.

35. *Rollamo,* 1954, 97.

36. "Many Awards at Honors Convocation," *The Missouri Miner,* April 30, 1954.

37. Royal Society of Chemistry. The Merck Index Online - chemicals, drugs and biologicals (rsc.org), (accessed July 6, 2021).

38. Levings, Grand Historian, email to author, September 20, 2021.

39. "Heads Alpha Chi Sigma," *MSM Alumnus,* July-August 1954. 6.

40. A record of Egan's initiation date could not be found. But the Missouri Miner records him as the Reporter in the spring of 1953 and he appears in the Alpha Chi Sigma pictures of the Rollamo. See also, "Damp Party Held by Pikers Complete with Bats and Drippings," *The Missouri Miner,* October 22, 1954.

41. "Members of AXS Attend Founder's Day Meeting in St. Louis," *The Missouri Miner,* December 10, 1954.

42. "Dr. Schrenk Speaks to Kansas City Paint Group," *MSM Alumnus,* January-February 1955, 9.

43. "Members of Campus Organizations and Honor Societies Lauded; Thousands of Dollars Given in Scholarships," *The Missouri Miner,* April 29, 1955; and "Honors Bestowed at Christmas Convocation," *The Missouri Miner*, December 16, 1955.

44. Information provided by the National Office of Alpha Chi Sigma and Beta Delta Membership Records. See also, Beta Delta Chapter of Alpha Chi Sigma, End of 1955-1956 School Year Message from the MA, document. Beta Delta Archives.

45. Rollamo, 1955, 117; and Report from the MA 1956. Beta Delta Archives. The MA's Report shows only Maurice LeGrand as Chapter Historian.

46. KOMU-TV. Wikipedia, (accessed May 21, 2021). See also "KOMU change to ABC involves more than a flip of a switch," Columbia Missiourian. 74th year. No. 258, July 17, 1982.

47. "Chemical Engineering TV Program From MSM to be Shown Tonight," *The Missouri Miner*, March 02, 1956.

48. "Robert Bridger Awarded Atlas Powder Scholarship," *The Missouri Miner*, May 18, 1956.

49. Information provided by the National Office of Alpha Chi Sigma and

Beta Delta Membership records. See also, Beta Delta Chapter of Alpha Chi Sigma, End of 1955-1956 School Year Message from the MA. Beta Delta Archives.

50. "Chem Department Receives New Paint Equipment." *The Missouri Miner*, May 18, 1956.

51. "MSM has 41 New Faculty Members for Coming Semester," *The Missouri Miner*, September 21, 1956.

52. "J. Johnson of Rolla Wins 56-57 A.P.M. Scholarship," *The Missouri Miner,* September 21, 1956.

53. "MSM Profs. Awarded Research Grants Totaling $16,500," *The Missouri Miner*, September 28, 1956.

54. "MSM Student First from St. Louis Area to Get Grant Under Wars Orphan Act," *The Missouri Miner*, October 5, 1956; and "Many Awards Given at Christmas Convocation," *The Missouri Miner*, January 11, 1957. See Also AIChE.org. CEP Magazine | AIChE. https://www.aiche.org/publications, (accessed July 8, 2021).

55. Rollamo, 1956, 125; and Beta Delta Chapter of Alpha Chi Sigma, Report from the MA 1956, document. Beta Delta Archives. The MA's report only shows Dr. R. L. Hicks as the Chapter Historian.

56. "Chem. Dept. May Now Grant Ph.D. Degree," *The Missouri Miner*, January 11, 1957.

57. Information provided by the National Office of Alpha Chi Sigma and Beta Delta Membership Records. Also, "Many Awards Given at Christmas Convocation," *The Missouri Miner,* January 11, 1957.

58. David Bunch, Recorder, *Meeting Minutes of March 20, 1957*, meeting minutes. Beta Delta Archives.

59. "Doc Schrenk." *The Missouri Miner*, March 29, 1957.

60. Bunch, Recorder, *Meeting Minutes of April 3 and April 4, 1957*, meeting minutes; Bunch, Recorder, *Meeting Minutes of April 17, 1957*, meeting minutes, Beta Delta Archives; and Allen Pope, Recorder, *Meeting Minutes of May 15, 1957*, meeting minutes. Beta Delta Archives.

61. "James Johnson Given Scholarship in Nuclear Technology," *The Missouri Miner*, April 5, 1957.

62. Bunch, Recorder, *Meeting Minutes of April 10, 1957—Formal Pledging*, meeting minutes. Beta Delta Archives.

63. Allen Pope, Recorder, *Meeting Minutes of October 2, 1957,* meeting minutes. Beta Delta Archives.

64. Pope, Recorder, *Meeting Minutes of October 16, 1957*, meeting minutes. Beta Delta Archives.

65. Recorder, Meeting Minutes of October 2, 1957, meeting minutes; Pope, Recorder, Meeting Minutes (Smoker) of November 6, 1957, meeting minutes; Pope, Recorder, Meeting Minutes of October 30, 1957, meeting minutes; and Pope, Recorder, Meeting Minutes of November 14, 1957, meeting minutes. Beta Delta Archives.

66. Pope, Recorder, *Meeting Minutes of December 8, 1957,* meeting minutes. Beta Delta Archives.

67. John Donaldson, Recorder, *Meeting Minutes of December 18, 1957*, meeting minutes. Beta Delta Archives.

68. "Xmas Honors Convocation Held Thursday Morning," *The Missouri Miner*, December 20, 1957.

69. "Alpha Chi Sigma," Rollamo, 1957. Assumed this officer list was for the spring since Dale Harris was reported as Master Alchemist in the fall.

70. Donaldson, Recorder, *Meeting Minutes of January 15, 1958*, meeting minutes. Beta Delta Archives.

71. Donaldson, Recorder, *Meeting Minutes of February 5, 1958*, meeting minutes. Beta Delta Archives.

72. "Three Students Have Benefitted Under Kelly Scholarships," *The Missouri Miner,* February 7, 1958.

73. Donaldson, Recorder, *Meeting Minutes of February 19, 1958*, meeting minutes; and Donaldson, Recorder, *Meeting Minutes of March 5, 1958*, meeting minutes. Beta Delta Archives.

74. "Armstrong Fills Auditorium to Overflow For Concert," *The Missouri Miner,* March 21, 1958.

75. Donaldson, Recorder, *Meeting Minutes of March 19, 1958*, meeting minutes. Beta Delta Archives.

76. Donaldson, Recorder, *Meeting Minutes of April 2, 1958*, meeting minutes. Beta Delta Archives.

77. "President's Column," *MSM Alumnus*, March-April 1958, 2.

78. "'Doc' Schrenk Honored as Great Teacher and Leader; at MSM 35 Years," *MSM Alumnus*, May-June 1958, 7-8.

79. "Dr. Schrenk Honored at a Banquet Held in His Honor," *The Missouri Miner*, April 25, 1958.

80. "Prof. Jensen Opens 9th Annual Honors Convocation," *The Missouri Miner*, May 9, 1958.

81. "Alpha Chi Sigma Initiates Thirteen Members Sunday" and "Prof. Jensen Opens 9th Annual Honors Convocation," *The Missouri Miner*, May 9, 1958. Also, information provided by the National Office of Alpha Chi Sigma and Beta Delta Membership Records.

82. John Donaldson, Recorder, *Meeting Minutes of April 2, 1958*, meeting minutes. Beta Delta Archives.

83. "MSM Alumnus Receives Steel Research Grant," *The Missouri Miner*, May 16, 1958.

84. "Work Begins on New Student Union Building," *The Missouri Miner*, September 19, 1958; and "Dr. Eppelsheimer Announces Future Plans for Building of Nuclear Reactor," *The Missouri Miner*, September 26, 1958.

85. Risdon Hankinson, Recorder, *Meeting Minutes of October 1, 1958*, meeting minutes. Beta Delta Archives.

86. "AIChE," *The Missouri Miner*, October 17, 1958.

87. "Campus News: AIChE," *The Missouri Miner*, October 17, 1958.

88. Hankinson, Recorder, *Meeting Minutes of October 22, 1958*, meeting minutes. Beta Delta Archives.

89. "Dean Wilson Announces Scholarships Awarded To Paint Chemistry Students," *The Missouri Miner*, October 24, 1958.

90. Hankinson, Recorder, *Meeting Minutes of November 5, 1958*, and *Meeting Minutes of November 19,* 1958, meeting minutes. Beta Delta Archives.

91. Hankinson, Recorder, *Meeting Minutes of December 3, 1958*; and Kenneth Powell, Recorder, *Meeting Minutes of December 17, 1958*, meeting minutes. Beta Delta Archives.

92. "Top MSM Students Receive Honors for Superior Work," *The Missouri Miner*, January 9, 1959.

93. *The Missouri Miner,* April 11, 1958.

94. Powell, Recorder, *Meeting Minutes of January 7, 1959*, meeting minutes. See also, Powell, Recorder, *Meeting Minutes of February 4, 1959*, meeting minutes. Beta Delta Archives.

95. "Prototype of Nuclear Fuel Processing in Progress," *The Missouri Miner*, February 13, 1959.

96. Powell, Recorder, *Meeting Minutes of February 18, 1959*, meeting minutes. Beta Delta Archives.

97. "Lynn Rockwell Elected New President of the "M" Club," And "Campus News: AIChE," *The Missouri Miner*, February 20, 1959.

98. Powell, Recorder, *Meeting Minutes of March 18, 1959*, meeting minutes. Beta Delta Archives.

99. Powell, Recorder, *Meeting Minutes of April 1, 1959*, meeting minutes. Beta Delta Archives.

100. Powell, Recorder, *Meeting Minutes of April 16, 1959*, meeting minutes. Beta Delta Archives.

101. Powell, Recorder, *Meeting Minutes of May 6, 1959*, meeting minutes. Beta Delta Archives.

102. Powell, Recorder, *Meeting Minutes of May 20, 1959*, meeting minutes. Beta Delta Archives.

103. Powell, Recorder, *Meeting Minutes of September 30, 1959*, meeting minutes Beta Delta Archives.

104. James, Recorder, *Meeting Minutes of October 21, 1959* and *Meeting Minutes of October 28, 1959,* meeting minutes. Beta Delta Archives.

105. James, Recorder, *Meeting Minutes of November 4, 1959*, meeting minutes. Beta Delta Archives.

106. "Alumnus is Manager in Chemical Society," *The Missouri Miner*, November 6, 1959.

107. "Blue Key Chooses Jerry Stone as Man of the Month," *The Missouri Miner,* December 4, 1959.

108. James, Recorder, *Meeting Minutes of November 18, 1959*, meeting minutes. Beta Delta Chapter Archives.

109. James, Recorder, *Initiation and Banquet—November 22, 1959*, meeting minutes. Beta Delta Archives. Also, information provided by the National Office of Alpha Chi Sigma and Beta Delta Membership Records.

110. Levings, Beta Delta Timeline.

Chapter 4: The 1960s

1. "First Nuclear Reactor in Missouri Nears Completion on MSM Campus," *The Missouri Miner*, September 23, 1960.

2. "Old Chemistry Building Destroyed Firemen Fight Blaze for Seven Hours," *The Missouri Miner*, October 22, 1969; and "Fire Destroys Records, Research Notes, Books In Old Chemistry Building," *The Missouri Miner*, October 29, 1969.

3. Levings, "Looking Back," The Hexagon, Fall 2013, 70.

4. Levings, "Looking Back," The Hexagon, Summer 2016, 56-57.

5. Levings, "Looking Back," The Hexagon, Winter 2016, 93.

6. Levings, "Looking Back," The Hexagon, Winter 2018, 62.

7. Roy W. Loan, Grand Recorder, letter to the Collegiate Chapter MAs and Professional Chapter Presidents of Alpha Chi Sigma, Mary 4, 1960.

8. "Dr. Charles J. Thelen to Speak at AIChE Meeting on Explosives," *The Missouri Miner*, March 4, 1960.

9. J. D. Commerferd, Chairman of the Midwest Award, letter to Dr. Frank Conrad, April 1, 1960.

10. "Alpha Chi Sigma Holds Help Sessions," *Rollamo*, 1961, 146. The University of Missouri School of Mines and Metallurgy.

11. John S. McAnally, Chairman Efficiency Rating System Committee, letter to Mr. Gary Achenbach, July 1, 1960.

12. "Summer Paint Courses In Chem. Dept. Are Success," *The Missouri Miner*, September 16, 1960.

13. "Joe Gay Named Man-of-Month," *The Missouri Miner*, October 28, 1960.

14. "AIChE Presents Chapter Award," *The Missouri Miner*, February 17, 1961; and "Baptist Student Union Earns $431 for Mission," *The Missouri Miner*, May 11, 1962.

15. Alpha Chi Sigma Announces Officers," *The Missouri Miner*, April 14, 1961.

16. "Four MSM Students Receive St. Joseph Lead Scholarships," *The Missouri Miner*, October 6, 1961.

17. "New Officers," *The Missouri Miner*, October 13, 1961.

18. "Gov. Dalton Visits MSM to Celebrate Reactor Dedication," *The Missouri Miner*, October 27, 1961.

19. Klinger, T.; et al. (2019), "Overview of First Wendelstein 7-X High-Performance Operation," Nuclear Fusion. 59: 112004.

20. "Five Miners Get Scholarships," *The Missouri Miner*, October 27, 1961.

21. "General Motors Awards Four Scholarships," *The Missouri Miner*, November 3, 1961.

22. "MSM Senior Participates in P&G Training Program," *The Missouri Miner*, November 10, 1961.

23. The signature in the Beta Delta Membership Records reads Needels whereas the National Records has the spelling of Needles.

24. "ChE Dept. to Host Summery Paint Chemistry Course," *The Missouri Miner*, May 18, 1962.

25. "Missouri School of Mines Students Receive Scholarships for School Year," *The Missouri Miner*, October 5, 1962.

26. "Louis Pasteur: Father of Research and Processes," *The Missouri Miner*, April 5, 1963.

27. "MSM From 1871 to 1963," *The Missouri Miner*, March 15, 1963.

28. "Speech on Space to be Given by Dr. Von Braun," *The Missouri Miner*, March 29, 1963; "Wernher Von Braun to Speak at High School Auditorium," *The Missouri Miner*, April 5, 1963; and "Capacity Crowd Present to Hear Dr. Von Braun," *The Missouri Miner*, April 19, 1963.

29. Levings, Beta Delta Timeline. Also National Office of Alpha Chi Sigma records and Beta Delta Membership Records.

30. "IFC Chooses Clint Clark as Fraternity Man of the Year," *The Missouri Miner,* May 10, 1963.

31. "Scholarship to Chem Engineer," *The Missouri Miner,* February 21, 1964.

32. "MSM Alumnus to Dean's Post at Washington Univ.," *The Missouri Miner,* April 10, 1964; and Beta Delta Data, Fall 1978.

33. National Office of Alpha Chi Sigma's records. See also Beta Delta Membership Records. The National Office records the initiation date for Engemen and Brunson as January 1, 1964.

34. "Official Name Changed to 'University of Missouri at Rolla,'" *The Missouri Miner,* April 24, 1964.

35. "George McLellan Speaks on Glass," *The Missouri Miner,* May 1, 1964.

36. "Dr. Bosch Announces Offering Of Summer Paint Chemistry Courses," *The Missouri Miner*, April 17, 1964.

37. Levings, Beta Delta Timeline; and "Dr. Baker Makes Appointment of New Department Chairmen," *The Missouri Miner*, September 25, 1964.

38. Fifty-five Members Added to Faculty," *The Missouri Miner*, December 11, 1964.

39. "Hanna Receives A. P. Green Award," *The Missouri Miner,* November 6, 1964.

40. "Sophomore Wins Mann Scholarship," *The Missouri Miner*, November 20, 1964.

41. According to the records of the National Office of Alpha Chi Sigma Thurman was initiated on December 23. See also Beta Delta Membership Records.

42. Thomas Dunning, Reporter, letters to Office of the Grand Recorder March 5, 1964, and November 2, 1964; and Letter William E. McCracken, Treasurer, letter to the Grand Recorder Office, April 8, 1964.

43. "St. Louis Society Gives Bosch Award," *The Missouri Miner,* February 5, 1965.

44. Merle Griffin, Grand Recorder, letter to George Breuer, Reporter, May 12, 1965.

45. George Breuer, Reporter, Beta Delta, letter to Merle Griffin, Grand Recorder, May 7, 1965.

46. The names Missouri Valley District and Midwest District were interchangeable according Supreme Council Proposition 1887, July 1, 1960.

47. "Alpha Chi Sigma Honors Initiates With Banquet," *The Missouri Miner*, May 21, 1965.

48. GMA Burton E. Tiffany, letter to Grand Chapter Members, October 19, 1965.

49. Breuer, Reporter, letter to the St. Louis Professional Chapter and collegiate chapters, October 9, 1965; and Mark Potts, Reporter, Alpha Epsilon, letter to George Breuer, Reporter, Beta Delta, October 16, 1965.

50. "Alpha Chi Sigma Holds Initiation," *The Missouri Miner*, December 17, 1965.

51. Grand Recorder Office letter to G. Breuer, February 3, 1965.

52. "Blue Key Announces 'Man of the Month' Awards," *The Missouri Miner,* February 25, 1966.

53. "Tsimpris and Bauer Receive AIChE Scholarship Awards," *The Missouri Miner,* March 25, 1966.

54. Levings, Beta Delta Conclave Attendance.

55. "Alpha Chi Sigma Officers Elected; Events Planned," *The Missouri Miner*, September 23, 1966; and Invitation from Delta Chapter to Beta Delta Chapter dated October 7, 1966.

56. "Scholarships, Awards Given to Honored University Students," *The Missouri Miner*, November 18, 1966. According to the records of the National Office of Alpha Chi Sigma Eshbaugh was initiated on December 14.

57. Alpha Chi Sigma, Constitutional Interpretation No. 49, Eligibility of Students in Science Engineering Program Courses at University of Michigan for Election in Alpha Chi Sigma, document, October 11, 1956. Also, Constitutional Interpretation No. 50, Eligibility for membership with respect to "allied professions in which chemistry predominates," document, December 27, 1966.

58. "Blue Key Chooses Fall Men of the Month," *The Missouri Miner,* January 13, 1967.

59. "Fifty-Year Certificate Presented to Dr. Schrenk," *The Missouri Miner*, March 3, 1967.

60. Peter Gebauer, Chair, Study Committee on Selective Service, Zeta Chapter of Alpha Chi Sigma, letter to the chapters, May 10, 1967.

61. "Koederitz Chosen by Blue Key as January Man of the Month," *The Missouri Miner*, February 2, 1968.

62. "Two Sets of Twins Achieve Academic Excellence at UMR," *The Missouri Miner*, May 3, 1968.

63. Levings, Beta Delta Conclave Attendance, document.

64. "Dr. Webb Earns National Patent on Radioactivity," *The Missouri Miner*, September 18, 1968.

65. James Ziegenmier, Recorder, September 18, 1968, *Proceedings of Beta Delta of Alpha Chi*, meeting minutes. Beta Delta Archives.

66. Ziegenmier, Recorder, October 16 and October 30, 1968, *Proceedings of Beta Delta of Alpha Chi Sigma*, meeting minutes. Beta Delta Archives.

67. Ziegenmier. Recorder, November 6, 1968, *Proceedings of Beta Delta of Alpha Chi Sigma*, meeting minutes. Beta Delta Archives.

68. Ziegenmier, Recorder, December 4, 1968, *Proceedings of Beta Delta of Alpha Chi Sigma*, meeting minutes. Beta Delta Archives.

69. Ziegenmier, Recorder, January 7, 1969, *Proceedings of the Beta Delta of Alpha Chi Sigma*, meeting minutes; and Thomas Bell, Chapter Recorder, February 19, 1969, *Proceedings of the Beta Delta of Alpha Chi Sigma*, meeting minutes. Beta Delta Archives.

70. "AIChE Holds Regional; Haseltine Wins First," *The Missouri Miner*, March 19, 1969. Thomas Bell, Chapter Recorder, March 5, 1969, *Proceedings of the Beta Delta of Alpha Chi Sigma,* meeting minutes; Bell, Chapter Recorder, March 19, 1969, *Proceedings of the Beta Delta of Alpha Chi Sigma*, meeting minutes; and Bell, Chapter Recorder, March 24, 1969, *Proceedings of the Beta Delta of Alpha Chi Sigma*, meeting minutes. Beta Delta Archives.

71. Bell, Chapter Recorder, April 1, 1969, *Proceedings of the Beta Delta of Alpha Chi Sigma*, meeting minutes. Beta Delta Archives.

72. Bell, Chapter Recorder, April 16, 1969, *Proceedings of the Beta Delta of Alpha Chi Sigma*, meeting minutes. Beta Delta Archives.

73. "Head of UMR Graduate School to be Named Dean Emeritus," *The Missouri Miner*, April 30, 1969.

74. Bell, Chapter Recorder, April 1, 1969, *Proceedings of the Beta Delta of Alpha Chi Sigma*, meeting minutes. Beta Delta Archives.

75. Bell, Chapter Recorder, April 30, 1969, *Proceedings of the Beta Delta of Alpha Chi Sigma*, Meeting minutes. . Beta Delta Archives.

76. Bell, Chapter Recorder, May 7, 1969, *Proceedings of the Beta Delta of Alpha Chi Sigma*, meeting minutes. Beta Delta Archives.

77. Keith Ashby, Chapter Recorder, October 1, 1969, *Proceedings of the Beta Delta of Alpha Chi Sigma*, meeting minutes; and Ashby, Chapter Recorder, October 15, 1969, *Proceedings of the Beta Delta of Alpha Chi Sigma,* meeting minutes. Beta Delta Archives.

78. Ashby, Chapter Recorder, November 15, 1969, *Proceedings of the Beta Delta of Alpha Chi Sigma*, meeting minutes. Beta Delta Archives.

79. Ashby, Chapter Recorder, December 3, 1969, *Proceedings of the Beta Delta of Alpha Chi Sigma*, meeting minutes. Beta Delta Archives.

80. Ashby, Chapter Recorder, December 9, 1969, *Proceedings of the Beta Delta of Alpha Chi Sigma*, meeting minutes. Beta Delta Archives.

81. Missouri S&T, "Mailand Strunk," Chemical and Biochemical Engineering, Missouri S&T. – Chemical and Biochemical Engineering | Missouri S&T (mst.edu).

82. "Dr. Baker Makes Appointment of New Department Chairmen," *The Missouri Miner,* September 25, 1964.

83. Missouri S&T, "Dr. Dudley Thompson," Missouri S&T – Chemistry | Missouri S&T (mst.edu).

84. "Head of UMR Graduate School to be Named Dean Emeritus," *The Missouri Miner,* April 30, 1969; and Missouri S&T, "Wouter Bosch," Missouri S&T, – Chemistry | Missouri S&T (mst.edu).

85. "Alpha Chi Sigma Ask Your Vote for 'Professor Snarf,'" *The Missouri Miner*, April 23, 1965.

Chapter 5: The 1970s

1. "Chemistry, Chem-Engr. Building Dedicated," *The Missouri Miner,* May 1, 1974.

2. Levings, "Looking Back," *The Hexagon,* Spring 2020, 13.

3. Levings, "Looking Back," *The Hexagon*, Spring 2001, 14; and Levings, "Looking Back," *The Hexagon*, Winter 2001, 78.

4. Alpha Chi Sigma, "Important Events in the History of Alpha Chi Sigma (1902-2012)," https:// alphachisigma.org. (Accessed February 25, 2021).

5. Levings, "Looking Back," *The Hexagon*, Spring Fall 2004, 54.

6. Frank J. Doering, Recorder, February 18, 1970, *Proceedings of the Beta Delta Chapter of Alpha Chi Sigma*, meeting minutes. Beta Delta Archives.

7. Doering, Recorder, March 4, 1970, *Proceedings of the Beta Delta Chapter of Alpha Chi Sigma*, meeting minutes; and Doering, Recorder, March 9, 1970, *Proceedings of the Beta Delta Chapter of Alpha Chi Sigma*, meeting minutes. Beta Delta Archives.

8. Doering, Recorder, March 18, 1970, *Proceedings of the Beta Delta Chapter of Alpha Chi Sigma*, meeting minutes. Beta Delta Archives.

9. Doering, Recorder, April 1, 1970, *Proceedings of the Beta Delta Chapter of Alpha Chi Sigma*, meeting minutes. Beta Delta Archives.

10. Doering, Recorder, April 15, 1970, *Proceedings of the Beta Delta Chapter of Alpha Chi Sigma*, meeting minutes. Beta Delta Archives.

11. Doering, Recorder, April 29, 1970, *Proceedings of the Beta Delta Chapter of Alpha Chi Sigma*, meeting minutes; and Doering, Recorder, May 6, 1970, *Proceedings of the Beta Delta Chapter of Alpha Chi Sigma,* meeting minutes. Beta Delta Archives.

12. Alpha Chi Sigma, Alpha Chi Sigma Source Book. 24. Home - Alpha Chi Sigma (accessed February 25, 2021).

13. Veo Peoples, Recorder, September 2, 1970, *Proceedings of the Beta Delta Chapter of Alpha Chi Sigma*, meeting minutes. September 2, 1970. Beta Delta Archives.

14. Peoples, Recorder, September 30, 1970, *Proceedings of the Beta Delta Chapter of Alpha Chi Sigma*, meeting minutes. Beta Delta Archives; and Peoples, Recorder, October 7, 1970, *Proceedings of the Beta Delta Chapter of Alpha Chi Sigma,* meeting minutes. Beta Delta Archives.

15. "Preliminary Plans Approved for New Building at Rolla," *The Missouri Miner*, September 30, 1970.

16. Peoples, Recorder, November 18, 1970, *Proceedings of the Beta Delta Chapter of Alpha Chi Sigma*, meeting minutes. Beta Delta Archives.

17. Robert C. Haiducek, Recorder, December 2, 1970, *Proceedings of the Beta Delta Chapter of Alpha Chi Sigma,* meeting minutes. Beta Delta Archives.

18. *Rollamo,* 1970, 245.

19. Haiducek, Recorder, January 3, 1971, *Proceedings of the Beta Delta Chapter of Alpha Chi Sigma,* meeting minutes. Beta Delta Archives. See also, Beta Delta Chapter of Alpha Chi Sigma, February 24, 1971, Notes taken during meeting with Jim Miller, Grand Recorder, document; and, Beta Delta Membership Registration February 5, 1971.

20. Haiducek, Recorder, March 17, 1971, *Proceedings of the Beta Delta Chapter of Alpha Chi Sigma,* meeting minutes; and Haiducek, Recorder, March 31 1971, *Proceedings of the Beta Delta Chapter of Alpha Chi Sigma,* meeting minutes.

21. National Office of Alpha Chi Sigma's records and Beta Delta Membership Records. Also, Robert C. Haiducek, Recorder, March 17, 1971, *Proceedings of the Beta Delta Chapter of Alpha Chi Sigma,* meeting minutes; Haiducek, Recorder, March 31, 1971, *Proceedings of the Beta Delta Chapter of Alpha Chi Sigma,* meeting minutes; and Haiducek, Recorder, April 21, 1971, *Proceedings of the Beta Delta Chapter of Alpha Chi Sigma,* meeting minutes.

22. Haiducek, Recorder, April 27, and May 5, 1971, *Proceedings of the Beta Delta Chapter of Alpha Chi Sigma,* meeting minutes.

23. Levings, "Looking Back," *The Hexagon,* Fall 2016, 56-57; and Levings, David M., email to author, October 24, 2021. See also, National Office of Alpha Chi Sigma's records and Beta Delta Membership Records.

24. Davies, Carol (Langemach), email to author, November 28, 2021.

25. Levings, *Supreme Council Positions,* document; and John Adams, email to author, December 7, 2021.

26. These sources included material shared with the author by Gary Bland, surveys returned from alumni, and information shared in emails from alumni.

27. "Dr. Schrenk Alpha Chi Sigma 'Man of the Year,'" *MSM Alumnus,* June 1972, 12. According to custom, the author(s) of the nominating letter are kept in confidence, only known to the committee.

28. Apparently the loan fund initiated in 1970 was not continued for 1971 and 1972. Records could not be located which could resolve this question.

29. Beta Delta Chapter of Alpha Chi Sigma, *Beta Delta Data*, Fall 1973; and *Rollamo 1973*.

30. Joe Never, "Looking Back On…" *The Missouri Miner*, March 6, 1975.

31. Beta Delta Chapter of Alpha Chi Sigma, *Beta Delta Data*, Fall 1973.

32. Beta Delta Chapter of Alpha Chi Sigma, Beta Delta Committee List Fall 1974, document.

33. "Alumnus and Wife Keep Tradition Alive," *MSM Alumnus,* December 1974.

34. National Office of Alpha Chi Sigma's and Beta Delta's Membership Records, and Tony Messina, letter to Gary Bland, District Counselor, May 14, 1974.

35. Beta Delta Chapter of Alpha Chi Sigma, *Beta Delta Membership Registration Spring 1975*, document.

36. Suzanne Duncan, Recorder, March 20, 1975, *Proceedings of the Beta Delta Chapter of Alpha Chi Sigma*, meeting minutes; and Duncan, Recorder, January 13, 1975, *Proceedings of the Beta Delta Chapter of Alpha Chi Sigma*, meeting minutes.

37. Duncan, Recorder, January 29, and February 10, 1975, *Proceedings of the Beta Delta Chapter of Alpha Chi Sigma,* meeting minutes.

38. Duncan, Recorder, April 16, 1975, *Proceedings of the Beta Delta Chapter of Alpha Chi Sigma*, meeting minutes.

39. National Museum of American Diplomacy, "The Fall of Saigon (1975): The Bravery of American Diplomats," https://diplomacy.state.gov/u-s-diplomacy-stories/fall-of-saigon-1975-american-diplomats-refugees/ The Fall of Saigon (1975): The Bravery of American Diplomats and Refugees - National Museum of American Diplomacy (state.gov) (accessed October 30, 2021).

40. Melanie Miller, Recorder, April 30, 1975, *Proceedings of the Beta Delta Chapter of Alpha Chi Sigma*, meeting minutes.

41. John Adams, email to author, December 7, 2021.

42. Levings, Looking Back, document emailed to author, April 12, 2021.

43. Miller, Recorder, September 3, 1975, *Proceedings of the Beta Delta Chapter of Alpha Chi Sigma*, meeting minutes. September 3, 1975.

44. Miller, Recorder, September 17, 1975, *Proceedings of the Beta Delta Chapter of Alpha Chi Sigma*, meeting minutes; Miller, Recorder, September 25, and September 29, 1975, *Proceedings of the Beta Delta Chapter of Alpha Chi Sigma*, meeting minutes; and, Miller, Recorder, October 15, 1975, *Proceedings of the Beta Delta Chapter of Alpha Chi Sigma*, meeting minutes.

45. Miller, Recorder, September 25, 1975, *Proceedings of the Beta Delta Chapter of Alpha Chi Sigma*, meeting minutes.

46. Levings, Response to the Survey, document.

47. Miller, Recorder, November 15, 1975, *Proceedings of the Beta Delta Chapter of Alpha Chi Sigma*, meeting minutes.

48. Information provided by the National Office of Alpha Chi Sigma, and Beta Delta Membership Records. See also, Miller, Recorder, October 15, 1975, *Proceedings of the Beta Delta Chapter of Alpha Chi Sigma*, meeting minutes.

49. Levings, *Supreme Council Positions*, document.

50. Miller, Recorder, November 19, 1975, *Proceedings of the Beta Delta Chapter of Alpha Chi Sigma*, meeting minutes.

51. Rita Stockhecker, Recorder, December 3, 1975, *Proceedings of the Beta Delta Chapter of Alpha Chi Sigma*, meeting minutes.

52. Stockhecker, Recorder, January 21, 1976, *Proceedings of the Beta Delta Chapter of Alpha Chi Sigma,* meeting minutes; and Stockhecker, Recorder, February 4, February 12, February 23, and February 26, 1976, *Proceedings of the Beta Delta Chapter of Alpha Chi Sigma*, meeting minutes.

53. Stockhecker, Recorder, February 26, 1976, Proceedings of the Beta Delta Chapter of Alpha Chi Sigma, meeting minutes.

54. Stockhecker, Recorder, March 3, and March 17, 1976, *Proceedings of the Beta Delta Chapter of Alpha Chi Sigma*, meeting minutes; and Stockhecker, Recorder, March 31, 1976, *Proceedings of the Beta Delta Chapter of Alpha Chi Sigma,* meeting minutes.

55. Stockhecker, Recorder, April 7, 1976, *Proceedings of the Beta Delta Chapter of Alpha Chi Sigma*, meeting minutes.

56. When a collegiate group is at a successful level, their District Counselor will ask the Grand Collegiate Alchemist to request that the Supreme Council move the group from a collegiate group to a colony. Once the group becomes a colony, it recruits, educates and initiates pledges under

the supervision its parent (sponsoring) chapter, but will do so more on their own. The colony also will host regular chapter meetings, professional events, and social events. Alpha Chi Sigma website. https//:www.alphachisigma.org/prospective-members/start-a-chapter?.

57. Kay Thornton, Recorder, April 21, 1976, *Proceedings of the Beta Delta Chapter of Alpha Chi Sigma*, meeting minutes.

58. Thornton, Recorder, September 29, 1976, *Proceedings of the Beta Delta Chapter of Alpha Chi Sigma,* meeting minutes.

59. "AIChE," *The Missouri Miner*, September 2, 1976. "Chemistry Help Sessions," *The Missouri Miner*, October 21, 1976.

60. Thornton, Recorder, September 15, September 23, and September 27, 1976, *Proceedings of the Beta Delta Chapter of Alpha Chi Sigma*, meeting minutes.

61. Thornton, Recorder, September 2, 1976, *Proceedings of the Beta Delta Chapter of Alpha Chi Sigma*, meeting minutes.

62. Kay Thornton, Recorder, September 15, September 23, and September 27, 1976, *Proceedings of the Beta Delta Chapter of Alpha Chi Sigma*, meeting minutes.

63. Thornton, Recorder, September 29, 1976, *Proceedings of the Beta Delta Chapter of Alpha Chi Sigma*, meeting minutes.

64. Thornton, Recorder, October 6, and October 20, 1976, *Proceedings of the Beta Delta Chapter of Alpha Chi Sigma*, meeting minutes.

65. Thornton, Recorder, November 17, 1976, *Proceedings of the Beta Delta Chapter of Alpha Chi Sigma*, meeting minutes.

66. Levings, conversation with author, October 18, 2021.

67. Jana Trampe, Recorder, January 19, 1977, *Proceedings of the Beta Delta Chapter of Alpha Chi Sigma*, meeting minutes; and Trampe, Recorder, March 15, and April 12, 1977, *Proceedings of the Beta Delta Chapter of Alpha Chi Sigma*, meeting minutes.

68. Trampe, Recorder, February 16, 1977, *Proceedings of the Beta Delta Chapter of Alpha Chi Sigma*, meeting minutes.

69. Information provided by the National Office of Alpha Chi Sigma. Beta Delta Membership Records include Marjorie Riggins. See also, Trampe, Recorder, March 29, 1977, *Proceedings of the Beta Delta Chapter of Alpha Chi Sigma,* meeting minutes.

70. Trampe, Recorder, April 20, 1977, *Proceedings of the Beta Delta Chapter of Alpha Chi Sigma*, meeting minutes.

71. Trampe, Recorder, May 4, 1977, *Proceedings of the Beta Delta Chapter of Alpha Chi Sigma*, meeting minutes.

72. The Shillelagh Newsletter, Who we are | Missouri S&T (mst.edu). See also, "Order of the Golden Shillelagh," *The Missouri Miner*, March 16, 1977.

73. Dave Mees, Recorder, October 5, and November 30, 1977, *Proceedings of the Beta Delta Chapter of Alpha Chi Sigma*, meeting minutes.

74. Beta Delta Chapter of Alpha Chi Sigma, *Beta Delta Data*, Spring 1978; and Beta Delta Chapter of Alpha Chi Sigma, Fall 1977 Committee List, document.

75. Mees, Recorder, November 30, 1977, *Proceedings of the Beta Delta Chapter of Alpha Chi Sigma*, meeting minutes.

76. Mees, Recorder, December 7, 1977, *Proceedings of the Beta Delta Chapter of Alpha Chi Sigma*, meeting minutes.

77. Stan Heimburger, Recorder, April 18, 1977, *Proceedings of the Beta Delta Chapter of Alpha Chi Sigma*, meeting minutes. See also, Levings, Response to Survey, document.

78. Heimburger, Recorder, January 18, 1978, *Proceedings of the Beta Delta Chapter of Alpha Chi Sigma*, meeting minutes.

79. Heimburger, Recorder, March 1, 1978, *Proceedings of the Beta Delta Chapter of Alpha Chi Sigma*, meeting minutes.

80. Heimburger, Recorder, March 1, and March 15, 1978, *Proceedings of the Beta Delta Chapter of Alpha Chi Sigma*, meeting minutes.

81. Heimburger, Recorder, April 18, 1978, *Proceedings of the Beta Delta Chapter of Alpha Chi Sigma*, meeting minutes; Michael Haynes, Recorder, September 12, and September 18, 1978, *Proceedings of the Beta Delta Chapter of Alpha Chi Sigma*, meeting minutes; and *Beta Delta Data Fall 1978*.

82. Haynes, Recorder, April 30, 1978, *Proceedings of the Beta Delta Chapter of Alpha Chi Sigma*, meeting minutes; and Haynes, Recorder, April 30, 1978, *Proceedings of the Beta Delta Chapter of Alpha Chi Sigma*, meeting minutes.

83. Beta Delta's District at the time.

84. Levings, "Looking Back," *The Hexagon*, Summer 2003, 94.

85. Levings, email to author, October 31, 2021; and Levings, "Looking Back," *The Hexagon*, Fall 2016, 56-57.

86. Greek Week Queen Candidates," *The Missouri Miner*, April 20, 1978.

87. Haynes, Recorder, August 30, 1978, *Proceedings of the Beta Delta Chapter of Alpha Chi Sigma*, meeting minutes.

88. Beta Delta Chapter of Alpha Chi Sigma, Fall 1978 Committee List, document.

89. Valerie Brenner, Acting Recorder, September 20, September 21, October 4, and November 1, 1978, *Proceedings of the Beta Delta Chapter of Alpha Chi Sigma*, meeting minutes.

90. Anne Fulton, Acting Recorder November 29, 1978, *Proceedings of the Beta Delta Chapter of Alpha Chi Sigma*, meeting minutes.

91. Fulton, Acting Recorder November 29, and December 6, 1978, *Proceedings of the Beta Delta Chapter of Alpha Chi Sigma*, meeting minutes.

92. *Beta Delta Data Fall 1978.*

93. Fulton, Acting Recorder, January 31, February 1, February 7, and February 21, 1979, *Proceedings of the Beta Delta Chapter of Alpha Chi Sigma*, meeting minutes.

94. Beta Delta Chapter of Alpha Chi Sigma, Spring 1979 Committee List, document; and Fulton, Acting Recorder, January 17, 1979, *Proceedings of the Beta Delta Chapter of Alpha Chi Sigma*, meeting minutes.

95. Fulton, Acting Recorder, February 21, March 7, and March 21, 1979, *Proceedings of the Beta Delta Chapter of Alpha Chi Sigma*, meeting minutes; and Fulton, Acting Recorder, February 8, and March 21, 1979, *Proceedings of the Beta Delta Chapter of Alpha Chi Sigma*, meeting minutes.

96. Robert Stevens, email to author, January 6, 2020; and Levings, email to author, January 7, 2022. *Supreme Council Proposition 3612*, August 6, 1996 proposed: "The Saint Louis Professional Chapter be reactivated. Justification: They held a meeting on June 1, 1996 at which they elected officers and adopted by-laws. They indicate their primary goals are to aid Collegiate chapters in their area and the reactivation of inactive chapters such as Alpha Epsilon at Washington University in St. Louis."

97. Fulton, Acting Recorder, February 8, 1979, *Proceedings of the Beta Delta Chapter of Alpha Chi Sigma,* meeting minutes; and *Beta Delta Data Spring 1979.*

98. Beta Delta Chapter of Alpha Chi Sigma, *AXΣ Bulletin*, March 28, 1979; and Fulton, Acting Recorder, April 4, 1979, *Proceedings of the Beta Delta Chapter of Alpha Chi Sigma*, meeting minutes.

99. Fulton, Acting Recorder, April 18, 1979, Proceedings of the Beta Delta Chapter of Alpha Chi Sigma, meeting minutes.

100. Kevin Wiese, Recorder, May 2, 1979, *Proceedings of the Beta Delta Chapter of Alpha Chi Sigma*, meeting minutes.

101. Wiese, Recorder, August 22, September 5, and September 19, 1979, *Proceedings of the Beta Delta Chapter of Alpha Chi Sigma*, meeting minutes.

102. Wiese, Recorder, September 26, October 17, and November 7, 1979, *Proceedings of the Beta Delta Chapter of Alpha Chi Sigma,* meeting minutes. Also, information provided by the National Office of Alpha Chi Sigma, and Beta Delta Membership Records.

103. Wiese, Recorder, December 5, 1979, *Proceedings of the Beta Delta Chapter of Alpha Chi Sigma*, meeting minutes.

104. "Faculty Personals," and "Walter T. Schrenk Memorial.," *MSM Alumnus*, February 1980. 18 and 25.

105. "Chem.-ChE Building Renamed," *The Missouri Miner*, August 28, 1980. See also, Robert Stevens, Response to Survey, document.

106. "Dr. Walter Schrenk Honored by Portrait," *The Missouri Miner*, January 21, 1982; and "'Doc' Schrenk's Lessons Last a Lifetime," *MSM-UMR Alumnus*, Winter 1996, 11.

107. "Alpha Chi Sigma Initiates Ten," *The Missouri Miner*, January 14, 1942; and Missouri S&T, "Edward Schneider," Chemical and Biochemical Engineering Department, Missouri S&T, https://www.chemeng.mst.edu/facultystaffand facilities/schneider/.

108. Legacy.com. Edward Schneider Obituary - (2011) - Kirkwood, MO - St. Louis Post-Dispatch (legacy.com) (Accessed February 25, 2021).

109. Alpha Phi Omega," *Rollamo*, 1942, The University of Missouri School of Mines and Metallurgy.

Notes 469

110. Judy Flebbe, "Vapor pressures of some C4 hydrocarbons and their mixtures" (doctoral thesis, University of Missouri-Rolla, 1980).

111. "Judy Flebbe earns PhD. In Chem Eng.," *The Missouri Miner*, December 6, 1979; "AIChE Awards," The Missouri Miner, March 20, 1975.; and "UMR Names Who's Who," *The Missouri Miner,* November 13, 1975.

112. *Rollamo*, 1976, 128, 248, 257; and "Fall Concert by UMR Orchestra," *The Missouri Miner*, November 9, 1978.

113. "Judy Flebbe earns PhD. In Chem Eng.," *The Missouri Miner,* December 6, 1979.

114. Ibid.

115. Gary Fischer, conversation with author, February 5, 2021.

116. Dave Barclay, email to author, January 29, 2021.

117. Missouri S&T, Department Scholarships and Fellowships, https//www.chemeng.mst.edu/studentopp/scholarship. Scholarship – Chemical and Biochemical Engineering | Missouri S&T (mst.edu) (accessed, February 11, 2021). Also, "1985-1986 UMR Development Fund Named Scholarship Recipients," *MSM Alumnus*, August 1986, 12.

118. Missouri S&T, "Harvey Grice," https//www.chemeng.mst.edu/facultystaffand facilities/grice. Missouri S&T. – Chemical and Biochemical Engineering | Missouri S&T (mst.edu), (accessed October 22, 2021).

Chapter 6: The 1980s-1990s

1. "Chem.-ChE. Building Renamed," *The Missouri Miner,* August 28, 1980.

2. Ken Hardy, "Building Renovation Start," *The Missouri Miner*, September 25, 1980; and *Beta Delta Data*. Fall 1982. VMA Report; and, Julie Achurch, "University to Renovate Electrical Engineering," and "Schrenk," *The Missouri Miner*, September 21, 1994.

3. "Chemistry Department Receives Gift," *The Missouri Miner*, March 28, 1990.

4. Supreme Council Proposition 3095, July 2, 1983, and Proposition 3170, March 8, 1985; and Levings, "Looking Back," *The Hexagon*, Winter 2008, 78.

5. The Welch Foundation, "The Welch Award," https//www.welch1.org/awards/welch-award-in-chemistry. Welch Award in Chemistry (welch1.org), (accessed December 13, 2021); and Levings, "Looking Back," *The Hexagon*, Fall 2010, 61., and "Looking Back," *The Hexagon*, Fall 2013, 70.

6. Levings, "Looking Back," *The Hexagon*, Winter 2001, 78, and, "Looking Back," *The Hexagon*, Winter 2005, 82.

7. Levings, Beta Delta Timeline. See also Leo Reisberg, "Fraternities in Decline," *The Chronicle of Higher Education*, January 2000, 46. Reisberg ascribes the decline to changing demographics, bad publicity about alcohol abuse and hazing incidents, and changing student values.

8. Howard Mizuki, "MA Report," *Beta Delta Data*, Fall 1983; Beta Delta Chapter of Alpha Chi Sigma, "Officer Reports," *Beta Delta Data*, Spring 1984; and John Hume, Chair, "Safety Committee Report," *Beta Delta Data*, Spring 1985.

9. DeWayne Gerber, interview by the author, November 7, 2021.

10. Jon Wenzel, District Counselor 2002-2010, interview by the author, July 26, 2021.

11. Levings, "Looking Back," *The Hexagon*, Fall 2017, 61.

12. Wenzel, Assistant Grand Recorder, Central District Counselor from 2000 to 2010, interview by the author, July 26, 2021; and Pete Ritter, Gamma Theta 1989, CDC, 1998-2000 Biennial Report for the Central District, document.

13. "Tutoring Services," *The Missouri Miner*, January 21, 1987.

14. Peggy Taylor, "VMA Report," *Beta Delta Data,* Spring 1980; and Peter Scholtes, "VMA Report," *Beta Delta Data*, Fall 1980.

15. Beta Delta Chapter of Alpha Chi Sigma, "Officer Reports," *Beta Delta Data*, Spring 1985.

16. Carol Kenesey, Chair, "Safety Report," *Beta Delta Data*, Fall 1986.

17. Dale Abrahams, "MA Report," *Beta Delta Data*, Spring 1983; and Beta Delta Chapter of Alpha Chi Sigma, "Drink to Me!" *Beta Delta Data*, Fall 1983.

18. Dale Kyser, "MC Report," *Beta Delta Data*, Spring 1982.

19. Beta Delta Chapter of Alpha Chi Sigma, December 5, 1979, *Proceedings of the Beta Delta Chapter of Alpha Chi Sigma*, meeting minutes; and Beta Delta Chapter of Alpha Chi Sigma, *Beta Delta Data*, Spring and Fall 1982.

20. *Beta Delta Data*, Fall 1982.

21. *Beta Delta Data's* from 1983, 1984, 1985, 1986, 1987, and 1989.

22. Levings, Response to the Survey, document.

23. *Beta Delta Data*, Spring 1984; and Stephen Guck, "Alumni Secretary," *Beta Delta Data*, Fall 1985.

24. Beta Delta Chapter of Alpha Chi Sigma, "MA Report," *Beta Delta Data*, Fall 1982.

25. Natalie Betz was nominated by Theta Xi and Susan Schumacher was nominated by Kappa Delta. "1986 UMR Homecoming Queen Candidates," *The Missouri Miner*, October 14, 1986; "Homecoming Queen Candidates," *The Missouri Miner*, September 28, 1988; and "Homecoming Queen Crowned," *The Missouri Miner*, October 12, 1988.

26. "Bob Linke GDI," *The Missouri Miner*, March 8, 1989.

27. Beta Delta Chapter of Alpha Chi Sigma, "Flebbe Memorial," *Beta Delta Data*, Spring 1981; and *Beta Delta Data*, Fall 1982. See also Appendix Judith L. Flebbe Memorial Scholarship.

28. Beta Delta Chapter of Alpha Chi Sigma, November 29, 1989, December 6, 1989, and January 17, 1990, *Meeting Minutes*, meeting minutes; Beta Delta Chapter of Alpha Chi Sigma, April 21, 1990, Membership Record Spring 1991, document; and Beta Delta Chapter of Alpha Chi Sigma, Membership Record Fall 1991, document.

29. "St. Pat's Queen Candidates," *The Missouri Miner*, February 1990.

30. Beta Delta Chapter of Alpha Chi Sigma, August 29, 1990, *Meeting Minutes*, meeting minutes.

31. Levings, "Looking Back," *The Hexagon*, Fall 2016, 56-57.

32. William H. Webb, "The reactions of acid halides with sodium, magnesium, zinc and amalgams," (master thesis, University of Missouri School of Mines and Metallurgy, 1939).

33. "Alpha Chi Sigma Holds Initiation," *The Missouri Miner*, February 23, 1938; "Alpha Chi Sigma to Install Officers," *The Missouri Miner,* January 21, 1941; "Alpha Chi Sigma Installs Officers," *The Missouri Miner,* January 31, 1942; and "Johnson to Head Alpha Chi Sigma," *The Missouri Miner*, April 18, 1942.

34. Levings, email to author, March 24, 2021; and "Alpha Chi Sigma Holds Initiation," *The Missouri Miner,* December 17, 1965.

35. Levings, email to author, March 24, 2021.

36. "Curators Promote Seven MDM Faculty," *The Missouri Miner*, May 21, 1948; "Here's What the Faculty Members of MSM Are Doing and Have Done This Summer," *MSM Alumnus*, July-August 1952, 9-10; "3 Atomic Problems Carried On by MSM," *MSM Alumnus*, November-December 1952, 11; and "Faculty Promotions Announced," *The Missouri Miner*, May 3, 1957.

37. "Met. Dept. Finishes Air Force Contract," *The Missouri Miner*, February 10, 1956.

38. "MSM to Staff Mineral Research Lab in Rolla," *The Missouri Miner*, May 11, 1956; and "First Nuclear Reactor in Missouri Nears Completion on MSM Campus," *The Missouri Miner*, September 23, 1960.

39. "American Chemical Society Holds First Meeting of Golden Anniversary on MSM Campus," *MSM Alumnus*, September-October 1959, 3.

40. "MSM to Host Institute for High School Science Teachers," *The Missouri Miner*, January 11, 1963.

41. "Dr. Webb Earns National Patent on Radioactivity," *The Missouri Miner,* September 18, 1968.

42. "Meet the New Department Chairmen," *MSM Alumnus,* August 1964, 3-5; "Two Institutes for Teachers," *MSM Alumnus*, December 1964, 15; "Summer Enrollment Tops 900-Mark," *MSM Alumnus*, June 1965, 6-7; "Four Summer Institutes Planned," *MSM Alumnus*, December 1966, 5; and "ACS Area Chapter Receives Charter, Elects Officers," *The Missouri Miner,* October 14, 1966.

43. "Spotlight on Professor Emeritus," *The Missouri Miner*, November 03, 1977; and "1977 Alumni Awards Banquet," *MSM Alumnus*, December 1977, 4-8.

44. "Homecoming 1988," *MSM Alumnus*, December 1988, 3; "William H. Webb," *MSM Alumnus*, June 1977, 23-24; and "Century Club," *MSM Alumnus*, February 1989, 3.

45. Find a Grave, "Capt. William Hamlet Webb (1912-1989)," https://findagrave.com. Capt. William Hamlet Webb (1912-1989) - Find A Grave Memorial.

46. Porter Funeral Home, "Ruby Webb Obituary," Obituary | Ruby Webb | Porter Funeral Home, Ruby Fogleman Webb (1916-2019) - Find A Grave Memorial; and Chemistry Department Missouri S&T, Chemmunicator, 2010 Spring Semester. http://chem.mst.edu.

47. Texas A&M, "Mary Kay O'Connor Process Safety Center," https://psc.tamu.edu/about-the-center/history, History (tamu.edu) (accessed February 11, 2021).

48. Pillips Disaster of 1989. Wikipedia. Phillips disaster of 1989 – Wikipedia.

49. Evan Flores, and Sam Scott, "Center Emphasizes Engineering Safety," The Battalion, September 29, 2015, https//:thebatt.com, (accessed February 11, 2021).

50. Texas A&M, "Mary Kay O'Connor Process Safety Center."

51. *Beta Delta Data*, Fall 1982.

Chapter 7: The 2000s

1. Missouri S&T website. Index – Office of the Chancellor | Missouri S&T (mst.edu) (accessed November 26, 2021).

2. Andrew Careaga, Missouri S&T, "Missouri S&T receives $300 million gift from June and Fred Kummer," News and Events, posted October 12, 2020, https://Missouri S&T.edu. Post by Missouri S&T – News and Events – Missouri S&T receives $300 million gift from June and Fred Kummer (mst.edu).

3. Missouri S&T – News and Events – Bertelsmeyer Hall dedication to be held Oct. 17 (mst.edu) (accessed December 1, 2021).

4. Levings, "Transmutation 2002 or Evolution 2002," *The Hexagon*, Winter 2001, 66.

5. Alchemy Outreach—Science and Engineering from a Historical Perspective," *The Hexagon*, Fall 2008. 52-53.

6. Levings, "Looking Back," *The Hexagon*, Fall 2020, 46.

7. Alpha Chi Sigma, Supreme Council Proposition 4679, January 12, 2018.

8. Alpha Chi Sigma, "Alpha Chi Sigma Hall of Fame," Educational Foundation - Alpha Chi Sigma (accessed December 12, 2021); Alpha Chi Sigma, Alpha Chi Sigma Source Book, Current Sourcebook - Alpha Chi Sigma, (accessed December 12, 2021); and Maddie Hines, Recorder, March 20, 2018, *Meeting Minutes of March 20, 2018*, meeting minutes.

9. Levings, "Looking Back," *The Hexagon*, Winter 2003, 59.

10. Levings, "Looking Back," *The Hexagon*, Summer 2010, 30.

11. Jon Wenzel, Assistant Grand Recorder, interview by author, July 26, 2021.

12. Levings, "Looking Back," *The Hexagon*, Fall 2016, 56-57.

13. Alpha Chi Sigma, Supreme Council Proposition 4010, May 10, 2004.

14. Rachel Palasky, Survey Response, document. Also Nicole Moon and Matthew Senter, interview by author, March 13, 2021.

15. Matthew Senter, email to author, November 24, 2021.

16. Beta Delta Chapter of Alpha Chi Sigma, *Meeting Minutes*, January 20, 2016, and February 10, 2016, meeting minutes; and Matthew Senter, email to the author, December 3, 2021.

17. Science Olympiad, "Background," https://www.soinc.org/about/background; and Matthew Senter and Nicole Moon, email to author, December 3, 2021.

18. Matthew Senter and Michael Smith communications with Nicole Moon emailed to author February 15, 2022.

19. Senter, District Counselor, Central District, email to author. December 4, 2021.

20. Beta Delta Chapter of Alpha Chi Sigma, spring *Meeting Minutes* including January 21, 28, February 4, 11, 18, 25, March 4, 18, April 1, 8, 15, 22, 29, and May 6, meeting minutes.

21. Senter, fall *Meeting Minutes* including August 25, September 1, 8, 15, 22, 29, October 6, 13, 27, November 3, 10, and December 12, meeting minutes.

22. Senter, email to author, December 17, 2021.

23. Beta Delta Chapter of Alpha Chi Sigma, March 23, 2016, *Meeting Minutes March 23, 2016*, meeting minutes.

24. Beta Delta Chapter of Alpha Chi Sigma, March 2, 2106, Meeting Minutes March 2, 2016. See also Meeting Minutes April 30, 2016, meeting minutes; and Matthew Senter, email to author November 21, 2021.

25. Matthew Senter, email to author, November 24, 2021; and Kari Knobbe, email to author, November 21, 2021.

26. Alpha Chi Sigma website, "Alpha Chi Sigma Awards," Awards - Star Chapter - Alpha Chi Sigma. (accessed November 23, 2021.

27. Alpha Chi Sigma, Supreme Council Proposition 4594, August 9, 2016.

28. Kari Knobbe, email to author, November 14, 2021; Matthew Senter, email to author, November 21, 2021; Beta Delta Chapter of Alpha Chi Sigma, August 23, 2016, *Meeting Minutes August 23, 2016*, meeting minutes; and *Meeting Minutes, September 6, 2016*, meeting minutes.

29. Beta Delta Chapter of Alpha Chi Sigma, August 30, 2016, Meeting Minutes of August 30, 2016, meeting minutes; Beta Delta Chapter of Alpha Chi Sigma, September 6, 2016, Meeting Minutes September 6, 2016, meeting minutes; and Anna Schneider, November 14, 2018, Meeting Minutes November 14, 2018, meeting minutes.

30. Senter, District Counselor, email to author, March 5, 2021; Beta Delta Chapter of Alpha Chi Sigma, September 20, 2016, *Meeting Minutes September 20, 2016*, and Beta Delta Chapter of Alpha Chi Sigma, October 4, 2016, *Meeting Minutes October 4, 2016*, meeting minutes.

31. Beta Delta Chapter of Alpha Chi Sigma, September 20, 2016, *Meeting Minutes September 20, 2016*, meeting minutes. Beta Delta Archives.

32. Beta Delta Chapter of Alpha Chi Sigma, October 4, 2016, *Meeting Minutes October 4, 2016*, meeting minutes; and Beta Delta Chapter of Alpha Chi Sigma, November 29, 2016, *Meeting Minutes November 29, 2016*, meeting minutes. Beta Delta Archives.

33. Beta Delta Membership List and National Office of Alpha Chi Sigma Records; Beta Delta Chapter of Alpha Chi Sigma, November 11, 2016, *Meeting Minutes November 11, 2016*, and Beta Delta Chapter of Alpha Chi Sigma, October 18, 2016, *Meeting Minutes October 18, 2016*, meeting minutes. Beta Delta Archives.

34. Russell House, Russell House | Phelps County Family Crisis Services (russellhousemo.org) (accessed November 27, 2021).

35. Knobbe, email to author, November 14, 2021, and Matthew Senter, email to author, November 21, 2021.

36. Beta Delta Chapter of Alpha Chi Sigma. *Meeting Minutes January 25, 2017*, meeting minutes; and *Meeting Minutes February 1, 2017*, meeting minutes. Beta Delta Archives.

37. Knobbe, email to author, November 14, 2021; and Missouri S&T, "Celebration of Nations," https://www.nations.mst.edu. Celebration of Nations – Celebration of Nations | Missouri S&T (mst.edu) (accessed December 2, 2021).

38. Beta Delta Chapter of Alpha Chi Sigma, April 5, 2017, *Meeting Minutes April 5, 2017*, meeting minutes; and Beta Delta Chapter of Alpha Chi Sigma, February 22, 2017, *Meeting Minutes February 22, 2017*, meeting minutes. Beta Delta Archives.

39. Nicole Moon and Matthew Senter, interview by author, March 13, 2021; and Matthew Senter, email to author, November 24, 2021.

40. Maddie Hines, Recorder, January 23, 2018, *Meeting Minutes of January 23, 2018*, meeting minutes. Beta Delta Archives.

41. Hines, Recorder, February 13, 2018, Meeting Minutes of February 13, 2018, meeting minutes. Beta Delta Archives.

42. Hines, January 23, *January 30, February 6, and February 27, 2018, Meeting Minutes*, meeting minutes. Beta Delta Archives.

43. Supreme Council Proposition 4725, July 27, 2018; and Senter, email to author, December 17, 2021.

44. Anna Schneider, Recorder, August 22 and September 5, 2018, *Meeting Minutes of August 22, 2018 and September 5, 2018*, meeting minutes. Beta Delta Archives.

45. Schneider, Recorder, August 22, 2018, *Meeting Minutes of August 22, 2018*, meeting minutes; Anna Schneider, September 19, 2018, *Meeting Minutes September 19, 2018*, meeting minutes; Schneider, September

26, 2018, *Meeting Minutes September 26, 2018*, meeting minutes; Schneider, November 7, 2018, *Meeting Minutes November 7, 2018*, meeting minutes. Beta Delta Archives; and Matthew Senter, email to author, December 17, 2021.

46. Jacob Brownfield, Recorder, *February 14, 2019, and February 27, 2019, Meeting Minutes*, meeting minutes; and Kari Knobbe, Recorder, August 28, 2019, *Meeting Minutes*, meeting minutes. Beta Delta Archives.

47. Knobbe, Recorder, September 11, 2019, *Meeting Minutes*, meeting minutes; and Knobbe, Recorder, October 9, 2019, *Meeting Minutes*, meeting minutes. Beta Delta Archives.

48. Prior to 2015 there was a push by several districts to curb or eliminate the use of purposefully difficult, unpassable finals and make them strictly about material in the Alpha Chi Sigma Sourcebook. Anna Dorner, communicated to Nicole Moon, and communicated in an email from Nicole Moon to the author, February 15, 2022.

49. Moon, email to author, February 10, 2022.

50. Ibid.

51. Nicole Moon and Matthew Senter, interview by author, March 13, 2021; and Derek Dillinger, MA, interview by author, March 20, 2021.

52. "Report from the 55th Biennial Conclave," *The Hexagon*, Winter 2020; and Alpha Chi Sigma, "Alpha Chi Sigma Health and Safety," https://alphachisigma.org/about-us/health-and-safety. Alpha Chi Sigma Health and Safety - Alpha Chi Sigma, (accessed March 24, 2021).

53. Whitney Sheffield, Recorder, January 23, 2020; Sheffield, Recorder, February 6, 2020, *Meeting Minutes*, meeting minutes; and Sheffield, Recorder, April 16, 2020, *Meeting Minutes*, meeting minutes. Beta Delta Archives.

54. Moon, Recorder, September 3, and September 10, 2020, *Meeting Minutes*, meeting minutes. Beta Delta Archives.

55. Moon, email to author, December 2, 2021.

56. Moon, email to author, December 16, 2021.

57. Vaughn Foreman, Spring 2020, Meeting Minutes, meeting minutes. Beta Delta Archives.

58. Knobbe, email to author, December 17, 2021.

59. Missouri S&T, "Missouri S&T to Host StemFest Oct. 2," https://www.news.mst.edu/2021/09/missouri-st-to-hold-stemfest-oct-2," Missouri S&T – News and Events – Missouri S&T to host STEMFest Oct. 2 (mst.edu), (accessed December 13, 2021).

60. Caroline Williams, Recorder, Fall *Meeting Minutes* including September 1, 8, 15, 22, October 6, October 13, 20, 27, November 3, and November 10, meeting minutes. Beta Delta Archives.

61. Beta Delta Chapter of Alpha Chi Sigma, Fall *Meeting Minutes* including August 27, September 10, 17, October 8, 15, 22, 29, November 5, 12, 19, and December 3, meeting minutes. Beta Delta Archives.

62. Beta Delta Membership List and National Office of Alpha Chi Sigma records.

63. Hines, Recorder, April 3, 2018, *Meeting Minutes of April 3, 2018*, meeting minutes. Beta Delta Archives.

Appendix A—Epsilon Pi Omicron Members, Initiates and Officers

1. "New Society is Organized," *The Missouri Miner*, January 31, 1933.

2. "Chem Fraternity Initiates," *The Missouri Miner*, May 9, 1933.

3. *Rollamo*, 1934. The University of Missouri School of Mines and Metallurgy; and "Eight Initiated by Epsilon Pi Omicron," *The Missouri Miner*, May 1, 1934.

4. *Rollamo*, 1935. The University of Missouri School of Mines and Metallurgy; and "8 Chemists Pledged," *The Missouri Miner*, November 13, 1935.

5. *Rollamo,* 1936. The University of Missouri School of Mines and Metallurgy.

Appendix C—Beta Delta Kuebler Award Recipients and Order of Altotus Members

1. Levings, David M. Looking Back, *The Hexagon*, Fall 2007, 62.

Appendix D—Judith L. Flebbe Memorial Scholarship Recipients and Initial Donors

1. "1985-1986 UMR Development Fund Named Scholarship Recipients," *MSM Alumnus*, August 1986, 11-13.

2. "Flebbe Memorial," *Beta Delta Data*, Spring 1981.

ACKNOWLEDGEMENTS

A work of this nature cannot be accomplished alone. This history could not have been written without the dedicated efforts and input of others to whom I am greatly indebted. First, I would like to express my gratitude to my friend and editor, Dennis Uhlig, for his insights, recommendations and patience, which transformed my dry technical approach into a more appealing read.

The writing, however, could not have occurred without the research and retrieval of records. For their diligent digging into Beta Delta's file, scanning records for my review, and answering questions which I liberally flung at them from time to time, I offer my deepest appreciation to Nicole Moon and Kari Knobbe. Along with Nicole and Kari, many other brothers in the chapter graciously responded to my requests for information, including Matthew Senter, Derek Dillinger, Rae Boillat, Christina Arens, and Dr. Douglas Ludlow. Without them this history would have only been a timeline.

Equally, I was dependent on the input and recommendations of my friend and Beta Delta brother, Mitch Levings, Grand Historian of Alpha Chi Sigma, for whom I had the pleasure of being pledge master. I am grateful for Mitch's patience during those times when I would call and ask, "Hey, Mitch do you have a minute?" and he understood our conversation would be more like an hour or so. He graciously accepted my physics of time-dilation.

I would also like to thank DeWayne Gerber, another of my wonderful pledges, for whom I also had the honor of being pledge master, and Jon Wenzel, Assistant Grand Recorder, who provided a clearer picture of the trends and central concerns of the chapter during the 1980s and 1990s. But details of specific events and people of the 1970s and 1980s would have been lost, had it not been for Gary Bland, who was so kind as to box up his Beta Delta Datas, and other records, and Fed-Ex them to me.

Many others contributed through emails, surveys, or phone conversations, providing valuable details that clarified issues or brought cut-and-dried meeting minutes to life. Thank you to John Rasche, John Adams, Gary Fischer, Dave Barclay, Tony Messina, Nicole Talbot, Carol (Langemach) Davies, Bob and Melanie Naeger, John DeGood, Bob Stevens, Rachel Palasky, and Jennifer Ward Whalen.

Finally, I would like to thank Erin Goodwin, Assistant Director of Fraternity Operations, and Allison Wisher, of the National Office of Alpha Chi Sigma, who early on provided Beta Delta alumni information and initiation records, which opened many avenues for further research, and Sarah Baggett from the Financial Aid Office, Missouri S&T, who provided information in regard to the Judith L. Flebbe Memorial Scholarship.

THE AUTHOR

Keith Schuette is a 1977 graduate of the University of Missouri-Rolla (currently the Missouri University of Science and Technology), where he earned a BS degree in Metallurgical Engineering. He also holds a Masters of Divinity degree from Eden Theological Seminary in St. Louis. He was initiated into Alpha Chi Sigma in the spring of 1974 and served the Beta Delta chapter as Vice-Master Alchemist and Master of Ceremonies.

A father of a daughter and a son, and a grandfather of four, he currently resides with his wife, Linda, in West Bend, Wisconsin.

www.ingramcontent.com/pod-product-compliance
Lightning Source LLC
Chambersburg PA
CBHW050511170426
43201CB00013B/1919